P9-CQZ-092

Linux Firewalls

New Riders Professional Library

Linux Firewalls

New Riders

201 West 103rd Street,
Indianapolis, Indiana 46290

Robert L. Ziegler

Linux Firewalls

Robert L. Ziegler

Copyright © 2000 by New Riders Publishing

All rights reserved. No part of this book shall be reproduced, stored in a retrieval system, or transmitted by any means, electronic, mechanical, photocopying, recording, or otherwise, without written permission from the publisher. No patent liability is assumed with respect to the use of the information contained herein. Although every precaution has been taken in the preparation of this book, the publisher and author(s) assume no responsibility for errors or omissions. Neither is any liability assumed for damages resulting from the use of the information contained herein.

International Standard Book Number: 0-7357-0900-9

Library of Congress Catalog Card Number: 99-65384

Printed in the United States of America

First Printing: November, 1999

03   02   01   00   7   6   5   4   3   2

Interpretation of the printing code: The rightmost double-digit number is the year of the book's printing; the rightmost single-digit number is the number of the book's printing. For example, the printing code 99-1 shows that the first printing of the book occurred in 1999.

Trademarks

All terms mentioned in this book that are known to be trademarks or service marks have been appropriately capitalized. New Riders Publishing cannot attest to the accuracy of this information. Use of a term in this book should not be regarded as affecting the validity of any trademark or service mark.

Warning and Disclaimer

Every effort has been made to make this book as complete and as accurate as possible, but no warranty or fitness is implied. The information provided is on an as-is basis. The authors and the publisher shall have neither liability nor responsibility to any person or entity with respect to any loss or damages arising from the information contained in this book.

Publisher
David Dwyer

Executive Editor
Laurie Petrycki

Acquisitions Editor
Katie Purdum

Development Editor
Kitty Wilson Jarrett

Managing Editor
Sarah Kearns

Project Editor
Caroline Wise

Copy Editor
Nancy Albright

Indexers
Craig Small
Cheryl Lenser

Technical Reviewers
Debbie Dailey
Dr. Craig Hollabaugh

Compositor
Ron Wise

About the Author

Robert L. Ziegler graduated from the University of Wisconsin–Madison with an undergraduate degree in psychology, following near completions in both German and philosophy. After taking educational and career trips in several directions, he decided to make his hobby his career and earned a master's degree in computer science, also from the University of Wisconsin–Madison.

Out of school, Bob became one of a team of two UNIX operating system developers working for a company developing a mini-supercomputer. He developed a multiprocessor version of BSD 4.3 UNIX as a side project to the team's ongoing uniprocessor development efforts. Since then, he has worked as a UNIX operating system kernel developer for R&D companies in the Boston area.

The advent of Linux and consumer access to 24/7 Internet connectivity gave Bob the keys to a dream he'd had since 1982—to have his own UNIX server and LAN at home. What began as a pragmatic effort to make his system secure on the Internet quickly grew into a passion for the home UNIX user. He offers free, Web-based Linux firewall design services to the public, as well as a popular firewall and LAN FAQ to help people quickly get their Linux systems set up securely.

Now a principal engineer with Nokia, Bob is designing and developing firewall products for Nokia's Ipsilon product family.

About the Reviewers

Debbie Dailey is currently a UNIX system administrator for a world leader in plumbing products. She worked with mainframes for six years before returning to school to study computer science, with an emphasis on network security. Debbie began her UNIX career as a system administrator student intern while attending classes full time. She recently received her B.S. in computer science from Purdue University.

Dr. Craig Hollabaugh has loved UNIX since his first talk session in 1985. He administered Sun workstations while pursuing a doctoral electrical engineering degree in interactive analog simulation at Georgia Institute of Technology. He then developed interface tools and the C++ wrapper to the distributed parallel gradient iterative solver at the University of Texas Computation Fluid Dynamics Laboratory. In 1995, at his first startup company, Wireless Scientific, he developed a wireless industrial telemetry application centered around Linux. Later, Craig's successful consulting career brought him to Cambridge, Massachusetts, where he's now the vice president of engineering at Kiava Systems. He oversees Kiava's integration and embedded DSP hardware development. His personal research interest is in interactive simulation in elementary math and science education.

One of my two lifelong best friends died while the book was being written. To Gloria Frawley, who across the lifetimes has been friend, lover, brother, sister, parent, child, husband, wife. Until we walk together again, thank you for the purest, most trusting, nonjudgmental love I've known, and the best playmate I could ever hope for.

Acknowledgments

I've never understood just why people write thank you and acknowledgment sections. Who bothers to read them? Well, I have a better idea why now.

So, I want to thank Bill Sommerfeld for giving me my first tutorial when he realized just how clueless I was; Gary Zaidenweber for pounding the need for security into my head, and for helping set up my system initially; my other friends at Hewlett-Packard, who encouraged me to go after my passion, especially Mary MacGregor and my manager Cindy Buhner, who are far more appreciated than they might know; Paul Fox for sending me a copy of his own firewall when I was first starting out; Craig Hollabaugh for donating weeks of editorial review on the FAQ this book is inspired by; Karl Runge for donating weeks of firewall rule review; numerous customers in the NorthEast Mediaone newsgroups; my mom, who trusted me to find my own way as I struggled with career transition issues for over a year; Regina Weyer for always being there across the miles and across all the years; Jonathan Kaplan for being a steady source of belief and support; Old Person for being a constant friend and source of encouragement over the past few years; Alan Small for kindly reworking the hardest piece of text in this book; and last but not least, Kitty Jarrett, my editor, who somehow survived all my inexperience. Kitty speaks softly, and carries no stick. She simply observes and asks, often with humor.

Contents

Tell Us What You Think!

As the reader of this book, *you* are our most important critic and commentator. We value your opinion and want to know what we're doing right, what we could do better, what areas you'd like to see us publish in, and any other words of wisdom you're willing to pass our way.

As the Executive Editor for the Linux team at New Riders Publishing, I welcome your comments. You can fax, email, or write me directly to let me know what you did or didn't like about this book—as well as what we can do to make our books stronger.

Please note that I cannot help you with technical problems related to the topic of this book, and that due to the high volume of mail I receive, I might not be able to reply to every message.

When you write, please be sure to include this book's title and author, as well as your name and phone or fax number. I will carefully review your comments and share them with the author and editors who worked on the book.

Fax:	317-581-4663
Email:	newriders@mcp.com
Mail:	Laurie Petrycki
	Executive Editor
	Linux/Open Source
	New Riders Publishing
	201 West 103rd Street
	Indianapolis, IN 46290 USA

Introduction

Linux is enjoying growing popularity among home hobbyists and small, home-based businesses. Continual, direct Internet access is becoming more widespread in the home as cable modem and DSL connection services expand into the consumer market.

Not only is UNIX a popular server platform, especially for Web servers, but it's also excellent as the gateway to a home LAN. Behind that gateway, continually connected to the Internet, are other UNIX machines, Windows and NT platforms, Macintoshes, and shared printers. As a result, small system users are being exposed to security issues they've never had to think about before.

Network security is an especially important issue for Linux users with direct Internet connections. Unlike a simple personal computer system, UNIX is a full-fledged, powerful operating system. Its founding purpose and philosophy was to promote information sharing in a research and development environment. As such, it's grown to be large, cryptic, and not for the inexperienced or unprotected.

Connecting a UNIX system to the Internet is much like advertising an open house to the public, leaving your front door wide open, and going on an extended vacation. Without precautions, unwanted intruders will enter in both cases, and it will happen sooner than later.

The average home or small system user doesn't have the time, interest, or patience to learn all the facets of security needed. This book's goal is to help home and small business Linux users get their Internet security measures in place quickly, without the need to become a network security expert. The necessary precautions are not difficult to implement, but finding all the information in one place, with an emphasis on *how to do it*, is not an easy task.

What This Book Covers

For small system users, security issues are almost exclusively concerned with external security, with protecting themselves against unintended network access from the outside. There are exceptions, of course. For example, some families might be concerned with limiting certain kinds of system and Internet access by their children, but that tends to be about the extent of it. For the most part, the home environment is considered to be a trusted environment.

This book guides home and small business users through the basic steps of designing and implementing a packet-filtering firewall. A firewall is only one step toward creating a secure system, however. Higher-level security measures are needed as well.

Computer security requires a multitiered approach. No single layer of a security scheme is sufficient by itself. Each successive layer depends on the protections offered by the levels below it. The services you enable, along with the firewall, form the basis for your system security. Thus, the book is concerned with disabling unnecessary services, selecting services to make public, and identifying dangerous local services that need to be protected behind the firewall.

The types of firewall protection a small system can easily and economically support are examined. Topics include the idea behind packet-level filtering, how to set up your own firewall, how to set some services up more securely in terms of the firewall and communication protocols, IP masquerading to hide your internal computers' identities when they access the Internet, and ensuring that the firewall is working.

Although not the primary topic of the book, Part III, "System-Level Security and Monitoring," discusses higher-level forms of access control. Topics include access control lists supported by `tcp_wrappers` and `portmap`, server configuration, proxies, and general system administration practices.

Finally, the book covers system security and integrity monitoring, detecting preliminary probes and unauthorized access attempts before an intrusion occurs. Also covered are tools for detecting signs of a compromise, and how to recover if a compromise is discovered.

The text and examples in this book are based on Red Hat Linux 6.0. The firewall examples are written in `ipchains` semantics. Because the conversion from `ipfwadm` to `ipchains` is in process at this moment, and Linux systems are using both versions today, examples in `ipfwadm` semantics are included in Appendix B, "Firewall Examples and Support Scripts."

What This Book Doesn't Cover

The security policies and procedures a large business needs to emphasize are almost opposite what a small system user needs to emphasize. External Internet security represents only a small percentage of the security issues facing a larger business. It's estimated that around 90% of business-level security breaches originate from inside corporate LANs, not from the outside Internet.

This book doesn't attempt to address issues of internal system security, large-scale, multiuser LAN security, complex proxy configurations, corporate-level authentication methods and technologies, virtual private networks, encryption, or commercial-level firewall and network architectures.

Hacking Attempts: The Scope of the Problem

Current estimates of the number of intrusion attempts are difficult to come by. Perhaps this is because unsuccessful attempts largely go unnoticed, and many sites have habituated to them and have come to consider them to be life-as-usual on the Internet. Estimates in documents at CERT range from growth consistent with the growth of the Internet all the way to exponential growth in 1998.

Whatever the actual numbers may be, global Internet hacking attempts, and their level of sophistication, are undeniably growing. The patterns of port scans have changed from simple probes for a few common security flaws to domainwide scans of the entire service port range. The latest hacking tools are shared over the Internet through Web sites, mailing lists, and news groups. Groups of hacking aficionados use Internet Relay Chat to coordinate cooperative group scans and attacks, often to reduce the risk of detection. Newly detected vulnerabilities are rapidly publicized across the Internet and immediately taken advantage of. The vendors and security monitoring organizations are in a perpetual race with the hacker community to each keep one step ahead of the other.

What a Hacker Has to Gain

So who are these hackers and what do they hope to gain? There is no single answer.

Much of what passes for a hacking attempt is really the result of curiosity, a mistake, poorly written software, and poorly configured systems. Much of the hacking activity originates with curious teenagers and students. Much originates from compromised systems, especially at university sites. The system's owner is unaware that his or her computer is being used as a base of operations by an uninvited guest. Then there's the aforementioned groups of loosely cooperating hackers, people for whom this is their idea of a good time. Corporate and political espionage can play a part in it, even for the home user.

As for what the hacker hopes to gain, some people want the challenge of solving the puzzle. Some want the bragging rights. Some simply like to break in and destroy. Then there are tangible gains. A new base of operations from which to launch further attacks, appearing to be the compromised site, is a major find. In a similar vein, a compromised site provides a base or system resources for sending bulk email. A nastier goal is finding a site to establish as a WAREZ repository. Finally, there's the obvious goal of theft, of stealing software and other intellectual property.

What You Have to Lose

When a system is compromised, the average home user is most often inconvenienced and frightened. Data loss is a common problem, because many hackers manage to ineptly wipe people's hard drives. Data loss also covers any files that haven't been backed up, because a compromised system needs to be reloaded from scratch, whether damage was done or not.

Loss of service is another common problem. An ISP will usually shut the account down until the problem has been corrected. The system owner first has to understand the security flaw and learn how to make the system secure before he or she can implement the critical security procedure. This takes time. For a small business, both of these outcomes means loss of revenue as well as inconvenience.

Not only will the ISP view the owner with suspicion, but the owner can suffer loss of reputation from anyone else who was bothered by actions the hacker launched from the system. If your ISP doesn't believe in your personal innocence, it will likely drop you as a customer. If your site was identified as a WAREZ site, or if the hacker attacked the wrong sites, you could face legal bills and social embarrassment.

Finally, personal information and proprietary information can be stolen or disseminated.

Firewalls Versus Hacking in an Ideal World

Conceptually, many or most hacking attempts could be stopped at the source by the ISPs or gateway service providers. A standard set of filtering procedures, applied in routers and gateways as a matter a course, would end most of this type of attempted security breach. Unfortunately, this is practical only in an ideal world at this point. Not only would all service providers everywhere have to be convinced of the importance of their role and responsibility in the effort, but network routers would have to be able to handle the extra load of packet filtering on a massive scale. Hardware just isn't there yet.

Nevertheless, these kinds of filtering procedures can easily be implemented in your home and small business systems without any noticeable performance degradation. Not only will these procedures help you maintain a more secure site, but they'll also help protect other people from your mistakes.

I

Preliminary Considerations

Preliminary Concepts
Underlying Packet-Filtering
Firewalls

A SMALL SITE MAY HAVE INTERNET ACCESS through a cable modem, a DSL line, ISDN, or often, a PPP connection to a phone line dial-up account. The computer connected directly to the Internet is the focus for security issues. Whether you have one computer or a small local area network (LAN) of linked computers, the focus for a small site will be on the machine with the direct Internet connection. This machine will be the firewall machine.

The term *firewall* has a number of meanings depending on its implementation and purpose. At this opening point in the book, firewall means the Internet-connected machine. This is where your security policies will be implemented. The firewall machine's external network interface card is the connection point, or gateway, to the Internet. The purpose of a firewall is to protect what's on your side of this gateway from what's on the other side.

A simple firewall setup is sometimes called a *bastion firewall* because it's the main line of defense against attack from the outside. All your security measures are mounted from this one defender of your realm. Consequently, everything possible is done to protect this system. It's your one and only bastion of defense.

Behind this line of defense is your single computer or your group of computers. The purpose of the firewall machine might simply be to serve as the connection point to the Internet for other machines on your LAN. You might be running local, private services behind this firewall, such as a shared printer or shared file systems. Or you might want all your computers to have access to the World Wide Web. One of your machines might host your private financial records. You might want to have Internet access from this machine, but you won't want anyone getting in. At some point, you might want to offer your own services to the Internet. One of the machines might be hosting your own Web site for the Internet. Your setup and goals will determine your security policies.

The firewall's purpose is to enforce the security policies you define. These policies reflect the decisions you've made about which Internet services you want to be accessible to your computers, which services you want to offer the world from your computers, which services you want to offer to specific remote users or sites, and which services and programs you want to run locally for your own private use. Security policies are all about access control and authenticated use of private or protected services, programs, and files on your computers.

Home and small business systems don't face all the security issues of a large, corporate site. The basic ideas and steps are the same. There just aren't so many factors to consider. The emphasis is on protecting your site from unwelcome access from the Internet. (A corporate site would emphasize internal security, which isn't much of an issue for a home-based site.) A packet-filtering firewall is one common approach to—and one piece of—network security and controlling access from the outside.

Before going into the details of developing a firewall, this chapter introduces basic underlying concepts and mechanisms a packet-filtering firewall is based on. These concepts include a general frame of reference for what network communication is, how network-based services are identified, what a packet is, and the types of messages and information sent between computers on a network.

The TCP/IP Reference Networking Model

In order to provide a framework for this chapter, and for the rest of the book, I'm going to use a few terms before they're defined in the following sections of this chapter. The definitions are old hat to computer science and networking people, but they might be new to less technically inclined people. If this is all new to you, don't worry. Right now, I'm just trying to give you a conceptual place to hang the upcoming definitions on so that they make more sense.

If you've had formal academic training in networking, you're familiar with the Open Systems Interconnection (OSI) reference model. The OSI reference model was developed in the late 1970s and early 1980s to provide a framework for network interconnection standards. The OSI model is a formal, careful, academic model. Textbooks and academicians use this model as their conceptual framework when talking about networking.

Networking was taking off in the late 1970s and early 1980s, so the world went on during the seven years the OSI reference model was being hammered out. As TCP/IP became the de facto standard for Internet communication between UNIX machines during this time, a second, informal model called the TCP/IP reference model developed. Rather than being an academic ideal, the TCP/IP reference model is based on what manufacturers and developers finally came to agree upon for communication across the Internet. Because the model focuses on TCP/IP from a practical, real-world, developer's point of view, the model is simpler than the OSI model. So where OSI explicitly delineates seven layers, the TCP/IP model clumps them into four layers.

This book uses the TCP/IP reference model. As with most people with a computer science background, I tend to use the OSI vocabulary, but map it into the TCP/IP conceptual model.

Network communication is conceptualized as a layered model, with communication taking place between adjacent layers on an individual computer, and between parallel layers on communicating computers. The program you're running (e.g., your Web browser) is at the top, at the application layer, talking to another program on another computer (e.g., a Web server).

In order for your Web browser client application to send a request for a Web page to the Web server application, it has to make library and system calls that take the information from the Web browser and encapsulate it in a message suitable for transport between the two programs across the network. These messages are either transport-layer TCP segments or UDP datagrams. To construct these messages, the application layer calls the transport layer to provide this service. The transport-layer messages are sent between the Web browser client and the Web server. The transport layer knows how to deliver messages between a program on one computer and a program on the other end of the network. Both the OSI model and TCP/IP model call this layer the transport layer, although the OSI model breaks this layer into several different layers functionally.

In order for these transport-layer messages to be delivered between the two programs, the messages have to be sent between the two computers. To do this, the transport layer calls functions in the operating system that take the TCP or UDP transport message and encapsulate it in an Internet datagram suitable for sending to the other computer. These datagrams are IP packets. The IP packets are sent between the two computers across the Internet. The Internet layer knows how to talk to the computer on the other other end of the network. The TCP/IP reference model calls this layer the Internet layer. The OSI reference model vocabulary is commonly used for this layer, so it's more commonly called the network layer. They are one and the same.

Beneath the network layer is the subnet layer. Again, the packet is encapsulated in an Ethernet header. At the subnet level, the message is now called an Ethernet frame. From the TCP/IP point of view, the subnet layer is a clump of everything that happens to get the IP packet delivered to the next computer. This clump includes all the addressing and delivery details associated with routing the frame between the computers, from one router to the next, until the destination computer is finally found. This layer includes translating the network frame from one kind of network to another along the way. Most networks today are Ethernet networks, but along the way are ATM networks, FIDI networks, token ring networks, and so forth—whatever network technology is being used to carry the frames between two computers. This clump includes the hardware, the physical wires connecting two computers, and the signals, the voltage changes representing the individual bits of a frame, and the control information required to frame an individual byte.

The summary idea, as shown in Figure 1.1, is that the application layer represents communication between two programs. The transport layer represents how this communication is delivered between the two programs. Programs are identified by numbers called *service ports*. The network layer represents how this communication is carried between the two end computers. Computers, or their individual network interface cards, are identified by numbers called *IP addresses*. The subnet layer represents how this communication is carried between each individual computer along the way. On an Ethernet network, these computer network interfaces are identified by numbers called *Ethernet addresses,* which you are probably familiar with as your network card's burned-in hardware MAC address.

The next section describes the information these layers pass among themselves that ends up being used by a packet-filtering firewall.

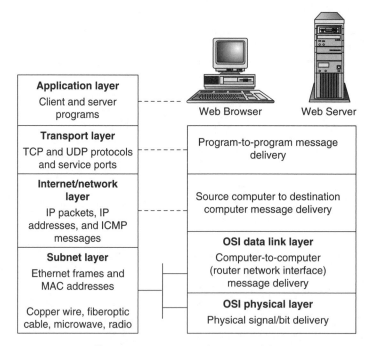

Figure 1.1   TCP/IP reference model.

Service Ports: The Door to the Programs on Your System

Network-based services are programs running on a machine that other computers on the network can access. The service ports identify the programs and individual sessions or connections taking place. Service ports are the numeric names for the different network-based services. They are also used as numeric identifiers for the endpoints of a particular connection. Service port numbers range from 0 through 65535.

Server programs (that is, *daemons*) listen for incoming connections on a service port assigned to them. By historical convention, major network services are assigned well-known, or famous, port numbers in the lower range from 1 to 1023. These port number–to–service mappings are coordinated by the Internet Assigned Numbers Authority (IANA) as a set of universally agreed-upon conventions or standards.

These lower-ranged ports are called *privileged ports* because they are owned by programs running with system-level (that is, `superuser` or `root`) privileges. The idea is to increase confidence that the client program is really connecting to the intended, advertised service. This is the intention—it's not a guarantee. You can never be absolutely certain that a remote machine or service is who or what it claims to be.

An advertised service is simply a service available over the Internet from its assigned port. If your machine isn't offering a particular service and someone tries to connect to the port associated with that service, nothing will happen. They are knocking on the door, but no one lives there to answer. For example, Web servers are assigned to port 80. If your machine isn't running a Web server and someone tries to connect to port 80, the client program receives an error message from your machine indicating that the service isn't offered.

The higher port numbers from 1024 to 65535 are called *unprivileged ports*. They serve a dual purpose. For the most part, these ports are dynamically assigned to the client end of a connection. The combination of client and server port number pairs, the transport protocol used, along with their respective IP host addresses, uniquely identify the connection.

Additionally, ports in the 1024-through-49151 range are registered with the IANA. These ports can be used as part of the general unprivileged pool, but they are also associated with particular services such as SOCKS or X Window servers. Originally, the idea was that services offered on the higher ports were not running with root privilege. They were for use by user-level, nonprivileged programs. The convention may or may not hold in any individual case.

Service Name-to-Port Number Mappings

Linux distributions are supplied with a list of common service port numbers. The list is found in the /etc/services file.

Each entry consists of a symbolic name for a service, the port number assigned to it, the protocol (TCP or UDP) the service runs over, and any optional nicknames for the service. The following table lists some common service name-to-port number mappings, taken from the Red Hat Release 6.0:

Port Name	Port Number/Protocol	Alias
ftp	21/tcp	
telnet	23/tcp	
smtp	25/tcp	mail
whois	43/tcp	nicname
domain	53/tcp	nameserver
domain	53/udp	nameserver
finger	79/tcp	
pop-3	110/tcp	
nntp	119/tcp	readnews
www	80/tcp	http
auth	113/tcp	ident
ntp	123/udp	
https	443/tcp	

Note that the symbolic names associated with the port numbers vary by Linux distribution and release. Names and aliases differ. Port numbers do not.

Also note that port numbers are associated with a protocol. The IANA has attempted to assign the same service port number to both the TCP and UDP protocols, regardless of whether a particular service uses both protocols. Most services use one protocol or the other. The *domain* service uses both protocols.

Packets: IP Network Messages

The term *packet* refers to an Internet Protocol (IP) network message. The IP standard defines the structure of a message sent between two computers over the network. It's the name given to a single, discrete message or piece of information that is sent across a network. Structurally, a packet contains an information header and a message body containing the data being transferred. The body of the IP packet—its data—is all or a piece (a fragment) of a higher-level protocol message.

The IP firewall (IPFW) mechanism included in Linux supports three IP message types: ICMP, UDP, and TCP. An ICMP (Internet Control Message Protocol) packet is a network-level, IP control and status message. At the network level, ICMP messages contain information about the communication between the two endpoint computers. A UDP (User Datagram Protocol) IP packet carries UDP transport-level data between two network-based programs, without any guarantees regarding successful delivery or packet delivery ordering. Sending a UDP packet is akin to sending a postcard to another program. A TCP (Transmission Control Protocol) IP packet carries TCP transport-level data between two network-based programs, as well, but the packet header contains additional state information for maintaining an ongoing, reliable connection. Sending a TCP packet is akin to carrying on a phone conversation with another program. Most Internet network services use the TCP communication protocol rather than the UDP communication protocol. In other words, most Internet services are based on the idea of an ongoing connection with two-way communication between a client program and a server program.

All IP packet headers contain the source and destination IP addresses and the type of IP protocol message (ICMP, UDP, or TCP) this packet contains. Beyond this, a packet header contains slightly different fields depending on the protocol type. ICMP packets contain a type field identifying the control or status message type, along with a second code field for defining the message more specifically. UDP and TCP packets contain source and destination service port numbers. TCP packets contain additional information about the state of the connection and unique identifiers for each packet. (The header contains other fields, as well. The other fields are either not visible or else not generally useful at the IP packet-filtering level.) (Almost any book on TCP/IP networking defines the remaining header fields. One reference is *TCP/IP Clearly Explained* by Pete Loshin, published by Academic Press.)

IP Message Types: ICMP

An ICMP packet is a network layer, IP control and status message. Its header contains the source and destination IP addresses, the ICMP protocol identifier, and an ICMP message type. An ICMP message type indicates whether the packet is a command, a response to a command, status information, or an error condition. Individual ICMP message types are covered in Chapter 3, "Building and Installing a Firewall." ICMP messages do not contain source and destination ports. They are not sent between programs; they are sent between source and destination endpoint computers.

An example ICMP message is an error status message. If you attempted to connect to a remote Web server, and a Web server wasn't running on the remote host, the remote host would return an ICMP error message indicating that the service didn't exist. The fields of interest in the packet header are shown in Figure 1.2.

IP Message Types: UDP

UDP is a stateless (that is, connectionless) and unreliable transport delivery protocol. A program sends a UDP message, which may or may not be received or responded to. No acknowledgment of receipt is returned. No flow control is provided, so a UDP datagram is silently dropped if it can't be processed along the way.

A UDP packet header contains the source and destination IP addresses, the UDP protocol type, and the source and destination service port numbers.

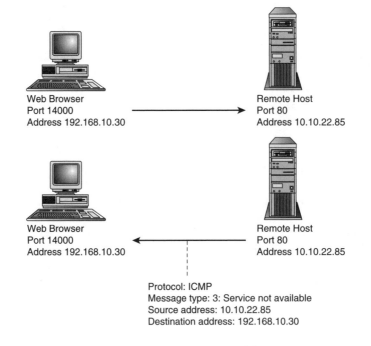

Web Browser
Port 14000
Address 192.168.10.30

Remote Host
Port 80
Address 10.10.22.85

Web Browser
Port 14000
Address 192.168.10.30

Remote Host
Port 80
Address 10.10.22.85

Protocol: ICMP
Message type: 3: Service not available
Source address: 10.10.22.85
Destination address: 192.168.10.30

Figure 1.2   Incoming ICMP error message.

Unreliable UDP?

UDP is referred to as an *unreliable datagram service*. *Unreliable* doesn't carry any negative connotations as to UDP's usability. Unreliable, in this case, means that no effort is made to ensure proper delivery. As a result, without the reliable, connection-oriented overhead of TCP, UDP-based data transfer is several times faster than TCP-based data transfer. Consequently, UDP lends itself well to simple query and response types of communication.

As an example, your machine could periodically attempt to contact a remote network time server. Internet time servers are assigned UDP service port 123. The time server will return the current time of day. Your system could update its system clock with the information from the more accurate network time server. If the exchange is unsuccessful because the time server isn't running on the remote machine or the remote machine is down at the time, an ICMP error message, `Service or Host Not Available`, is returned.

As shown in Figure 1.3, the client program on your system initiates the request. An unprivileged port is assigned to the request. An outgoing UDP request packet is constructed with the unprivileged port as the source port. The destination port is the well-known time service port, 123.

The time server responds with a UDP packet containing the current time. An incoming UDP response packet will arrive from the time server's IP address from source port 123, addressed to your IP address and the unprivileged destination port you initially provided.

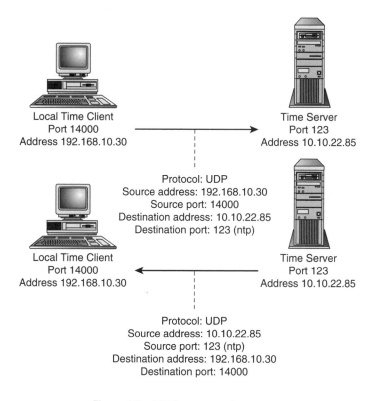

Figure 1.3   UDP request and response.

IP Message Types: TCP

The vast majority of network services run over TCP. Messages are sent reliably in both directions as part of an ongoing connection between two programs—without error, without loss or duplication, and delivered in order. Every TCP segment is acknowledged upon receipt. Every TCP segment is identified by a unique sequence number. Flag bits are used to define the state of the connection.

If an IP-encapsulated TCP segment will be larger than the maximum transmission unit (MTU) of the underlying network, the segment is broken up into fragments. (Because most networks are Ethernet networks, the MTU is 1500 bytes maximum per Ethernet frame.) The fragments are identified as belonging to a particular segment and sent individually, to be reconstructed into the original TCP segment by the final destination computer.

When a client program initiates a connection to a server, a port is selected from the unprivileged pool on the client's end. The combination of the client's IP address, port number, and transport protocol defines the client's socket. On the server side, the combination of host IP, address, the server's famous port number, and transport protocol forms the server's socket. The connection between client and server is uniquely defined by this socket pair.

Each individual connection between a given client and server, possibly just one in a set of simultaneous connections to that server (e.g., a Web server), is uniquely identified by the source address and port number of the client in conjunction with the server's IP address and assigned port number, along with the transport protocol used by the application.

A TCP packet header contains the source and destination IP addresses, the TCP protocol message type, the source and destination service ports, and sequence and acknowledgment numbers, and control flags used to create and maintain a reliable virtual circuit, or ongoing two-way connection.

A Typical TCP Connection: Visiting a Remote Web Site

As an illustration, a common TCP connection example is going to a Web site through your Netscape browser (i.e., connecting to a Web server). This section illustrates the aspects of connection establishment and ongoing communication that will be relevant to IP packet filtering in later chapters.

What happens? As shown in Figure 1.4, a Web server is running on a machine somewhere, waiting for a connection request on TCP service port 80. You click on the link for a URL in Netscape. Part of the URL is parsed into a hostname; the hostname is translated into the Web server's IP address; and your browser is assigned an unprivileged port (e.g., 14000) for the connection. An HTTP message for the Web server is constructed. It's encapsulated in a TCP message, wrapped in an IP packet header, and sent out. For our purposes, the header contains the fields shown in Figure 1.4.

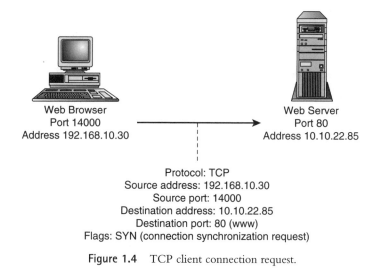

Web Browser
Port 14000
Address 192.168.10.30

Web Server
Port 80
Address 10.10.22.85

Protocol: TCP
Source address: 192.168.10.30
Source port: 14000
Destination address: 10.10.22.85
Destination port: 80 (www)
Flags: SYN (connection synchronization request)

Figure 1.4   TCP client connection request.

Additional information is included in the header that isn't visible at the packet-filtering level. Nevertheless, describing the sequence numbers associated with the SYN and ACK flags helps clarify what's happening during the three-way handshake. When the client program sends its first connection request message, the SYN flag is accompanied by a synchronization sequence number. The client is requesting a connection with the server, and passes along a starting sequence number it will use as the starting point to number all the rest of the messages the client will send.

The packet is received at the server machine. It's sent to service port 80. The server is listening to port 80, so it's notified of an incoming connection request (the SYN connection synchronization request flag) from the source IP address and port socket pair (192.168.10.30). The server allocates a new socket on its end, (10.10.22.85), and associates it with the client socket.

The Web server responds with an acknowledgment (ACK) to the SYN message, along with its own synchronization request (SYN), as shown in Figure 1.5. Now the connection is half-open.

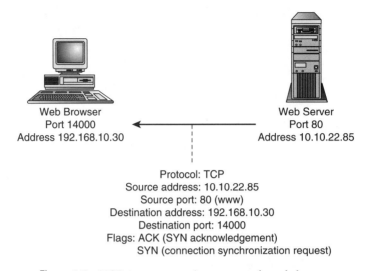

Web Browser
Port 14000
Address 192.168.10.30

Web Server
Port 80
Address 10.10.22.85

Protocol: TCP
Source address: 10.10.22.85
Source port: 80 (www)
Destination address: 192.168.10.30
Destination port: 14000
Flags: ACK (SYN acknowledgement)
SYN (connection synchronization request)

Figure 1.5 TCP server connection request acknowledgment.

Two fields not visible to the packet–filtering level are included in the SYN–ACK header. Along with the ACK flag, the server includes the client's sequence number incremented by one. The purpose of the acknowledgment is to acknowledge the message the client referred to by its sequence number. The server acknowledges this by incrementing the client's sequence number, effectively saying it received the message, and sequence number + 1 is the next message the server expects to receive. The client is free to throw its copy of the original SYN message away now that the server has acknowledged receipt of it.

The server also sets the SYN flag in its first message. As with the client's first message, the SYN flag is accompanied by a synchronization sequence number. The server is passing along its own starting sequence number for its half of the connection.

This first message is the only message the server will send with the SYN flag set. This and all subsequent messages have the ACK flag set. The presence of the ACK flag in all server messages, as compared to the lack of an ACK flag in the client's first message, will be a critical difference when we get to the information available for constructing a firewall.

Your machine receives this message and replies with its own acknowledgment, after which, the connection is established. Figure 1.6 shows a graphic representation. From here on, both the client and server set the ACK flag. The SYN flag won't be set again by either program.

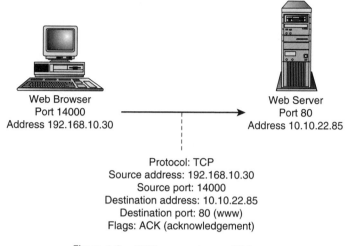

Figure 1.6   TCP connection establishment.

With each acknowledgment, the client and server programs increment their partner process's sequence number by the number of sequentially contiguous packets received since the last ACK was sent, indicating receipt of the packets, and indicating the next message the program expects to receive.

As your browser receives the Web page, your machine receives data messages from the Web server with packet headers, as shown in Figure 1.7.

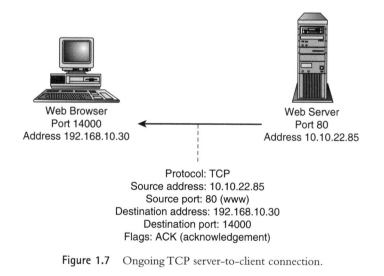

Figure 1.7   Ongoing TCP server-to-client connection.

Additional messages with flags for closing the connection are sent at the end, but those flags aren't available at the packet-filtering level. The important flags are the SYN and ACK flags. The SYN flag is set when a client and server exchange their first two messages during connection establishment. All subsequent messages between client and server have the ACK flag set.

Summary

The simple examples in this chapter illustrate the information that IP packet-filtering firewalls are based on. Chapter 2, "Packet-Filtering Concepts," builds on this introduction, describing how the ICMP, UDP, and TCP message types and service port numbers are used to define a packet-filtering firewall.

II

Packet-Filtering and Basic Security Measures

2

Packet-Filtering Concepts

THE TERM *FIREWALL* HAS A NUMBER OF DIFFERENT meanings depending on the mechanisms used to implement the firewall, the level of the TCP/IP protocol stack the firewall is operating on, and the network and routing architectures used. Three of the most common meanings refer to a packet-filtering firewall; an application gateway, also called a screened-host firewall; and an application-level circuit gateway, also called a proxy firewall.

A packet-filtering firewall is normally implemented within the operating system and operates at the IP network and transport protocol layers. It protects the system by making routing decisions after filtering packets based on information in the IP packet header.

An application gateway, or screened-host firewall, is implemented at the network architecture and system configuration levels. Network traffic is never passed through the application gateway machine. External access is allowed only to the gateway machine. Internal access is allowed only to the gateway machine. Local users must log in to the gateway machine and access the Internet from there. Additionally, the gateway machine may be protected by packet-filtering firewalls on both its external and internal interfaces.

A proxy firewall is usually implemented as separate applications for each service being proxied. Each proxy application appears to be the server to the client program, and appears to be the client to the real server. Special client programs, or specially configured client programs, connect to the proxy server instead of a remote server. The proxy establishes the connection to the remote server on the client application's behalf, after substituting the client's source address with its own. Proxy applications can ensure data integrity—that is, that data appropriate to the service is being exchanged—filter against viruses, and enforce high-level, detailed access control policies.

This book covers the ideas behind a packet-filtering firewall. All three approaches control which services can be accessed and by whom. Each approach has its strengths and advantages based on the differing information available at the various TCP/IP reference model layers. Large, commercial firewall products often incorporate some combination of packet filtering, protected screened hosts, and application proxying functionality into a multi-tiered security package.

Chapter 1, "Preliminary Concepts Underlying Packet-Filtering Firewalls," introduced the concepts and information a firewall is based on. This chapter introduces how this information is used to implement firewall rules. Much of this chapter focuses on filtering incoming packets, the types of packets to be filtered out and why. Less emphasis is placed on filtering outgoing packets under the assumption that a small site is a reasonably trusted environment without the additional internal security issues a larger corporate site would face. In fact, not all commercial firewalls provide the capability of filtering outgoing packets. In part, this is due to the appreciable performance cost packet filtering imposes on large routers. Hardware isn't quite fast enough—yet.

Both Chapter 1 and this chapter talk at length about the TCP and UDP service ports. The last section of this chapter, "Private Versus Public Network Services," describes the common network services found on a UNIX machine, what they do, and recommendations for whether you might consider running these services on a firewall machine.

A Packet-Filtering Firewall

An IPFW packet-filtering firewall consists of a list of acceptance and denial rules. These rules explicitly define which packets will and will not be allowed through the network interface. The firewall rules use the packet header fields described in Chapter 1 to decide whether to route a packet through to its destination, to silently throw the packet away, or to block the packet and return an error condition to the sending machine. These rules are based on the specific network interface card and host IP address, the network layer's source and destination IP addresses, the transport layer's TCP and UDP service ports, TCP connection flags, the network layer's ICMP message types, and whether the packet is incoming or outgoing.

Using a hybrid of the TCP/IP reference model, a packet-filtering firewall functions at the network and transport layers, as shown in Figure 2.1.

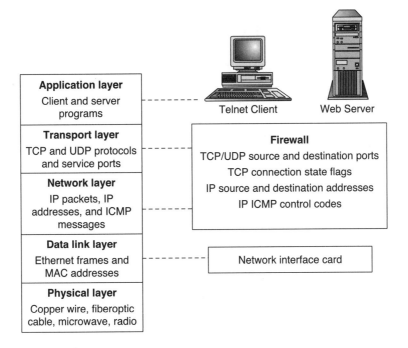

Figure 2.1   Firewall placement in the TCP/IP reference model.

The overall idea is that you need to very carefully control what passes between the Internet and the machine you have connected directly to the Internet. On the external interface to the Internet, you will individually filter what's coming in from the outside and what's going out from the machine as exactly and as explicitly as possible.

For a single machine setup, it might be helpful to think of the network interface as an I/O pair. The firewall independently filters what comes in and what goes out through the interface. The input filtering and the output filtering can have completely different rules. The lists of rules defining what can come in and what can go out are called *chains*. The I/O pair is the list of rules on the input chain and the list of rules on the output chain. The lists are called chains because a packet is matched against each rule in the list, one-by-one, until a match is found or the list is exhausted, as depicted in Figure 2.2.

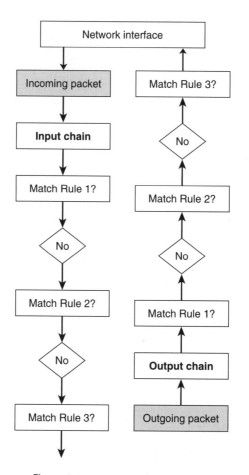

Figure 2.2 Input and output chains.

This sounds pretty powerful, and it is, but it isn't a surefire security mechanism. It's only part of the story, one layer in a full security scheme. Not all application communication protocols lend themselves to packet filtering. This type of filtering is too low-level to allow fine-grained authentication and access control. These security services must be furnished at higher levels. IP doesn't have the ability to verify that the sender is who or what it claims to be. The only identifying information available at this level is the source address in the IP packet header. The source address can easily be modified. Neither the network nor transport layers can verify that the application data is correct. Nevertheless, the packet level allows greater, simpler control over direct port access, packet contents, and correct communication protocols than can easily or conveniently be done at higher levels.

Without packet-level filtering, higher-level filtering and proxy security measures are either crippled or potentially ineffective. To some extent at least, they must rely on the correctness of the underlying communication protocol. Each layer in the security protocol stack adds another piece that other layers can't easily provide.

Choosing a Default Packet-Filtering Policy

Each firewall chain has a default policy and a collection of actions to take in response to specific message types. Each packet is checked against each rule in the list in turn until a match is found. If the packet doesn't match any rule, it falls through and the default policy is applied to the packet.

There are two basic approaches to a firewall:

- Deny everything by default and explicitly allow selected packets through.
- Accept everything by default and explicitly deny selected packets through.

The deny-everything policy is the recommended approach. This approach makes it easier to set up a secure firewall, but each service and related protocol transaction you want must be enabled explicitly. (See Figure 2.3.) This means you have to understand the communication protocol for each service you enable. The deny-everything approach requires more work up front to enable Internet access. Some commercial firewall products support only the deny-everything policy.

The accept-everything policy makes it much easier to get up and running right away, but forces you to anticipate every conceivable access type you might want to disable. (See Figure 2.4.) The danger is that you won't anticipate a dangerous access type until it's too late, or later enable an insecure service without first blocking external access to it. In the end, developing a secure accept-everything firewall is much more work, much more difficult, and therefore much more error-prone.

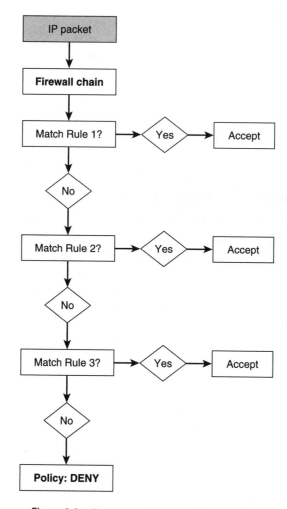

Figure 2.3 Deny-everything-by-default policy.

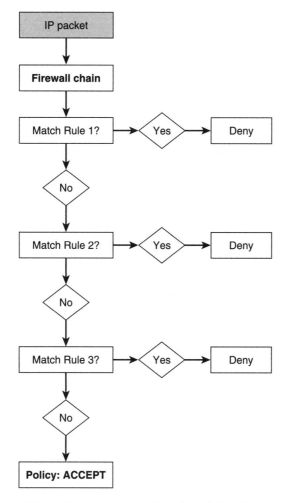

Figure 2.4   Accept-everything-by-default policy.

Rejecting Versus Denying a Packet

The IPFW firewall mechanism gives you the option of either rejecting or denying packets. What's the difference? As shown in Figure 2.5, when a packet is rejected, the packet is thrown away and an ICMP error message is returned to the sender. When a packet is denied, the packet is simply thrown away without any notification to the sender.

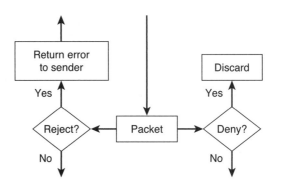

Figure 2.5   Rejecting versus denying a packet.

Denial is almost always the better choice. There are three reasons for this. First, sending an error response doubles the network traffic. The majority of dropped packets are dropped because they are malevolent, not because they represent an innocent attempt to access a service you don't happen to offer. Second, any packet you respond to can be used in a denial-of-service attack. Third, any response, even an error message, gives the would-be hacker potentially useful information.

Filtering Incoming Packets

The input side of the external interface I/O pair, the input chain, is the more interesting in terms of securing your site. As mentioned earlier, you can filter based on source address, destination address, source port, destination port, and TCP status flag. We'll use all these pieces of information at one point or another in the following sections.

Remote Source Address Filtering

At the packet level, the only means of identifying the IP packet's sender is the source address in the packet header. This fact opens the door to source address spoofing, where the sender places an incorrect address, rather than his or her own address, in the source field. The address might be a nonexistent address or it might be a legitimate address belonging to someone else. This can allow unsavory types to break into your system, appear to be you while attacking other sites, pretend to be someone else while attacking you, or otherwise mislead you as to the source of incoming messages.

Source Address Spoofing and Illegal Addresses

There are six major classes of source addresses you should deny on your external interface in all cases. These are incoming packets claiming to be from the following:

- Your IP address—You will never see legal incoming packets claiming to be *from* your machine. Because the source address is the only information available, and it can be modified, this is one of the few forms of spoofing you can detect at the packet-filtering level. Incoming packets claiming to be from your machine are spoofed. You can't be certain whether other incoming packets are coming from where they claim to be.

- Class A, B, and C *private* IP addresses—A set of addresses in each of the Class A, B, and C ranges are reserved for use in private LANs. They aren't intended for use on the Internet. As such, these addresses can be used by any site internally without the need to purchase registered IP addresses. Your machine should never see incoming packets from these source addresses.

  (In fact, private source addresses are seen quite often on local ISP subnets due to misconfigured systems, as well as from intentionally spoofed sites. If someone is leaking these addresses, you'll see them.)

  - Class A private addresses are assigned the range from `10.0.0.0` to `10.255.255.255`.

  - Class B private addresses are assigned the range from `172.16.0.0` to `172.31.255.255`.

  - Class C private addresses are assigned the range from `192.168.0.0` to `192.168.255.255`.

- Class D multicast IP addresses—IP addresses in the Class D range are set aside for use as destination addresses when participating in a multicast network broadcast, such as an audio- or videocast. They range from `224.0.0.0` to `239.255.255.255`. Your machine should never see packets from these source addresses.

- Class E reserved IP addresses—IP addresses in the Class E range were set aside for future and experimental use and are not assigned publicly. They range from `240.0.0.0` to `247.255.255.255`. Your machine should never see packets from these source addresses, and mostly likely won't. The defense and intelligence networks are quite good at not leaking their packets.

- Loopback interface addresses—The loopback interface is a private network interface used by the UNIX system for local, network-based services. Rather than send local traffic through the network interface driver, the operating system takes a shortcut through the loopback interface as a performance improvement. By definition, loopback traffic is targeted for the system generating it. It doesn't go out on the network. The loopback address range is `127.0.0.0` to `127.255.255.255`. You'll usually see it referred to as `127.0.0.1`, localhost, or the loopback interface, `lo`.

- Malformed broadcast addresses—Broadcast addresses are special addresses applying to all machines on a network. Address `0.0.0.0` is a special broadcast source address. The broadcast source address will either be `0.0.0.0` or a regular IP address. DHCP clients will see incoming broadcast packets from source address `0.0.0.0`. I'm unaware of any other situations where broadcast address `0.0.0.0` will be seen. It is not a legitimate point-to-point source address. When seen as the source address in a regular, point-to-point, nonbroadcast packet, the address is forged.

Blocking Problem Sites

Another common but less frequently used source address filtering scheme is to block all access from a selected machine, or more typically, from an entire network's IP address block. This is how the Internet community tends to deal with problem sites and ISPs that don't police their users. If a site develops a reputation as a bad Internet neighbor, other sites tend to block it across the board.

On the individual level, blocking all access from selected networks is convenient when individuals in the remote network are habitually making a nuisance of themselves.

Limiting Incoming Packets to Selected Remote Hosts

You might want to accept certain kinds of incoming packets from only specific external sites or individuals. In these cases, the firewall rules will define either specific IP addresses or a limited range of IP source addresses these packets will be accepted from.

The first class of incoming packets is from remote servers responding to your requests. Although some services, such as Web or FTP services, can be expected to be coming from anywhere, other services will legitimately be coming from only your ISP or specially chosen trusted hosts. Examples of servers that are probably offered only through your ISP are POP mail service, DHCP dynamic IP address assignment, and possibly Domain Name Service (DNS) name server responses.

The second class of incoming packets is from remote clients accessing services offered from your site. Again, while some incoming service connections, such as connections to your Web server, can be expected to be coming from anywhere, other local services will be offered to only a few trusted remote users or friends. Examples of restricted local services might be `telnet`, `ssh`, and `finger`.

Local Destination Address Filtering

Filtering incoming packets based on the destination address is not much of an issue. Your network interface card ignores regular packets that aren't addressed to it. The exception is broadcast packets, which are broadcast to all hosts on the network.

Address `255.255.255.255` is the general broadcast destination address. This address can be defined more explicitly as your network address followed by `255` in the remaining address quads. For example, if your ISP's network address is `192.168.0.0` and your

IP address is 192.168.10.30, you might see broadcast packets addressed to either 192.168.255.255 or 255.255.255.255 from your ISP.

Broadcast-to-destination address 0.0.0.0 is similar to the situation of point-to-point packets claiming to be from the broadcast source address mentioned earlier in the section "Source Address Spoofing and Illegal Addresses." Here, broadcast packets are directed to source address 0.0.0.0 rather than to the destination address, 255.255.255.255. In this case, there is little question about the packet's intent. This is an attempt to identify your system as a UNIX machine. For historical reasons, networking code derived from BSD UNIX returns an error type 3 ICMP message in response to 0.0.0.0 being used as the broadcast destination address. Other operating systems silently discard the packet. As such, this is a good example of why denying versus rejecting a packet makes a difference. In this case, the error message itself is what the hacker is looking for.

Remote Source Port Filtering

The source port in incoming packets identifies the program on the remote host that is sending the message. Generally speaking, all incoming requests from remote clients to your services follow the same pattern, and all incoming responses from remote servers to your local clients follow a different pattern.

Incoming requests and connections from remote clients to your local servers will have a source port in the unprivileged range. If you are hosting a Web server, all incoming connections to your Web server should have a source port between 1024 and 65535.

Incoming responses from remote servers that you contacted will have the source port that is assigned to the particular service. If you connect to a remote Web site, all incoming messages from the remote server will have the source port set to 80, the http service port number.

Local Destination Port Filtering

The destination port in incoming packets identifies the program or service on your computer that the packet is intended for. As with the source port, generally speaking, all incoming requests from remote clients to your services follow the same pattern, and all incoming responses from remote services to your local clients follow a different pattern.

Incoming requests and connections from remote clients to your local servers will set the destination port to the service number assigned to the particular service. An incoming packet destined for your local Web server will have the destination port set to 80, the http service port number.

Incoming responses from remote servers that you contacted will have a destination port in the unprivileged range. If you connect to a remote Web site, all incoming messages from the remote server will have a destination port between 1024 and 65535.

Incoming TCP Connection-State Filtering

Incoming TCP packet acceptance rules can make use of the connection state flags associated with TCP connections. All TCP connections adhere to the same set of connection states. These states differ between client and server due to the three-way handshake during connection establishment.

Incoming TCP packets from remote clients will have the SYN flag set in the first packet received as part of the three-way connection establishment handshake. The first connection request will have the SYN flag set, but not the ACK flag. All incoming packets after the first connection request will have only the ACK flag set. Your local server firewall rules will allow incoming packets, regardless of the state of the SYN and ACK flags.

Incoming packets from remote servers will always be responses to the initial connection request initiated from your local client program. Every packet received from a remote server will have the ACK flag set. Your local client firewall rules will require all incoming packets from remote servers to have the ACK flag set. Legitimate servers do not usually attempt to initiate connections to client programs.

Probes and Scans

A probe is an attempt to connect to or get a response from an individual service port. A scan is a series of probes to a set of different service ports. Scans are often automated.

In and of themselves, probes and scans are harmless. On the Internet, the only way to find out whether a site offers a particular service is to probe the port. How do you know whether a site has a Web server if you don't have its URL? You try to go to its Web site. In other words, you probe its http port.

Unfortunately, probes and scans are rarely innocent anymore. They are most likely the initial information-gathering phase, looking for interesting vulnerabilities prior to launching a hacking attempt. In 1998, in particular, we saw an exponential rise in scans worldwide. Automated scan tools are widespread, and coordinated efforts by groups of hackers are common.

General Port Scans

General port scans are indiscriminate probes across a large block of service ports, possibly the entire range (see Figure 2.6). These scans, probably generated by older network maintenance tools, such as satan or strobe, are becoming less frequent as more sophisticated, targeted tools, such as mscan, sscan, and nscan, become available.

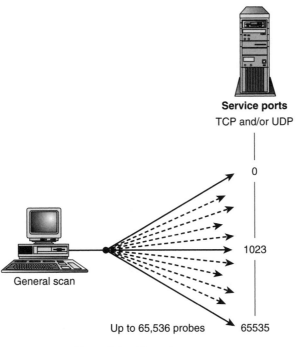

Figure 2.6   General port scan.

Targeted Port Scans

Targeted port scans look for specific vulnerabilities (see Figure 2.7). The newer, more sophisticated tools attempt to identify the hardware, operating system, and software versions. These tools are designed to zero in on known vulnerabilities on specific targets.

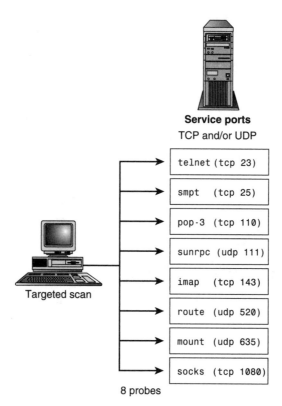

Figure 2.7   Targeted port scan.

Common Service Port Targets

Common targets are often individually probed as well as scanned. The hacker may be looking for a specific vulnerability, such as an insecure mail server or an open RPC `portmap` daemon.

An extensive list of ports is presented in Chapter 6, "Verifying That the System Is Running as You Expect" in the section "Interpreting the System Logs." Only a few common ports are mentioned here to give you the idea:

- Incoming packets from `reserved` port 0 are always bogus. This port isn't used legitimately.

- Probes of TCP ports 0 to 5 are a signature of the `sscan` program.

- `telnet` (23/tcp), `smtp` (25/tcp), `pop-3` (110/tcp), `sunrpc` (111/udp/tcp), `imap` (143/tcp), `snmp` (161/udp), `route` (520/udp) and `mount` (635/udp) are favorite target ports. They represent some of the most potentially vulnerable openings to a system. Because these services are so common, they are good examples of why you want to either not offer them to the outside world or very carefully control outside access to these services.

- NetBIOS (137, 138/`tcp`/`udp`, 139/`tcp`), Netbus (12345/`tcp`), and Back Orifice (31337/`udp`) probes are tediously common. They pose no threat to a UNIX system. The target is a Windows system in this case.

Avoiding Paranoia—Responding to Port Scans

Every day or so, the firewall logs in /`var`/`log`/`messages` show all kinds of failed connection attempts.

Are people trying to hack your system this often? Yes, they are. Is your system compromised? No, it isn't. The ports are blocked. The firewall is doing its job. These are failed connection attempts that the firewall denied.

At what point do you personally decide to report unwanted access attempts? At what point is it important enough to you to take the time to report them? At what point do you say enough is enough and get on with your life, or should you be writing `abuse@some.system` each time?

There are no "right" answers. How you respond is a personal judgment call. The topic itself can lead to religious wars. For obvious probes and scans, there is no clearcut answer. It's going to depend on your own personality and comfort level, how you personally define a serious probe, and your social conscience.

With that in mind, these are some workable guidelines.

The most common attempts are a combination of automated probing, mistakes, legitimate attempts based on the history of the Internet, ignorance, curiosity, and misbehaving software.

You should ignore individual, isolated, single connection attempts to `telnet`, `ssh`, `ftp`, `finger` or any other port for a common service that you're not providing. Probes and scans are a fact of life on the Internet, all too frequent, and usually don't pose a risk. They are kind of like door-to-door salespeople, commercial phone calls, wrong phone numbers, and junk postal mail. There isn't enough time in the day to respond to each one.

On the other hand, some probers are more persistent. You might decide to add firewall rules to block them completely, or possibly even their entire domain address space if their domain has a bad reputation or they use multiple source addresses.

Scans of a subset of the ports known to be potential security holes are typically the precursor to a hacking attempt if an open port is found. More inclusive scans are usually part of a broader scan for openings throughout a domain or subnet. Current hacking tools probe a subset of these ports one after the other.

Occasionally, you'll see serious hacking attempts. This is unquestionably a time to take action. Write them. Report them. Double-check your security. Observe what they're doing. Block them. Block their IP address block. Take your system offline, if it comes to that.

Historically Dangerous Ports

For further information on historically dangerous ports, see the "Packet Filtering for Firewall Systems" paper available at www.`cert.org`.

Some system administrators take every occurrence seriously, because even if *their* machine is secure, other people's machines might not be. The next guy might not even have the capability of knowing that he is being probed. Reporting probes is the socially responsible thing to do, for everyone's sake.

How should you respond to port scans? If you write these people, their postmaster, their uplink service provider NOC, or the network address block coordinator, try to be polite. Give them the benefit of the doubt. Overreactions are misplaced more often than not. What might appear as a serious hacking attempt to you is often a curious kid playing with a new program. A polite word to the abuse, root, or postmaster will usually take care of the problem. More people need to be educated about Netiquette than need their network accounts rescinded. And, they might be innocent of anything. Just as often, the person's system is compromised and they have no idea of what's going on. They'll be grateful for the information.

Denial-of-Service Attacks

Denial-of-service attacks are based on the idea of flooding your system with packets in such a way as to disrupt or seriously degrade your Internet connection, tying up local servers to the extent that legitimate requests can't be honored, or in the worst case, crashing your system altogether. The two most common results are keeping the system too busy to do anything useful and tying up critical system resources.

You can't protect against denial-of-service attacks completely. They can take as many different forms as the hacker's imagination allows. Anything that results in a response from your system, anything that results in your system allocating resources, anything that induces a remote site to stop communicating with you—all can be used in a denial-of-service attack.

These attacks usually involve one of several classic patterns, however, including TCP SYN flooding, ping flooding, UDP flooding, and ICMP routing redirect bombs.

TCP SYN Flooding

A TCP SYN flooding attack consumes your system resources until no more incoming TCP connections are possible. The attack makes use of the basic TCP three-way handshaking protocol during connection establishment, in conjunction with IP source address spoofing.

Denial-of-Service Attacks

For further information on denial-of-service attacks, see the "Denial of Service" paper available at www.cert.org.

The attacker spoofs his or her source address and initiates a connection to one of your TCP-based services. As a client attempting to open a TCP connection, the attacker sends you a SYN message. Your machine responds by sending an acknowledgment, a SYN-ACK. However, in this case, the address you're replying to isn't the attacker's address. It's a nonexistent address. The final stage of TCP connection establishment, receiving an ACK in response, will never happen. Consequently, finite network connection resources are consumed. The connection remains in a half-opened state until the connection attempt times out. The hacker floods your port with connection request after connection request, faster than the TCP timeouts release the resources. If this continues, all resources will be in use and no more incoming connection requests can be accepted. If the target is your smtp port, you can't receive email. If the target is your http port, people can't connect to your Web site.

Several aids are available to Linux users. The first is the source address filtering described previously. This filters out the most commonly used spoofed source addresses, but there is no guarantee that the spoofed address falls within the categories we can anticipate and filter against. The second is to compile your kernel with SYN cookies enabled; this is a specific retardant to SYN flooding. SYN cookies are enabled by default in Red Hat 6.0. You don't need to do anything. Earlier versions require you to explicitly configure the option into the kernel using make config, make menuconfig, or make xconfig, and then recompile and reinstall the kernel.

ping Flooding

Any message that elicits a response from your machine can be used to degrade your network connection by forcing the system to spend most of its time responding. The ICMP echo request message sent by ping is a common culprit.

Additionally, an older exploit called the *Ping of Death* involved sending very large ping packets. Vulnerable systems could crash as a result. Linux is not vulnerable to this exploit, nor are many other current UNIX operating systems. If your firewall is protecting older systems, those systems could be vulnerable.

The Ping of Death exploit gives an idea of how the simplest protocols and message interactions can be used by the creative hacker. Not all hacking attempts are attempts to break into your computer. Some are merely destructive. In this case, the goal is to crash the machine.

ping is a very useful, basic networking tool. You might not want to disable ping altogether. In today's Internet environment, conservative folks recommend disabling incoming ping, or at least severely limiting whom you accept echo requests from. Because of ping's history of involvement in denial-of-service attacks, many sites no longer respond to external ping requests.

SYN Flooding and IP Spoofing

For more information on SYN flooding and IP spoofing, see CERT_Advisory_CA-96.21, "TCP SYN Flooding and IP Spoofing Attacks" at ftp://info.cert.org/pub/cert_advisories/CA-96.21.tcp_syn_flooding.

UDP Flooding

The UDP protocol is especially useful as a denial-of-service tool. Unlike TCP, UDP is stateless. Flow control mechanisms aren't included. There are no connection state flags. Datagram sequence numbers aren't used. No information is maintained on which packet is expected next. It's relatively easy to keep a system so busy responding to incoming UDP probes that no bandwidth is left for legitimate network traffic.

Because UDP services are inherently less secure than TCP services, many sites disable all UDP ports that aren't absolutely necessary. As mentioned earlier, almost all common Internet services are TCP-based. The firewall we'll build in Chapter 3, "Building and Installing a Firewall," carefully limits UDP traffic to only those remote hosts providing necessary UDP services.

ICMP Redirect Bombs

ICMP redirect message type 5 tells the target system to change its routing tables in favor of a shorter route. If you run `routed` or `gated` and honor redirect messages, it's possible for a hacker to fool your system into thinking that the hacker's machine is one of your local machines or one of your ISP's machines, or even fool your system into forwarding all traffic to some other remote host.

Denial-of-Service Attacks and Other System Resources

Network connectivity isn't the only concern in denial-of-service attacks. Here are some examples of other areas to keep in mind while configuring your system:

- Your file system can overflow if your system is forced to write enormous numbers of messages to the error logs, or if your system is flooded with many copies of large email messages. You may want to configure resource limits and set up a separate partition for rapidly growing or changing file systems.

- Servers can be crashed if large amounts of data are sent to them and overflow the input buffers, or if unexpected data is sent to them. CGI scripts are especially vulnerable unless you take precautions. Many of the current vulnerabilities in servers are due to buffer overflows. It's important to keep up-to-date and install all the newest patches and software revisions.

UDP Port Denial-of-Service Attacks

For a description of a denial-of-service exploit using these UDP services, see CERT Advisory CA-96.01, "UDP Port Denial-of-Service Attack" at www.cert.org.

Email Denial-of-Service Exploits

For a description of a denial-of-service exploit using email, see "Email Bombing and Spamming" at www.cert.org.

- System memory, process table slots, CPU cycles, and other resources can be exhausted by repeated, rapid invocations of network services. There's little you can do about this other than setting any configurable limits for each individual service, enabling SYN cookies, and denying rather than rejecting packets sent to unsupported service ports.

Miscellaneous Considerations for Filtering Incoming Packets

Source routing and fragmentation are not packet-filtering firewall issues in the Linux implementation of IPFW, but they are security issues related to packets. Both are addressed at the operating system level.

Source-Routed Packets

Source-routed packets employ a rarely used IP option that allows the originator to define the route taken between two machines, rather than let the intermediate routers determine the path. As with ICMP redirects, this feature can allow a hacker to fool your system into thinking it's talking to a local machine, an ISP machine, or some other trusted host.

Red Hat Linux 6.0 discards source-routed packets by default. Earlier releases must be recompiled to deny source-routed packets. Enabling this feature in the kernel compilation configuration is highly recommended. Source routing has few legitimate uses. Some routers even ignore the option.

Packet Fragmentation

Different underlying networks (e.g., Ethernet, ATM, token ring) define different limits on the size of a frame. As a packet is passed on from one router to the next along the path from the source machine to the destination machine, network gateway routers may need to cut the packet into smaller pieces, called *fragments*, before passing them on to a new network. The first fragment contains the usual source and destination port numbers. The following fragments do not.

Firewall machines and machines that do IP masquerading for other local hosts should be configured to reassemble the packets before delivering them to the local target. This feature is enabled automatically in Red Hat 6.0. Prior releases required you to explicitly compile the defragmentation feature into the kernel.

CGI Denial-of-Service Exploits

For a description of a denial-of-service exploit using CGI scripts, see "How to Remove Meta-characters from User-Supplied Data in CGI Scripts" at www.cert.org and "The World Wide Web Security FAQ" at www.w3.org.

Filtering Outgoing Packets

If your environment represents a trusted environment, filtering outgoing packets isn't as critical as filtering incoming packets. Your system won't respond to incoming messages the firewall doesn't pass through. Still, symmetric filtering is more secure. It also protects other people, and you, from mistakes on your end.

What can go wrong on your end? In a worst-case scenario, a hacker could succeed in getting an account on your system. Filtering outgoing packets provides a bit more protection, at least until the hacker gets `root` access and figures out how to disable the firewall.

Filtering outgoing messages also allows you to run LAN services without leaking local packets onto the Internet where these packets don't belong. It's not only a question of disallowing external access to LAN services. It's also a question of not broadcasting local system information onto the Internet. Examples of this would be if you were running a local `dhcpd`, `timed`, `routed`, or `rwhod` server for internal use. Other obnoxious services might be broadcasting `wall` or `syslogd` messages.

Another area is blocking mischief originating from your machines. A year ago, I was taking a somewhat cavalier approach to outgoing filters in a Usenet security discussion. Someone wrote to tease me that I obviously didn't have teenage children...

A final problem area that is showing up on my ISP's network is coming from people running test or experimental software. They've brought a program home from work to try out or work on, and the software isn't behaving well.

A related source is some of the older personal computer software, which sometimes ignores the Internet service port protocols and reserved assignments. This is the personal computer equivalent of running a program designed for LAN use on an Internet-connected machine.

Local Source Address Filtering

Filtering outgoing packets based on the source address is easy. For a small site or a single computer connected to the Internet, the source address is always your computer's IP address during normal operation. There is no reason to allow an outgoing packet to have any other source address.

For people whose IP address is dynamically assigned by their ISP via DHCP, a brief exception exists during address assignment. This exception is specific to DHCP and is covered in Chapter 3.

For people with a LAN and multiple public server machines, each with its own statically assigned IP address, the issue is not so clear-cut. LAN topics are covered in Chapter 4, "LAN Issues, Multiple Firewalls, and Perimeter Networks." For people with a LAN whose firewall machine has a dynamically assigned IP address, limiting outgoing packets to contain the source address of the firewall machine's IP address is mandatory. It protects you from several fairly common configuration mistakes, covered in Chapter 4, that appear as cases of source address spoofing or illegal source addresses to remote hosts.

Remote Destination Address Filtering

As with incoming packets, you might want to allow certain kinds of outgoing packets to be addressed only to specific remote networks or individual machines. In these cases, the firewall rules will define either specific IP addresses or a limited range of IP destination addresses to which these packets will be allowed.

The first class of outgoing packets to filter by destination address is packets destined to remote servers you've contacted. Although some packets, such as those going to Web or FTP servers, can be expected to be destined to anywhere on the Internet, other remote services will legitimately be offered from only your ISP or specially chosen trusted hosts. Examples of servers that are probably offered only through your ISP are POP mail service, DHCP dynamic IP address assignment, and Usenet news service.

The second class of outgoing packets to filter by destination address is packets destined to remote clients who are accessing a service offered from your site. Again, although some outgoing service connections can be expected to be going anywhere, such as responses from your local Web server, other local services will be offered to only a few trusted remote sites or friends. Examples of restricted local services might be telnet, ssh, and finger. Not only will the firewall rules deny general incoming connections to these services, but the rules also don't allow outgoing responses from these services to just anyone.

Local Source Port Filtering

Explicitly defining which service ports on your end can be used for outgoing connections serves two purposes—one for your client programs and one for your server programs. Specifying the source ports allowed for your outgoing connections helps ensure that your programs are behaving correctly, and protects other people from any local network traffic that doesn't belong on the Internet.

Outgoing connections from your local clients will almost always originate from an unprivileged source port. Limiting your clients to the unprivileged ports in the firewall rules helps protect other people from potential mistakes on your end by ensuring that your client programs are behaving as expected.

Outgoing packets from your local server programs will always originate from their assigned service port. Limiting your servers to their assigned ports at the firewall level ensures that your server programs are functioning correctly at the protocol level. More importantly, it helps protect any private, local network services you might be running from outside access. It also helps protect remote sites from being bothered by network traffic that should remain confined to your local systems.

Remote Destination Port Filtering

Your local client programs are designed to connect to network servers offering their services from their assigned service ports. From this perspective, limiting your local clients to connect only to their associated server's service port ensures protocol correctness. Limiting your client connections to specific destination ports serves a couple of other purposes as well. One, it helps guard against local, private network client programs inadvertently attempting to access servers on the Internet. Two, it does much to disallow outgoing mistakes, port scans, and other mischief potentially originating from your site.

Your local server programs will almost always participate in connections originating from unprivileged ports. The firewall rules limit your servers' outgoing traffic to only unprivileged destination ports.

Outgoing TCP Connection-State Filtering

Outgoing TCP packet acceptance rules can make use of the connection state flags associated with TCP connections, just as the incoming rules do. All TCP connections adhere to the same set of connection states, which differs between client and server.

Outgoing TCP packets from local clients will have the SYN flag set in the first packet sent as part of the three-way connection establishment handshake. The initial connection request will have the SYN flag set, but not the ACK flag. All outgoing packets after the first connection request will only have the ACK flag set. Your local client firewall rules will allow outgoing packets with either the SYN or ACK flags set.

Outgoing packets from local servers will always be responses to an initial connection request initiated from a remote client program. Every packet sent from your servers will have the ACK flag set. Your local server firewall rules will require all outgoing packets from your servers to have the ACK flag set.

Private Versus Public Network Services

One of the easiest ways to inadvertently allow uninvited intrusions is to allow outside access to local services that are designed only for LAN use. Some services, if offered locally, should never cross the boundary between your LAN and the big, bad Internet beyond. Some of these services annoy your neighbors, some provide information you'd be better off keeping to yourself, and some represent glaring security holes if they're available outside your LAN.

Some of the earliest network services, the BSD remote access commands in particular, were designed for local sharing and ease-of-access across multiple lab machines in a trusted environment. Some of the later services were intended for Internet access, but they were designed at a time when the Internet was basically an extended community of academicians and researchers. The Internet was a relatively open, safe place. As the Internet grew into a global network including general public access, it developed into a completely untrusted environment.

Many UNIX network services are designed to provide local information about user accounts on the system, which programs are running and which resources are in use, system status, network status, and similar information from other machines connected over the network. Not all these informational services represent security holes in and of themselves. It's not that a hacker can use them directly to gain unauthorized access to your system. It's that they provide information about your system and user accounts that can be useful to a hacker who is looking for known vulnerabilities. They might also supply information such as usernames, addresses, phone numbers, and so forth, which you don't want to be readily available to everyone who asks.

Some of the more dangerous network services are designed to provide LAN access to shared file systems and devices, such as a networked printer or fax machine.

Some services are difficult to configure correctly, and some are difficult to configure securely. Entire books are devoted to configuring some of the more complicated UNIX services. Specific service configuration is beyond the scope of this book.

Some services just don't make sense in a home or small office setting. Some are intended to manage large networks, provide Internet routing service, provide large database informational services, support two-way encryption and authentication, and so forth.

Protecting Nonsecure Local Services

The easiest way to protect yourself is to not offer the service. But what if you need one of these services locally? Not all services can be protected adequately at the packet-filtering level. Multiconnection services, such as RealAudio and ICQ, and UDP-based RPC services are notoriously difficult to secure at the packet-filtering level.

One way to safeguard your computer is to not host network services on the firewall machine that you don't intend for public use. If the service isn't available, there's nothing for a remote client to connect to. Small sites such as those in the home often won't have a supply of computers available to enforce access security policies by running private services on other machines. Compromises have to be made.

Another way to safeguard your computer is to implement a firewall of some sort. A packet-filtering firewall adds protection at the service port access level. It allows you to run many of the local, insecure network services, particularly TCP services, with less danger of outside access; it can help control which outside parties can access local services; and by enforcing low-level communication protocols, it can help ensure that your programs are talking to whom and what you expect.

A packet-filtering firewall doesn't offer complete security however. Some programs require higher-level security measures than can be provided at the packet-filtering level. Some programs are too problematic to risk running on a firewall machine.

Selecting Services to Run

When all is said and done, only you can decide which services you need or want. The first step in securing your system is deciding which services and daemons you intend to run on the firewall machine. Each service has its own security considerations. When it comes to selecting services to run under UNIX, the general rule of thumb is to run only the network services you need and understand. It's important to understand a network service, what it does and who it's intended for, before you run it—especially on a machine connected directly to the Internet.

The following sections list the most common network services available on a Red Hat Linux system. The services are categorized by how and when the services are started. Stated differently, the services are categorized by the mechanism UNIX uses to start them, which also determines how these services are organized from a system administration point of view.

Network services are started from three major places in a UNIX system. One, basic services are managed by the runlevel manager and started automatically at boot time from shell scripts under the /etc/rc.d directory. Two, some of the more elective network services are managed by inetd and started upon request from a client program. These services are defined in inetd's configuration file, /etc/inetd.conf. Three, some network services are local to your specific site and must be started explicitly through your local configuration scripts. These services are usually not part of the standard Linux distribution. Instead, they are usually programs you've downloaded from some software repository and installed yourself.

Runlevel Manager

A *runlevel* is a booting and system state concept taken from System V UNIX. Red Hat Linux incorporates seven different runlevels. The subdirectories under /etc/rc.d are associated with the various runlevels and contain symbolic links to configuration scripts in /etc/rc.d/init.d. The symbolic links follow a naming convention indicating whether a service is to be stopped (names starting with *K*) or started (names starting with *S*) when entering a runlevel, and the order the scripts are to be executed in.

You won't use all seven runlevels. Your system will operate at one of runlevels 2, 3, or 5. Runlevel 3 is the default, normal, multiuser system state. Runlevel 2 is the same as 3, without Network File System (NFS) services running. Runlevel 5 is the same as 3, with the addition of the X Window Display Manager, which presents an X-based login and host selection screen. (Ideally, a firewall machine should not run the X Window Display Manager.)

For the curious, the remaining runlevels represent specialized system states. Runlevel 0 defines the final cleanup actions to take before halting the system. Runlevel 1 defines the actions to take when entering and exiting single-user mode. Runlevel 4 isn't used. You could set it up as a customized state of your own. Runlevel 6 defines the final cleanup actions to take before rebooting the system.

When you first install your system, and later when using the runlevel manager available through the control-panel program, you are given the opportunity to define which system services will start automatically when the system boots. Both of these configuration tools provide graphic interfaces to managing the system startup files in /etc/rc.d.

As a little background on this, when the system boots, the master system process, `init`, reads its configuration file, `/etc/inittab`. This file tells `init` to execute several scripts in `/etc/rc.d`, including `rc.sysinit` and `rc`. `/etc/rc.d/rc.sysinit` runs once at boot time to initialize the system, load modules, check the file systems, read systemwide configuration settings, and so forth. `/etc/rc.d/rc` is executed each time the runlevel is changed. Its job is first to stop services that aren't defined to be running at this runlevel, and then to kick off the services that *are* defined to run at this particular runlevel (runlevel 3 or 5, usually). The default runlevel is defined in `/etc/inittab`. It is preconfigured as `id:3:initdefault`. Runlevel 2 is the best choice for a firewall machine.

When you start the runlevel editor, you see a window divided into nine lists of alphabetized names, which are the names of system service initialization scripts. The leftmost list is titled "Available" and contains the names of all the scripts available in `/etc/rc.d/init.d`. The rest of the window is divided into two rows, labeled "Start" and "Stop". Both rows are divided into four columns labeled from 2 to 5, referring to services to start or stop upon entry to each of the runlevels, 2 through 5. Table 2.1 lists the service initialization scripts available in the leftmost column. The exact contents depend on the specific service packages you've installed on the system.

Table 2.1   Network Services Available at Different Runlevels

	amd
Description	Enables the NFS automount daemon, `amd`.
Considerations	NFS was designed as a LAN service. It contains numerous security vulnerabilities if used over the Internet. Do not allow Internet access to your NFS-mounted file systems. In fact, don't run NFS on your firewall machine. NFS is made up of several daemons. Within the runlevel editor, the initialization scripts are called `amd`, `nfs` and `nfsfs`.
Recommendation	Don't run `amd` on the firewall machine.

	arpwatch
Description	Enables the `arpwatch` daemom to log and build a database of Ethernet address/IP address pairings it sees on a LAN interface.

continues

Table 2.1 Continued

arpwatch

Considerations	Properly configured, the `arpwatch` daemon is not a security problem. `arpwatch` listens on a private UNIX domain socket. By default, however, `arpwatch` will put your external network interface into promiscuous mode as a packet sniffer, enabling the interface to examine packets not addressed to it. Finding your network interface in promiscuous mode is a telltale sign of a compromised system. If your interface is in promiscuous mode as a normal part of your system state, security information is lost, and you are not learning anything about your LAN you don't already know.
Recommendation	Don't run `arpwatch` on the firewall machine.

autofs

Description	Enables the automount management process, `automount`.
Considerations	NFS is an RPC-based LAN service. Both NFS and any network service relying on the `portmap` daemon are potentially severe security holes and should not be accessible from the Internet. Ideally, these servers should not be running on a firewall machine. Additionally, `automount` relies on Network Information Service (NIS) if the service is available. NIS is another LAN service that is best not run on a firewall machine.
Recommendation	Don't run `automount` on the firewall machine.

bootparamd

Description	Enables the boot parameter server.
Considerations	The `bootparamd` daemon provides boot-related information to diskless workstations on a LAN. A home or small business system is not likely to have diskless workstations. In any case, this server should not be run on a firewall machine.
Recommendation	Don't run `bootparamd`.

dhcpd

Description	Starts a local DHCP server.
Considerations	This service assigns dynamically allocated IP addresses to its client hosts. This service is often used within an ISP or a corporate LAN.

Recommendation	If your ISP dynamically assigns IP addresses, running a local DHCP server is a quick way to get your ISP account shut down. Some people have good reasons for running a local server, but care must be taken at both the firewall level and at the server configuration level. Don't enable the dhcpd server unless you know what you are doing. Don't run dhcpd unless you really need it. Don't run it until you understand its configuration. Don't run it without a firewall in place.

gated

Description	Enables the gateway routing daemon.
Considerations	The gated daemon handles network routing protocols. Routing in a small LAN is better and more safely managed by using static IP addresses. Firewall machines should use static routing only. If you must run a routing daemon, choose gated over the older and less secure routed, because gated supports the newer OSPF routing protocol; routed supports only the older RIP routing protocol. While RIP and OSPF are LAN routing protocols, firewall machines should not function as dynamic routers. gated should not be run on the firewall machine.
Recommendation	Don't run gated.

httpd

Description	Starts the Apache Web server to host a Web site.
Considerations	Web server security is beyond the scope of this book. However, as with any kind of file access service, the basic issue is limiting access to only those parts of your file system that you intend to make public, and running the servers as unprivileged users. Additionally, avoid any CGI script unless you understand the serious security issues these scripts can represent. Because CGI scripts can execute programs on your system, the basic issues involve stringent input checking, running as an unprivileged user, and using full pathnames to any programs or scripts the CGI program executes.

continues

More Information on Web Server Issues

For information on Web server issues, see the Apache Web Site at www.apache.org, *Apache Server for Dummies* by Ken Coar (IDG Books), and "How to Remove Meta-characters from User-Supplied Data in CGI Scripts" at www.cert.org.

Table 2.1   Continued

	httpd
Recommendation	Run httpd later if you decide to host a Web site. Read the Apache Web server documentation and the comments in the configuration files first.

	inet
Description	The inetd daemon is at the heart of providing many network services. Instead of having at least one of every service daemon continually running, whether the service is being used or not, inetd replaces these daemons with a single program—itself. inetd listens for incoming connections to the service ports it manages, decides which service the request should be connected to, possibly uses a helper program to do access permission checking, starts the requested program if it isn't running continually, and establishes the ongoing connection between the client program making the request and the server program that will service that request.
Considerations	You need inetd if you use common services, such as ftp or telnet, locally or if you offer these services to remote sites.
Recommendation	Run inetd.

	innd
Description	Enables a local Usenet news server.
Considerations	You don't need to worry about anything if you have a firewall in place. Few small sites have a use for a local news server. News server configuration is difficult. If you need a local server, be certain to deny remote access from anyone except specific, trusted remote sites.
Recommendation	Don't run innd.

	linuxconf
Description	Allows you to configure your machine using a local Web server as the user interface.
Considerations	linuxconf listens on TCP port 98. By default, linuxconf listens on only the loopback interface. You don't need to worry about anything if you maintain the default configuration. Don't change the linuxconf access configuration to allow external access.

Recommendation	None.

lpd

Description	Enables the printer server.
Considerations	At first glance, you might think that access to your printer is necessarily limited to the local machine. With UNIX, your printers are treated as network devices. Be sure that both your printer access configuration files and your firewall block remote access to your printer if you have one.
Recommendation	Run lpd if you are sharing a printer among local UNIX machines.

mars-nwe

Description	Enables the mars-nwe file and print server for Novell NetWare Windows clients on the LAN.
Considerations	Local file and printer servers should not run on a firewall machine. To enable NetWare support, you'd have to recompile your kernel with IPX network layer support, SPX transport layer support, and NCP file system support. As the kernel configuration help document says, if you don't understand it, don't enable it.
Recommendation	Don't run mars-nwe on the firewall machine.

mcserv

Description	Enables the Midnight Commander file server.
Considerations	mcserv manages access to the Midnight Commander networked file system. It is an insecure file server intended for LAN use. Do not allow external Internet access to your Midnight Commander file systems. mcserv is a UDP RPC-based service, which relies on the portmap daemon. Ideally, the service should not be running on the firewall machine.
Recommendation	Don't run mcserv on the firewall machine.

named

Description	The named daemon provides the server half of the network DNS, translating between symbolic machine names and their numeric IP addresses. The client half of DNS, the resolver, isn't visible as a distinct program. It's part of the network libraries compiled into your programs.

continues

Table 2.1 Continued

	named
Considerations	DNS services are most likely provided by your ISP. Running a local server can improve network performance. Simple DNS servers do not pose security risks if configured correctly.
Recommendation	Run named after you understand the server and how to configure it. DNS configuration can be complicated and arcane. In the meantime, point your name resolver to your ISP's name servers.

	netfs
Description	Mounts NFS, Samba, and NetWare networked file systems.
Considerations	netfs is not a service daemon. It's a shell script that runs once to mount networked file systems locally. The caveat remains that network file system services should not generally be used on a firewall machine.
Recommendation	Don't run netfs on the firewall machine.

	network
Description	The network configuration script runs at boot time to activate the network interfaces you've configured. It is not a server, per se.
Considerations	You need to run this script.
Recommendation	Run network.

	nfs
Description	Enables NFS services.
Considerations	NFS was designed as a LAN service. It contains numerous security vulnerabilities if used over the Internet. Do not allow Internet access to your NFS-mounted file systems. In fact, don't run NFS on your firewall machine. NFS is made up of several daemons. Within the runlevel editor, the initialization scripts are called amd, nfs and nfsfs.
Recommendation	Don't run nfs on the firewall machine.

More Information on DNS

For information on DNS, see *DNS and BIND* by Paul Albitz and Cricket Liu (O'Reilly), the "DNS HOWTO" by Nicolai Langfeldt, available in your online documentation in /usr/doc/, and man pages named(8), resolver(5), and hostname(7).

	nscd
Description	Enables the Name Switch Cache daemon.
Considerations	nscd is a support service for NIS that caches user passwords and group memberships. NIS is an inherently insecure LAN service that should not being running on a firewall machine.
Recommendation	Don't run nscd on the firewall machine.

	portmap
Description	Enables the RPC portmap manager.
Considerations	The RPC portmap daemon is somewhat similar to inetd. It manages connections to RPC-based services, such as NFS and NIS. If you aren't using these services locally, disable the portmap daemon. If you are using these services, make certain that your firewall blocks outside access to portmap. The newer portmap honors access control information in /etc/hosts.allow and /etc/hosts.deny.
Recommendation	Don't run portmap on the firewall machine.

	postgresql
Description	Starts a local SQL database server.
Considerations	SQL is a TCP-based service associated with port 5432. The main server, postmaster, can be configured to use either Internet domain sockets or local UNIX domain sockets. As a service designed to access local files, SQL should not generally be offered from a firewall machine without firewall and security configuration precautions. Refer to the man pages postmaster(1), postgres(1) and psql(1), and the online document, PostgreSQL-HOWTO.
Recommendation	Don't run postgresql on the firewall machine.

continues

Commonly Exploited Vulnerabilities
The portmap daemon represents a family of the most commonly exploited vulnerabilities in a UNIX system.

Table 2.1   Continued

	routed
Description	Enables the `routed` daemon to automatically update dynamic kernel routing tables.
Considerations	Both `routed` and `gated` represent serious security holes, `routed` even more so than `gated`. It's unlikely that you will need to manage your firewall's routing table dynamically using RIP. That's a service provided by your ISP. Just use static IP addresses locally on the firewall machine.
Recommendation	Don't run `routed`.

	rstatd
Description	Enables the `rstatd` daemon to collect and provide system information for other machines on the LAN.
Considerations	System status information should not be shared with remote Internet machines. The service should not be run on a firewall machine.
Recommendation	Don't run `rstatd` on the firewall machine.

	ruserd
Description	Enables the remote user locator service. This is an RPC-based service that provides information about individual users currently logged into one of the machines on the LAN.
Considerations	A small site has little need for this LAN service. Additionally, the `rpc.rusersd` daemon depends on RPC services, which should not be used on a firewall machine.
Recommendation	Don't run `ruserd` on the firewall machine.

	rwalld
Description	Enables the `rpc.rwalld` service daemon. This is an RPC-based service that allows users to write messages to the terminals of everyone else logged in to a machine on the LAN.
Considerations	A small site has little need for this LAN service. Additionally, the `rpc.rwalld` daemon depends on RPC services, which should not be used on a firewall machine.
Recommendation	Don't run `rwalld` on the firewall machine.

<table>
<tr><td colspan="2" align="center">*rwhod*</td></tr>
<tr><td>Description</td><td>Enables the rwhod service daemon. The rwhod daemon supports the rwho and ruptime services for a LAN. As such, the service provides information about who is logged in, what they are doing, which systems are running and connected to the LAN, and so forth.</td></tr>
<tr><td>Considerations</td><td>A small site has little need for this LAN service. Ideally, the rwhod daemon should not be used on a firewall machine.</td></tr>
<tr><td>Recommendation</td><td>Don't run rwhod on the firewall machine.</td></tr>
</table>

	sendmail
Description	Local mail service is handled by sendmail.
Considerations	You need sendmail if you host your own mail services. Properly configured, sendmail is relatively secure today. Nevertheless, sendmail remains a frequent hacker target. Security updates are made available as problems are discovered and fixed.
	SMTP services have a long history of security vulnerabilities, both in terms of allowing general system access and in terms of being used as a spam relay. Much effort has gone into making current versions of sendmail more secure. As distributed by Red Hat, the default configuration is quite secure, at least in terms of unauthorized mail relaying.
Recommendation	Run sendmail if you want local mail services independent of your ISP. Don't run sendmail if you use you ISP-provided mail service exclusively.

	smb
Description	Enables Samba file sharing and printer sharing service.
Considerations	File system and device sharing services are LAN services and shouldn't be run on a firewall machine. Samba services should not be remotely available under any circumstances.
Recommendation	Don't run smb on a firewall machine.

continues

Table 2.1   Continued

	snmpd
Description	Enables the local Simple Network Management Daemon. The **snmpd** daemon manages SNMP network administration.
Considerations	SNMP is a LAN management service. For safety, as a local UDP service, **snmpd** should not be running on a firewall machine. A small LAN is very unlikely to need this. If you must use it, view it as a dangerous service and make certain to block all SNMP traffic between your LAN and the Internet. You don't want outsiders managing your network for you, and they won't appreciate seeing packets originating from your SNMP daemon.
Recommendation	Don't run **snmpd**.
	squid
Description	Enables the Squid Internet Object Cache. If you aren't running the Apache Web server locally, **squid** can serve as a local HTTP proxy server and local Web cache for Web pages retrieved from remote Web sites. Some amount of effort is required to configure **squid**.
Considerations	Properly configured, **squid** has no special security considerations with a firewall in place.
Recommendation	Run **squid** later if you want Web pages cached locally and you aren't using the Apache server's caching features.
	syslog
Description	The **syslog** configuration script starts up the **syslogd** and **klogd** system logging daemons at boot time. You really want this service so that system status and error messages are written to the log files. **syslogd** can be configured to run as a LAN service.
Considerations	You need this service.
Recommendation	Run **syslog**.
	xfs
Description	Enables the X Window font server, which is new in Red Hat 6.0, to serve fonts to local and remote X servers.

Considerations	Although xfs can be configured to listen on a TCP Internet domain socket for remote servers, in its default configuration, xfs listens on a private UNIX domain socket. As such, xfs is not a security risk by default. The X Window server depends on xfs. Ideally, the service should not be run on a firewall machine.
Recommendation	Do not run xfs on a firewall machine if possible.

xntpd

Description	Enables a local network time server.
Considerations	You don't need to worry about anything if you have a firewall in place. Some sites schedule cron to periodically run the ntpd or ntpdate client program to get the current time from an official remote time server. The local xntpd server is run to disseminate the current system time among local machines on the internal LAN.
Recommendation	Run xntpd later after you understand the configuration issues, if you want a local time server for LAN machines.

ypbind

Description	Enables the ypbind daemon for machines running as NIS clients.
Considerations	The NIS package includes the boot-time configuration scripts ypbind, yppasswdd, and ypserv. NIS is a LAN service providing centralized network, user, and machine administration functions. A small LAN is unlikely to need this. If you must use it, consider it to be a dangerous service and make certain to block all NIS and RPC traffic between your LAN and the Internet.
Recommendation	Don't run ypbind on the firewall machine.

yppasswdd

Description	Enables the NIS password server.
Considerations	The NIS package includes the boot-time configuration scripts ypbind, yppasswdd, and ypserv. NIS is a LAN service providing centralized network, user, and machine administration functions. A small LAN is unlikely to need this. If you must use it, consider it to be a dangerous service and make certain to block all NIS and RPC traffic between your LAN and the Internet.
Recommendation	Don't run yppasswdd on the firewall machine.

continues

Table 2.1   Continued

	ypserv
Description	Enables the NIS master server.
Considerations	The NIS package includes the boot-time configuration scripts `ypbind`, `yppasswdd`, and `ypserv`. NIS is a LAN service providing centralized network, user and machine administration functions. A small LAN is unlikely to need this. If you must use it, consider it to be a dangerous service and make certain to block all NIS and RPC traffic between your LAN and the Internet.
Recommendation	Don't run `ypserv` on the firewall machine.

inetd **Managed Services**

Now that you know more about the runlevel manager and which basic system services are automatically started when the machine boots up, we can move on to discuss network services. Network services can be both local and public, and are started by `inetd`. Some, but not all, network services you offer from your site are made available through the `inetd` superserver. Services managed by `inetd` are specified in the `/etc/inetd.conf` configuration file.

Practically all the services in this file are LAN services and should be commented out on a firewall machine. `/etc/inetd.conf` occasionally changes with new Linux releases. The default configuration provided with recent versions of Red Hat Linux, including 6.0, are not secure for a system connected directly to the Internet.

The exact contents of the `/etc/inetd.conf` file differs by vendor and by release version. Generally, `/etc/inetd.conf` contains the services described in the following sections, in this order.

Network Testing Services

The first set of services are provided internally by the `inetd` daemon itself for use in local network testing and trouble-shooting. Probably no one reading this book will ever need these testing facilities:

```
#echo       stream  tcp    nowait  root    internal
#echo       dgram   udp    wait    root    internal
#discard    stream  tcp    nowait  root    internal
#discard    dgram   udp    wait    root    internal
#daytime    stream  tcp    nowait  root    internal
#daytime    dgram   udp    wait    root    internal
#chargen    stream  tcp    nowait  root    internal
#chargen    dgram   udp    wait    root    internal
#time       stream  tcp    nowait  root    internal
#time       dgram   udp    wait    root    internal
```

If you look into them, the services sound harmless. However, `discard` and `chargen` together have been used in a well-publicized UDP denial-of-service attack. See the section "UDP Flooding" earlier in this chapter for a pointer to the CERT advisory describing these attacks.

Standard Services

A handful of standard UNIX services are managed by `inetd`, most notably the `ftp` and `telnet` servers:

- `ftp`—`ftp` is one of the most common means of sharing files across the Internet. However, `ftp` is full of security holes and has often been exploited when it isn't configured securely. Proper configuration is detailed; it requires study:

    ```
    #ftp    stream  tcp    nowait  root    /usr/sbin/tcpd in.ftpd -l -a
    ```

    If you want to offer general FTP services to the Internet, wait until you've read the configuration documentation and some of the papers from CERT covering FTP's security issues. If all you want is to offer a few files from your site to anonymous users, you might consider using a Web server instead to make these files available. Anonymous FTP services are more prone to security breaches due to misconfigurations than authenticated FTP services. I'd recommend not even installing the anonymous FTP package. Authenticated `ftp` should not be offered to remote users from a firewall machine, ideally.

    If you want to offer FTP services to only your LAN, you will need to enable the service in `/etc/inetd.conf`. Outside access can be disabled in the `ftp` configuration files, in your firewall, and in the `tcp_wrapper` configuration. `tcp_wrapper` documentation can be found in man pages `tcpd(8)`, `hosts_access(5)`, `inetd.conf(5)`, `hosts_options(5)` and `syslog.conf(5)`.

- `telnet`—`telnet` is one of the most common means of logging in to remote systems, both over the Internet and locally between UNIX and non-UNIX machines. If you have a LAN, chances are you'll want to enable this service unless you can use `ssh` on all your local machines. If you want to access your machine from remote accounts over the Internet, you need `telnet` unless the remote host provides some more secure service, such as SSH:

    ```
    #telnet stream tcp    nowait  root    /usr/sbin/tcpd in.telnetd
    ```

    `telnet` is considered to be insecure over the Internet because it passes information in ASCII clear text, including your login name and password. Packet sniffers can and have been used to capture this kind of information.

FTP Security Issues

For information on FTP security issues, see the following papers available at www.cert.org: "Anonymous FTP Configuration Guidelines," "Anonymous FTP Abuses," and "Problems with the FTP PORT Command."

If you need `telnet` access internally, but don't need to allow login access from remote sites, access can be limited to your local machines by your firewall, by `tcp_wrappers`, and in the `/etc/security/access.conf` file.

- gopher—The `gopher` information retrieval service is a standard service. Some people still use it, but it has largely been replaced by Web servers and search engines. Most people won't have a need to offer this service. `gopher` has been dropped from `/etc/inetd.conf` as of Red Hat release 6.0:

  ```
  #gopher  stream  tcp    nowait  root    /usr/sbin/tcpd  gn
  ```

BSD Remote Access Services

The BSD services developed as part of the standard Berkeley UNIX distribution to make access among accounts on multiple LAN machines more convenient:

- Remote shell services—BSD remote access services (called `shell`, `login` and `exec` in `/etc/inetd.conf`) are accessed through the `rsh` and `rlogin` programs and the `rexec` library call. These are LAN services designed to make local access between machines by the same user easy, without the need to reauthenticate. A firewall system shouldn't use these services. Make sure these services are disabled on the firewall machine. If you do need them, be sure to block all outside access through your firewall and in the `tcp_wrapper` configuration. *Never* allow external access to these services, or you'll be hacked in no time:

  ```
  #shell  stream  tcp    nowait  root    /usr/sbin/tcpd  in.rshd
  #login  stream  tcp    nowait  root    /usr/sbin/tcpd  in.rlogind
  #exec   stream  tcp    nowait  root    /usr/sbin/tcpd  in.rexecd
  ```

- Talk services—The talk services are not insecure in and of themselves, but do you really want people on the Internet to be able to write messages to your terminal, or even know which accounts exist on your system? A small system probably won't need these. The talk services have largely been replaced over the Internet by services such as IRC or Instant Messenger:

  ```
  #comsat dgram   udp    wait    root    /usr/sbin/tcpd  in.comsat
  #talk   dgram   udp    wait    root    /usr/sbin/tcpd  in.talkd
  #ntalk  dgram   udp    wait    root    /usr/sbin/tcpd  in.ntalkd
  #dtalk  stream  tcp    wait    nobody  /usr/sbin/tcpd  in.dtalkd
  ```

sunrpc **and** *mountd* **Exploits**

For more information on `sunrpc` (111/udp/tcp) and `mountd` (635/udp) exploits, see `www.cert.org/advisories/CA-98.12.mountd.html`. For more information on `imap` (143/tcp) exploits, see `www.cert.org/advisories/CA-98.09.imapd.html`. For more information on pop-3 (110/tcp) exploits, see `www.cert.org/advisories/CA-98.08.qpopper_vul.html`.

Mail Delivery Services

Mail delivery servers, both POP and IMAP services, are notorious security holes when not configured properly. Along with `portmap` and `mountd`, the `pop-3` and `imap` servers are the three most frequently compromised servers today:

- `pop-2`—`pop-2` has mostly been replaced by the newer `pop-3` protocol. There's probably no reason for anyone to offer this service:

    ```
    #pop-2   stream tcp    nowait root    /usr/sbin/tcpd ipop2d
    ```

- `pop-3`—You may need to offer POP services. Most people don't need to. Some will want to offer POP services to a few remote users, or you may want to offer POP services locally as a means of retrieving email from a central mail server. Again, if you need only a local POP server, be sure to block external access in your firewall, `tcp_wrapper`, and POP configuration files under `/etc/ppp`:

    ```
    #pop-3   stream tcp    nowait root    /usr/sbin/tcpd ipop3d
    ```

- `imap`—As with `pop-3`, you may need to offer `imap` mail service. Most people won't need to enable this service:

    ```
    #imap    stream tcp    nowait root    /usr/sbin/tcpd imapd
    ```

uucp

Don't enable uucp! The UUCP service used to be a very common way of sending files between remote machines. Some news servers rely on uucp to get their news feeds. A few sites still use it as an alternative to ftp, under carefully controlled security conditions, but uucp is dying out:

```
#uucp   stream tcp    nowait uucp    /usr/sbin/tcpd /usr/lib/uucp/uucico -l
```

Remote Boot Services

Remote boot services are used to assign IP addresses and boot diskless machines over the LAN. Diskless workstations and routers use these services:

- `tftp`—As the comment in `/etc/inetd.conf` says, don't enable this service! Its purpose is to load the operating system into a remote, diskless system or router over the local, trusted network. Unfortunately, quite a few people use `tftp` as an alternative to `ftp`, thinking it is more secure because it doesn't use authentication. Just the opposite is true:

    ```
    #tftp dgram  udp    wait    root    /usr/sbin/tcpd in.tftpd
    ```

- `bootps`—BOOTP is used by diskless workstations to discover their IP address, the location of the boot server, and to initiate the system download over `tftp` prior to booting. I can't imagine why the average home or small business setup would ever need this service. Leave it disabled:

    ```
    #bootps dgram   udp    wait    root    /usr/sbin/tcpd bootpd
    ```

Information Services

The services commented as information services in /etc/inetd.conf provide user account, process, and network connection and configuration information. If used, these services should be limited to other machines on your LAN. These services listen on two sets of sockets, inet domain sockets for remote hosts and UNIX domain sockets for local queries. Disabling these services in /etc/inetd.conf disables access from remote hosts. Local access is not affected:

- finger—finger is an informational service. It isn't so much that it's a security hole, but that it provides information about your user accounts, login times, pending mail, machine names, and so on. Although this information isn't necessarily sensitive, it can be useful to a hacker. Allowing access to your finger service isn't recommended in today's Internet environment:

    ```
    #finger    stream tcp    nowait root   /usr/sbin/tcpd in.fingerd
    ```

- System Information Services—Along with finger, cfinger, systat, and netstat provide user account and system information that is potentially useful to a hacker. Disabling these services in /etc/inetd.conf disables network access to these services. Local access remains available:

    ```
    #cfinger   stream tcp    nowait root    /usr/sbin/tcpd in.cfingerd
    #systat    stream tcp    nowait guest   /usr/sbin/tcpd /bin/ps -
    auwwx
    #netstat   stream tcp    nowait guest   /usr/sbin/tcpd /bin/netstat
    -f inet
    ```

RARP, BOOTP, and DHCP

The bootpd and dhcpd servers share the same service port in /etc/services. They are distinct services.

Historically, diskless machines knew their Ethernet interface's hardware address, but didn't know their software IP address. The Reverse Address Resolution Protocol (RARP) was developed to enable diskless machines to ask a server for their IP address based on their MAC hardware address. RARP was replaced by BOOTP, the Bootstrap Protocol. BOOTP not only provides the IP address, but also provides the address of the file server to download the workstation's boot image from via tftp. BOOTP has not been replaced, but the protocol evolved into DHCP, the Dynamic Host Configuration Protocol. DHCP includes a superset of BOOTP's features, providing additional router and name server address information beyond the host's IP address, as well as providing dynamic allocation of reusable IP addresses.

Authentication

The AUTH service is somewhat similar to finger in that it provides user information, usually to mail and news servers for logging purposes when you send mail or post a news article. FTP servers sometimes infrequently require a valid identd lookup, as well. Whether you choose to enable the AUTH identd user authentication service is up to you. The topic is open for debate, with people on both sides of the issue having good reasons for their own choices. Some people insist on enabling the service as a matter of courtesy. Other people disable the service to keep user account information private:

```
auth    stream  tcp     nowait    nobody    /usr/sbin/in.identd in.identd -l -e -o
```

Locally Defined Services

Beyond the automatic service and daemon startup management done by the runlevel manager and inetd, other services and daemons not part of your standard Linux distribution must be explicitly started by you. These programs are usually started from /etc/rc.d/rc.local.

At boot time, the /etc/rc.d/rc.local script is run to execute any local configuration options you've defined. By default, it creates the files used to provide the login banner. Other possible uses include starting local programs, such as the sshd server, or updating the system time from a remote time service.

Summary

With the basics of the IP protocols and server considerations out of the way, Chapter 3 takes you through the process of constructing an actual firewall for your site. The firewall script uses the information available in the network packets described in Chapter 1 to construct specific firewall input and output rules that implement the concepts presented in this chapter.

3

Building and Installing a Firewall

CHAPTER 2, "PACKET-FILTERING CONCEPTS," COVERS the background ideas and concepts behind a packet-filtering firewall. Each firewall rule chain has its own default policy. Each rule applies not only to an individual input or output chain, but to a specific network interface, message protocol type (i.e., TCP, UDP, ICMP), and service port number. Individual acceptance, denial, and rejection rules are defined for the input chain and the output chain, as well as for the forward chain, which you'll learn about at the end of this chapter and in Chapter 4, "LAN Issues, Multiple Firewalls, and Perimeter Networks." This chapter pulls those ideas together to demonstrate how to build a simple, single-system, custom-designed firewall for your site.

The firewall you'll build in this chapter is based on a deny-everything-by-default policy. All network traffic is blocked by default. Services are individually enabled as exceptions to the policy.

After the single-system firewall is built, the chapter closes by demonstrating how to extend the standalone firewall to a formal bastion firewall. A *bastion firewall* has at least two network interfaces. It insulates an internal LAN from direct communication with the Internet. Only minor extensions are required to make the single-system firewall function as a simple, dual-homed bastion firewall. It protects your internal LAN by applying packet-filtering rules at the external interface, acting as a proxying gateway between the LAN and the Internet.

The single-system and bastion firewalls are the least-secure forms of firewall architecture. If the firewall host were to be compromised, any local machines would be open to attack. As a standalone firewall, it's an all-or-nothing proposition. Because this book is targeted at the home and small business user, the assumption is that the majority of home users have a single computer connected to the Internet, or a single firewall machine protecting a small, private LAN. "Least-secure," however, does not imply an insecure firewall. These firewalls are less flexible than more complicated architectures involving multiple machines. Chapter 4 introduces more flexible configurations that allow for additional internal security protecting more complicated LAN and server configurations than a single-system firewall can.

ipchains: The Linux Firewall Administration Program

This book is based on Red Hat Linux 6.0. Linux comes supplied with a firewall mechanism called IPFW (IP firewall). The major Linux distributions either have or are in the process of converting to `ipchains`, a rewrite of IPFW version 4. This new version is usually referred to as `ipchains`, its administration program's name. Previous Linux distributions used an earlier IPFW implementation. Their firewall mechanism is usually referred to as `ipfwadm`, the earlier version's administration program's name.

`ipchains` is used in the examples in this book. Because `ipfwadm` remains in widespread use on older Linux systems, `ipfwadm` versions of the examples are presented in Appendix B, "Firewall Examples and Support Scripts." Although the syntax differs between `ipchains` and `ipfwadm`, they are functionally the same. `ipchains` includes the `ipfwadm` feature set, along with additional features found in the new IPFW implementation. The features new to `ipchains` won't be used in this book. Only the features common to both versions are used in the examples.

As a firewall administration program, `ipchains` creates the individual packet filter rules for the `input` and `output` chains composing the firewall. One of the most important aspects of defining firewall rules is that the order in which the rules are defined is important.

Packet-filtering rules are stored in kernel tables, in an `input`, `output`, or `forward` chain, in the order in which they are defined. Individual rules are inserted at the beginning of the chain or appended to the end of the chain. All rules are appended in the examples in this chapter (with one exception at the end of the chapter). The order you define the rules in is the order they'll be added to the kernel tables, and thereby the order the rules will be compared against each packet.

As each externally originating packet arrives at a network interface, its header fields are compared against each rule in the interface's `input` chain until a match is found. Conversely, as each internally originating packet is sent to a network interface, its header fields are compared against each rule in the interface's `output` chain until a match is found. In either direction, when a match is found, the comparison stops and the rule's packet disposition is applied: ACCEPT, REJECT, or DENY. If the packet doesn't match any rule on the chain, the default policy for that chain is applied. The bottom line is that *the first matching rule wins*.

The numeric service port numbers, rather than their symbolic names, as listed in /etc/services, are used in all the examples of rules in this chapter. ipchains supports the symbolic service port names. The examples in this chapter use the numeric values because the symbolic names are not consistent across Linux distributions, or even from one release to the next. You could use the symbolic names for clarity in your own rules, but remember that your firewall could break with the next system upgrade.

ipchains is a compiled C program. It must be invoked once for each individual firewall rule you define. This is done from a shell script. The examples in this chapter assume that the shell script is named /etc/rc.d/rc.firewall. In cases where shell semantics differ, the examples are written in Bourne (sh), Korn (ksh), or Bourne Again (bash) shell semantics.

The examples are not optimized. They are spelled out for clarity and to maintain conceptual and feature-set compatibility between ipchains and ipfwadm. The two programs use different command-line arguments to reference similar features, and offer slightly different shortcuts and optimization capabilities. The examples are presented using the features common to both programs.

ipchains Options Used in the Firewall Script

ipchains options aren't covered in full in this chapter. Only the features used in the examples in this book, features common to ipfwadm, are covered. Table 3.1 lists the ipchains command-line arguments used here:

```
ipchains -A¦I [chain] [-i interface] [-p protocol] [ [!] -y]
         [-s address [port[:port]]]
         [-d address [port[:port]]]
         -j policy [-l]
```

For a description of the complete ipchains feature set, refer to the online man page, ipchains, and to IPCHAINS-HOWTO.

Table 3.1 *ipchains* **Options Used in the Firewall Script**

Option	Description
-A [*chain*]	Append a rule to the end of a chain. The examples use the built-in chains: input, output, and forward. If a chain isn't specified, the rule applies to all chains.
-I [*chain*]	Insert a rule at the beginning of a chain. The examples use the built-in chains: input, output, and forward. If a chain isn't specified, the rule applies to all chains.
-i <*interface*>	Specify the network interface the rule applies to. If an interface isn't specified, the rule applies to all interfaces. Common interface names are eth0, eth1, lo, and ppp0.
-p <*protocol*>	Specify the IP protocol the rule applies to. If the -p option isn't used, the rule applies to all protocols. The supported protocol names are tcp, udp, icmp, and all. Any of the protocol names or numbers from /etc/protocols are also allowed.
-y	The SYN flag must be set, and the ACK flag must be cleared in a TCP message, indicating a connection establishment request. If -y isn't given as an argument, the TCP flag bits aren't checked.
! -y	The ACK flag must be set in a TCP message, indicating an initial response to a connection request or an ongoing, established connection. If ! -y isn't given as an argument, the TCP flag bits aren't checked.
-s <*address*> [<*port*>]	Specify the packet's source address. If a source address isn't specified, all unicast source addresses are implied. If a port or range of ports is given, the rule applies to only those ports. Without a port specifier, the rule applies to all source ports. A range of ports is defined by a beginning and ending port number, separated by a colon (e.g., 1024:65535). If a port is given, an address must be specified.
-d <*address*> [<*port*>]	Specify the packet's destination address. If a destination address isn't specified, all unicast destination addresses are implied. If a port or range of ports is given, the rule applies to only those ports. Without a port specifier, the rule applies to all destination ports. A range of ports is defined by a beginning and ending port number, separated by a colon (e.g., 1024:65535). If a port is given, an address must be specified.

Option	Description
-j *<policy>*	Specify the packet disposition policy for this rule: ACCEPT, DENY, or REJECT. The forward chain can take the MASQ (masquerade) policy, as well.
-l	Write a kernel informational (KERN_INFO) message in the system log, /var/log/messages by default, whenever a packet matches this rule.

Source and Destination Addressing Options

Both a packet's source and destination addresses can be specified in a firewall rule. Only packets with that specific source or destination address match the rule. Addresses may be a specific IP address, a fully qualified hostname, a network (domain) name, a limited range of addresses, or all-inclusive.

An IP address is a 32-bit numeric value, divided into four individual 8-bit bytes, ranging from 0 through 255. In dotted-decimal notation, each of the four bytes making up the 32-bit value is represented as one of the quads in the IP address. The private Class C IP address 192.168.10.30 is used as the local host address in the figures throughout this book.

ipchains allows the address to be suffixed with a bit mask specifier. The mask's value can range from 0 through 32, indicating the number of bits to mask. Bits are counted from the left, or most significant, quad. This mask specifier indicates how many of the leading bits in the address must exactly match the IP address defined in the rule.

A mask of 32, /32, means that all the bits must match. The address must exactly match what you've defined in the rule. Specifying an address as 192.168.10.30 is the same as specifying the address as 192.168.10.30/32. The /32 mask is implied by default. You don't need to specify it.

IP Addresses Expressed As Symbolic Names

Remote hosts and networks may be specified as fully qualified host or network names. Using a hostname is especially convenient for firewall rules that apply to an individual remote host. This is particularly true for hosts whose IP address can change, or that invisibly represent multiple IP addresses, such as ISP mail servers sometimes do. In general, however, remote addresses are better expressed in dotted quad notation because of the possibility of DNS hostname spoofing.

Symbolic hostnames can't be resolved until DNS traffic is enabled in firewall rules. If hostnames are used in the firewall rules, those rules must follow the rules enabling DNS traffic.

An example using masking would be to allow only a given connection type to be made between you and your ISP's server machines. Let's say that your ISP uses addresses in the range of 192.168.24.0 through 192.168.27.255 for its server address space. In this case, the address/mask pair would be 192.168.24/22. As shown in Figure 3.1, the first 22 bits of all addresses in this range are identical, so any address matching on the first 22 bits will match. Effectively, you are saying that you will allow connections to the service only when offered from machines in the address range 192.168.24.0 through 192.168.27.255.

A mask of 0, /0, means that no bits in the address are required to match. In other words, because no bits need to match, using /0 is the same as not specifying an address. Any unicast address matches. ipchains has a built-in alias for 0.0.0.0/0, any/0.

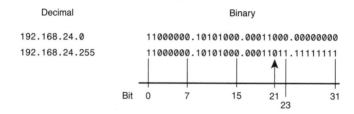

Figure 3.1   The first matching 22 bits in the masked IP address range 192.168.24.0/22.

Initializing the Firewall

A firewall is implemented as a series of packet-filtering rules defined by options on the ipchains command line. ipchains is executed once for each individual rule. (Different firewalls can range from a dozen rules to hundreds.)

The ipchains invocations should be made from an executable shell script and not directly from the command line. You should invoke the complete firewall shell script. Do not attempt to invoke specific ipchains rules from the command line because this could cause your firewall to accept or deny packets inappropriately. When the chains are initialized and the default deny policy is enabled, all network services are blocked until an acceptance filter is defined to allow the individual service.

Likewise, you should execute the shell script from the console. Do not execute the shell script from either a remote machine or from an X Window xterm session. Not only is remote network traffic blocked, but access to the local loopback interface used by X Window is blocked until access to the interface is explicitly reenabled.

Furthermore, remember that firewall filters are applied in the order in which you've defined them on the input or output chain. The rules are appended to the end of their chain in the order you define them. The first matching rule wins. Because of this, firewall rules must be defined in a hierarchical order from most specific to more general rules.

Firewall initialization is used to cover a lot of ground, including defining global constants used in the shell script, clearing out any existing rules in the firewall chains, defining default policies for the input and output chains, reenabling the loopback interface for normal system operation, denying access from any specific hosts or networks you've decided to block, and defining some basic rules to protect against bad addresses and to protect certain services running on unprivileged ports.

Symbolic Constants Used in the Firewall Examples

A firewall shell script is easiest to read and maintain if symbolic constants are used for recurring names and addresses. The following constants are either used throughout the examples in this chapter, or else are universal constants defined in the networking standards:

```
EXTERNAL_INTERFACE="eth0"              # Internet-connected interface
LOOPBACK_INTERFACE="lo"                # however your system names it

IPADDR="my.ip.address"                 # your IP address
ANYWHERE="any/0"                       # match any IP address
MY_ISP="my.isp.address.range"          # ISP server & NOC address range

LOOPBACK="127.0.0.0/8"                 # reserved loopback address range
CLASS_A="10.0.0.0/8"                   # class A private networks
CLASS_B="172.16.0.0/12"                # class B private networks
CLASS_C="192.168.0.0/16"               # class C private networks
CLASS_D_MULTICAST="224.0.0.0/4"        # class D multicast addresses
CLASS_E_RESERVED_NET="240.0.0.0/5"     # class E reserved addresses
```

```
BROADCAST_SRC="0.0.0.0"              # broadcast source address
BROADCAST_DEST="255.255.255.255"     # broadcast destination address
PRIVPORTS="0:1023"                   # well-known, privileged port range
UNPRIVPORTS="1024:65535"             # unprivileged port range
```

Constants not listed here are defined within the context of the specific rules they are used with.

Removing Any Preexisting Rules

The first thing to do when defining a set of filtering rules is to remove any existing rules from their chain. Otherwise, any new rules you define would be added to the end of existing rules. Packets could easily match a preexisting rule before reaching the point in the chain you are defining from this point on.

Removal is called *flushing* the chain. Without a directional argument referring to a specific chain, the following command flushes the rules of all three built-in chains—input, output, and forward—at once:

```
# Flush any existing rules from all chains
ipchains -F
```

The chains are empty. You're starting from scratch. The system is in its default accept-everything policy state.

Defining the Default Policy

A side effect of flushing all the rules is that the system is returned to its default state, including the default accept-everything policy for each chain. Until new default policies are defined, the system allows everything through the network interfaces. No filtering is done.

By default, you want the firewall to deny everything coming in and reject everything going out. Unless a rule is defined to explicitly allow a matching packet through, incoming packets are silently denied without notification to the remote sender, and outgoing packets are rejected and an ICMP error message is returned to the local sender. The difference for the end user is that, for example, if someone at a remote site attempts to connect to your Web server, that person's browser hangs until his or her system returns a TCP timeout condition. He or she has no indication whether your site or your Web server exist. If you, on the other hand, attempt to connect to a remote Web server, your browser receives an immediate error condition indicating that the operation isn't allowed:

```
# Set the default policy to deny
ipchains -P input   DENY
ipchains -P output  REJECT
ipchains -P forward REJECT
```

At this point, all network traffic is blocked.

Enabling the Loopback Interface

You need to enable unrestricted loopback traffic. This allows you to run any local network services you choose—or that the system depends on—without having to worry about getting all the firewall rules specified.

Loopback is enabled immediately in the firewall script. It's not an externally available interface. Local network-based services, such as the X Window system, will hang until loopback traffic is allowed through.

The rules are simple when everything is allowed. You simply need to undo the effect of the default deny policies for the loopback interface by accepting everything on that interface:

```
# Unlimited traffic on the loopback interface
ipchains -A input  -i $LOOPBACK_INTERFACE -j ACCEPT
ipchains -A output -i $LOOPBACK_INTERFACE -j ACCEPT
```

System logging, X Window, and other local, UNIX-domain, socket-based services are available again.

Source Address Spoofing and Other Bad Addresses

This section establishes some input chain filters based on source and destination addresses. These addresses will never be seen in a legitimate incoming packet from the Internet.

The Linux kernel offers some support against incoming spoofed packets in addition to what can be done at the firewall level. Also, in case TCP SYN Cookie protection is not enabled, the following lines enable both kernel support modules:

```
echo 1 >/proc/sys/net/ipv4/tcp_syncookies

# Setting up IP spoofing protection
# turn on Source Address Verification
for f in /proc/sys/net/ipv4/conf/*/rp_filter; do
    echo 1 > $f
done
```

Default Policy Rules and the First Matching Rule Wins

The default policies appear to be exceptions to the first-matching-rule-wins scenario. The default policy commands are not position-dependent. They aren't rules, per se. A chain's default policy is applied after a packet has been compared to each rule on the chain without a match.

The default policies are defined first in the script to define the default packet disposition before any rules to the contrary are defined. If the policy commands were executed at the end of the script, and the firewall script contained a syntax error causing it to exit prematurely, the default accept-everything policy would be in effect. If a packet didn't match a rule, (and rules are usually accept rules in a deny-everything-by-default firewall) the packet would fall off the end of the chain and be accepted by default. The firewall rules would not be accomplishing anything useful.

At the packet-filtering level, one of the few cases of source address spoofing you can identify with certainty as a forgery is your own IP address. This rule denies incoming packets claiming to be from you:

```
# Refuse spoofed packets pretending to be from
# the external interface's IP address
ipchains -A input  -i $EXTERNAL_INTERFACE -s $IPADDR -j DENY -l
```

There is no need to block outgoing packets destined to yourself. They won't return, claiming to be from you and appearing to be spoofed. Remember, if you send packets to your own external interface, those packets arrive on the loopback interface's input queue, not on the external interface's input queue. Packets containing your address as the source address never arrive on the external interface, even if you send packets to the external interface.

As explained in Chapter 2, spare private IP addresses are set aside in each of the Class A, B, and C address ranges for use in private LANs. They are not intended for use on the Internet. Routers are not supposed to route packets with private source addresses. Routers cannot route packets with private destination addresses. Nevertheless, many routers do allow packets through with private source addresses.

Additionally, if someone on your ISP's subnet (i.e., on your side of the router you share) is leaking packets with private destination IP addresses, you'll see them even if the router doesn't forward them. Machines on your own LAN could also leak private source addresses if your IP masquerading or proxy configuration is set up incorrectly.

The next three sets of rules disallow incoming and outgoing packets with any of the Class A, B, or C private network addresses as their source or destination addresses.

Firewall Logging

The -l option enables logging for packets matching the rule. When a packet matches the rule, the event is logged in /var/log/messages. Firewall logging is available by default in Red Hat 6.0. Releases prior to version 6.0 required you to recompile the kernel with the kernel logging module included in order to use the ipchains/ipfwadm logging option.

None of these packets should be seen outside a private LAN:

```
# Refuse packets claiming to be to or from a Class A private network
ipchains -A input  -i $EXTERNAL_INTERFACE -s $CLASS_A -j DENY
ipchains -A input  -i $EXTERNAL_INTERFACE -d $CLASS_A -j DENY
ipchains -A output -i $EXTERNAL_INTERFACE -s $CLASS_A -j DENY -l
ipchains -A output -i $EXTERNAL_INTERFACE -d $CLASS_A -j DENY -l

# Refuse packets claiming to be to or from a Class B private network
ipchains -A input  -i $EXTERNAL_INTERFACE -s $CLASS_B -j DENY
ipchains -A input  -i $EXTERNAL_INTERFACE -d $CLASS_B -j DENY
ipchains -A output -i $EXTERNAL_INTERFACE -s $CLASS_B -j DENY -l
ipchains -A output -i $EXTERNAL_INTERFACE -d $CLASS_B -j DENY -l

# Refuse packets claiming to be to or from a Class C private network
ipchains -A input  -i $EXTERNAL_INTERFACE -s $CLASS_C -j DENY
ipchains -A input  -i $EXTERNAL_INTERFACE -d $CLASS_C -j DENY
ipchains -A output -i $EXTERNAL_INTERFACE -s $CLASS_C -j DENY -l
ipchains -A output -i $EXTERNAL_INTERFACE -d $CLASS_C -j DENY -l
```

Your external network interface won't recognize a destination address other than its own if your routing table is configured correctly. But if you configured automatic routing and had a LAN using these addresses and someone on your ISP's subnet was leaking packets, your firewall could conceivably forward the packets to your LAN.

The next two rules disallow packets with a source address reserved for the loopback interface:

```
# Refuse packets claiming to be from the loopback interface
ipchains -A input  -i $EXTERNAL_INTERFACE -s $LOOPBACK -j DENY
ipchains -A output -i $EXTERNAL_INTERFACE -s $LOOPBACK -j DENY -l
```

Because loopback addresses are assigned to a local software interface, which system software handles internally, any packet claiming to be from such an address is intentionally forged. Notice that I've chosen to log the event if a local user attempts to spoof the address.

As with addresses set aside for use in private LANs, routers are not supposed to forward packets originating from the loopback address range. A router cannot forward a packet with a loopback destination address.

The next two rules block broadcast packets containing illegal source or destination broadcast addresses. The firewall's default policy is to deny everything. As such, broadcast destination addresses are denied by default and must be explicitly enabled in the cases where they are wanted:

```
# Refuse malformed broadcast packets
ipchains -A input  -i $EXTERNAL_INTERFACE -s $BROADCAST_DEST -j DENY -l
ipchains -A input  -i $EXTERNAL_INTERFACE -d $BROADCAST_SRC  -j DENY -l
```

The first of these rules logs and denies any packet claiming to come from
255.255.255.255, the address reserved as the broadcast destination address. A packet
will never legitimately originate from address 255.255.255.255.

The second of these rules logs and denies any packet directed to destination address
0.0.0.0, the address reserved as a broadcast source address. Such a packet is not a mistake; it is a specific probe intended to identify a UNIX machine running network
software derived from BSD. Because most UNIX operating system network code
is derived from BSD, this probe is effectively intended to identify machines
running UNIX.

Multicast addresses are legal only as destination addresses. The next rule pair denies
and logs spoofed multicast network packets:

```
# Refuse Class D multicast addresses
# illegal only as a source address
# Multicast uses UDP
ipchains -A input  -i $EXTERNAL_INTERFACE \
        -s $CLASS_D_MULTICAST -j DENY -l
ipchains -A output -i $EXTERNAL_INTERFACE \
        -s $CLASS_D_MULTICAST -j REJECT -l
```

Legitimate multicast packets are always UDP packets. As such, multicast messages
are sent point-to-point, just as any other UDP message is. The difference between unicast and multicast packets is the class of destination address used. The next rule denies
outgoing multicast packets from your machine:

```
ipchains -A output -i $EXTERNAL_INTERFACE \
        -d $CLASS_D_MULTICAST -j REJECT -l
```

Multicast functionality is a configurable option when you compile the kernel, and
your network interface card can be initialized to recognize multicast addresses. The
functionality is enabled by default in Red Hat 6.0, but not in earlier releases. You
might want to enable these addresses if you subscribe to a network conferencing service that provides multicast audio and video broadcasts.

You won't see legitimate multicast destination addresses unless you've registered
yourself as a recipient. Multicast packets are sent to multiple, but specific, targets by
prior arrangement. I have seen multicast packets sent out from machines on my ISP's
local subnet, however. You can block multicast addresses altogether if you don't subscribe to multicast services. The next rule denies incoming multicast packets:

```
ipchains -A input  -i $EXTERNAL_INTERFACE -d $CLASS_D_MULTICAST -j REJECT -l
```

Clarification on the Meaning of IP Address *0.0.0.0*

Address 0.0.0.0 is reserved for use as a broadcast source address. The IPFW convention of specifying a
match on any address, any/0, 0.0.0.0/0, or 0.0.0.0/0.0.0.0, doesn't match the broadcast
source address. The reason is that a broadcast packet has a bit set in the packet header indicating that
it's a broadcast packet destined for all interfaces on the network, rather than a point-to-point, unicast
packet destined for a particular destination. Broadcast packets are handled differently from nonbroadcast
packets. There is no legitimate nonbroadcast IP address 0.0.0.0.

Multicast registration and routing is a complicated process managed by its own IP layer control protocol, the Internet Group Management Protocol (IGMP, protocol 2). For more information on multicast communication, refer to an excellent white paper, "How IP Multicast Works," by Vicki Johnson and Marjory Johnson. The paper is available at `http://www.ipmulticast.com/community/whitepapers/howipmcworks.html`.

Class D IP addresses range from `224.0.0.0` to `239.255.255.255`. The `CLASS_D_MULTICAST` constant, `224.0.0.0/4`, is defined to match on the first four bits of the address. As shown in Figure 3.2, in binary, the decimal values 224 (11100000B) to 239 (11101111B) are identical through the first four bits (1110B).

The next rule in this section denies and logs packets claiming to be from a Class E reserved network:

```
# Refuse Class E reserved IP addresses
ipchains -A input  -i $EXTERNAL_INTERFACE \
         -s $CLASS_E_RESERVED_NET -j DENY -l
```

Class E IP addresses range from `240.0.0.0` to `247.255.255.255`. The `CLASS_E_RESERVED_NET` constant, `240.0.0.0/5`, is defined to match on the first five bits of the address. As shown in Figure 3.3, in binary, the decimal values 240 (11110000B) to 247 (11110111B) are identical through the first five bits (1111 0B).

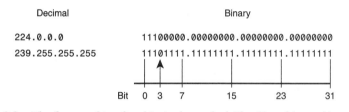

Figure 3.2 The first matching four bits in the masked Class D multicast address range `224.0.0.0/4`.

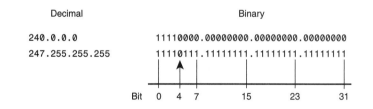

Figure 3.3 The first matching five bits in the masked Class E reserved address range `240.0.0.0/5`.

The IANA ultimately manages the allocation and registration of the world's IP address space. For more information on IP address assignments, see `http://www.isi.edu/in-notes/iana/assignments/ipv4-address-space`. Some blocks of addresses are defined as reserved by the IANA. These addresses should not appear on the public Internet. The final set of rules deny this class of potentially spoofed packets:

```
# refuse addresses defined as reserved by the IANA
# 0.*.*.*, 1.*.*.*, 2.*.*.*, 5.*.*.*, 7.*.*.*, 23.*.*.*, 27.*.*.*
# 31.*.*.*, 37.*.*.*, 39.*.*.*, 41.*.*.*, 42.*.*.*, 58-60.*.*.*

ipchains -A input -i $EXTERNAL_INTERFACE -s 1.0.0.0/8 -j DENY -l
ipchains -A input -i $EXTERNAL_INTERFACE -s 2.0.0.0/8 -j DENY -l
ipchains -A input -i $EXTERNAL_INTERFACE -s 5.0.0.0/8 -j DENY -l
ipchains -A input -i $EXTERNAL_INTERFACE -s 7.0.0.0/8 -j DENY -l
ipchains -A input -i $EXTERNAL_INTERFACE -s 23.0.0.0/8 -j DENY -l
ipchains -A input -i $EXTERNAL_INTERFACE -s 27.0.0.0/8 -j DENY -l
ipchains -A input -i $EXTERNAL_INTERFACE -s 31.0.0.0/8 -j DENY -l
ipchains -A input -i $EXTERNAL_INTERFACE -s 37.0.0.0/8 -j DENY -l
ipchains -A input -i $EXTERNAL_INTERFACE -s 39.0.0.0/8 -j DENY -l
ipchains -A input -i $EXTERNAL_INTERFACE -s 41.0.0.0/8 -j DENY -l
ipchains -A input -i $EXTERNAL_INTERFACE -s 42.0.0.0/8 -j DENY -l
ipchains -A input -i $EXTERNAL_INTERFACE -s 58.0.0.0/7 -j DENY -l
ipchains -A input -i $EXTERNAL_INTERFACE -s 60.0.0.0/8 -j DENY -l


# 65: 01000001   - /3 includes 64 - need 65-79 spelled out
ipchains -A input -i $EXTERNAL_INTERFACE -s 65.0.0.0/8 -j DENY -l
ipchains -A input -i $EXTERNAL_INTERFACE -s 66.0.0.0/8 -j DENY -l
ipchains -A input -i $EXTERNAL_INTERFACE -s 67.0.0.0/8 -j DENY -l
ipchains -A input -i $EXTERNAL_INTERFACE -s 68.0.0.0/8 -j DENY -l
ipchains -A input -i $EXTERNAL_INTERFACE -s 69.0.0.0/8 -j DENY -l
ipchains -A input -i $EXTERNAL_INTERFACE -s 70.0.0.0/8 -j DENY -l
ipchains -A input -i $EXTERNAL_INTERFACE -s 71.0.0.0/8 -j DENY -l
ipchains -A input -i $EXTERNAL_INTERFACE -s 72.0.0.0/8 -j DENY -l
ipchains -A input -i $EXTERNAL_INTERFACE -s 73.0.0.0/8 -j DENY -l
ipchains -A input -i $EXTERNAL_INTERFACE -s 74.0.0.0/8 -j DENY -l
ipchains -A input -i $EXTERNAL_INTERFACE -s 75.0.0.0/8 -j DENY -l
ipchains -A input -i $EXTERNAL_INTERFACE -s 76.0.0.0/8 -j DENY -l
ipchains -A input -i $EXTERNAL_INTERFACE -s 77.0.0.0/8 -j DENY -l
ipchains -A input -i $EXTERNAL_INTERFACE -s 78.0.0.0/8 -j DENY -l
ipchains -A input -i $EXTERNAL_INTERFACE -s 79.0.0.0/8 -j DENY -l


# 80: 01010000   - /4 masks 80-95
ipchains -A input -i $EXTERNAL_INTERFACE -s 80.0.0.0/4 -j DENY -l


# 96: 01100000   - /4 masks 96-111
ipchains -A input -i $EXTERNAL_INTERFACE -s 96.0.0.0/4 -j DENY -l
```

```
# 126: 01111110  - /3 includes 127 - need 112-126 spelled out
ipchains -A input -i $EXTERNAL_INTERFACE -s 112.0.0.0/8 -j DENY -l
ipchains -A input -i $EXTERNAL_INTERFACE -s 113.0.0.0/8 -j DENY -l
ipchains -A input -i $EXTERNAL_INTERFACE -s 114.0.0.0/8 -j DENY -l
ipchains -A input -i $EXTERNAL_INTERFACE -s 115.0.0.0/8 -j DENY -l
ipchains -A input -i $EXTERNAL_INTERFACE -s 116.0.0.0/8 -j DENY -l
ipchains -A input -i $EXTERNAL_INTERFACE -s 117.0.0.0/8 -j DENY -l
ipchains -A input -i $EXTERNAL_INTERFACE -s 118.0.0.0/8 -j DENY -l
ipchains -A input -i $EXTERNAL_INTERFACE -s 119.0.0.0/8 -j DENY -l
ipchains -A input -i $EXTERNAL_INTERFACE -s 120.0.0.0/8 -j DENY -l
ipchains -A input -i $EXTERNAL_INTERFACE -s 121.0.0.0/8 -j DENY -l
ipchains -A input -i $EXTERNAL_INTERFACE -s 122.0.0.0/8 -j DENY -l
ipchains -A input -i $EXTERNAL_INTERFACE -s 123.0.0.0/8 -j DENY -l
ipchains -A input -i $EXTERNAL_INTERFACE -s 124.0.0.0/8 -j DENY -l
ipchains -A input -i $EXTERNAL_INTERFACE -s 125.0.0.0/8 -j DENY -l
ipchains -A input -i $EXTERNAL_INTERFACE -s 126.0.0.0/8 -j DENY -l

# 217: 11011001  - /5 includes 216 - need 217-219 spelled out
ipchains -A input -i $EXTERNAL_INTERFACE -s 217.0.0.0/8 -j DENY -l
ipchains -A input -i $EXTERNAL_INTERFACE -s 218.0.0.0/8 -j DENY -l
ipchains -A input -i $EXTERNAL_INTERFACE -s 219.0.0.0/8 -j DENY -l

# 223: 11011111  - /6 masks 220-223
ipchains -A input -i $EXTERNAL_INTERFACE -s 220.0.0.0/6 -j DENY -l
```

Filtering ICMP Control and Status Messages

ICMP control messages are generated in response to a number of error conditions, and they are produced by network analysis programs, such as ping and traceroute. Table 3.2 lists the common ICMP message types of most interest to a small site.

Table 3.2   Common ICMP Message Types

Type Code	Symbolic Name	Description
0	echo-reply	A ping response.
3	destination-unreachable	A general error status message; a router along the path to the destination is unable to deliver the packet to its next destination; used by traceroute.
4	source-quench	IP network layer flow control between two routers, or between a router and a host.

continues

Table 3.2   Continued

Type Code	Symbolic Name	Description
5	`redirect`	A routing message returned to the sender when a router determines that a shorter path exists.
8	`echo-request`	A `ping` request.
11	`time-exceeded`	A routing message returned when a packet's maximum hop count (TTL) is exceeded; used by `traceroute`.
12	`parameter-problem`	Unexpected values that are found in the IP packet header.

Error Status and Control Messages

Four ICMP control and status messages need to pass through the firewall: Source Quench, Parameter Problem, incoming Destination Unreachable, and outgoing Destination Unreachable, subtype Fragmentation Needed. Four other ICMP message types are optional: Echo Request, Echo Reply, other outgoing Destination Unreachable subtypes, and Time Exceeded. Other message types can be ignored, to be filtered out by the default policy.

Of the message types that can—or should—be ignored, only Redirect is listed in Table 3.2 because of its role in denial-of-service attacks as a Redirect bomb. (See Chapter 2 for more information on Redirect bombs.) As with Redirect, the remaining ICMP message types are specialized control and status messages intended for use between routers.

ICMP Code Differences Between *ipchains* **and** *ipfwadm*

ipchains in Red Hat 6.0 supports the use of either the ICMP numeric message type or the alphabetic symbolic name. Earlier releases using `ipfwadm` supported only the numeric message type.

`ipchains` also supports use of the message subtypes, or codes. This is especially useful for finer filtering control over type 3 `destination-unreachable` messages. For example, you could specifically disallow outgoing `port-unreachable` messages to disable an incoming `traceroute`, or specifically allow only outgoing `Fragmentation Needed` status messages. `ipfwadm` does not support the message subtype codes.

To see a list of all supported ICMP symbolic names in `ipchains`, run `ipchains -h icmp`. To see the official RFC assignments, go to `http://www.isi.edu/in-notes/iana/assignments/icmp-parameters`.

The following sections describe the message types important to an endpoint host machine, as opposed to an intermediate router, in more detail.

Source Quench Control (Type 4) Messages

ICMP message type 4, Source Quench, is sent when a connection source, usually a router, is sending data faster than the next destination router can handle it. Source Quench is used as a primitive form of flow control at the IP network layer, usually between two adjacent, point-to-point machines:

```
ipchains -A input  -i $EXTERNAL_INTERFACE -p icmp \
         -s $ANYWHERE 4 -d $IPADDR -j ACCEPT

ipchains -A output -i $EXTERNAL_INTERFACE -p icmp \
         -s $IPADDR 4 -d $ANYWHERE -j ACCEPT
```

The router's next hop or destination machine sends a Source Quench command. The originating router responds by sending packets at a slower rate, gradually increasing the rate until it receives another Source Quench message.

Parameter Problem Status (Type 12) Messages

ICMP message type 12, Parameter Problem, is sent when a packet is received containing illegal or unexpected data in the header, or when the header checksum doesn't match the checksum generated by the receiving machine:

```
ipchains -A input  -i $EXTERNAL_INTERFACE -p icmp \
         -s $ANYWHERE 12 -d $IPADDR -j ACCEPT

ipchains -A output -i $EXTERNAL_INTERFACE -p icmp \
         -s $IPADDR 12 -d $ANYWHERE -j ACCEPT
```

Destination Unreachable Error (Type 3) Messages

ICMP message type 3, Destination Unreachable, is a general error status message:

```
ipchains -A input  -i $EXTERNAL_INTERFACE -p icmp \
         -s $ANYWHERE 3 -d $IPADDR -j ACCEPT

ipchains -A output -i $EXTERNAL_INTERFACE -p icmp \
         -s $IPADDR 3 -d $ANYWHERE -j ACCEPT
```

The ICMP packet header for type 3, Destination Unreachable, messages contains an error code field identifying the particular kind of error. Ideally, you'd want to drop outgoing type 3 messages. This message type is what is sent in response to a hacker's attempt to map your service ports or address space. An attacker can create a denial-of-service condition by forcing your system to generate large numbers of these messages by bombarding your unused UDP ports. Worse, an attacker can spoof the source address, forcing your system to send them to the spoofed hosts. Unfortunately, the Destination Unreachable message creates a Catch-22 situation. One of the message subtypes, Fragmentation Needed, is used to negotiate packet fragment size. Your network performance can be seriously degraded without this negotiation.

If you want to respond to incoming traceroute requests, you must allow outgoing ICMP Destination Unreachable messages, subtype code Port Unreachable.

Time Exceeded Status (Type 11) Messages

ICMP message type 11, Time Exceeded, indicates a timeout condition, or more accurately, that a packet's maximum hop count has been exceeded. On networks today, incoming Time Exceeded is mostly seen as the ICMP response to an outgoing UDP traceroute request:

```
ipchains -A input  -i $EXTERNAL_INTERFACE -p icmp \
        -s $ANYWHERE 11 -d $IPADDR -j ACCEPT

ipchains -A output -i $EXTERNAL_INTERFACE -p icmp \
        -s $IPADDR 11 -d $MY_ISP -j ACCEPT
```

If you want to respond to incoming traceroute requests, you must allow outgoing ICMP Time Exceeded messages. In the previous rules, only traceroutes from your ISP's machines are allowed. If you want to use traceroute yourself, you must allow incoming ICMP Time Exceeded messages. Because your machine is not an intermediate router, you have no other use for Time Exceeded messages.

ping Echo Request (Type 8) and Echo Reply (Type 0) Control Messages

ping uses two ICMP message types. The request message, Echo Request, is message type 8. The reply message, Echo Reply, is message type 0. ping is a simple network analysis tool dating back to the original DARPANET. The name ping was taken from the idea of the audible ping played back by sonar systems. (DARPA is the Defense Advanced Research Projects Agency, after all.) Similar to sonar, an Echo Request message broadcast to all machines in a network address space generates Echo Reply messages, in return, from all hosts responding on the network.

> ### *ipchains* Only: Using the ICMP Message Subtype Codes
> For ipchains users only: The general, ipfwadm-compatible ruleset mentioned previously could be replaced with more specific rules allowing any outgoing type 3 messages to your ISP, and Fragmentation Needed messages to any address:
>
> ```
> ipchains -A input  -i $EXTERNAL_INTERFACE -p icmp \
>         -s $ANYWHERE 3 -d $IPADDR -j ACCEPT
>
> ipchains -A output -i $EXTERNAL_INTERFACE -p icmp \
>         -s $IPADDR 3 -d $MY_ISP -j ACCEPT
>
> ipchains -A output -i $EXTERNAL_INTERFACE -p icmp \
>         -s $IPADDR fragmentation-needed -d $ANYWHERE -j ACCEPT
> ```

Outgoing *ping* to Remote Hosts

The following rule pair allows you to `ping` any host on the Internet:

```
# allow outgoing pings to anywhere
ipchains -A output -i $EXTERNAL_INTERFACE -p icmp \
        -s $IPADDR 8 -d $ANYWHERE -j ACCEPT

ipchains -A input  -i $EXTERNAL_INTERFACE -p icmp \
        -s $ANYWHERE 0 -d $IPADDR -j ACCEPT
```

Incoming *ping* from Remote Hosts

The approach shown here allows only selected external hosts to `ping` you:

```
# allow incoming pings from trusted hosts
ipchains -A input  -i $EXTERNAL_INTERFACE -p icmp \
        -s $MY_ISP 8 -d $IPADDR -j ACCEPT

ipchains -A output -i $EXTERNAL_INTERFACE -p icmp \
        -s $IPADDR 0 -d $MY_ISP -j ACCEPT
```

For the purposes of example, external hosts allowed to `ping` your machine are machines belonging to your ISP. Chances are good that your network operations center or customer support will want to `ping` your external interface. Other than from your local network neighbors, other incoming Echo Requests are denied. `ping` is used in several different types of denial-of-service attacks.

Blocking Incoming and Outgoing *smurf* Attacks

`smurf` attacks have used `ping` packets historically, continually broadcasting Echo Request messages to intermediate hosts with the source address spoofed to be the intended victim's IP address. As a result, every machine in the intermediary's network continually bombards the victim machine with Echo Reply messages, choking off all available bandwidth.

The following rule logs `smurf` attacks. Because the broadcast ICMP packets are not explicitly allowed, the firewall's deny-everything-by-default policy drops these packets anyway. Notice that all ICMP message types are denied, rather than just Echo Request messages. `ping` packets are typically used in `smurf` attacks, but other ICMP message types can be used as well. You can never be too careful in a firewall rule set:

```
# smurf attack
ipchains -A input  -i $EXTERNAL_INTERFACE -p icmp \
        -d $BROADCAST_DEST -j DENY -l

ipchains -A output -i $EXTERNAL_INTERFACE -p icmp \
        -d $BROADCAST_DEST -j REJECT -l
# smurf attack - network mask
ipchains -A input -i $EXTERNAL_INTERFACE -p icmp\
        -d $NETMASK -j DENY -l

ipchains -A output -i $EXTERNAL_INTERFACE -p icmp\
        -d $NETMASK -j REJECT -l
```

```
#smurf attack - network address
ipchains -A input -i $EXTERNAL_INTERFACE -p icmp\
        -d $NETWORK -j DENY -l

ipchains -A output -i $EXTERNAL_INTERFACE -p icmp\
        -d $NETWORK -j REJECT -l
```

Protecting Services on Assigned Unprivileged Ports

LAN services, in particular, often run on unprivileged ports. For TCP-based services, a connection attempt to one of these services can be distinguished from an ongoing connection with a client using one of these unprivileged ports through the state of the SYN and ACK bits. You should block incoming connection attempts to these ports for your own security protection. You want to block outgoing connection attempts to protect yourself and others from mistakes on your end, and to log potential internal security problems.

What kinds of mistakes might you need protection from? The worst mistake is offering dangerous services to the world, whether inadvertently or intentionally, and is discussed in Chapter 2. A common mistake is running local network services that leak out to the Internet and bother other people. Another is allowing questionable outgoing traffic, such as port scans, whether this traffic is generated by accident or intentionally sent out by someone on your machine. A deny-everything-by-default firewall policy protects you from most mistakes of these types.

A deny-everything-by-default firewall policy allows you to run many private services behind the firewall without undo risk. These services must explicitly be allowed through the firewall to be accessible to remote clients. This generalization is only an approximation of reality, however. Although TCP services on privileged ports are reasonably safe from all but a skilled and determined hacker, UDP services are inherently less secure, and some services are assigned to run on unprivileged ports. RPC services, usually run over UDP, are even more problematic. RPC-based services are bound to some port, often an unprivileged port. The portmap daemon maps between the RPC service number and the actual port number. A port scan can show where these RPC-based services are bound without going through the portmap daemon.

Smurf **Attacks**

Don't broadcast anything out unto the Internet. The ping broadcast mentioned previously is the basis of the smurf IP denial-of-service attack. See CERT Advisory CA-98.01.smurf at www.cert.org for more information on smurf attacks.

Official Service Port Number Assignments

Port numbers are assigned and registered by the IANA. The information was originally maintained as RFC 1700, "Assigned Numbers." That RFC is now obsolete. The official information is dynamically maintained by the IANA at http://www.isi.edu/in-notes/iana/assignments/port-numbers.

Common Local TCP Services Assigned to Unprivileged Ports

Some services, usually LAN services, are offered through an officially registered, well-known unprivileged port. Additionally, some services, such as FTP and IRC, use complicated communication protocols that don't lend themselves well to packet filtering. The rules described in the following sections disallow local or remote client programs from initiating a connection to one of these ports.

FTP is a good example of how the deny-by-default policy isn't always enough to cover all the possible cases. The FTP protocol is covered later in this chapter. For now, the important idea is that FTP allows connections between two unprivileged ports. Because some services listen on registered unprivileged ports, and the incoming connection request to these services are originating from an unprivileged client port, the rules allowing FTP inadvertantly allow incoming connections to these other, local, services, as well. This situation is also an example of how firewall rules are logically hierarchial and order-dependent. The rules explicitly protecting a LAN service running on an unprivileged port must precede the FTP rules allowing access to the entire unprivileged port range.

As a result, some of these rules appear to be redundant, and will be redundant for some people. For other people running other services, the following rules are necessary to protect private services running on local unprivileged ports.

Disallowing Open Window Connections (TCP Port 2000)

Outgoing client connections to a remote Open Window manager should not be allowed. By specifying the -y flag, indicating the SYN bit, only a connection establishment attempt made from your machine is rejected. Other in-progress connections with remote client programs that are using the unprivileged port 2000 are not affected by the rule, because remote unprivileged ports are the endpoint of a connection initiated by a remote client to a server on your machine.

The following rule blocks local clients from initiating a connection request to a remote Open Window manager:

```
OPENWINDOWS_PORT="2000"                    # (TCP) OpenWindows

# Open Windows: establishing a connection
ipchains -A output -i $EXTERNAL_INTERFACE -p tcp -y \
        -s $IPADDR \
        -d $ANYWHERE $OPENWINDOWS_PORT -j REJECT
```

Incoming connections to port 2000 don't need to be explicitly blocked. Linux is not distributed with the Open Window manager.

The Problem with Port Scans

Port scans are not harmful in themselves. They're generated by network analysis tools. The problem with port scans today is that they are usually generated by people with less-than-honorable intentions. They are "analyzing" your network, not their own. Unfortunately, this leaves the merely curious looking guilty as well.

Disallowing X Window Connections (TCP Ports 6000:6063)

Connections to remote X Window servers should be made over SSH, which automatically supports X Window connections. By specifying the -y flag, indicating the SYN bit, only connection establishment to the remote server port is being rejected. Other connections initiated using the port as a client port are not affected.

X Window port assignment begins at port 6000 with the first running server. If additional servers are run, each is assigned to the next incremental port. As a small site, you'll probably run a single X server, so your server will only listen on port 6000. Port 6063 is the highest assigned port, allowing 64 separate X Window managers running on a single machine:

```
XWINDOW_PORTS="6000:6063"                  # (TCP) X Window
```

The first rule ensures that no outgoing connection attempts to remote X Window managers are made from your machine:

```
# X Window: establishing a remote connection
ipchains -A output -i $EXTERNAL_INTERFACE -p tcp -y \
        -s $IPADDR \
        -d $ANYWHERE $XWINDOW_PORTS -j REJECT
```

The next rule logs and blocks incoming connection attempts to your X Window manager. Local connections are not affected because local connections are made over the loopback interface:

```
# X Window: incoming connection attempt
ipchains -A input -i $EXTERNAL_INTERFACE -p tcp -y \
        -d $IPADDR $XWINDOW_PORTS -j DENY -l
```

Disallowing SOCKS Server Connections (TCP Port 1080)

SOCKS is a local proxy server freely available from http://www.socks.nec.com/. Your SOCKS-aware client programs connect to the server instead of directly connecting to remote servers. The SOCKS server connects to remote servers, as a client, on your behalf.

Attempts to connect to remote SOCKS servers are fairly common and often involve intrusion exploits. The following rules allow port 1080 as a local or remote client port, but disallow port 1080 as a local or remote server port:

```
SOCKS_PORT="1080"                          # (TCP) socks
```

The first rule ensures that no outgoing connection attempts to remote SOCKS servers are made from your machine:

```
# SOCKS: establishing a connection
ipchains -A output -i $EXTERNAL_INTERFACE -p tcp -y \
        -s $IPADDR \
        -d $ANYWHERE $SOCKS_PORT -j REJECT -l
```

The next rule blocks incoming connection attempts to your SOCKS server:

```
# SOCKS: incoming connection
ipchains -A input -i $EXTERNAL_INTERFACE -p tcp -y \
        -d $IPADDR SOCKS_PORT -j DENY -l
```

Common Local UDP Services Assigned to Unprivileged Ports

TCP protocol rules can be handled more precisely than UDP protocol rules, due to TCP's connection establishment protocol. As a datagram service, UDP doesn't have a connection state associated with it. Access to UDP services should simply be blocked. Explicit exceptions are made to accommodate DNS and any of the few other UDP-based Internet services you might use. Fortunately, the common UDP Internet services are often the type that are used between a client and a specific server. The filtering rules can often allow exchanges with one specific remote host.

NFS is the main UDP service to be concerned with. NFS runs on unprivileged port 2049. Unlike the previous TCP-based services, NFS is primarily a UDP-based service. It can be configured to run as a TCP-based service, but usually isn't.

Disallowing NFS (UDP/TCP Port 2049) Connections

The first rule blocks NFS UDP port 2049 from any incoming access. The rule is unnecessary if you aren't running NFS. You shouldn't be running NFS on a firewall machine, but if you are, external access is denied:

```
NFS_PORT="2049"                          # (TCP/UDP) NFS

# NFS: UDP connections
ipchains -A input -i $EXTERNAL_INTERFACE -p udp \
        -d $IPADDR $NFS_PORT -j DENY -l
```

The next two TCP rules cover the little-used NFS TCP connection mode. Both incoming and outgoing connection establishment attempts are blocked, just as in the previous TCP sections:

```
# NFS: TCP connections
ipchains -A input -i $EXTERNAL_INTERFACE -p tcp -y \
        -d $IPADDR $NFS_PORT -j DENY -l

ipchains -A output -i $EXTERNAL_INTERFACE -p tcp -y \
        -d $ANYWHERE $NFS_PORT -j DENY -l
```

The TCP and UDP Service Protocol Tables

The remainder of this chapter is devoted to defining rules to allow access to specific services. Client/server communication, both for TCP- and UDP-based services, involves some kind of two-way communication using a protocol specific to the service. As such, access rules are always represented as an I/O pair. The client program makes a query, and the server sends a response. Rules for a given service are categorized as client rules or server rules. The client category represents the communication required for your local clients to access remote servers. The server category represents the communication required for remote clients to access the services hosted from your machines.

The application messages are encapsulated in either TCP or UDP transport protocol messages. Because each service uses an application protocol specific to itself, the particular characteristics of the TCP or UDP exchange is, to some extent, unique to the given service.

The exchange between client and server is explicitly described by the firewall rules. Part of the firewall rules' purpose is to ensure protocol integrity at the packet level. Firewall rules, expressed in `ipchains` syntax, are not overly human-readable, however. In each of the following sections, the service protocol at the packet-filtering level is presented as a table of state information, followed by the `ipchains` rules expressing those states.

Each row in the table lists a packet type involved in the service exchange. A firewall rule is defined for each individual packet type. The table is divided into columns:

- `Description` contains a brief description of whether the packet is originating from the client or the server, and the packet's purpose.

- `Protocol` is the transport protocol in use, TCP or UDP, or the IP protocol's control messages, ICMP.

- `Remote Address` is the legal address, or range of addresses, the packet can contain in the remote address field.

- `Remote Port` is the legal port, or range of ports, the packet can contain in the remote port field.

- `In/Out` describes the packet's direction, that is, whether it is coming into the system from a remote location or whether it is going out from the system to a remote location.

- `Local Address` is the legal address, or range of addresses, the packet can contain in the local address field.

- `Local Port` is the legal port, or range of ports, the packet can contain in the local port field.

- TCP protocol packets contain a final column, TCP Flag, defining the legal **SYN-ACK** states the packet may have.

The table describes packets as either incoming or outgoing. Addresses and ports are described as either remote or local, relative to your machine's network interface. Notice that for incoming packets, remote address and port refer to the source fields in the IP packet header. Local address and port refer to the destination fields in the IP packet header. For outgoing packets, remote address and port refer to the destination fields in the IP packet header. Local address and port refer to the source fields in the IP packet header.

Finally, in the few instances where the service protocol involves ICMP messages, notice that the IP network layer ICMP packets are not associated with the concept of a source or destination port, as is the case for transport layer TCP or UDP packets. Instead, ICMP packets use the concept of a control or status message type. ICMP messages are not sent to programs bound to particular service ports. Instead, ICMP messages are sent from one computer to another. Consequently, the few ICMP packet entries presented in the tables use the source port column to contain the message type. For incoming ICMP packets, the source port column is the Remote Port column. For outgoing ICMP packets, the source port column is the Local Port column.

Enabling Basic, Required Internet Services

Only two services are truly required: the Domain Name Service (DNS) and the IDENT user identification service. DNS translates between hostnames and their associated IP addresses. You can't locate a remote host without DNS. identd provides the username or ID associated with a connection. This is commonly requested by a remote mail server when you send email. You don't need to offer identd service, but you must account for incoming connection requests in some way to avoid lengthy timeouts.

Allowing DNS (UDP/TCP Port 53)

DNS uses a communication protocol that relies on both UDP and TCP. Connection modes include regular client-to-server connections, peer-to-peer traffic between forwarding servers and full servers, and primary and secondary name server connections.

Query lookup requests are normally done over UDP, both for client-to-server lookups and peer-to-peer server lookups. The UDP communication can fail for a client-to-server lookup if the information being returned is too large to fit in a single UDP DNS packet. The server sets a flag bit in the DNS message header indicating that the data is truncated. In this case, the protocol allows for a retry over TCP. Figure 3.4 shows the relationship between UDP and TCP during a DNS lookup. In practice, TCP isn't normally needed for queries. TCP is conventionally used for administrative zone transfers between primary and secondary name servers.

Zone transfers are the transfer of a name server's complete information about a network, or the piece (zone) of a network, the server is authoritative for (i.e., the official server). The authoritative name server is referred to as the primary name server. Secondary, or backup, name servers periodically request zone transfers from their primary to keep their DNS caches up-to-date.

For example, one of your ISP's name servers is the primary, authoritative server for the ISP's LAN address space. ISPs often have multiple DNS servers to balance the load, as well as for backup redundancy. The other name servers are secondary name servers, refreshing their information from the master copy on the primary server.

Zone transfers are beyond the scope of this book. A small system isn't likely to be an authoritative name server for a public domain's name space, nor is it likely to be a public backup server for that information.

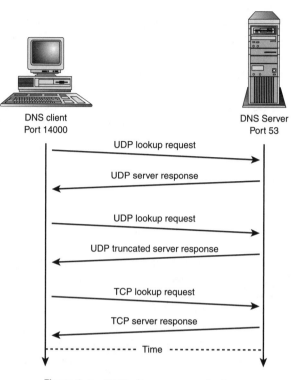

Figure 3.4   DNS client-to-server lookup.

Table 3.3 lists the complete DNS protocol for which the firewall rules account.

Table 3.3   DNS Protocol

Description	Protocol	Remote Address	Remote Port	In/ Out	Local Address	Local Port	TCP Flag
Local client query	UDP	NAMESERVER	53	Out	IPADDR	1024:65535	—
Remote server response	UDP	NAMESERVER	53	In	IPADDR	1024:65535	—
Local client query	TCP	NAMESERVER	53	Out	IPADDR	1024:65535	Any
Remote server response	TCP	NAMESERVER	53	In	IPADDR	1024:65535	Ack
Local server query	UDP	NAMESERVER	53	Out	IPADDR	53	—
Remote server response	UDP	NAMESERVER	53	In	IPADDR	53	—
Local zone transfer request	TCP	Primary	53	Out	IPADDR	1024:65535	Any
Remote zone transfer request	TCP	Primary	53	In	IPADDR	1024:65535	ACK
Remote client query	UDP	DNS client	1024:65535	In	IPADDR	53	—
Local server response	UDP	DNS client	1024:65535	Out	IPADDR	53	—
Remote client query	TCP	DNS client	1024:65535	In	IPADDR	53	Any
Local server response	TCP	DNS client	1024:65535	Out	IPADDR	53	ACK
Remote client query	UDP	DNS client	53	In	IPADDR	53	—
Local server response	UDP	DNS client	53	Out	IPADDR	53	—
Remote zone transfer request	TCP	Secondary	1024:65535	In	IPADDR	53	Any
Local zone transfer response	TCP	Secondary	1024:65535	Out	IPADDR	53	ACK

Allowing DNS Lookups as a Client

The DNS resolver client isn't a specific program. The client is incorporated into the network library code compiled into network programs. When a hostname requires a lookup, the resolver requests the lookup from a `named` server. Many small systems are configured only as a DNS client. The server runs on a remote machine. For a home user, the name server is usually a machine owned by your ISP.

DNS sends a lookup request as a UDP datagram:

```
NAMESERVER ="my.name.server"                # (TCP/UDP) DNS

ipchains -A output -i $EXTERNAL_INTERFACE -p udp \
        -s $IPADDR $UNPRIVPORTS \
        -d $NAMESERVER 53 -j ACCEPT

ipchains -A input  -i $EXTERNAL_INTERFACE -p udp \
        -s $NAMESERVER 53 \
        -d $IPADDR $UNPRIVPORTS -j ACCEPT
```

If an error occurs because the returned data is too large to fit in a UDP datagram, DNS retries using a TCP connection.

The next two rules are included for the rare occasion when the lookup response won't fit in a DNS UDP datagram. They won't be used in normal, day-to-day operations. You could run your system without problem for months on end without the TCP rules. Unfortunately, every so often—perhaps once or twice a year—your DNS lookups hang without these rules due to a poorly configured remote DNS server. More typically, these rules are used by a secondary name server requesting a zone transfer from its primary name server:

```
ipchains -A output -i $EXTERNAL_INTERFACE -p tcp \
        -s $IPADDR $UNPRIVPORTS \
        -d <my.dns.primary> 53 -j ACCEPT

ipchains -A input -i $EXTERNAL_INTERFACE -p tcp ! -y \
        -s <my.dns.primary> 53 \
        -d $IPADDR $UNPRIVPORTS -j ACCEPT
```

Allowing Your DNS Lookups as a Peer-to-Peer, Forwarding Server

Peer-to-peer transactions are exchanges between two servers. In the case of DNS, when your local name server doesn't have the information a client requested stored locally, it contacts a remote server and forwards the request to it.

Configuring a local forwarding name server can be a big performance gain. As shown in Figure 3.5, when `named` is configured as a caching and forwarding name server, it functions both as a local server and as a client to a remote DNS server. The difference between a direct client-to-server exchange and a forwarded local server–to–remote server exchange (peer-to-peer) is in the source and destination ports used. Instead of initiating an exchange from an unprivileged port, `named` initiates the exchange from its own DNS port 53. A second difference is that peer-to-peer server lookups of this type are always done over UDP.

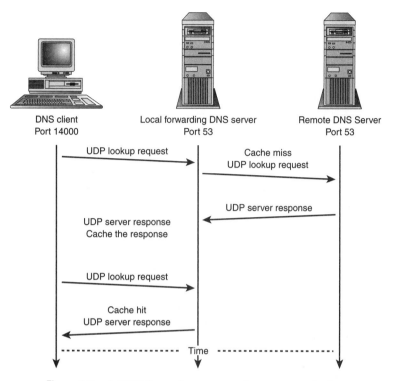

DNS client
Port 14000

Local forwarding DNS server
Port 53

Remote DNS Server
Port 53

UDP lookup request

Cache miss
UDP lookup request

UDP server response

UDP server response
Cache the response

UDP lookup request

Cache hit
UDP server response

Time

Figure 3.5   A DNS forwarding server and peer-to-peer lookup.

Local client requests are sent to the local DNS server. The first time, named won't have the lookup information, so it forwards the request to a remote name server. named caches the returned information and passes it on to the client. The next time the same information is requested, named finds it in its local cache and doesn't make a remote request:

```
ipchains -A output -i $EXTERNAL_INTERFACE -p udp \
         -s $IPADDR 53 \
         -d $NAMESERVER 53 -j ACCEPT

ipchains -A input  -i $EXTERNAL_INTERFACE -p udp \
         -s $NAMESERVER 53 \
         -d $IPADDR 53 -j ACCEPT
```

Allowing Remote DNS Lookups to Your Server

The average home-based site has little reason to provide DNS service to remote machines. Unless your site is an ISP, your clients will be machines local to your LAN, your subnet, your router, your network address space, or whatever terms are in use for the size of network and organization you're looking at.

Assuming you are a home or small business offering DNS to the outside world, you would limit the clients to a select group. You would not allow connections from just anywhere:

```
# client-to-server DNS transaction
ipchains -A input  -i $EXTERNAL_INTERFACE -p udp \
        -s <my.dns.clients> $UNPRIVPORTS \
        -d $IPADDR 53 -j ACCEPT

ipchains -A output -i $EXTERNAL_INTERFACE -p udp \
        -s $IPADDR 53 \
        -d <my.dns.clients> $UNPRIVPORTS -j ACCEPT

# peer-to-peer server DNS transaction
ipchains -A input  -i $EXTERNAL_INTERFACE -p udp \
        -s <my.dns.clients> 53 \
        -d $IPADDR 53 -j ACCEPT

ipchains -A output -i $EXTERNAL_INTERFACE -p udp \
        -s $IPADDR 53 \
        -d <my.dns.clients> 53 -j ACCEPT
```

The next two rules apply to client request retries when the data is too large to fit in a UDP DNS packet. They also apply to a secondary name server requesting zone transfers from a primary name server. TCP is used almost exclusively for zone transfers, and zone transfers represent a number of potential security holes. If used, it's important to limit the client source addresses:

```
ipchains -A input  -i $EXTERNAL_INTERFACE -p tcp \
        -s <my.dns.secondaries> $UNPRIVPORTS \
        -d $IPADDR 53 -j ACCEPT

ipchains -A output -i $EXTERNAL_INTERFACE -p tcp ! -y \
        -s $IPADDR 53 \
        -d <my.dns.secondaries> $UNPRIVPORTS -j ACCEPT
```

Filtering the AUTH User Identification Service (TCP Port 113)

The AUTH, or IDENTD, user identification service is most often used when sending mail or posting a Usenet article. Some FTP sites are also configured to require a resolvable AUTH lookup. For logging purposes, the server initiates an AUTH request back to your machine to get the account name of the user who initiated the mail or news connection. Table 3.4 lists the complete client/server connection protocol for the AUTH service.

DNS Zone Transfers over TCP

Large-scale network services, such as DNS zone transfers, should not be allowed by small sites. Undoubtedly, someone somewhere is an exception. For the exceptions, and for those individuals who are "going to do it anyway," limit the list of secondaries you accept connections from. Share your DNS tables with only trusted remote sites.

Table 3.4 *identd* **Protocol**

Description	Protocol	Remote Address	Remote Port	In/ Out	Local Address	Local Port	TCP Flag
Local client query	TCP	ANYWHERE	113	Out	IPADDR	1024:65535	Any
Remote server response	TCP	ANYWHERE	113	In	IPADDR	1024:65535	Ack
Remote client query	TCP	ANYWHERE	1024:65535	In	IPADDR	113	Any
Local server response	TCP	ANYWHERE	1024:65535	Out	IPADDR	113	Ack

Allowing Your Outgoing AUTH Requests as a Client

Your machine would act as an AUTH client if you ran a mail or FTP server. There is no reason not to allow your system to be an AUTH client:

```
ipchains -A output -i $EXTERNAL_INTERFACE -p tcp \
        -s $IPADDR $UNPRIVPORTS \
        -d $ANYWHERE 113 -j ACCEPT

ipchains -A input -i $EXTERNAL_INTERFACE -p tcp ! -y \
        -s $ANYWHERE 113 \
        -d $IPADDR $UNPRIVPORTS -j ACCEPT
```

Filtering Incoming AUTH Requests to Your Server

Offering AUTH services is the subject of ongoing debate. There appear to be no overwhelming arguments to make the case for either side, other than that a few FTP sites require it, and AUTH provides user account information. Whether you decide to offer the service or not, you will receive incoming requests for the service every time you send mail.

If you run the `identd` server out of `/etc/inetd.conf`, the following rules enable incoming `identd` connection requests:

```
ipchains -A input  -i $EXTERNAL_INTERFACE -p tcp \
        -s $ANYWHERE $UNPRIVPORTS \
        -d $IPADDR 113 -j ACCEPT

ipchains -A output -i $EXTERNAL_INTERFACE -p tcp ! -y \
        -s $IPADDR 113 \
        -d $ANYWHERE $UNPRIVPORTS -j ACCEPT
```

If you decide not to offer the service, you can't just deny the incoming requests. The result would be a long wait each time you tried to send mail or post a Usenet article. Your mail client won't be notified that the mail or article was received for delivery until the identd request timed out. Instead, you need to reject the connection request to avoid waiting for the TCP connection timeout. This is the only case where an incoming packet is rejected rather than denied in these examples:

```
ipchains -A input -i $EXTERNAL_INTERFACE -p tcp \
        -s $ANYWHERE \
        -d $IPADDR 113 -j REJECT
```

Enabling Common TCP Services

Possibly no one will want to enable all the services listed in this section, but everyone will want to enable some subset of them. These are the services most often used over the Internet today. As such, this section is more of a reference section than anything else. This section provides rules for the following:

- Email
- Usenet
- telnet
- ssh
- ftp
- Web services
- finger
- whois
- gopher Information Service
- Wide Area Information Service (WAIS)

Many other services are available that aren't covered here. Some of them are used on specialized servers, some by large businesses and organizations, and some are designed for use in local, private networks.

Email (TCP SMTP Port 25, POP Port 110, IMAP Port 143)

Email is a service almost everyone wants. How mail is set up depends on your ISP, your connection type, and your own choices. Email is sent across the network using the SMTP protocol assigned to TCP service port 25. Email is commonly received locally through one of three different protocols—SMTP, POP, or IMAP—depending on the services your ISP provides and on your local configuration.

SMTP is the general mail protocol. Mail is delivered to the destination host machine. The endpoint mail server determines whether the mail is deliverable (addressed to a valid user account on the machine) and delivers it to the user's local mailbox.

POP and IMAP are mail retrieval services. POP runs on TCP port 110. IMAP runs on TCP port 143. ISPs commonly make incoming mail available to their customers using one of these two services. Both services are authenticated. They are associated with the ISP customer's user account and password. As far as mail retrieval is concerned, the difference between SMTP and POP or IMAP is that SMTP receives incoming mail and queues it in the user's local mailbox. POP and IMAP retrieve mail into the user's local mail program from the user's ISP, where the mail had been queued remotely in the user's SMTP mailbox at the ISP. Table 3.5 lists the complete client/server connection protocols for SMTP, POP, and IMAP.

Table 3.5   SMTP, POP, and IMAP Mail Protocols

Description	Protocol	Remote Address	Remote Port	In/ Out	Local Address	Local Port	TCP Flag
Send outgoing mail	TCP	ANYWHERE	25	Out	IPADDR	1024:65535	Any
Remote server response	TCP	ANYWHERE	25	In	IPADDR	1024:65535	Ack
Receive incoming mail	TCP	ANYWHERE	1024:65535	In	IPADDR	25	Any
Local server response	TCP	ANYWHERE	1024:65536	Out	IPADDR	25	Ack
Local client query	TCP	POP SERVER	110	Out	IPADDR	1024:65535	Any
Remote server response	TCP	POP SERVER	110	In	IPADDR	1024:65535	Ack
Remote client query	TCP	POP client	1024:65535	In	IPADDR	110	Any
Local server response	TCP	POP client	1024:65535	Out	IPADDR	110	ACK
Local client query	TCP	IMAP SERVER	143	Out	IPADDR	1024:65535	Any
Remote server response	TCP	IMAP SERVER	143	In	IPADDR	1024:65535	ACK
Remote client query	TCP	IMAP client	1024:65535	In	IPADDR	143	Any
Local server response	TCP	IMAP client	1024:65535	Out	IPADDR	143	ACK

Sending Mail Over SMTP (TCP Port 25)

Mail is sent over SMTP. But whose SMTP server do you use to collect your mail and send it onward? ISPs offer SMTP mail service to their customers. The ISP's mail server acts as the mail gateway. It knows how to collect your mail, find the recipient host, and relay the mail. With UNIX, you can host your own local mail server if you want. Your server will be responsible for routing the mail to its destination.

Relaying Outgoing Mail Through an External (ISP) Gateway SMTP Server

When you relay outgoing mail through an external gateway SMTP server, your client mail program sends all outgoing mail to your ISP's mail server. Your ISP acts as your mail gateway to the rest of the world. Your system doesn't need to know how to locate your mail destinations or the routes to them. The ISP mail gateway serves as your relay.

The following two rules allow you to relay mail through your ISP's SMTP gateway:

```
SMTP_GATEWAY="my.isp.server"            # external mail server or relay

ipchains -A output -i $EXTERNAL_INTERFACE -p tcp \
        -s $IPADDR $UNPRIVPORTS \
        -d $SMTP_GATEWAY 25 -j ACCEPT

ipchains -A input -i $EXTERNAL_INTERFACE -p tcp ! -y \
        -s $SMTP_GATEWAY 25 \
        -d $IPADDR $UNPRIVPORTS -j ACCEPT
```

Sending Mail to Any External Mail Server

Alternatively, you can bypass your ISP's mail server and host your own. Your local server is responsible for collecting your outgoing mail, doing the DNS lookup on the destination hostname, and relaying the mail to its destination. Your client mail program points to your local SMTP server rather than to the ISP's server.

The following two rules allow you to send mail directly to the remote destinations:

```
ipchains -A output -i $EXTERNAL_INTERFACE -p tcp \
        -s $IPADDR $UNPRIVPORTS \
        -d $ANYWHERE 25 -j ACCEPT

ipchains -A input -i $EXTERNAL_INTERFACE -p tcp ! -y \
        -s $ANYWHERE 25 \
        -d $IPADDR $UNPRIVPORTS -j ACCEPT
```

Proxy Servers As Both Client and Server

The current SMTP mail server is `sendmail`, which is a proxy server. It acts as a server to the client mail program sending the mail. It acts as a client to the remote server it's sending the mail to. The terms *client* and *server* can be confusing in this context. `sendmail` acts as both, depending on which program it's talking to.

Receiving Mail

How you receive mail depends on your situation. If you run your own local mail server, you can collect incoming mail directly on your Linux machine. If you retrieve your mail from your ISP account, you may or may not retrieve mail as a POP or IMAP client, depending on how you've configured your ISP email account, and depending on the mail delivery services the ISP offers.

Receiving Mail as a Local SMTP Server (TCP Port 25)

If you want to receive mail sent directly to your local machines from anywhere in the world, you need to run `sendmail` and use these server rules:

```
ipchains -A input  -i $EXTERNAL_INTERFACE -p tcp \
        -s $ANYWHERE $UNPRIVPORTS \
        -d $IPADDR 25 -j ACCEPT

ipchains -A output -i $EXTERNAL_INTERFACE -p tcp ! -y \
        -s $IPADDR 25 \
        -d $ANYWHERE $UNPRIVPORTS -j ACCEPT
```

Alternatively, if you'd rather keep your local email account relatively private and use your work or ISP email account as your public address, you could configure your work and ISP mail accounts to forward mail to your local server. In this case, you could replace the previous single rule pair, accepting connections from anywhere, with separate, specific rules for each mail forwarder.

Retrieving Mail as a POP Client (TCP Port 110)

Connecting to a POP server is a very common means of retrieving mail from a remote ISP or work account. If your ISP uses a POP server for customer mail retrieval, you need to allow outgoing client-to-server connections.

The server's address will be a specific hostname or address, rather than the global ANYWHERE specifier. POP accounts are user accounts associated with a specific user and password:

```
POP_SERVER="my.isp.pop.server"          # external pop server, if any

ipchains -A output -i $EXTERNAL_INTERFACE -p tcp \
        -s $IPADDR $UNPRIVPORTS \
        -d $POP_SERVER 110 -j ACCEPT

ipchains -A input -i $EXTERNAL_INTERFACE -p tcp ! -y \
        -s $POP_SERVER 110 \
        -d $IPADDR $UNPRIVPORTS -j ACCEPT
```

Receiving Mail as an IMAP Client (TCP Port 143)

Connecting to an IMAP server is another common means of retrieving mail from a remote ISP or work account. If your ISP uses an IMAP server for customer mail retrieval, you need to allow outgoing client-to-server connections.

The server's address will be a specific hostname or address, rather than the global ANYWHERE specifier. IMAP accounts are user accounts associated with a specific user and password:

```
IMAP_SERVER="my.isp.imap.server"       # external imap server, if any

ipchains -A output -i $EXTERNAL_INTERFACE -p tcp \
        -s $IPADDR $UNPRIVPORTS \
        -d $IMAP_SERVER 143 -j ACCEPT

ipchains -A input -i $EXTERNAL_INTERFACE -p tcp ! -y \
        -s $IMAP_SERVER 143 \
        -d $IPADDR $UNPRIVPORTS -j ACCEPT
```

Examples of Real-World Client and Server Email Combinations

Four common approaches to client and server email combinations are described in this section:

- Sending mail as an SMTP client and receiving mail as a POP client
- Sending mail as an SMTP client and receiving mail as an IMAP client
- Sending mail as an SMTP client and receiving mail as an SMTP server
- Sending mail as an SMTP server and receiving mail as an SMTP server

The first two are useful if you rely completely on your ISP's SMTP and POP or IMAP email services. The third example is a mixed approach, relaying outgoing mail through your ISP's SMTP mail server, but receiving mail directly through your local SMTP server. The fourth approach supports running your own complete, independent mail server for both outgoing and incoming mail.

Sending Mail as an SMTP Client and Receiving Mail as a POP Client

If you are sending mail as an SMTP client and receiving mail as a POP client, you are relying completely on a remote site for your mail services. The remote site hosts both an SMTP server for relaying your outgoing mail, and a POP server for local mail retrieval:

```
SMTP_GATEWAY="my.isp.server"            # external mail server or relay

ipchains -A output -i $EXTERNAL_INTERFACE -p tcp \
        -s $IPADDR $UNPRIVPORTS \
        -d $SMTP_GATEWAY 25 -j ACCEPT

ipchains -A input -i $EXTERNAL_INTERFACE -p tcp ! -y \
        -s $SMTP_GATEWAY 25 \
        -d $IPADDR $UNPRIVPORTS -j ACCEPT

POP_SERVER="my.isp.pop.server"          # external pop server, if any
```

```
ipchains -A output -i $EXTERNAL_INTERFACE -p tcp \
        -s $IPADDR $UNPRIVPORTS \
        -d $POP_SERVER 110 -j ACCEPT

ipchains -A input -i $EXTERNAL_INTERFACE -p tcp ! -y \
        -s $POP_SERVER 110 \
        -d $IPADDR $UNPRIVPORTS -j ACCEPT
```

Sending Mail as an SMTP Client and Receiving Mail as an IMAP Client

If you are sending mail as an SMTP client and receiving mail as an IMAP client, you are relying completely on a remote site for your mail services. The remote site hosts both an SMTP server for relaying outgoing mail and an IMAP server for local mail retrieval:

```
SMTP_GATEWAY="my.isp.server"           # external mail server or relay

ipchains -A output -i $EXTERNAL_INTERFACE -p tcp \
        -s $IPADDR $UNPRIVPORTS \
        -d $SMTP_GATEWAY 25 -j ACCEPT

ipchains -A input -i $EXTERNAL_INTERFACE -p tcp ! -y \
        -s $SMTP_GATEWAY 25 \
        -d $IPADDR $UNPRIVPORTS -j ACCEPT

IMAP_SERVER="my.isp.imap.server"       # external imap server, if any

ipchains -A output -i $EXTERNAL_INTERFACE -p tcp \
        -s $IPADDR $UNPRIVPORTS \
        -d $IMAP_SERVER 143 -j ACCEPT
ipchains -A input -i $EXTERNAL_INTERFACE -p tcp ! -y \
        -s $IMAP_SERVER 143 \
        -d $IPADDR $UNPRIVPORTS -j ACCEPT
```

Sending Mail as an SMTP Client and Receiving Mail as an SMTP Server

If you are sending mail as an SMTP client and receiving mail as an SMTP server, you are relying on a remote site to offer SMTP service to relay your outgoing mail to remote destinations. You run sendmail locally as a local SMTP server allowing remote hosts to send mail to your machine directly. Outgoing mail is relayed through your ISP, but the local sendmail daemon knows how to deliver incoming mail to local user accounts:

```
SMTP_GATEWAY="my.isp.server"              # external mail server or relay

ipchains -A output -i $EXTERNAL_INTERFACE -p tcp \
        -s $IPADDR $UNPRIVPORTS \
        -d $SMTP_GATEWAY 25 -j ACCEPT
```

```
ipchains -A input -i $EXTERNAL_INTERFACE -p tcp ! -y \
        -s $SMTP_GATEWAY 25 \
        -d $IPADDR $UNPRIVPORTS -j ACCEPT

ipchains -A input  -i $EXTERNAL_INTERFACE -p tcp \
        -s $ANYWHERE $UNPRIVPORTS \
        -d $IPADDR 25 -j ACCEPT

ipchains -A output -i $EXTERNAL_INTERFACE -p tcp ! -y \
        -s $IPADDR 25 \
        -d $ANYWHERE $UNPRIVPORTS -j ACCEPT
```

Sending Mail as an SMTP Server and Receiving Mail as an SMTP Server

If you are sending mail as an SMTP server and receiving mail as an SMTP server, you provide all your own mail services. Your local sendmail daemon is configured to relay outgoing mail to the destination hosts itself, as well as collect and deliver incoming mail:

```
ipchains -A output -i $EXTERNAL_INTERFACE -p tcp \
        -s $IPADDR $UNPRIVPORTS \
        -d $ANYWHERE 25 -j ACCEPT

ipchains -A input -i $EXTERNAL_INTERFACE -p tcp ! -y \
        -s $ANYWHERE 25 \
        -d $IPADDR $UNPRIVPORTS -j ACCEPT

ipchains -A input  -i $EXTERNAL_INTERFACE -p tcp \
        -s $ANYWHERE $UNPRIVPORTS \
        -d $IPADDR 25 -j ACCEPT

ipchains -A output -i $EXTERNAL_INTERFACE -p tcp ! -y \
        -s $IPADDR 25 \
        -d $ANYWHERE $UNPRIVPORTS -j ACCEPT
```

Hosting a Mail Server for Remote Clients

Hosting public POP or IMAP services is unusual for a small system. You might do this if you offered remote mail services to a few friends, for example, or if their ISP mail service was temporarily unavailable. In any case, it's important to limit the clients your system will accept connections from, both on the packet-filtering level and on the server configuration level. You should also consider using an encrypted authentication method, or allow mail retrieval only over an SSH connection.

Hosting a POP Server for Remote Clients

POP servers are one of the three most common and successful points of entry for hacking exploits.

If you use a local system as a central mail server and run a local popd server to provide mail access to local machines on a LAN, you don't need the server rules in this example. Incoming connections from the Internet should be denied. If you do need to host POP service for a limited number of remote individuals, the next two rules allow incoming connections to your POP server. Connections are limited to your specific clients' IP addresses:

```
ipchains -A input  -i $EXTERNAL_INTERFACE -p tcp \
        -s <my.pop.clients> $UNPRIVPORTS \
        -d $IPADDR 110 -j ACCEPT

ipchains -A output -i $EXTERNAL_INTERFACE -p tcp ! -y \
        -s $IPADDR 110 \
        -d <my.pop.clients> $UNPRIVPORTS -j ACCEPT
```

Hosting an IMAP Server for Remote Clients

IMAP servers are one of the three most common and successful points of entry for hacking exploits.

If you use a local system as a central mail server and run a local `imapd` server to provide mail access to local machines on a LAN, you don't need a server rule. Incoming connections from the Internet should be denied. If you do need to host IMAP service for a limited number of remote individuals, the next two rules allow incoming connections to your IMAP server. Connections are limited to your specific clients' IP addresses:

```
ipchains -A input  -i $EXTERNAL_INTERFACE -p tcp \
        -s <my.imap.clients> $UNPRIVPORTS \
        -d $IPADDR 143 -j ACCEPT

ipchains -A output -i $EXTERNAL_INTERFACE -p tcp ! -y \
        -s $IPADDR 143 \
        -d <my.imap.clients> $UNPRIVPORTS -j ACCEPT
```

Accessing Usenet News Services (TCP NNTP Port 119)

Usenet news is accessed over NNTP running on top of TCP through service port 119. Reading news and posting articles are handled by your local news client. Few systems require the server rules. Table 3.6 lists the complete client/server connection protocol for the NNTP Usenet news service.

Table 3.6 **NNTP Protocol**

Description	Protocol	Remote Address	Remote Port	In/ Out	Local Address	Local Port	TCP Flag
Local client query	TCP	NEWS SERVER	119	Out	IPADDR	1024:65535	Any
Remote server response	TCP	NEWS SERVER	119	In	IPADDR	1024:65535	Ack
Remote client query	TCP	NNTP clients	1024:65535	In	IPADDR	119	Any
Local server response	TCP	NNTP clients	1024:65535	Out	IPADDR	119	Ack
Local server query	TCP	News feed	119	Out	IPADDR	1024:65535	Any
Remote server response	TCP	News feed	119	In	IPADDR	1024:65535	Ack

Reading and Posting News as a Usenet Client

The client rules allow connections to your ISP's news server. Both reading news and posting articles are handled by these rules:

```
NEWS_SERVER="my.news.server"              # external news server, if any

ipchains -A output -i $EXTERNAL_INTERFACE -p tcp \
        -s $IPADDR $UNPRIVPORTS \
        -d $NEWS_SERVER 119 -j ACCEPT

ipchains -A input -i $EXTERNAL_INTERFACE -p tcp ! -y \
        -s $NEWS_SERVER 119 \
        -d $IPADDR $UNPRIVPORTS -j ACCEPT
```

Hosting a Usenet News Server for Remote Clients

A small site is very unlikely to host a news server for the outside world. Even hosting a local news server is unlikely. For the rare exception, the server rules should be configured to allow incoming connections only from a select set of clients:

```
ipchains -A input  -i $EXTERNAL_INTERFACE -p tcp \
        -s <my.news.clients> $UNPRIVPORTS \
        -d $IPADDR 119 -j ACCEPT

ipchains -A output -i $EXTERNAL_INTERFACE -p tcp ! -y \
        -s $IPADDR 119 \
        -d <my.news.clients> $UNPRIVPORTS -j ACCEPT
```

Allowing Peer News Feeds for a Local Usenet Server

A small, home-based site is unlikely to have a peer-to-peer news feed server relationship with an ISP. Although news servers used to be fairly accessible to the general Internet, few open news servers are available anymore due to SPAM and server load issues.

If your site is large enough or rich enough to host a general Usenet server, you have to get your news feed from somewhere. The next two rules allow your local news server to receive its news feed from a remote server. The local server contacts the remote server as a client. The only difference between the peer-to-peer news feed rules and the regular client rules is the name or address of the remote host:

```
ipchains -A output -i $EXTERNAL_INTERFACE -p tcp \
         -s $IPADDR $UNPRIVPORTS \
         -d <my.news.feed> 119 -j ACCEPT

ipchains -A input -i $EXTERNAL_INTERFACE -p tcp ! -y \
         -s <my.news.feed> 119 \
         -d $IPADDR $UNPRIVPORTS -j ACCEPT
```

telnet (TCP Port 23)

`telnet` has been the de facto standard means of remote login over the Internet for many years. As the nature of the Internet community has changed, `telnet` has come to be viewed more and more as an insecure service, because it communicates in ASCII clear text. Nevertheless, `telnet` may be the only tool available to you for remote connections, depending on the connection options available at the other end. If you have the option, you should always use an encrypted service, such as `ssh`, rather than `telnet`.

The client and server rules here allow access to and from anywhere. If you use `telnet`, you can probably limit the external addresses to a select subset at the packet-filtering level. Table 3.7 lists the complete client/server connection protocol for the TELNET service.

Table 3.7 TELNET Protocol

Description	Protocol	Remote Address	Remote Port	In/ Out	Local Address	Local Port	TCP Flag
Local client request	TCP	ANYWHERE	23	Out	IPADDR	1024:65535	Any
Remote server response	TCP	ANYWHERE	23	In	IPADDR	1024:65535	Ack
Remote client request	TCP	telnet clients	1024:65535	In	IPADDR	23	Any
Local server response	TCP	telnet clients	1024:65535	Out	IPADDR	23	Ack

Allowing Outgoing Client Access to Remote Sites

If you need to use `telnet` to access your accounts on remote systems, the next two rules allow outgoing connections to remote sites. If your site has multiple users, you might limit outgoing connections to the specific sites your users have accounts on, rather than allowing outgoing connections to `anywhere`:

```
ipchains -A output -i $EXTERNAL_INTERFACE -p tcp \
         -s $IPADDR $UNPRIVPORTS \
         -d $ANYWHERE 23 -j ACCEPT

ipchains -A input -i $EXTERNAL_INTERFACE -p tcp ! -y \
         -s $ANYWHERE 23 \
         -d $IPADDR $UNPRIVPORTS -j ACCEPT
```

Allowing Incoming Access to Your Local Server

Even if you need client access to remote servers, you may not need to allow incoming connections to your TELNET server. If you do, the next two rules allow incoming connections to your server:

```
ipchains -A input   -i $EXTERNAL_INTERFACE -p tcp \
         -s $ANYWHERE $UNPRIVPORTS \
         -d $IPADDR 23 -j ACCEPT

ipchains -A output -i $EXTERNAL_INTERFACE -p tcp ! -y \
         -s $IPADDR 23 \
         -d $ANYWHERE $UNPRIVPORTS -j ACCEPT
```

Rather than allow connections from anywhere, it is preferable to define server rules for each specific host or network an incoming connection can legitimately originate from.

ssh (TCP Port 22)

SSH, secure shell, isn't included in Linux distributions due to export limitations on cryptographic technology, but it is freely available from software sites on the Internet. SSH is considered far preferable to using `telnet` for remote login access, because both ends of the connection use authentication keys for both hosts and users, and data is encrypted. Additionally, SSH is more than a remote login service. It can automatically direct X Window connections between remote sites, and FTP and other TCP-based connections can be directed over the more secure SSH connection. Provided that the other end of the connection allows SSH connections, it's possible to route all TCP connections through the firewall using SSH. As such, SSH is something of a poor man's virtual private network (VPN).

The ports used by SSH are highly configurable. The rules in this example apply to the default SSH port usage. By default, connections are initiated between a client's unprivileged port and the server's assigned service port 22. The server forks off a copy of itself for the connection, and the client end of the connection is then reassigned to

a privileged port in the descending range from 1023 to 513 in order to support
.rhosts and hosts.equiv authentication. The first available port is used. The SSH
client will optionally use the unprivileged ports exclusively. The SSH server will accept
connections from either the privileged or unprivileged ports.

The client and server rules here allow access to and from anywhere. In practice, you
would limit the external addresses to a select subset, particularly because both ends of
the connection must be configured to recognize each individual user account for
authentication. Table 3.8 lists the complete client/server connection protocol for the
SSH service.

Table 3.8   SSH Protocol

Description	Protocol	Remote Address	Remote Port	In/ Out	Local Address	Local Port	TCP Flag
Local client request	TCP	ANYWHERE	22	Out	IPADDR	1024:65535	Any
Remote server response	TCP	ANYWHERE	22	In	IPADDR	1024:65535	Ack
Local client request	TCP	ANYWHERE	22	Out	IPADDR	513:1023	Any
Remote server response	TCP	ANYWHERE	22	In	IPADDR	513:1023	Ack
Remote client request	TCP	SSH clients	1024:65535	In	IPADDR	22	Any
Local server response	TCP	SSH clients	1024:65535	Out	IPADDR	22	Ack
Remote client request	TCP	SSH clients	513:1023	In	IPADDR	22	Any
Local server response	TCP	SSH clients	513:1023	Out	IPADDR	22	Ack

SSH, *tcp_wrappers,* **and** *rhost* **Authentication**

SSH cannot be started under tcp_wrappers directly, but it can be compiled to honor the access list
information in /etc/hosts.allow and /etc/hosts.deny.

.rhosts and hosts.equiv authentication should simply not be available on a firewall machine.
System security analysis tools discussed in Chapter 8, "Intrusion Detection and Incident Reporting" warn
you if these files exist on the system.

For more information on SSH, refer to http://www.ssh.fi/.

When selecting a privileged server port for the ongoing connection, the first free port between 1023 to 513 is used. The range of ports you allow equates to the number of simultaneous incoming SSH connections you allow:

```
SSH_PORTS="1020:1023"                    # (TCP) 4 simultaneous connections
```

Allowing Client Access to Remote SSH Servers

These rules allow you to connect to remote sites using ssh:

```
ipchains -A output -i $EXTERNAL_INTERFACE -p tcp \
        -s $IPADDR $UNPRIVPORTS \
        -d $ANYWHERE 22 -j ACCEPT

ipchains -A input -i $EXTERNAL_INTERFACE -p tcp ! -y \
        -s $ANYWHERE 22 \
        -d $IPADDR $UNPRIVPORTS -j ACCEPT

ipchains -A output -i $EXTERNAL_INTERFACE -p tcp \
        -s $IPADDR $SSH_PORTS \
        -d $ANYWHERE 22 -j ACCEPT

ipchains -A input  -i $EXTERNAL_INTERFACE -p tcp ! -y \
        -s $ANYWHERE 22 \
        -d $IPADDR $SSH_PORTS -j ACCEPT
```

Allowing Remote Client Access to Your Local SSH Server

These rules allow incoming connections to your sshd server:

```
ipchains -A input  -i $EXTERNAL_INTERFACE -p tcp \
        -s $ANYWHERE $UNPRIVPORTS \
        -d $IPADDR 22 -j ACCEPT

ipchains -A output -i $EXTERNAL_INTERFACE -p tcp ! -y \
        -s $IPADDR 22 \
        -d $ANYWHERE $UNPRIVPORTS -j ACCEPT

ipchains -A input -i $EXTERNAL_INTERFACE -p tcp \
        -s $ANYWHERE $SSH_PORTS \
        -d $IPADDR 22 -j ACCEPT

ipchains -A output -i $EXTERNAL_INTERFACE -p tcp ! -y \
        -s $IPADDR 22 \
        -d $ANYWHERE $SSH_PORTS -j ACCEPT
```

ftp (TCP Ports 21, 20)

FTP remains one of the most common means of transferring files between two networked machines. Web-based interfaces to FTP have become common, as well.

FTP uses two privileged ports, one for sending commands and one for sending data. Port 21 is used to establish the initial connection to the server and pass user commands. Port 20 is used to establish a data channel over which files and directory listings are sent as data.

FTP has two modes for exchanging data between a client and server, normal data channel port mode and passive data channel mode. Normal port mode is the original, default mechanism when using the ftp client program and connecting to a remote FTP site. Passive mode is a newer mechanism, and is the default when connecting through a Web browser. Occasionally, you might encounter an FTP site that supports only one mode or the other. Table 3.9 lists the complete client/server connection protocol for the FTP service.

Table 3.9 FTP Protocol

Description	Protocol	Remote Address	Remote Port	In/ Out	Local Address	Local Port	TCP Flag
Local client query	TCP	ANYWHERE	21	Out	IPADDR	1024:65535	Any
Remote server response	TCP	ANYWHERE	21	In	IPADDR	1024:65535	Ack
Remote server port data channel request	TCP	ANYWHERE	20	In	IPADDR	1024:65535	Any
Local client port data channel response	TCP	ANYWHERE	20	Out	IPADDR	1024:65535	Ack
Local client passive data channel request	TCP	ANYWHERE	1024:65535	Out	IPADDR	1024:65535	Any
Remote server passive data channel response	TCP	ANYWHERE	1024:65535	In	IPADDR	1024:65535	Ack
Remote client request	TCP	ANYWHERE	1024:65535	In	IPADDR	21	Any
Local server response	TCP	ANYWHERE	1024:65535	Out	IPADDR	21	ACK
Local server port data channel request	TCP	ANYWHERE	1024:65535	Out	IPADDR	20	Any
Remote client port data channel response	TCP	ANYWHERE	1024:65535	In	IPADDR	20	ACK
Remote client passive data channel request	TCP	ANYWHERE	1024:65535	In	IPADDR	1024:65535	Any
Local server passive data channel response	TCP	ANYWHERE	1024:65535	Out	IPADDR	1024:65535	ACK

Allowing Outgoing Client Access to Remote FTP Servers

It's almost a given that most sites will want FTP client access to remote file repositories. Most people will want to enable outgoing client connections to a remote server.

Outgoing FTP Requests

The next two rules allow an outgoing connection to a remote FTP server:

```
ipchains -A output -i $EXTERNAL_INTERFACE -p tcp \
        -s $IPADDR $UNPRIVPORTS \
        -d $ANYWHERE 21 -j ACCEPT

ipchains -A input -i $EXTERNAL_INTERFACE -p tcp ! -y \
        -s $ANYWHERE 21 \
        -d $IPADDR $UNPRIVPORTS -j ACCEPT
```

Normal Port Mode FTP Data Channels

The next two rules allow the standard data channel connection, where the remote server calls back to establish the data connection:

```
ipchains -A input  -i $EXTERNAL_INTERFACE -p tcp \
        -s $ANYWHERE 20 \
        -d $IPADDR $UNPRIVPORTS -j ACCEPT

ipchains -A output -i $EXTERNAL_INTERFACE -p tcp ! -y \
        -s $IPADDR $UNPRIVPORTS \
        -d $ANYWHERE 20 -j ACCEPT
```

This unusual callback behavior, where the remote server establishes the secondary connection with your client, is part of what makes FTP difficult to secure at the packet-filtering level. There is no mechanism to assure that the incoming connection is truly originating from the remote FTP server you've contacted. Unless you've explicitly blocked incoming connections to local services running on unprivileged ports, such as an X Window or SOCKS server, remote access to these services is allowed by the FTP client rules for port mode data channels.

Passive Mode FTP Data Channels

The next two rules allow the newer passive data channel mode used by Web browsers:

```
ipchains -A output -i $EXTERNAL_INTERFACE -p tcp \
        -s $IPADDR $UNPRIVPORTS \
        -d $ANYWHERE $UNPRIVPORTS -j ACCEPT

ipchains -A input  -i $EXTERNAL_INTERFACE -p tcp ! -y \
        -s $ANYWHERE $UNPRIVPORTS \
        -d $IPADDR $UNPIRVPORTS -j ACCEPT
```

Passive mode is considered more secure than port mode because the ftp client initiates both the control and data connections, even though the connection is made between two unprivileged ports.

Allowing Incoming Access to Your Local FTP Server

Whether to offer FTP services to the world is a difficult decision. Although FTP sites abound on the Internet, FTP server configuration requires great care. Numerous FTP security exploits are possible.

If your goal is to offer general read-only access to some set of files on your machine, you might consider making these files available through a Web server. If your goal is to allow file uploads to your machine from the outside, FTP server access should be severely limited on the firewall level, on the `tcp_wrapper` level, and on the FTP configuration level.

In any case, if you decide to offer FTP services, and if you decide to allow incoming file transfers, write access should not be allowed via Anonymous FTP. Remote write access to your file systems should be allowed only from specific, authenticated FTP user accounts, from specific remote sites, and to carefully controlled and limited FTP areas reserved in your file system. Chapter 7, "Issues At the UNIX System Administration Level," discusses these FTP issues.

Incoming FTP Requests

The next two rules allow incoming connections to your FTP server:

```
ipchains -A input   -i $EXTERNAL_INTERFACE -p tcp \
         -s $ANYWHERE $UNPRIVPORTS \
         -d $IPADDR 21 -j ACCEPT

ipchains -A output -i $EXTERNAL_INTERFACE -p tcp ! -y \
         -s $IPADDR 21 \
         -d $ANYWHERE $UNPRIVPORTS -j ACCEPT
```

Normal Port Mode FTP Data Channel Responses

The next two rules allow the FTP server to call back the remote client and establish the secondary data channel connection:

```
ipchains -A output -i $EXTERNAL_INTERFACE -p tcp \
         -s $IPADDR 20 \
         -d $ANYWHERE $UNPRIVPORTS -j ACCEPT

ipchains -A input  -i $EXTERNAL_INTERFACE -p tcp ! -y \
         -s $ANYWHERE $UNPRIVPORTS \
         -d $IPADDR 20 -j ACCEPT
```

Passive Mode FTP Data Channel Responses

The next two rules allow the remote FTP client to establish the secondary data channel connection with the local server:

```
ipchains -A input   -i $EXTERNAL_INTERFACE -p tcp \
         -s $ANYWHERE $UNPRIVPORTS \
         -d $IPADDR $UNPRIVPORTS -j ACCEPT

ipchains -A output -i $EXTERNAL_INTERFACE -p tcp ! -y \
         -s $IPADDR $UNPRIVPORTS \
         -d $ANYWHERE $UNPRIVPORTS -j ACCEPT
```

Web Services

Web services are based on Hypertext Transfer Protocol (HTTP). Client and server connections use the standard TCP conventions. Several higher-level, special-purpose communication protocols are available, in addition to the standard general HTTP access, including secure access over SSL, and access via an ISP-provided Web server proxy. These different access protocols use different service ports.

Standard HTTP Access (TCP Port 80)

In normal use, Web services are available over http service port 80. Table 3.10 lists the complete client/server connection protocol for the HTTP Web service.

Table 3.10   HTTP Protocol

Description	Protocol	Remote Address	Remote Port	In/ Out	Local Address	Local Port	TCP Flag
Local client request	TCP	ANYWHERE	80	Out	IPADDR	1024:65535	Any
Remote server response	TCP	ANYWHERE	80	In	IPADDR	1024:65535	Ack
Remote client request	TCP	ANYWHERE	1024:65535	In	IPADDR	80	Any
Local server response	TCP	ANYWHERE	1024:65535	Out	IPADDR	80	Ack

Accessing Remote Web Sites as a Client

It's almost inconceivable in today's world that a home-based site would not want to access the World Wide Web from a Web browser. The next two rules allow access to remote Web servers:

```
ipchains -A output -i $EXTERNAL_INTERFACE -p tcp \
        -s $IPADDR $UNPRIVPORTS \
        -d $ANYWHERE 80 -j ACCEPT

ipchains -A input -i $EXTERNAL_INTERFACE -p tcp ! -y \
        -s $ANYWHERE 80 \
        -d $IPADDR $UNPRIVPORTS -j ACCEPT
```

Caution: Don't Use *tftp* on the Internet

tftp offers a simplified, unauthenticated, UDP version of the FTP service. It is intended for loading boot software into routers and diskless workstations over a local network from trusted hosts. Some people confuse tftp as an alternative to ftp. Don't use it over the Internet, period.

Allowing Remote Access to a Local Web Server

If you decide to run a Web server of your own and host a Web site for the Internet, the general server rules allow all typical incoming access to your site. This is all most people need to host a Web site:

```
ipchains -A input -i $EXTERNAL_INTERFACE -p tcp\
        -s $ANYWHERE $UNPRIVPORTS \
        -d $IPADDR 80 -j ACCEPT

ipchains -A output -i $EXTERNAL_INTERFACE -p tcp ! -y \
        -s $IPADDR 80 \
        -d $ANYWHERE $UNPRIVPORTS -j ACCEPT
```

Secure Web Access (SSL) (TCP Port 443)

Secure Socket Layer (SSL) is used for secure, encrypted Web access. The SSL protocol uses TCP port 443. You will most often encounter this if you go to a commercial Web site to purchase something, use online banking services, or enter a protected Web area where you'll be prompted for personal information. Table 3.11 lists the complete client/server connection protocol for the SSL service.

Table 3.11   SSL Protocol

Description	Protocol	Remote Address	Remote Port	In/Out	Local Address	Local Port	TCP Flag
Local client request	TCP	ANYWHERE	443	Out	IPADDR	1024:65535	Any
Remote server response	TCP	ANYWHERE	443	In	IPADDR	1024:65535	Ack
Remote client request	TCP	ANYWHERE	1024:65535	In	IPADDR	443	Any
Local server response	TCP	ANYWHERE	1024:65535	Out	IPADDR	443	Ack

Accessing Remote Web Sites Over SSL as a Client

Most people will want client access to secure Web sites at some point or another:

```
ipchains -A output -i $EXTERNAL_INTERFACE -p tcp \
        -s $IPADDR $UNPRIVPORTS \
        -d $ANYWHERE 443 -j ACCEPT

ipchains -A input -i $EXTERNAL_INTERFACE -p tcp ! -y \
        -s $ANYWHERE 443 \
        -d $IPADDR $UNPRIVPORTS -j ACCEPT
```

Allowing Remote Access to a Local SSL Web Server

If you conduct some form of e-commerce, you'll mostly likely want to allow incoming connections to SSL-protected areas of your Web site. Otherwise, you won't need local server rules.

The basic Apache Web server distribution comes with SSL support, but the more secure SSL modules are not included due to Federal encryption regulations. Both free and commercial SSL support packages are available for the Apache Web server, however. See `www.apache.org` for more information.

The next two rules allow incoming access to your Web server using the SSL protocol:

```
ipchains -A input  -i $EXTERNAL_INTERFACE -p tcp \
          -s $ANYWHERE $UNPRIVPORTS \
          -d $IPADDR 443 -j ACCEPT

ipchains -A output -i $EXTERNAL_INTERFACE -p tcp ! -y \
          -s $IPADDR 443 \
          -d $ANYWHERE $UNPRIVPORTS-j ACCEPT
```

Web Proxy Access (TCP Ports 8008, 8080)

Publicly accessible Web server proxies are most common at ISPs. As a customer, you configure your browser to use a remote proxy service. Web proxies are often accessed through one of two unprivileged ports assigned for this purpose, port 8008 or 8080, as defined by the ISP. In return, you get faster Web page access when the pages are already cached locally at your ISP's server, and the anonymity of proxied access to remote sites. Your connections are not direct, but instead are initiated on your behalf by your ISP's proxy. Table 3.12 lists the local client to remote server connection protocol for the Web proxy service.

Table 3.12   Web Proxy Protocol

Description	Protocol	Remote Address	Remote Port	In/ Out	Local Address	Local Port	TCP Flag
Local client request	TCP	WEB PROXY SERVER	WEB PROXY PORT	Out	IPADDR	1024:65535	Any
Remote server response	TCP	WEB PROXY SERVER	WEB PROXY PORT	In	IPADDR	1024:65535	Ack

If you use a Web proxy service offered by your ISP, the specific server address and port number will be defined by your ISP. The client rules are:

```
WEB_PROXY_SERVER="my.www.proxy"        # ISP Web proxy server, if any
WEB_PROXY_PORT="www.proxy.port"        # ISP Web proxy port, if any
                                       # typically 8008 or 8080

ipchains -A output -i $EXTERNAL_INTERFACE -p tcp \
         -s $IPADDR $UNPRIVPORTS \
         -d $WEB_PROXY_SERVER $WEB_PROXY_PORT -j ACCEPT

ipchains -A input -i $EXTERNAL_INTERFACE -p tcp ! -y \
         -s $WEB_PROXY_SERVER $WEB_PROXY_PORT \
         -d $IPADDR $UNPRIVPORTS -j ACCEPT
```

finger (TCP Port 79)

From a connection point of view, the finger service is harmless. Due to the changing nature of privacy issues in relation to a growing and changing Internet community, offering finger service is generally discouraged today. finger provides user account information, including such things as user login name, real name, currently active logins, pending mail, and mail forwarding locations. Often, finger provides user-furnished (in a .plan file) personal information as well, including phone numbers, home addresses, tasks and plans, vacation status, and so forth. Table 3.13 lists the complete client/server connection protocol for the finger service.

Table 3.13 *finger* **Protocol**

Description	Protocol	Remote Address	Remote Port	In/ Out	Local Address	Local Port	TCP Flag
Local client request	TCP	ANYWHERE	79	Out	IPADDR	1024:65535	Any
Remote server response	TCP	ANYWHERE	79	In	IPADDR	1024:65535	Ack
Remote client request	TCP	finger clients	1024:65535	In	IPADDR	79	Any
Local server response	TCP	finger clients	1024:65535	Out	IPADDR	79	Ack

Accessing Remote *finger* Servers as a Client

There's no harm in enabling outgoing access to remote finger servers, and these are the rules to do so:

```
ipchains -A output -i $EXTERNAL_INTERFACE -p tcp \
        -s $IPADDR $UNPRIVPORTS \
        -d $ANYWHERE 79 -j ACCEPT

ipchains -A input -i $EXTERNAL_INTERFACE -p tcp ! -y \
        -s $ANYWHERE 79 \
        -d $IPADDR $UNPRIVPORTS -j ACCEPT
```

Allowing Remote Client Access to a Local *finger* Server

If you choose to allow outside access to your finger service, it's recommended that you limit access to specific client sites. finger access can be limited both at the firewall level and at the tcp_wrapper level.

The next rules allow incoming connections to your finger server, but only selected remote hosts are allowed to initiate the connection:

```
ipchains -A input  -i $EXTERNAL_INTERFACE -p tcp \
        -s <my.finger.clients> $UNPRIVPORTS \
        -d $IPADDR 79 -j ACCEPT

ipchains -A output -i $EXTERNAL_INTERFACE -p tcp ! -y \
        -s $IPADDR 79 \
        -d <my.finger.clients> $UNPRIVPORTS -j ACCEPT
```

whois (TCP Port 43)

The whois program accesses the InterNIC Registration Services database. It allows IP address and host and domain name lookups in human-readable form. Table 3.14 lists the local client to remote server connection protocol for the whois service.

Table 3.14 *whois* Protocol

Description	Protocol	Remote Address	Remote Port	In/ Out	Local Address	Local Port	TCP Flag
Local client request	TCP	ANYWHERE	43	Out	IPADDR	1024:65535	Any
Remote server response	TCP	ANYWHERE	43	In	IPADDR	1024:65535	Ack

The next two rules allow you to query an official remote server:

```
ipchains -A output -i $EXTERNAL_INTERFACE -p tcp \
         -s $IPADDR $UNPRIVPORTS \
         -d $ANYWHERE 43 -j ACCEPT

ipchains -A input -i $EXTERNAL_INTERFACE -p tcp ! -y \
         -s $ANYWHERE 43 \
         -d $IPADDR $UNPRIVPORTS -j ACCEPT
```

gopher (TCP Port 70)

The GOPHER information service is still available for low-overhead ASCII terminals, but its use has largely been replaced by Web-based search engines and hypertext links. It is unlikely that a Linux system would offer local GOPHER service instead of a Web site. Server rules are not included. Table 3.15 lists the local client to remote server connection protocol for the GOPHER service.

Table 3.15 *gopher* **Protocol**

Description	Protocol	Remote Address	Remote Port	In/Out	Local Address	Local Port	TCP Flag
Local client request	TCP	ANYWHERE	70	Out	IPADDR	1024:65535	Any
Remote server response	TCP	ANYWHERE	70	In	IPADDR	1024:65535	Ack

The following are the client rules that allow you to connect to a remote server:

```
ipchains -A output -i $EXTERNAL_INTERFACE -p tcp \
         -s $IPADDR $UNPRIVPORTS \
         -d $ANYWHERE 70 -j ACCEPT

ipchains -A input -i $EXTERNAL_INTERFACE -p tcp ! -y \
         -s $ANYWHERE 70 \
         -d $IPADDR $UNPRIVPORTS -j ACCEPT
```

WAIS (TCP Port 210)

Wide Area Information Servers (WAIS) are now known as search engines. Web browsers typically provide a graphical front-end to WAIS. Netscape contains the WAIS client code necessary to connect to WAIS. Table 3.16 lists the local client to remote server connection protocol for the WAIS service.

Table 3.16   WAIS Protocol

Description	Protocol	Remote Address	Remote Port	In/ Out	Local Address	Local Port	TCP Flag
Local client request	TCP	ANYWHERE	210	Out	IPADDR	1024:65535	Any
Remote server response	TCP	ANYWHERE	210	In	IPADDR	1024:65535	Ack

The following two rules allow client access to remote WAIS services:

```
ipchains -A output -i $EXTERNAL_INTERFACE -p tcp \
         -s $IPADDR $UNPRIVPORTS \
         -d $ANYWHERE 210 -j ACCEPT

ipchains -A input -i $EXTERNAL_INTERFACE -p tcp ! -y \
         -s $ANYWHERE 210 \
         -d $IPADDR $UNPRIVPORTS -j ACCEPT
```

Enabling Common UDP Services

The stateless UDP protocol is inherently less secure than the connection-based TCP protocol. Because of this, many security-conscious sites completely disable, or else limit as much as possible, all access to UDP services. Obviously, UDP-based DNS exchanges are necessary, but the remote name servers can be explicitly specified in the firewall rules. As such, this section provides rules for only three services:

- traceroute
- Dynamic Host Configuration Protocol (DHCP)
- Network Time Protocol (NTP)

traceroute **(UDP Port 33434)**

traceroute is a UDP service that causes intermediate systems to generate ICMP Time Exceeded messages to gather hop count information, and the target system to return a Destination Unreachable (port not found) message, indicating the endpoint of the route to the host. By default, the firewall being developed in this chapter blocks incoming UDP traceroute packets destined to the port range traceroute generally uses. As a result, outgoing ICMP responses to incoming traceroute requests won't be sent. Table 3.17 lists the complete client/server exchange protocol for the traceroute service.

Table 3.17 *traceroute* Protocol

Description	Protocol	Remote Address	Remote Port/ ICMP Type	In/ Out	Local Address	Local Port/ ICMP Typ
Outgoing traceroute probe	UDP	ANYWHERE	33434:33523	Out	IPADDR	32769:65535
Time Exceeded (intermediate hop)	ICMP	ANYWHERE	11	In	IPADDR	—
Port not found (termination)	ICMP	ANYWHERE	3	In	IPADDR	—
Incoming traceroute probe	UDP	ISP	32769:65535	In	IPADDR	33434:33523
Time Exceeded (intermediate hop)	ICMP	ISP	—	Out	IPADDR	11
Port not found (termination)	ICMP	ISP	—	Out	IPADDR	3

traceroute can be configured to use any port or port range. As such, it's difficult to block all incoming traceroute packets by listing specific ports. However, it often uses source ports in the range from 32769 to 65535 and destination ports in the range from 33434 to 33523. Symbolic constants are defined for traceroute's default source and destination ports:

```
TRACEROUTE_SRC_PORTS="32769:65535"
TRACEROUTE_DEST_PORTS="33434:33523"
```

Enabling Outgoing *traceroute* Requests

If you intend to use traceroute yourself, you must enable the UDP client ports. Note that you must allow incoming ICMP Time Exceeded and Destination Unreachable messages from anywhere for outgoing traceroute to work:

```
ipchains -A output -i $EXTERNAL_INTERFACE -p udp \
         -s $IPADDR $TRACEROUTE_SRC_PORTS \
         -d $ANYWHERE $TRACEROUTE_DEST_PORTS -j ACCEPT
```

Allowing Incoming *traceroute* Requests

Because traceroute is a less secure UDP service and can be used to attack other UDP services, the following example opens incoming traceroute from only your ISP and its associated Network Operations Center:

```
ipchains -A input -i $EXTERNAL_INTERFACE -p udp \
         -s $MY_ISP $TRACEROUTE_SRC_PORTS \
         -d $IPADDR $TRACEROUTE_DEST_PORTS -j ACCEPT
```

Note that you must allow outgoing ICMP Time Exceeded and Destination Unreachable messages to be targeted to your ISP for incoming `traceroute` to work.

Accessing Your ISP's DHCP Server (UDP Ports 67, 68)

DHCP exchanges, if any, between your site and your ISP's server will necessarily be local client to remote server exchanges. DHCP clients receive temporary, dynamically allocated IP addresses from a central server that manages the ISP's customer IP address space.

If you have a dynamically allocated IP address from your ISP, you need to run the DHCP client daemon (either `dhcpd` or `pump`) on your machine. It's not uncommon for bogus DHCP server messages to fly around your ISP's local subnet if someone runs the server by accident. For this reason, it's especially important to filter DHCP messages to limit traffic between your client and your specific ISP DHCP server as much as possible.

Table 3.18 lists the DHCP message type descriptions as quoted from RFC 2131, "Dynamic Host Configuration Protocol."

Table 3.18   DHCP Message Types

DHCP Message	Description
DHCPDISCOVER	Client broadcast to locate available servers.
DHCPOFFER	Server to client in response to `DHCPDISCOVER` with offer of configuration parameters.
DHCPREQUEST	Client message to servers either (a) requesting offered parameters from one server and implicitly declining offers from all others; (b) confirming correctness of previously allocated address after, e.g., system reboot; or (c) extending the lease on a particular network address.
DHCPACK	Server to client with configuration parameters, including committed network address.
DHCPNAK	Server to client indicating client's notion of network address is incorrect (e.g., client has moved to new subnet) or client's lease has expired.
DHCPDECLINE	Client to server indicating network address is already in use.
DHCPRELEASE	Client to server relinquishing network address and canceling remaining lease.
DHCPINFORM	Client to server, asking only for local configuration parameters; client already has externally configured address. (Not supported in Red Hat 6.0.)

In essence, when the DHCP client initializes, it broadcasts a `DHCPDISCOVER` query to discover whether any DHCP servers are available. Any servers receiving the query may respond with a `DHCPOFFER` message indicating their willingness to function as server to this client, and include the configuration parameters they have to offer. The client broadcasts a `DHCPREQUEST` message to both accept one of the servers and inform any remaining servers that it has chosen to decline their offers. The chosen server responds with a `DHCPACK` message, indicating confirmation of the parameters it originally offered. Address assignment is complete at this point. Periodically, the client will send a `DHCPREQUEST` message requesting a renewal on the IP address lease. If the lease is renewed, the server responds with a `DHCPACK` message. Otherwise, the client falls back to the initialization process. Table 3.19 lists the local client to remote server exchange protocol for the DHCP service.

The DHCP protocol is far more complicated than this brief summary, but the summary describes the essentials of the typical client and server exchange.

Table 3.19   DHCP Protocol

Description	Protocol	Remote Address	Remote Port	In/Out	Local Address	Local Port
`DHCPDISCOVER;` `DHCPREQUEST`	UDP	`255.255.255.255`	67	Out	`0.0.0.0`	68
`DHCPOFFER`	UDP	`0.0.0.0`	67	In	`255.255.255.255`	68
`DHCPOFFER`	UDP	`DHCP SERVER`	67	In	`255.255.255.255`	68
`DHCPREQUEST;` `DHCPDECLINE`	UDP	`DHCP SERVER`	67	Out	`0.0.0.0`	68
`DHCPACK;` `DHCPNAK`	UDP	`DHCP SERVER`	67	In	ISP/netmask	68
`DHCPACK`	UDP	`DHCP SERVER`	67	In	IPADDR	68
`DHCPREQUEST;` `DHCPRELEASE`	UDP	`DHCP SERVER`	67	Out	IPADDR	68

The following firewall rules allow communication between your DHCP client and a remote server:

```
DHCP_SERVER="my.dhcp.server"            # if you use one

# INIT or REBINDING: No lease or Lease time expired.

ipchains -A output -i $EXTERNAL_INTERFACE -p udp \
        -s $BROADCAST_0 68 \
        -d $BROADCAST_1 67 -j ACCEPT
```

```
# Getting renumbered

ipchains -A input  -i $EXTERNAL_INTERFACE -p udp \
        -s $BROADCAST_0 67 \
        -d $BROADCAST_1 68 -j ACCEPT

ipchains -A input  -i $EXTERNAL_INTERFACE -p udp \
        -s $DHCP_SERVER 67 \
        -d $BROADCAST_1 68 -j ACCEPT

ipchains -A output -i $EXTERNAL_INTERFACE -p udp \
        -s $BROADCAST_0 68 \
        -d $DHCP_SERVER 67 -j ACCEPT

# As a result of the above, we're supposed to change our IP
# address with this message, which is addressed to our new
# address before the dhcp client has received the update.

ipchains -A input  -i $EXTERNAL_INTERFACE -p udp \
        -s $DHCP_SERVER 67 \
        -d $MY_ISP 68 -j ACCEPT

ipchains -A input  -i $EXTERNAL_INTERFACE -p udp \
        -s $DHCP_SERVER 67 \
        -d $IPADDR 68 -j ACCEPT

ipchains -A output -i $EXTERNAL_INTERFACE -p udp \
        -s $IPADDR 68 \
        -d $DHCP_SERVER 67 -j ACCEPT
```

Notice that DHCP traffic cannot be completely limited to your DHCP server. During initialization sequences, when your client doesn't yet have an assigned IP address or even the server's IP address, packets are broadcast rather than sent point-to-point.

Accessing Remote Network Time Servers (UDP 123)

Network time services such as NTP allow access to one or more public Internet time providers. This is useful to maintain an accurate system clock, particularly if your internal clock tends to drift, and to establish the correct time and date at bootup or after a power loss. A small system user should use the service only as a client. Few, if any, small sites have a satellite link to Greenwich, England, a radio link to the United States atomic clock, or an atomic clock of their own lying around.

xntpd is the server daemon. In addition to providing time service to clients, xntpd also uses a peer-to-peer relationship among servers. Few small sites require the extra precision xntpd provides. ntpdate is the client program, and can use either client-to-server or peer-to-peer communication. The client program is all a small site will need. Table 3.20 lists only the client/server exchange protocol for the NTP service.

Table 3.20   NTP Protocol

Description	Protocol	Remote Address	Remote Port	In/Out	Local Address	Local Port
Local client query	UDP	timeserver	123	Out	IPADDR	1024:65535
Remote server response	UDP	timeserver	123	In	IPADDR	1024:65535

As a client, you can use `ntpdate` to periodically query a series of public time service providers from a `cron` job. These hosts would be individually specified in a series of firewall rules:

```
ipchains -A output -i $EXTERNAL_INTERFACE -p udp \
         -s $IPADDR $UNPRIVPORTS \
         -d <my.time.provider> 123 -j ACCEPT

ipchains -A input  -i $EXTERNAL_INTERFACE -p udp \
         -s <my.time.provider> 123 \
         -d $IPADDR $UNPRIVPORTS -j ACCEPT
```

Logging Denied Incoming Packets

Any packet matching a rule can be logged by adding the `-l` option to its `ipchains` rule. Some of the rules presented previously had logging enabled. The IP address spoofing rules are examples.

Rules can be defined for the explicit purpose of logging certain kinds of packets. Most typically, packets of interest are suspicious packets indicating some sort of probe or scan. Because all packets are denied by default, if logging is desired for certain packet types, explicit rules must be defined before the packet falls off the end of the chain and the default policy takes effect. Essentially, out of all the denied packets, you might be interested in logging some of them.

Which packets are logged is an individual matter. Some people want to log all denied packets. For other people, logging all denied packets could soon overflow their system logs. Some people, secure in the knowledge that the packets are denied, don't care about them and don't want to know about them. Other people are interested in the obvious port scans or some particular packet type.

Because of the first-matching-rule-wins behavior, you could log all denied incoming packets with a single rule:

```
ipchains -A input -i $EXTERNAL_INTERFACE -j DENY -l
```

For some people, this will produce too many log entries—or too many uninterest-ing log entries. For example, you might want to log all denied incoming ICMP traffic with the exception of ping, because it is a common service, regardless of whether your site responds to ping requests:

```
ipchains -A input -i $EXTERNAL_INTERFACE -p icmp \
        -s $ANYWHERE 1:7 -d $IPADDR -j DENY -l

ipchains -A input -i $EXTERNAL_INTERFACE -p icmp \
        -s $ANYWHERE 9:18 -d $IPADDR -j DENY -l
```

You might want to log denied incoming TCP traffic to all ports, and denied incoming UDP traffic to your privileged ports:

```
ipchains -A input -i $EXTERNAL_INTERFACE -p tcp \
        -d $IPADDR -j DENY -l

ipchains -A input -i $EXTERNAL_INTERFACE -p udp \
        -d $IPADDR $PRIVPORTS -j DENY -l
```

Then again, you might want to log all denied privileged port access, with the exception of commonly probed ports you don't offer service on anyway:

```
ipchains -A input -i $EXTERNAL_INTERFACE -p tcp \
        -d $IPADDR 0:19 -j DENY -l

# skip ftp, telnet, ssh
ipchains -A input -i $EXTERNAL_INTERFACE -p tcp \
        -d $IPADDR 24 -j DENY -l

# skip smtp
ipchains -A input -i $EXTERNAL_INTERFACE -p tcp \
        -d $IPADDR 26:78 -j DENY -l

# skip finger, www
ipchains -A input -i $EXTERNAL_INTERFACE -p tcp \
        -d $IPADDR 81:109 -j DENY -l

# skip pop-3, sunrpc
ipchains -A input -i $EXTERNAL_INTERFACE -p tcp \
        -d $IPADDR 112:136 -j DENY -l

# skip NetBIOS
ipchains -A input -i $EXTERNAL_INTERFACE -p tcp \
        -d $IPADDR 140:142 -j DENY -l

# skip imap
ipchains -A input -i $EXTERNAL_INTERFACE -p tcp \
        -d $IPADDR 144:442 -j DENY -l

# skip secure_web/SSL
ipchains -A input -i $EXTERNAL_INTERFACE -p tcp \
        -d $IPADDR 444:65535 -j DENY -l
```

```
#UDP rules
ipchains -A input -i $EXTERNAL_INTERFACE -p udp \
        -d $IPADDR 0:110 -j DENY -l

# skip sunrpc
ipchains -A input -i $EXTERNAL_INTERFACE -p udp \
        -d $IPADDR 112:160 -j DENY -l

# skip snmp
ipchains -A input -i $EXTERNAL_INTERFACE -p udp \
        -d $IPADDR 163:634 -j DENY -l

# skip NFS mountd
ipchains -A input -i $EXTERNAL_INTERFACE -p udp \
        -d $IPADDR 636:5631 -j DENY -l

# skip pcAnywhere
ipchains -A input -i $EXTERNAL_INTERFACE -p udp \
        -d $IPADDR 5633:31336 -j DENY -l

# skip BackOrifice
ipchains -A input -i $EXTERNAL_INTERFACE -p udp \
        -d $IPADDR 31338:33433 -j DENY -l

# skip traceroute
ipchains -A input -i $EXTERNAL_INTERFACE -p udp \
        -s $ANYWHERE 32679:65535 \
        -d $IPADDR 33434:33523 -j DENY -l

# skip the rest
ipchains -A input -i $EXTERNAL_INTERFACE -p udp \
        -d $IPADDR 33434:65535 -j DENY -l
```

Denying Access to Problem Sites Up Front

If some site is making a habit of scanning your machine or otherwise being a nuisance, you might decide to deny it access to everything, at least until the problem behavior is corrected.

One way to do this without editing the rc.firewall script each time is to include a separate file of specific denial rules. By inserting the rules into the input chain rather than appending them, the site will be blocked even if subsequent rules would otherwise allow them access to some service. The file is named /etc/rc.d/ rc.firewall.blocked. To avoid a possible runtime error, you check for the file's existence before trying to include it:

```
# Refuse packets claiming to be from the banned list
if [ -f /etc/rc.d/rc.firewall.blocked ]; then
    . /etc/rc.d/rc.firewall.blocked
fi
```

An example of a global denial rule in the `rc.firewall.blocked` file could be:

```
ipchains -I input -i $EXTERNAL_INTERFACE -s <address/mask> -j DENY
```

Any packet from this source address range is denied, regardless of message protocol type or source or destination port.

At this point, the firewall rules are defined. When the firewall rules are installed in the kernel as a functional firewall, you can connect your Linux machine to the Internet with a good measure of confidence that your system is secure against most outside attacks.

Enabling LAN Access

If the firewall machine sits between the Internet and a LAN, machines on the LAN have access neither to the firewall machine's internal network interface nor to the Internet. Chapter 4 covers LAN firewall issues in depth. A small site, particularily a home site, won't need or have the resources to implement the firewall architecture presented in Chapter 4. For the average home site, and for many small business sites as well, the single-machine firewall developed in this chapter is sufficient.

To support a LAN behind the firewall, a few more rules are needed to enable access to the firewall machine's internal network interface and to pass internal traffic through to the Internet. When the firewall machine serves in this capacity, with two or more network interfaces, it's called a bastion firewall, or a screened-subnet firewall.

Enabling LAN Access to the Firewall's Internal Network Interface

For a home or small business setup, there is probably little reason to limit direct access to the firewall machine from the internal LAN. This rule pair allows open communication between the firewall machine and the LAN:

```
LAN_INTERFACE_1="eth1"              # internal LAN interface

LAN_1="192.168.1.0/24"             # your (private) LAN address range
LAN__IPADDR_1="192.168.1.1"        # your internal interface address

ipchains -A input  -i $LAN_INTERFACE_1 \
         -s $LAN_1 -j ACCEPT

ipchains -A output -i $LAN_INTERFACE_1 \
         -d $LAN_1 -j ACCEPT
```

Notice that this rule pair allows LAN access to the firewall machine. The LAN does not yet have Internet access through the firewall. Because a firewall machine, by definition, does not route traffic dynamically, or automatically using static routes (unless the machine is misconfigured), additional firewall rules are necessary to route local traffic onward.

Enabling LAN Access to the Internet: IP Forwarding and Masquerading

At this point, selected ports are open for either client or server communication, or both, between remote machines and the firewall machine's external network interface. Local communication between the LAN and firewall machine is completely open through the firewall's internal network interface. Internal machines on the LAN do not yet have access to the Internet, however. Allowing Internet access is a two-step process. Communication between the LAN and the Internet must be both forwarded and masqueraded.

IP forwarding is a kernel service allowing the Linux machine to act as a router between two networks, forwarding traffic from one network to the other. With a LAN, IP forwarding must be enabled in the routing section of the network configuration. With a deny-everything-by-default firewall policy in force, however, forwarded packets can't cross between the two interfaces until specific rules allow it.

Few home-based systems should or will want to forward internal traffic directly. IP addresses taken from the Class A, B, or C private address ranges require IP masquerading (another kernel service), or application-level proxying to substitute the private LAN IP address with the public IP address of the firewall machine's external interface. Packets with private source addresses should not cross beyond the firewall machine out to the Internet, and if they do, they might not be routed to their destination indefinitely. Even if your site has registered, static IP addresses, IP masquerading and application-level proxy servers are two of the best ways to secure and transparently isolate your internal machines from the Internet.

On the `ipchains` administration level, forwarding and masquerading appear to be different aspects of the same service. (In fact, they are separate mechanisms. But the user interfaces to the two services are combined in the firewall administration program.) Forwarding routes LAN traffic from the firewall's internal interface out through the external interface to the Internet. Before the packets are placed on the firewall machine's external interface output queue, the masquerading service replaces the packet's source address with that of the firewall machine's external interface's public IP address. Forwarding and masquerading together let the firewall machine act as a filtering, proxying router.

The following rule demonstrates how to forward and masquerade all internal traffic out through the external interface. The `ACCEPT` and `DENY` rules for the external interface's `output` chain are applied after the forwarding rules are applied, so even though everything is allowed to be forwarded and masqueraded between the two network interfaces, only those packets allowed out by the firewall rules for the external interface will actually pass through:

```
ipchains -A forward -i $EXTERNAL_INTERFACE -s $LAN_1 -j MASQ
```

Masquerading rules can take source and destination address and port arguments, just as the other rules do. The network interface argument is the name of the forwarding (external) interface, not the packets' local network interface. Although the rules in the example allow everything, you could just as easily define specific rules to masquerade and forward only specific services, only TCP traffic, and so forth.

Installing the Firewall

As a shell script, installation is simple. The script should be owned by `root`:

```
chown root.root /etc/rc.d/rc.firewall
```

The script should be writable and executable by `root` alone. Ideally, the general user should not have read access:

```
chmod ug=rwx /etc/rc.d/rc.firewall
```

To initialize or reinitialize the firewall at any time, execute the script from the command line. There is no need to reboot:

```
sh /etc/rc.d/rc.firewall
```

How the script is executed at boot time varies based on whether you have a registered, static IP address or a dynamic, DHCP-assigned IP address.

Installing a Firewall with a Static IP Address

If you have a static IP address, the simplest way to initialize the firewall is to edit `/etc/rc.d/rc.local` and add the following line to the end of the file:

```
sh /etc/rc.d/rc.firewall
```

If hostnames are used in the firewall rules, the important thing to remember is that DNS traffic must be enabled before the hostnames are encountered in the script. If a local name server is configured, the system automatically starts `named` before running `rc.local` at boot time or later if changing runlevels.

Installing a Firewall with a Dynamic IP Address

If you have a dynamic IP address, you will discover that firewall installation support was (annoyingly) discontinued as of Red Hat 6.0. With luck, enough irate DHCP clients will complain to get firewall support reinstated. In the meantime, you have to reconfigure your system's default installation setup for DHCP. The following steps work for earlier versions of `/sbin/dhcpcd` prior to Red Hat 6.0. If you've upgraded from an earlier release, these steps reinstate your prior environment:

1. Red Hat 6.0 replaced the DHCP client, `dhcpcd`, with a new client, `pump`. `pump` doesn't provide a mechanism for executing a script when your IP address is assigned or reassigned. Consequently, without editing one of the network startup

scripts, `/sbin/ifup`, you have no means of storing the dynamic information the DHCP server has provided, nor do you have a way of automatically restarting the firewall script if your IP address is reassigned after a lease revocation. You have to edit the executable script, `/sbin/ifup`, to use the older `/sbin/dhcpcd` instead of `/sbin/pump`.

Refer to the section "`dhcpcd` Support in `/sbin/ifup`" in Appendix B for examples of code.

2. Create a new executable shell script, `/etc/sysconfig/network-scripts/ifdhcpc-done`. This file was provided as part of the Red Hat distribution until release 6.0. It was run by `dhcpcd` after IP address assignment or reassignment. `pump` doesn't support running a script.

   `ifdhcpc-done`'s original, primary purpose was to provide a mechanism to inform `/sbin/ifup` as to whether `dhcpcd` succeeded in getting its dynamic information from the DHCP server or not. Depending on the particular Red Hat release, the file also performed a few other file updates.

   `ifdhcpc-done` is the perfect place to execute `/etc/rc.d/rc.firewall` from because `ifdhcpc-done` is executed each time the IP address is assigned or changed. It's also a useful place from which to perform several other functions. Among them are setting the system's domain name, updating `/etc/hosts` with the current IP address, updating `/etc/resolv.conf` if you run your own name server, updating `/etc/named.conf` if you run your own name server and forward queries to your ISP's name servers, and providing a mechanism for relaying the current IP address and name server addresses to the firewall script.

   Refer to the section "Updating Dynamic Addresses and Installing the Firewall from `/etc/sysconfig/network-scripts/ifdhcpc-done`" in Appendix B for examples of code.

3. Create `dhcpcd`'s configuration directory, `/etc/dhcpc`:
   ```
   mkdir /etc/dhcpc
   ```

   `pump` doesn't use this directory. `dhcpcd` expects the directory to exist.

4. The firewall script itself needs to include `IPADDR` and the `NAMESERVER`s from `/etc/dhcpc/dhcpd-eth0.info`. These addresses are provided by the DHCP server. Name server addresses are quite stable. Your IP address can change relatively frequently, depending on your ISP's DHCP server configuration.

Summary

This chapter leads you through the processes involved in developing a standalone firewall using `ipchains`. The deny-by-default policy was established. Initial potential problems were addressed, such as source address spoofing and protecting services running on unprivileged ports. ICMP messages, the control and status messages used by the underlying IP network layer, were handled. DNS name service, which underlies all network services, and `AUTH` user identification service, which supports several common network services, were handled. Examples of rules for popular network services were shown. Examples of controlling the level of logging produced were demonstrated. Finally, the issues involved in firewall installation were described, both for sites with a static IP address and sites with a dynamically assigned IP address.

At the end, the firewall script was very slightly extended to add support to serve as a bastion firewall for a small LAN. Complete script examples for both `ipchains` and `ipfwadm` are included in Appendix B.

Chapter 4 uses the bastion firewall as the basis for building a more complicated firewall architecture. A screened subnet architecture using two firewalls separating a DMZ perimeter network is described in Chapter 4. A small business could easily have the need and the resources for this more elaborate configuration.

4

LAN Issues, Multiple Firewalls, and Perimeter Networks

A PACKET-FILTERING FIREWALL IS A STATIC ROUTER with traffic screening rules enforcing local policies concerning which packets are allowed through the network interfaces. The single-system firewall presented in Chapter 3, "Building and Installing a Firewall," is a basic bastion firewall. As a packet-filtering router on a dual-homed host (dual-homed means that your firewall machine has two or more network interfaces, one connected to the Internet and another connected to your LAN), the firewall applies rules to decide whether to forward or block packets crossing between the two interfaces. On a dual-homed system that masquerades LAN traffic, the machine acts as a simple screened-subnet firewall due to the proxying gateway effect of IP masquerading and the use of static routing.

For the dual-homed host setup with a LAN, the firewall rules applied to each network interface represent an I/O pair. In the case with a LAN, you have two pairs. The firewall filters what comes in and what goes out through the external interface. It also filters, to a greater or lesser degree, what comes in and what goes out through the internal interface to your LAN. The two interfaces are handled separately. Additionally, traffic is not routed directly between the Internet and the LAN. The filtering rules on the two interfaces act as a bastion firewall and static router between the two networks.

The firewall configuration presented in Chapter 3 is perfectly adequate for a home system. It's about the best that can be done with an individual, standalone system. More can be done with a dual-homed firewall and LAN. The question is, is the extra effort worth the increased security in a trusted environment?

As a bastion firewall, if the firewall machine is ever compromised, it's all over. Even if a second set of firewall rules is applied to the internal interface, if the system has been compromised, it won't be long before the hacker has gained root access. At that point, if not before, the internal systems are wide open as well. Chances are, a home system will never have to face this situation if the services offered to the Internet are chosen carefully and a stringent firewall policy is enforced. Still, a bastion firewall represents a single point of failure. It's an all-or-nothing situation.

Larger organizations and corporate LANs would not depend on the single-machine, bastion firewall architecture alone. They would use a screened-host architecture with no direct routing, or a screened-subnet architecture with proxy services, along with a perimeter DMZ network created between the external (bastion) firewall and an internal, secondary (choke) firewall. Public servers in the DMZ network have their own specialized firewalls, as well. This means that these sites have a lot more computers at their disposal, and a staff to manage them.

This chapter covers some of the basic issues underlying LAN security. Security policies are defined relative to the site's level of security needs, the importance of the data being protected, and the cost of lost data or privacy. This chapter opens by posing the types of questions the site's policy maker has to answer while choosing server placement and security policies.

First, the LAN options used in Chapter 3 for a small home LAN are discussed. Although the firewall architecture presented in Chapter 3 is fine for a home setup, some small businesses may require more elaborate measures, especially if some LAN machines offer public Internet services and others are used for internal development and business administration. So, the firewall example in Chapter 3 is extended to support more elaborate LAN options that offer greater flexibility than a home site might need.

Following that, the firewall example from Chapter 3 is used as the basis to develop a formal, elaborate, textbook type of firewall. The bastion firewall has two network interfaces: one connected to the Internet, and one connected to a perimeter network, or DMZ. Public Internet services are offered from machines in the DMZ network. A second firewall, a choke firewall, is also connected to the DMZ network, separating the internal, private networks from the quasi-public server machines in the perimeter network. Private machines are protected behind the choke firewall on the internal LAN. If the bastion firewall fails, the public server machines in the DMZ might be exposed. The choke firewall protects the internal LAN from the compromised bastion machine and from any other machine in the perimeter network.

DMZ: A Perimeter Network by Any Other Name

A perimeter network between two firewalls is called a DMZ, or demilitarized zone. The purpose of a DMZ is to establish a protected space from which to run public servers (or services), and to isolate that space from the rest of the private LAN.

LAN Security Issues

Security issues are largely dependent on the size of the LAN, its architecture, and what it's used for. Are services offered to the Internet? Are these services hosted on the firewall machine, or are they hosted on internal machines? For example, you might offer anonymous FTP from the bastion firewall machine, but serve a Web site from an internal machine in the DMZ. When services are hosted from internal machines, you might want to place those machines on a perimeter network and apply completely different packet filtering and access policies to those machines. If services are offered from internal machines, is this fact visible to the outside, or are the services proxied or transparently forwarded so they appear to be available from the firewall machine?

How much information do you want to make publicly available about the machines on your LAN? Do you intend to host local DNS services? Are local DNS database contents available from the bastion firewall machine?

Can people log in to your machines from the Internet? How many and which local machines are accessible to them? Do all user accounts have the same access rights? Will incoming connections be proxied for additional access control?

Are all internal machines equally accessible to local users and from all local machines? Are external services equally accessible from all internal machines? For example, if you were to use a screened- host firewall architecture, users would have to log in to the bastion firewall machine directly to have access to the Internet. No routing would be done at all.

Are private LAN services running behind the firewall? For example, is NFS used internally, or NIS, or network time servers, or the Berkeley remote commands, such as rsh, rlogin, and rcp? Do you need to keep any of these services from leaking information to the Internet, such as SNMP, DHCP, timed, xntpd, remote uptime, or rwho? Maintaining such services behind the secondary choke firewall ensures complete isolation of these services from the Internet.

Related to services designed for LAN use are questions about local access versus external access to services designed for Internet use. Will you offer FTP internally but not externally, or possibly offer different kinds of FTP services to both? Will you run a private Web server or configure different parts of the same site to be available to local users as opposed to remote users? Will you run a local mail server to send mail but use a different mechanism to retrieve incoming mail from the Internet (i.e., will your mail be delivered directly to your machine's user accounts, or will you explicitly retrieve mail from an ISP)?

Configuration Options for a Trusted Home LAN

There are two kinds of internal network traffic to consider. As shown in Figure 4.1, the first is local access to the bastion firewall, through the internal interface. The second is local access to the Internet, through the bastion machine's external interface.

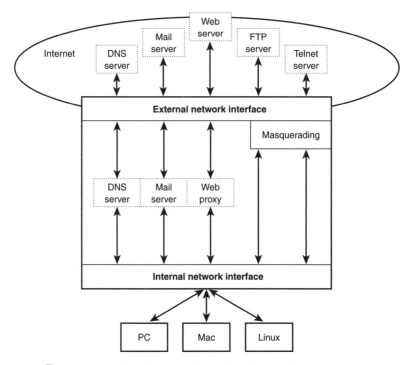

Figure 4.1 LAN traffic to the firewall machine and to the Internet.

Presumably, most small systems have no reason to filter packets between the firewall and local network in general. However, because most home-based sites are assigned a single IP address, one exception arises: IP masquerading. Presumably, the only internal filtering-related action you take will be to enable your own form of source address spoofing to masquerade packets moving between your internal machines and the Internet.

If you have a single public IP address for the firewall machine, and all internal machines use private class IP addresses, you will necessarily provide a form of proxying by virtue of the required IP masquerading. If your internal machines have registered IP addresses, you should still make certain not to forward traffic directly between the LAN and the Internet. Either use application-level proxies for outside connections or use IP masquerading.

Effectively, IP masquerading is a low-level form of proxying. A proxy makes connections to remote servers on behalf of a local client. All outgoing connections appear to originate from the host running the proxy server. Outgoing packets from your LAN will be identified as coming from the bastion machine connected directly to the Internet, their source address being replaced with the address of the bastion's external network interface. Incoming packets destined for the LAN have their destination addresses translated back into the target addresses of your internal computers.

LAN Access to the Bastion Firewall

In a home environment, chances are you'll want to enable unrestricted access between the LAN machines and the bastion firewall.

Starting with the firewall developed in Chapter 3 as the basis, two more constants are needed in the firewall example to refer to the internal interface connecting to the LAN. This example defines the internal network interface as `eth1`; the LAN is defined as including Class C private addresses ranging from `192.168.1.0` through `192.168.1.255`:

```
LAN_INTERFACE_1="eth1"
LAN_1="192.168.1.0/24"
```

Allowing unrestricted access through the internal interface is a simple matter of allowing all protocols and all ports by default:

```
ipchains -A input  -i $LAN_INTERFACE_1 -s $LAN_1 -j ACCEPT
ipchains -A output -i $LAN_INTERFACE_1 -d $LAN_1 -j ACCEPT
```

LAN Access to Other LANs: Forwarding Local Traffic Among Multiple LANs

If the machines on your LAN, or on multiple LANs, require routing services among themselves, you need to allow access among the machines for the service ports they require, unless they have alternate internal connection paths through a hub. In the former case, any local routing done between LANs would be done by the firewall.

Two more constants are needed. This example defines a second internal network interface as `eth2`; the LAN is defined as including Class C private addresses ranging from `192.168.3.0` through `192.168.3.255`:

```
LAN_INTERFACE_2="eth2"
LAN_2="192.168.3.0/24"
```

The following rules allow access to the firewall machine:

```
ipchains -A input  -i $LAN_INTERFACE_1 -s $LAN_1 -j ACCEPT
ipchains -A output -i $LAN_INTERFACE_1 -d $LAN_1 -j ACCEPT

ipchains -A input  -i $LAN_INTERFACE_2 -s $LAN_2 -j ACCEPT
ipchains -A output -i $LAN_INTERFACE_2 -d $LAN_2 -j ACCEPT
```

The following rules forward traffic in both directions between the two LANs without masquerading:

```
ipchains -A forward -i $LAN_INTERFACE_2 \
         -s $LAN_1 -d $LAN_2 -j ACCEPT

ipchains -A forward -i $LAN_INTERFACE_1 \
         -s $LAN_2 -d $LAN_1 -j ACCEPT
```

LAN Access to the Internet: Forwarding Versus Masquerading

Forwarding routes traffic between network interfaces *as is*. Forwarding is routing traffic between networks. Traffic can be forwarded in either direction. If your internal machines have registered IP addresses, you could simply forward their traffic and they would appear as their own distinct machines to the Internet servers. Likewise, you could forward incoming traffic to a particular local machine. For example, you could forward all incoming mail to a mail server on a machine in the DMZ.

Masquerading sits on top of forwarding as a separate kernel service. Traffic is masqueraded in both directions, but not symmetrically. Only outgoing connections are allowed. Any traffic from machines on your LAN to an outside destination is passed through the firewall. In the process, the internal machine's IP address is replaced with the address of the firewall machine's external network interface. The process is reversed for incoming responses. Before the packet is forwarded to the internal machine, the firewall's destination IP address is replaced with the real IP address of the internal machine participating in the connection.

An incoming connection cannot be forwarded to a masqueraded internal address, because the internal address is invisible to the Internet. An incoming connection must be routed directly to a unique, officially registered, public internal interface.

Both forwarding and masquerading are kernel-level services; both must be configured and compiled into the kernel. To use masquerading, forwarding must be enabled as well. Configuration of the two services is separate, however. Forwarding is enabled in your network configuration in the /etc/sysconfig/network file. Look for a line that reads FORWARD_IPV4=yes. IP forwarding can be permanently configured by hand in /etc/sysconfig/network or through the control-panel GUI interface. The IP forwarding option is found in the routing section of the control-panel's network configuration dialogs. Neither of these configuration methods takes effect until the network is restarted. If IP forwarding wasn't enabled, you can enable it immediately by typing the following line as root:

```
echo "1" > /proc/sys/net/ipv4/ip_forward
```

Masquerading is enabled by the ipchains masquerade command.

When developing a Linux firewall, masquerading can be viewed as a special case of forwarding. In terms of ipchains semantics, masquerading is treated as if it were a special case of forwarding.

For a personal, home-based system, the following rule masquerades all traffic from machines on the LAN destined for external addresses:

```
ipchains -A forward -i $EXTERNAL_INTERFACE \
        -s $LAN_1 -j MASQ
```

The term *all traffic* is relative, however. Because of the firewall's hierarchical, first-matching-rule-wins behavior, only those packets allowed through the external network interface will be routed in either direction.

Whether you use officially registered IP addresses or private class IP addresses for local machines, you should use masquerading rather than direct forwarding for outgoing connections. Masquerading local addresses is a powerful security measure. Incoming connections from external machines directly to your local machines will not be possible. Your local machines aren't visible. They all appear to be the firewall machine.

A firewall machine must not route incoming traffic automatically. LAN addresses should all be masqueraded or proxied on the Internet.

For services based on atypical communication protocols, an additional, service-specific, kernel masquerade module, or a separate application-level proxy, is needed. Some services use multiple connections, such as FTP, where a secondary data connection is initiated by the remote server in response to the control stream initiated by the local client. Some services require that both client and server use unprivileged ports for communications. This is a particular problem when the exchanges use the UDP protocol, where a connection state does not exist to monitor.

These atypical communication protocols are examples of why some services are not easily handled at the packet-filtering level. Both multiconnection services and connectionless UDP services fall into this category. Both are good candidates for packet-filtering modules or application-level proxy services.

Linux distributions are released with a growing number of masquerading modules for specific services. As of Red Hat release 6.0, module support is included for FTP, Quake, CU-SeeMe, IRC, RealAudio, and LiveVideo. If forwarding and masquerading are enabled in the kernel compilation configuration, these special proxy modules are compiled for you automatically. You must explicitly load the modules you want to use, however.

The alternative, or an additional safeguard, is to use an application-level proxy filter, such as SOCKS. Again, all outgoing local traffic will appear to be originating from the firewall machine. Additionally, if your site requires finer-grained access control than packet filtering can provide, application-level proxies often provide that control. Proxies are usually application-specific. They understand the application's communication protocol and can do source and destination monitoring not possible at the packet-filtering level.

Configuration Options for a Larger or Less Trusted LAN

A larger business or organization would use more elaborate, specific mechanisms rather than the simple, generic forwarding and masquerading firewall rules presented in the last section for a trusted home LAN. In less trusted environments, firewall machines are protected from internal users as strongly as from external users. Port-specific firewall rules are defined for the internal interface as well as for the external interface. Those rules might be a mirror image of the rules for the external interface, or the rules might be more inclusive. What is allowed through the firewall machine's internal network interfaces depends on the types of systems running on the LAN and the types of local services running on the firewall machine, if any, you want to allow access to.

For example, you might want to block local broadcast messages from reaching the bastion firewall. If not all of your users are completely trusted, you might want to restrict what passes into the firewall from internal machines as strongly as what comes in from the Internet. Additionally, you should keep the number of user accounts to a bare minimum on the firewall machine.

The IP masquerading or proxying issues remain for the larger LAN as well as for a home LAN. A home-based business might have a single IP address, requiring LAN address masquerading. However, businesses often lease several publicly registered IP addresses, or an entire network address block. Public addresses are usually assigned to a business's public servers. With public IP addresses, outgoing connections are forwarded and incoming connections are routed normally. Rather than creating a private class network for internal public servers, a local subnet is defined to create a local, public, DMZ LAN.

Subnetting to Create Multiple Networks

IP addresses are divided into two pieces: a network address and a host address within that network. Class A, B, and C network addresses are defined by their first 8, 16, and 24 bits, respectively. Within each address class, the remaining bits define the host part of the IP address.

Subnetting is a local extension to the network address part of the local IP addresses. A local network mask is defined that treats some of the most significant host address bits as if they were part of the network address. These additional network address bits serve to define multiple networks locally. Remote sites are not aware of local subnets. They see the address range as normal Class A, B, or C addresses.

For example, let's take the Class C private address block, 192.168.1.0. 192.168.1.0 defines the address as a Class C network address, containing up to 254 hosts. The network mask for this network is 255.255.255.0, exactly matching the first 24 bits, the network address, of the 192.168.1.0 network.

This network can be subnetted into two local networks by defining the first 25 bits, rather than the first 24 bits, as the network address. The most significant bit of the host address field is now treated as part of the network address field. The host field now contains 7 bits, rather than 8. The network mask becomes 255.255.255.128. Two subnetworks are defined: 192.168.1.0, addressing hosts from 1 to 126, and 192.168.1.128, addressing hosts from 129 to 254. Each subnet loses 2 host addresses because each subnet uses the lowest host address, 0 or 128, as the network address, and the highest host address, 127 or 255, as the broadcast address. Table 4.1 shows this in tabular form.

Table 4.1   Class C Network *192.168.1.0* Subnetted into Two Subnets

Sub-net	Network Address	Network Mask	First Addressable Host	Last Addressable Hosts	Broadcast Address	Total Hosts
0	192.168.1.0	255.255.255.0	192.168.1.1	192.168.1.254	192.168.1.255	254
1	192.168.1.0	255.255.255.128	192.168.1.1	192.168.1.126	192.168.1.127	126
2	192.168.1.128	255.255.255.128	192.168.1.129	192.168.1.254	192.168.1.255	126

Subnetworks 192.168.1.0 and 192.168.1.128 can be assigned to 2 separate internal network interface cards. From the Internet's point of view, the site consists of a single network of up to 254 hosts. Internally, the site consists of two independent networks, each containing up to 126 hosts.

Subnetting allows creating multiple internal networks, each containing different classes of client or server machines, each with its own, independent routing. Different firewall policies can be applied to the two networks. Although it is possible to masquerade the LAN address, subnetted traffic is usually forwarded without masquerading.

Selective Internal Access by Host, Address Range, or Port

Traffic through a firewall machine's internal interface can be selectively limited, just as traffic through the external interface is. For example, rather than letting everything through on the internal interface, traffic could be limited to DNS, SMTP, AUTH, POP, and HTTP. In this case, let's say that the firewall machine provides these services for the LAN. Local machines are not allowed any other access to outside services.

Point of Interest

In this example, local hosts are limited to the specific services: DNS, SMTP, AUTH, POP, and HTTP. Because POP is a local mail retrieval service in this case, and DNS, SMTP, and HTTP are inherently proxy services, no direct Internet access is being made by local clients. In each case, the local clients are connecting to local servers. POP is a local LAN service. The three other servers establish remote connections on the client's behalf.

The following example considers a firewall machine with an internal interface connected to a LAN. Constants for the internal interface are

```
LAN_INTERFACE="eth1"              # internal interface to the LAN
FIREWALL="192.168.1.1"            # firewall machine's internal
                                  # interface address
LAN_ADDRESSES="192.168.1.0/24"    # range of addresses used on the LAN
```

LAN machines point to the firewall machine's internal interface as their name server:

```
ipchains -A input -i $LAN_INTERFACE -p udp \
        -s $LAN_ADDRESSES $UNPRIVPORTS \
        -d $FIREWALL 53 -j ACCEPT

ipchains -A output  -i $LAN_INTERFACE -p udp \
        -s $FIREWALL 53 \
        -d $LAN_ADDRESSES $UNPRIVPORTS -j ACCEPT

ipchains -A input -i $LAN_INTERFACE -p tcp \
        -s $LAN_ADDRESSES $UNPRIVPORTS \
        -d $FIREWALL 53 -j ACCEPT

ipchains -A output  -i $LAN_INTERFACE ! -y -p tcp \
        -s $FIREWALL 53 \
        -d $LAN_ADDRESSES $UNPRIVPORTS -j ACCEPT
```

LAN machines also point to the firewall as their SMTP and POP server:

```
# Sending mail - SMTP

ipchains -A input  -i $LAN_INTERFACE -p tcp \
        -s $LAN_ADDRESSES $UNPRIVPORTS \
        -d $FIREWALL 25 -j ACCEPT

ipchains -A output -i $LAN_INTERFACE ! -y -p tcp \
        -s $FIREWALL 25 \
        -d $LAN_ADDRESSES $UNPRIVPORTS -j ACCEPT

# Receiving Mail - POP

ipchains -A input  -i $LAN_INTERFACE -p tcp \
        -s $LAN_ADDRESSES $UNPRIVPORTS \
        -d $FIREWALL 110 -j ACCEPT

ipchains -A output -i $LAN_INTERFACE ! -y -p tcp \
        -s $FIREWALL 110 \
        -d $LAN_ADDRESSES $UNPRIVPORTS -j ACCEPT
```

The sendmail server will initiate an AUTH lookup request to the mail client:

```
ipchains -A output -i $LAN_INTERFACE -p tcp \
        -s $FIREWALL $UNPRIVPORTS  \
        -d $LAN_ADDRESSES 113 -j ACCEPT
ipchains -A input  -i $LAN_INTERFACE ! -y -p tcp \
        -s $LAN_ADDRESSES 113 \
        -d $FIREWALL $UNPRIVPORTS -j ACCEPT
```

Finally, a local proxying Web server is running on the firewall machine on port 8080. Internal machines point to the Web server on the firewall as their proxy, and the Web server forwards any outgoing requests on their behalf, along with caching any pages retrieved from the Internet:

```
ipchains -A input  -i $LAN_INTERFACE -p tcp \
         -s $LAN_ADDRESSES $UNPRIVPORTS \
         -d $FIREWALL 8080 -j ACCEPT

ipchains -A output -i $LAN_INTERFACE ! -y -p tcp \
         -s $FIREWALL 8080 \
         -d $LAN_ADDRESSES $UNPRIVPORTS -j ACCEPT
```

Configuration Options for Multiple LANs

Adding a second internal LAN allows this example to be developed further. As shown in Figure 4.2, the DNS, SMTP, AUTH, POP, and HTTP services are offered from server machines in a second LAN rather than from the firewall machine. In this case, traffic is routed between the two LANs by the internal interfaces on the firewall machine (but routing could be done directly via a hub or switch).

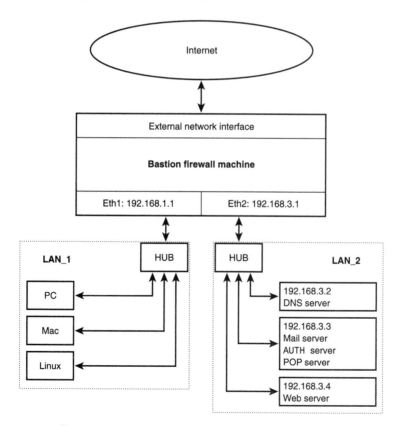

Figure 4.2   Separating clients and servers in multiple LANs.

The following variables are used to define the LANS, network interfaces, and server machines in this example:

```
CLIENT_LAN_INTERFACE="eth1"    # internal interface to the LAN
SERVER_LAN_INTERFACE="eth2"    # internal interface to the LAN
FIREWALL_1="192.168.1.1"       # firewall machine's internal
                               # interface address
FIREWALL_2="192.168.3.1"       # firewall machine's internal
                               # interface address
CLIENT_LAN="192.168.1.0/24"    # range of addresses used on the LAN
SERVER_LAN="192.168.3.0/24"    # range of addresses used on the LAN
DNS_SERVER="192.168.3.2"       # LAN DNS server
MAIL_SERVER="192.168.3.3"      # LAN Mail and POP server
POP_SERVER="192.168.3.3"       # LAN Mail and POP server
WEB_SERVER="192.168.3.4"       # LAN Web server
```

Internal machines point to the server's IP address on the server LAN as their name server. Just as with the rules between the firewall's internal interface and external interface, server access rules are defined for the client LAN's interface. Client access rules are defined for the server LAN's interface:

```
ipchains -A input -i $CLIENT_LAN_INTERFACE -p udp \
        -s $CLIENT_LAN $UNPRIVPORTS \
        -d $DNS_SERVER 53 -j ACCEPT

ipchains -A output -i $SERVER_LAN_INTERFACE -p udp \
        -s $CLIENT_LAN $UNPRIVPORTS \
        -d $DNS_SERVER 53 -j ACCEPT

ipchains -A input  -i $SERVER_LAN_INTERFACE -p udp \
        -s $DNS_SERVER 53 \
        -d $CLIENT_LAN $UNPRIVPORTS -j ACCEPT

ipchains -A output -i $CLIENT_LAN_INTERFACE -p udp \
        -s $DNS_SERVER 53 \
        -d $CLIENT_LAN $UNPRIVPORTS -j ACCEPT
```

Forwarding rules are needed to allow traffic routing between the two interfaces. In this case, the forwarding rules are specific to the interface, client address range and ports, and server address and port:

```
ipchains -A forward -i $SERVER_LAN_INTERFACE \
        -s $CLIENT_LAN $UNPRIVPORTS \
        -d $DNS_SERVER 53 -j ACCEPT

ipchains -A forward -i $CLIENT_LAN_INTERFACE \
        -s $DNS_SERVER 53  \
        -d $CLIENT_LAN $UNPRIVPORTS -j ACCEPT
```

The situation is more complicated than this, though. The DNS server on the second LAN needs to get its information from an external source. If the internal server were a masqueraded peer server to an external server, forwarding unresolved lookups to the external server, the firewall's UDP rules for its internal LAN interface and external Internet interface would be:

```
ipchains -A input   -i $SERVER_LAN_INTERFACE -p udp \
        -s $DNS_SERVER 53 \
        -d <external.name.server> 53 -j ACCEPT

ipchains -A output  -i $EXTERNAL_INTERFACE -p udp \
        -s $IPADDR 53 \
        -d <external.name.server> 53 -j ACCEPT

ipchains -A input   -i $EXTERNAL_INTERFACE -p udp \
        -s <external.name.server> 53 \
        -d $IPADDR 53 -j ACCEPT

ipchains -A output  -i $SERVER_LAN_INTERFACE -p udp \
        -s <external.name.server> 53 \
        -d $DNS_SERVER 53 -j ACCEPT

ipchains -A forward -i $EXTERNAL_INTERFACE -p udp \
        -s $DNS_SERVER 53 \
        -d <external.name.server> 53 -j MASQ
```

The clients in the CLIENT_LAN point to the MAIL_SERVER as their SMTP server for sending mail:

```
# Sending mail - SMTP
# ------------------

ipchains -A input   -i $CLIENT_LAN_INTERFACE -p tcp \
        -s $CLIENT_LAN $UNPRIVPORTS \
        -d $MAIL_SERVER 25 -j ACCEPT

ipchains -A output  -i $SERVER_LAN_INTERFACE -p tcp \
        -s $CLIENT_LAN $UNPRIVPORTS \
        -d $MAIL_SERVER 25 -j ACCEPT

ipchains -A input   -i $SERVER_LAN_INTERFACE ! -y -p tcp \
        -s $MAIL_SERVER 25 \
        -d $CLIENT_LAN $UNPRIVPORTS -j ACCEPT

ipchains -A output  -i $CLIENT_LAN_INTERFACE ! -y -p tcp \
        -s $MAIL_SERVER 25 \
        -d $CLIENT_LAN $UNPRIVPORTS -j ACCEPT

ipchains -A forward -i $SERVER_LAN_INTERFACE -p tcp \
        -s $CLIENT_LAN $UNPRIVPORTS \
        -d $MAIL_SERVER 25 -j ACCEPT

ipchains -A forward -i $CLIENT_LAN_INTERFACE -p tcp \
        -s $MAIL_SERVER 25 \
        -d $CLIENT_LAN $UNPRIVPORTS -j ACCEPT
```

The SMTP server on the SERVER_LAN needs to send the mail to remote destinations. The server requires access through the firewall to the Internet:

```
ipchains -A input   -i $SERVER_LAN_INTERFACE -p tcp \
        -s $MAIL_SERVER $UNPRIVPORTS \
        -d $ANYWHERE 25 -j ACCEPT

ipchains -A output  -i $SERVER_LAN_INTERFACE ! -y -p tcp \
        -s $ANYWHERE 25 \
        -d $MAIL_SERVER $UNPRIVPORTS -j ACCEPT

ipchains -A forward -i $EXTERNAL_INTERFACE -p tcp \
        -s $MAIL_SERVER $UNPRIVPORTS \
        -d $ANYWHERE 25 -j MASQ
```

The sendmail server will initiate an AUTH lookup request to the mail client:

```
ipchains -A output -i $CLIENT_LAN_INTERFACE -p tcp \
        -s $MAIL_SERVER $UNPRIVPORTS  \
        -d $CLIENT_LAN 113 -j ACCEPT

ipchains -A input  -i $CLIENT_LAN_INTERFACE ! -y -p tcp \
        -s $CLIENT_LAN 113 \
        -d $MAIL_SERVER $UNPRIVPORTS -j ACCEPT
```

Realistically, the SMTP server on the SERVER_LAN would need to receive mail from remote sources, as well. As presented here, receiving incoming mail directly via an internal sendmail daemon is not possible because the mail server is masqueraded. Solutions to this problem are discussed later in this chapter. For the sake of discussion, the solution based on the information presented so far in this chapter is to run a mail server on the bastion. The bastion server would relay mail between the MAIL_SERVER machine and remote machines.

The clients on the CLIENT_LAN point to the POP_SERVER machine to retrieve mail:

```
# Receiving Mail - POP
# --------------------

ipchains -A input   -i $CLIENT_LAN_INTERFACE -p tcp \
        -s $CLIENT_LAN $UNPRIVPORTS \
        -d $POP_SERVER 110 -j ACCEPT

ipchains -A output  -i $SERVER_LAN_INTERFACE -p tcp \
        -s $CLIENT_LAN $UNPRIVPORTS \
        -d $POP_SERVER 110 -j ACCEPT

ipchains -A input   -i $SERVER_LAN_INTERFACE ! -y -p tcp \
        -s $POP_SERVER 110 \
        -d $CLIENT_LAN $UNPRIVPORTS -j ACCEPT

ipchains -A output  -i $CLIENT_LAN_INTERFACE ! -y -p tcp \
        -s $POP_SERVER 110 \
        -d $CLIENT_LAN $UNPRIVPORTS -j ACCEPT
```

```
ipchains -A forward -i $SERVER_LAN_INTERFACE -p tcp \
         -s $CLIENT_LAN $UNPRIVPORTS \
         -d $POP_SERVER 110 -j ACCEPT

ipchains -A forward -i $CLIENT_LAN_INTERFACE -p tcp \
         -s $POP_SERVER_110  \
         -d $CLIENT_LAN $UNPRIVPORTS -j ACCEPT
```

Finally, a local Web proxy server is running on a server machine on the server LAN, bound to port 8080. Internal machines point to the Web server as their caching proxy, and the Web server forwards any outgoing requests on their behalf:

```
# WWW PROXY
# ---------

ipchains -A input   -i $CLIENT_LAN_INTERFACE -p tcp \
         -s $CLIENT_LAN $UNPRIVPORTS \
         -d $WEB_SERVER 8080 -j ACCEPT

ipchains -A output  -i $SERVER_LAN_INTERFACE -p tcp \
         -s $CLIENT_LAN $UNPRIVPORTS \
         -d $WEB_SERVER 8080 -j ACCEPT

ipchains -A input   -i $SERVER_LAN_INTERFACE ! -y -p tcp \
         -s $WEB_SERVER 8080 \
         -d $CLIENT_LAN $UNPRIVPORTS -j ACCEPT

ipchains -A output  -i $CLIENT_LAN_INTERFACE ! -y -p tcp \
         -s $WEB_SERVER 8080 \
         -d $CLIENT_LAN $UNPRIVPORTS -j ACCEPT

ipchains -A forward -i $SERVER_LAN_INTERFACE -p tcp \
         -s $CLIENT_LAN $UNPRIVPORTS \
         -d $WEB_SERVER 8080 -j ACCEPT

ipchains -A forward -i $CLIENT_LAN_INTERFACE -p tcp \
         -s $WEB_SERVER 8080  \
         -d $CLIENT_LAN $UNPRIVPORTS -j ACCEPT
```

The Web server on the server LAN needs Internet access to remote servers listening on TCP port 80, as well:

```
ipchains -A input   -i $SERVER_LAN_INTERFACE -p tcp \
         -s $WEB_SERVER $UNPRIVPORTS \
         -d $ANYWHERE 80 -j ACCEPT

ipchains -A output  -i $SERVER_LAN_INTERFACE ! -y -p tcp \
         -s $ANYWHERE 80 \
         -d $WEB_SERVER $UNPRIVPORTS -j ACCEPT

ipchains -A forward -i $EXTERNAL_INTERFACE -p tcp \
         -s $WEB_SERVER $UNPRIVPORTS \
         -d $ANYWHERE 80 -j MASQ
```

Masquerading LAN Traffic to the Internet

Several forwarding and masquerading rules have been used so far. A number of options are available in terms of how specific you want to make the rules.

Masquerading by Interface

For a personal home LAN, simply masquerading all traffic between the LAN and the Internet is the easiest. The following rule masquerades all traffic allowed through the external interface by the firewall's input and output rules:

```
ipchains -A forward -i $EXTERNAL_INTERFACE \
        -s $CLIENT_LAN -j MASQ
```

The generic masquerade rule is not allowing all LAN client traffic through the external interface. The rules for the external interface define what traffic can pass across the external interface. This rule enables masquerading of any traffic between the LAN and the Internet that the external interface rules allow to pass.

Masquerading by Service

If you prefer more explicit rules, or want to allow LAN access to only a subset of the external services available through the external interface's firewall filters, you can masquerade by service. Anything not specified by a forward and masquerade rule is not routed out to the Internet. The next rule specifically allows internal Web browsers to access external Web servers:

```
ipchains -A forward -i $EXTERNAL_INTERFACE -p tcp \
        -s $CLIENT_LAN $UNPRIVPORTS \
        -d $ANYWHERE 80 -j MASQ
```

Masquerading by Interface, Service, and Host

Firewall rule specificity can be taken all the way to interfaces, ports, and hosts. In the previous example showing two LANS, all machines on both LANs used a particular machine on the server LAN as the local name server, DNS_SERVER. Only DNS_SERVER is allowed access to an external DNS name server. Because this machine is running a forwarding name server, it uses UDP port 53 to 53, peer-to-peer communication with an external name server. Although SERVER_LAN_INTERFACE isn't defined explicitly in the masquerading rule, the interface is implied due to the fact that DNS_SERVER has a specific address relative to SERVER_LAN_INTERFACE. That is, no other machine on either LAN is allowed access to the external name server:

```
ipchains -A forward -i $EXTERNAL_INTERFACE -p udp \
        -s $DNS_SERVER 53 \
        -d <isp.dns.server> 53 -j MASQ
```

If the server machine were running as a DNS client to the external DNS server, the masquerading rules would be:

```
ipchains -A forward -i $EXTERNAL_INTERFACE -p udp \
        -s $DNS_SERVER $UNPRIVPORTS \
        -d <isp.dns.server> 53 -j MASQ

ipchains -A forward -i $EXTERNAL_INTERFACE -p tcp \
        -s $DNS_SERVER $UNPRIVPORTS \
        -d <isp.dns.server> 53 -j MASQ
```

Masquerading and Rule Precedence Hierarchy

The single-system, standalone firewall developed in Chapter 3 used specific input and output rules on the external interface. The easiest setup for a home LAN is to allow everything in and out on the internal interface, and forward and masquerade everything destined for a remote external address. Input, output and forwarding rules are being used for the LAN, but the rules applied to the external interface provide the filtering control for the entire site.

For any given chain, whether input, output, forward, or a site-defined chain, the packet is checked against the rules in the order the rules are defined in. The first matching rule wins. With a LAN and forwarding or masquerading, the question becomes which chain of rules is applied when?

As shown in Figure 4.3, each packet arrives on the input chain for that interface. The rules on the input chain are checked first. If the packet is accepted by the input filter, the next chain is determined by the packet's destination. If the destination is the local machine, the packet is placed on the loopback interface output chain. If the destination is a different machine's interface, the packet is passed to the forward chain first. If the packet is accepted by the forwarding filter, the packet is masqueraded and then placed on the output chain for the gateway interface. Finally, the output chain filters are checked. If the packet is accepted by the filter rules for that interface, it is sent on to its final destination (from the firewall's point of view).

Firewall Rule Precedence

For a more complete discussion of firewall rule precedence, refer to the IPCHAINS-HOWTO.

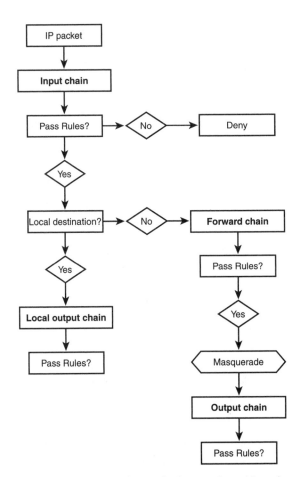

Figure 4.3   Masquerading and rule precedence hierarchy.

Port Redirection—Transparent Proxying

The port redirection features of `ipchains` are a limited, special case of *local* port forwarding and masquerading. Connections are not forwarded or masqueraded between
network interfaces. Instead, any traffic matching the rule, regardless of what the
packet's destination address or port is, is redirected to a local port.

This feature is useful for some of the application-level proxies you might run.
Often, application-level proxies require you to either reconfigure or replace the client
software with special applications that know about the local proxy service. Port redirection can make the redirection invisible to the client programs if they don't use a
special proxy protocol (e.g., direct HTTP protocol to a Web server is not the same as
the proxied HTTP protocol to a Web proxy server).

For example, let's say that you're running a `telnet` proxy server. It listens on the internal LAN interface to the regular `telnet` port, 23. Any outgoing `telnet` connection from the LAN is redirected to the local proxy. The proxy server then makes the connection on behalf of the local `telnet` client program:

```
ipchains -A input -i $CLIENT_LAN_INTERFACE -p tcp \
         -s $CLIENT_LAN $UNPRIVPORTS \
         -d $ANYWHERE 23 -j REDIRECT 23
```

Forwarding Incoming Connection Requests from the Internet to Internal Servers

Because masqueraded local machines are invisible to the outside world, services running on local machines are not available to remote clients. Experimental kernel code to enable incoming connections to servers running on internal, masqueraded machines is provided. The feature is enabled by compiling the masquerading module support and `ipportfw masq` support into the kernel. These experimental features require the use of `ipmasqadm`, a third-party application. `ipmasqadm` is not part of the Linux distribution. It must be downloaded separately from the Internet.

As an example, assume you want to forward incoming connections to your Web server to a server running on an internal, masqueraded machine. Two `ipmasqadm` commands are required in addition to the regular firewall rules. The first rule flushes the port forwarding chain initially. The second rule forwards incoming remote TCP connections targeted to the firewall machine's HTTP port 80 to an internal Web server at the masqueraded IP address `192.168.3.5`:

```
ipmasqadm portfw -f
ipmasqadm portfw -a -P tcp -L $IPADDR 80 -R 192.168.3.5 80
```

Transparent Proxy Kernel Support

Transparent proxying requires that transparent proxy support be enabled in the kernel's networking options configuration. This feature is enabled by default in Red Hat release 6.0. It must be explicitly enabled and the kernel recompiled in earlier releases.

Port Forwarding

Additional information on these experimental services can be found at `http://juanjox.linuxhq.com`, `http://www.monmouth.demon.uk/ipsubs/portforwarding.html`, `ftp://ftp.compsoc.net/users/steve/ipportfw/Linux21`, `http://ipmasq.cjb.net`, and online in the IP Masquerade HOWTO, `/usr/doc/HOWTO/mini/IP-Masquerade`.

An alternative is to use a local proxy server for the service you want to make available. Proxy servers can be used for both outgoing and incoming connections. Often, a proxy server is thought of as an application-level gateway program that masquerades outgoing connections to external services. Proxy servers for incoming connections to local services are usually used to enforce adherence to communication protocol specifications and finer-grained access control than can be accomplished at the packet-filtering level. The proxy server forwards the incoming connection to a local, masqueraded server. However, proxies usually require special client applications or special client configurations

A final alternative is available to sites with multiple registered IP addresses. The external interface accepts incoming packets addressed to any address in the local network address space. The firewall forwards specific connection types to specific internal servers. For example, the following rule forwards incoming connections to a Web server running in a LAN:

```
ipchains -A forward -i $SERVER_LAN_INTERFACE -p tcp \
        -s $ANYWHERE $UNPRIVPORTS \
        -d $WEB_SERVER 80 -j ACCEPT
```

In this setup, only external connections to the Web server are allowed. Remote machines have no other access to the internal server machine.

A Formal Screened-Subnet Firewall

A small- or medium-sized business might have reason to invest in a more elaborate firewall architecture. A dual-homed machine serves as a bastion firewall between the Internet and the internal LAN, just as it did at the close of Chapter 3. However, its internal interface connects to a perimeter network, a DMZ, rather than the private LAN. Public services are hosted from machines on the perimeter DMZ network, each with a separate firewall and security policy. The public servers may or may not have publicly visible interfaces, depending on how your public IP addresses are assigned.

A DMZ is usually configured in one of two basic ways. In the first method, the bastion firewall machine has three network interfaces, one connecting to the Internet and two internal interfaces connecting to two separate LANs. One LAN is a DMZ LAN for public servers. The other LAN is the private, internal LAN. Figure 4.4 shows this type of DMZ configuration.

The second DMZ configuration uses a second firewall machine, called a *choke* firewall. The choke machine sits on the other end of the perimeter network, forming a gateway between the DMZ network and the private LAN. Its internal interface connects to the private LAN. The internal machines are masqueraded, all appearing as the choke firewall's external interface address to the bastion and DMZ machines.

The bastion firewall masquerades all private LAN traffic, so masquerading LAN machines at the choke firewall is unnecessary. However, the bastion's firewall rules are simpler when the single choke IP address represents all private machines, distinguishing them from the public servers in the DMZ.

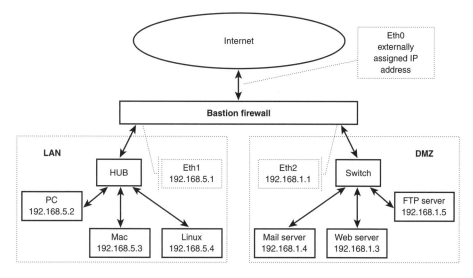

Figure 4.4 A DMZ network separated from a private LAN.

Unlike the firewall example in Chapter 3, this setup does not have a potential single point of failure. Services with different security policies can be hosted from different security zones within the internal networks.

The main idea is to physically isolate the private LAN from the external bastion firewall machine through the use of an internal choke firewall. The perimeter network shown in Figure 4.5 does not have to be a full network with its own servers; it's a conceptualization. The perimeter network could be implemented as simply as a crossover cable between the bastion's internal interface and the choke's external interface.

Implementing a DMZ as a simple crossover cable might sound silly. It buys a smaller site two firewalls, just as a full perimeter network does. Two firewalls don't represent a single point of failure. Local LAN services are hosted on the choke machine, completely isolated from the bastion or the Internet.

Using a crossover cable, the bastion's internal interface doesn't require a full set of separate firewall rules. The choke's external interface filters would suffice.

The remainder of this chapter assumes that the bastion and choke machines serve as the gateways to a DMZ network. The DMZ contains public and semipublic servers. Each of the network interfaces in the two firewall machines has its own, individualized ruleset.

This setup uses a minimum of four sets of firewall rules—one each for the external and internal interfaces of both firewall machines. The bastion firewall's external interface rules are nearly identical to the external interface rules in the example in Chapter 3. (The choke firewall's internal interface rules could be identical to the internal interface rules in the dual-homed example in Chapter 3, although I've extended them slightly to illustrate an internal DHCP server.)

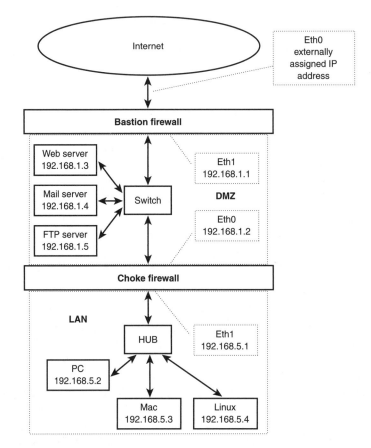

Figure 4.5   A perimeter network and a screened subnet behind a choke firewall.

The real difference between this example and the example in Chapter 3 is the addition of the DMZ perimeter network—the new rules applied to the bastion's internal interface and to the choke firewall's external interface. The rules for these two interfaces are mirror images of each other. Public servers on the DMZ network have their own individualized firewall rules, as well. Public servers in the DMZ are usually specialized, dedicated, single-service machines. Their firewall rules are simple and highly restrictive to the particular services they host.

The choke firewall's symbolic constants and initial rules are largely identical to the bastion's. Because the bastion's external rules remain the same as those in the example in Chapter 3, this chapter notes the differences between the external interface rulesets when they occur. The major emphasis of this example is on the choke's firewall rules, and on the symmetry between the bastion's internal interface and the choke's external interface.

Symbolic Constants Used In the Firewall Examples

As with the firewall example in Chapter 3, the bastion's external interface is assigned to eth0, leading to the Internet. The internal interface address is 192.168.1.1 on eth1, leading to the perimeter DMZ network. The choke's external interface address is 192.168.1.2 on eth0, leading to the perimeter DMZ network. The choke's internal interface address is 192.168.5.1 on eth1, leading to the private LAN.

Symbols for the Public Bastion Firewall

The following constants are added to the bastion's firewall script to refer to the bastion's internal interface, the choke's IP address, and the network address block for the DMZ:

```
BASTION_DMZ_INTERFACE="eth1"           # internal broadcast address
BASTION_DMZ_IPADDR="192.168.1.1"       # internal broadcast address
CHOKE_DMZ_IPADDR="192.168.1.2"         # internal choke firewall
DMZ_ADDRESSES="192.168.1.0/24"         # your (private) range
DMZ_BROADCAST="192.168.1.255"          # internal broadcast address
```

Symbols for the Private Choke Firewall

A firewall shell script is easiest to read and maintain if symbolic constants are used for recurring names and addresses. The following constants are either used throughout the examples in this chapter, or else are universal constants defined in the networking standards:

```
CHOKE_DMZ_INTERFACE="eth0"             # whichever you use
CHOKE_LAN_INTERFACE="eth1"             # whichever you use
LOOPBACK_INTERFACE="lo"                # however your system names it

CHOKE_DMZ_IPADDR="192.168.1.2"         # external interface address
BASTION_DMZ_IPADDR="192.168.1.1"       # bastion firewall
DMZ_ADDRESSES="192.168.1.0/24"         # your (private) range
DMZ_BROADCAST="192.168.1.255"          # external broadcast address
CHOKE_LAN_IPADDR="192.168.5.1"         # your internal interface address
CHOKE_LAN_ADDRESSES="192.168.5.0/24"   # your (private) range
ANYWHERE="any/0"                       # match any IP address

LOOPBACK="127.0.0.0/8"                 # reserved loopback address range
CLASS_A="10.0.0.0/8"                   # class A private networks
CLASS_B="172.16.0.0/12"                # class B private networks
CLASS_C="192.168.0.0/16"               # class C private networks
CLASS_D_MULTICAST="224.0.0.0/4"        # class D multicast addresses
CLASS_E_RESERVED_NET="240.0.0.0/5"     # class E reserved addresses
BROADCAST_SRC="0.0.0.0"                # broadcast source address
BROADCAST_DEST="255.255.255.255"       # broadcast destination address
PRIVPORTS="0:1023"                     # well-known, privileged
                                       # port range
UNPRIVPORTS="1024:65535"               # unprivileged port range
```

Constants not listed here are defined within the context of the specific rules they are used with.

Removing Any Preexisting Rules from the Choke Firewall

The first thing to do when defining a set of filtering rules is to remove any existing rules from the rule chains. Otherwise, any new rules you define will be added to the end of existing rules. Packets could easily match a preexisting rule before ever reaching the point in the chain you are defining from this point on. The following command flushes the rules of all three built-in chains—input, output, and forward—at once:

```
# Flush any existing rules from all chains
ipchains -F
```

The chains are empty. You're starting from scratch. The system is in its default accept-everything policy state.

Defining the Choke Firewall's Default Policy

The choke policy is to reject all traffic in either direction. An ICMP 3 error message is returned. This results in some kind of meaningful error message being delivered immediately, rather than forcing the local client to wait for a timeout.

Both firewalls drop everything by default, rather than accept everything by default:

```
# Set the default policy to reject
ipchains -P input   REJECT
ipchains -P output  REJECT
ipchains -P forward REJECT
```

At this point, all network traffic is blocked.

Enabling the Choke Machine's Loopback Interface

You need to enable unrestricted loopback traffic. This allows you to run any local network services you choose, or that the system depends on, without having to worry about getting all the firewall rules specified:

```
# Unlimited traffic on the loopback interface
ipchains -A input  -i $LOOPBACK_INTERFACE -j ACCEPT
ipchains -A output -i $LOOPBACK_INTERFACE -j ACCEPT
```

Source-Address Spoofing and Other Bad Addresses

This section establishes some filters based on source and destination addresses. These addresses will never been seen in a legitimate packet on the Internet.

At the packet-filtering level, one of the few cases of source address spoofing you can identify as a forgery with certainty is your own IP address. This rule denies incoming packets claiming to be from you:

```
# Refuse spoofed packets pretending to be from the interface addresses
ipchains -A input  -i $CHOKE_DMZ_INTERFACE \
         -s $CHOKE_DMZ_IPADDR -j REJECT -l

ipchains -A input  -i $CHOKE_LAN_INTERFACE \
         -s $CHOKE_LAN_IPADDR -j REJECT -l
```

The next two sets of rules disallow incoming and outgoing packets with any of the Class A or B private network addresses as their source or destination addresses. None of these packets should be seen outside a private LAN:

```
# Refuse packets claiming to be to or from a Class A private network
ipchains -A input  -i $CHOKE_DMZ_INTERFACE -s $CLASS_A -j REJECT -l
ipchains -A output -i $CHOKE_DMZ_INTERFACE -d $CLASS_A -j REJECT -l

ipchains -A input  -i $CHOKE_LAN_INTERFACE -s $CLASS_A -j REJECT -l
ipchains -A output -i $CHOKE_LAN_INTERFACE -d $CLASS_A -j REJECT -l

# Refuse packets claiming to be to or from a Class B private network
ipchains -A input  -i $CHOKE_DMZ_INTERFACE -s $CLASS_B -j REJECT -l
ipchains -A output -i $CHOKE_DMZ_INTERFACE -d $CLASS_B -j REJECT -l

ipchains -A input  -i $CHOKE_LAN_INTERFACE -s $CLASS_B -j REJECT -l
ipchains -A output -i $CHOKE_LAN_INTERFACE -d $CLASS_B -j REJECT -l
```

Class C private network addresses are used locally. The choke firewall can't block all Class C private addresses, because both its external and internal interfaces are assigned Class C addresses. (ipfwadm does not have the flexibility to block all Class C private addresses, with the exception of our own. ipchains does have the flexibility through the use of user-defined chains.)

The next two sets of rules disallow packets with a source address reserved for the loopback interface:

```
# Refuse packets claiming to be to or from the loopback interface
ipchains -A input  -i $CHOKE_DMZ_INTERFACE -s $LOOPBACK -j REJECT -l
ipchains -A input  -i $CHOKE_LAN_INTERFACE -s $LOOPBACK -j REJECT -l
```

The next two sets of rules primarily serve to log matching packets. The firewall's default policy is to reject everything. As such, broadcast addresses are rejected by default and must be explicitly enabled in the cases where they are wanted:

```
# Refuse malformed broadcast packets
ipchains -A input  -i $CHOKE_DMZ_INTERFACE \
      -s $BROADCAST_DEST -j REJECT -l
ipchains -A input  -i $CHOKE_DMZ_INTERFACE \
      -d $BROADCAST_SRC  -j REJECT -l

ipchains -A input  -i $CHOKE_LAN_INTERFACE \
      -s $BROADCAST_DEST -j REJECT -l
ipchains -A input  -i $CHOKE_LAN_INTERFACE \
      -d $BROADCAST_SRC  -j REJECT -l
```

Multicast addresses are legal only as destination addresses. The next rule pairs deny and log spoofed multicast network packets:

```
# Refuse Class D multicast & experimental addresses
ipchains -A input  -i $CHOKE_DMZ_INTERFACE -s $MULTICAST -j REJECT -l
ipchains -A output -i $CHOKE_DMZ_INTERFACE -s $MULTICAST -j REJECT -l

ipchains -A input  -i $CHOKE_LAN_INTERFACE -s $MULTICAST -j REJECT -l
ipchains -A output -i $CHOKE_LAN_INTERFACE -s $MULTICAST -j REJECT -l
```

The next rules in this section deny and log packets claiming to be from a Class E reserved network:

```
# Refuse reserved IP addresses
ipchains -A input -i $CHOKE_DMZ_INTERFACE -s $RESERVED_NET -j REJECT -l
ipchains -A input -i $CHOKE_LAN_INTERFACE -s $RESERVED_NET -j REJECT -l
```

Filtering ICMP Control and Status Messages

ICMP messages are handled differently when IP masquerading is enabled. Unless ICMP masquerading is enabled in the kernel compilation, along with general IP masquerading, only ICMP error messages are forwarded and masqueraded for existing connections. If ICMP Masquerading is also enabled, other control messages, such as those used by ping and traceroute, can be sent to the Internet from internal, masqueraded machines. Otherwise, these ICMP messages can be sent only between local hosts on the same network. ICMP masquerading is enabled by default in Red Hat release 6.0. It must be explicitly compiled into the kernel in earlier releases.

As with general masquerading, if ICMP masquerading is enabled, your local machines can initiate ICMP interactions with external machines, but external machines cannot initiate an ICMP message to any of your local machines. Only the external interface on the bastion machine is directly visible.

Source Quench Control (Type 4) Messages

ICMP message type 4, Source Quench, is sent when a connection source, usually a router, is sending data faster than the next destination router can handle it. Source Quench is used as a primitive form of flow control at the IP network layer, usually between two adjacent, point-to-point machines.

Bastion Source Quench Control DMZ Configuration

The bastion rules to accept all Source Quench messages are:

```
ipchains -A output -i $BASTION_DMZ_INTERFACE -p icmp \
         -s $BASTION_DMZ_IPADDR 4 -d $DMZ_ADDRESSES -j ACCEPT

ipchains -A input  -i $BASTION_DMZ_INTERFACE -p icmp \
         -s $DMZ_ADDRESSES 4 -d $BASTION_DMZ_IPADDR -j ACCEPT
```

Choke Source Quench Control DMZ Configuration

The choke rules to accept all Source Quench messages are:

```
ipchains -A input  -i $CHOKE_DMZ_INTERFACE -p icmp \
         -s $DMZ_ADDRESSES 4 -d $CHOKE_DMZ_IPADDR -j ACCEPT

ipchains -A output -i $CHOKE_DMZ_INTERFACE -p icmp \
         -s $CHOKE_DMZ_IPADDR 4 -d $DMZ_ADDRESSES -j ACCEPT
```

Parameter Problem Status (Type 12) Messages

ICMP message type 12, Parameter Problem, is sent when a packet is received containing illegal or unexpected data in the header, or when the header checksum doesn't match the checksum generated by the receiving machine.

Bastion Parameter Problem Status DMZ Configuration

The bastion rules to accept all Parameter Problem messages are:

```
ipchains -A output -i $BASTION_DMZ_INTERFACE -p icmp \
        -s $ANYWHERE 12 -d $DMZ_ADDRESSES -j ACCEPT

ipchains -A input  -i $BASTION_DMZ_INTERFACE -p icmp \
        -s $DMZ_ADDRESSES 12 -d $ANYWHERE -j ACCEPT
```

Choke Parameter Problem Status DMZ Configuration

The choke rules to accept all Parameter Problem messages are:

```
ipchains -A input  -i $CHOKE_DMZ_INTERFACE -p icmp \
        -s $ANYWHERE 12 -d $CHOKE_DMZ_IPADDR -j ACCEPT

ipchains -A output -i $CHOKE_DMZ_INTERFACE -p icmp \
        -s $CHOKE_DMZ_IPADDR 12 -d $ANYWHERE -j ACCEPT
```

Destination Unreachable Error (Type 3) Messages

ICMP message type 3, Destination Unreachable, is a general error status message.

Bastion Destination Unreachable Error Message DMZ Configuration

The bastion rules to accept all Destination Unreachable messages are:

```
ipchains -A output -i $BASTION_DMZ_INTERFACE -p icmp \
        -s $ANYWHERE 3 -d $DMZ_ADDRESSES -j ACCEPT

ipchains -A input  -i $BASTION_DMZ_INTERFACE -p icmp \
        -s $DMZ_ADDRESSES 3 -d $ANYWHERE -j ACCEPT
```

Choke Destination Unreachable Error Message DMZ Configuration

The choke rules to accept all Destination Unreachable messages are:

```
ipchains -A input  -i $CHOKE_DMZ_INTERFACE -p icmp \
        -s $ANYWHERE 3 -d $CHOKE_DMZ_IPADDR -j ACCEPT

ipchains -A output -i $CHOKE_DMZ_INTERFACE -p icmp \
        -s $CHOKE_DMZ_IPADDR 3 -d $ANYWHERE -j ACCEPT
```

Time Exceeded Status (Type 11) Messages

ICMP message type 11, Time Exceeded, indicates a timeout condition, or more accurately, that a packet's maximum hop count has been exceeded. On networks today, incoming Time Exceeded is mostly seen as the ICMP response to an outgoing UDP traceroute request.

Bastion Time Exceeded Status Message DMZ Configuration

The bastion rules to accept Time Exceeded messages with the choke firewall alone are:

```
ipchains -A output -i $BASTION_DMZ_INTERFACE -p icmp \
        -s $BASTION_DMZ_IPADDR 11 -d $DMZ_ADDRESSES -j ACCEPT

ipchains -A input  -i $BASTION_DMZ_INTERFACE -p icmp \
        -s $DMZ_ADDRESSES 11 -d $BASTION_DMZ_IPADDR -j ACCEPT
```

Choke Time Exceeded Status Message DMZ Configuration

The choke rules to accept Time Exceeded messages with the bastion firewall alone are:

```
ipchains -A input  -i $CHOKE_DMZ_INTERFACE -p icmp \
        -s $BASTION_DMZ_IPADDR 11 -d $CHOKE_DMZ_IPADDR -j ACCEPT

ipchains -A output -i $CHOKE_DMZ_INTERFACE -p icmp \
        -s $CHOKE_DMZ_IPADDR 11 -d $BASTION_DMZ_IPADDR -j ACCEPT
```

Echo Request (Type 8) and Echo Reply (Type 0) Control Messages

ping uses two ICMP message types. The request message, Echo Request, is message type 8. The reply message, Echo Reply, is message type 0. ping is a simple network analysis tool dating back to the original DARPANET.

Bastion ping DMZ Configuration

The following rule pair allows the machines in the DMZ to ping any host on the Internet:

```
ipchains -A input  -i $BASTION_DMZ_INTERFACE -p icmp \
        -s $DMZ_ADDRESSES 8 -d $ANYWHERE -j ACCEPT

ipchains -A output -i $BASTION_DMZ_INTERFACE -p icmp \
        -s $ANYWHERE 0 -d $DMZ_ADDRESSES -j ACCEPT
```

The approach shown here allows only the bastion machine to ping the DMZ machines:

```
ipchains -A output -i $BASTION_DMZ_INTERFACE -p icmp \
        -s $BASTION_DMZ_IPADDR 8 -d $DMZ_ADDRESSES -j ACCEPT

ipchains -A input  -i $BASTION_DMZ_INTERFACE -p icmp \
        -s $DMZ_ADDRESSES 0 -d $BASTION_DMZ_IPADDR -j ACCEPT
```

Choke ping DMZ Configuration

The following rule pair allows the choke machine to ping any host on the Internet:

```
ipchains -A output -i $CHOKE_DMZ_INTERFACE -p icmp \
        -s $CHOKE_DMZ_IPADDR 8 -d $ANYWHERE -j ACCEPT

ipchains -A input  -i $CHOKE_DMZ_INTERFACE -p icmp \
        -s $ANYWHERE 0 -d $CHOKE_DMZ_IPADDR -j ACCEPT
```

The approach shown here allows only the DMZ machines to ping the choke machine:

```
ipchains -A input  -i $CHOKE_DMZ_INTERFACE -p icmp \
        -s $DMZ_ADDRESSES 8 -d $CHOKE_DMZ_IPADDR -j ACCEPT

ipchains -A output -i $CHOKE_DMZ_INTERFACE -p icmp \
        -s $CHOKE_DMZ_IPADDR 0 -d $DMZ_ADDRESSES -j ACCEPT
```

Kernel Support for Masqueraded ICMP

If you have a LAN and are running a version of Red Hat Linux prior to release 6.0, ping ICMP messages are not forwarded between your LAN and remote machines, even if IP Forwarding is enabled. If you want to use ping from an internal machine, the kernel must be configured and compiled to include the ICMP Masquerading module. Other connection-related control and error messages are forwarded without this special module.

The TCP and UDP Service Protocol Tables

In each of the following sections, the service protocol at the packet-filtering level is first presented as a table of state information, followed by the ipchains rules expressing those states.

Each row in a service's protocol table lists a packet type involved in the service exchange. A firewall rule is defined for each packet type. The table is divided into columns:

- *Description* contains a brief description of whether the packet is originating from the client or the server, and the packet's purpose.
- *Protocol* is the transport protocol in use, TCP or UDP, or the IP protocol's control messages, ICMP.
- *Remote Address* is the legal address, or range of addresses, the packet can contain in the remote address field.
- *Remote Port* is the legal port, or range of ports, the packet can contain in the remote port field.
- *In/Out* describes the packet's direction, that is, whether it is coming into the system from a remote location or whether it is going out from the system to a remote location.
- *Local Address* is the legal address, or range of addresses, the packet can contain in the local address field.
- *Local Port* is the legal port, or range of ports, the packet can contain in the local port field.
- TCP protocol packets contain a final column, *TCP Flag*, defining the legal SYN-ACK states the packet may have.

The table describes packets as either incoming or outgoing. Addresses and ports are described as either remote or local, relative to your machine's network interface. Notice that for incoming packets, remote address and port refer to the source fields in the IP packet header. Local address and port refer to the destination fields in the IP packet header. For outgoing packets, remote address and port refer to the destination fields in the IP packet header. Local address and port refer to the source fields in the IP packet header.

Finally, in the few instances where the service protocol involves ICMP messages, notice that the IP network layer ICMP packets are not associated with the concept of a source or destination port, as is the case for transport layer TCP or UDP packets. Instead, ICMP packets use the concept of a control or status message type. ICMP messages are not sent to programs bound to particular service ports. Instead, ICMP messages are sent from one computer to another. Consequently, the few ICMP packet entries presented in the tables use the source port column to contain the message type. For incoming ICMP packets, the source port column is the Remote Port column. For outgoing ICMP packets, the source port column is the Local Port column.

Enabling DNS (UDP/TCP Port 53)

Access to remote Domain Name Service (DNS) is required for Internet access. DNS translates between hostnames and their associated IP addresses. You can't locate a remote host without DNS.

DNS uses a communication protocol that relies on both UDP and TCP. Connection modes include regular client-to-server connections, peer-to-peer traffic between forwarding servers and full servers, and primary and secondary full name server connections.

A home user has several DNS configuration options. If the firewall machine is not running `named`, but is operating purely as a DNS client, internal machines will be configured to point to the ISP's name servers, just as the firewall machine is. If the firewall machine is running a name server, the internal machines will be configured to point to the firewall machine's internal interface as their name server.

Classic DNS Setup for a LAN

Some sites need the additional sense of security that comes with a classic DNS setup that hides local host information. The attraction of this setup is that sensitive, local, personal, and account information can be centrally stored in the internal DNS database.

The idea is that the bastion firewall runs its own DNS server for the public. The server is configured as the authoritative source for the site, but the information is incomplete. The bastion name server knows nothing about internal machines. DNS clients on the bastion machine don't use the local name server. Instead, `/etc/resolv.conf` on the bastion points to the choke machine as the name server for bastion's local clients. Incoming queries from the Internet are handled by the public DNS server. Local queries are handled by the internal DNS server on the choke machine.

The choke machine hosts the real DNS server for the site. The internal server is also configured as the authoritative source for the site. In this case, the information is correct. Local queries, queries from the bastion's local clients, and queries from the private LAN are all handled by this internal, private DNS server. As shown in Figure 4.6, when the server doesn't have the requested lookup information, it queries the server on the bastion machine, which in turn forwards the query to an external name server.

If the firewall scripts use symbolic hostnames in some places, this mutually dependent configuration creates a chicken-and-egg dilemma when the servers are initializing. When the bastion comes up, it will try to use the choke as its name server. The choke will try to use the bastion as its name server.

When the bastion is first booted, it must use external name servers for its client requests. When the choke firewall's name server is running, the bastion clients can use the bastion server instead of the external servers.

Bastion DMZ Configuration As a Public Name Server

The bastion hosts the public name server. Local DNS clients running on the bastion use the private name server running on the choke machine. If the choke server can't service a query, it forwards the request to the server running on the bastion, which in turn forwards the query to designated remote servers. If none of the remote servers respond, the bastion server re-sends the query as a client to more authoritative remote name servers.

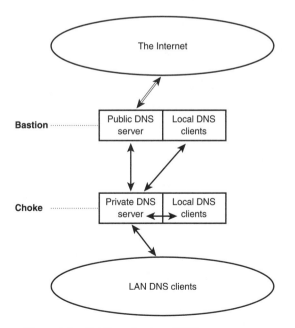

Figure 4.6 Public and private DNS name servers.

Table 4.2 lists the DNS protocol used by the bastion's DMZ interface.

Table 4.2   Bastion DNS Protocol on the DMZ Interface

Description	Protocol	Remote Address	Remote Port	In/ Out	Local Address	Local Port	TCP Flag
Choke server query	UDP	CHOKE_DMZ_IPADDR	53	In	BASTION_DMZ_IPADDR	53	—
Bastion server response	UDP	CHOKE_DMZ_IPADDR	53	Out	BASTION_DMZ_IPADDR	53	—
Bastion client query	UDP	CHOKE_DMZ_IPADDR	53	Out	BASTION_DMZ_IPADDR	1024:65535	—
Choke server response	UDP	CHOKE_DMZ_IPADDR	53	In	BASTION_DMZ_IPADDR	1024:65535	—
Bastion client query	TCP	CHOKE_DMZ_IPADDR	53	Out	BASTION_DMZ_IPADDR	1024:65535	Any
Choke server response	TCP	CHOKE_DMZ_IPADDR	53	In	BASTION_DMZ_IPADDR	1024:65535	ACK

The bastion's DNS server listens for peer-to-peer server requests from the choke's DNS server:

```
# DNS caching & forwarding name server (53)
# -------------------------------------

ipchains -A input  -i $BASTION_DMZ_INTERFACE -p udp \
        -s $CHOKE_DMZ_IPADDR 53 \
        -d $BASTION_DMZ_IPADDR 53 -j ACCEPT

ipchains -A output -i $BASTION_DMZ_INTERFACE -p udp \
        -s $BASTION_DMZ_IPADDR 53 \
        -d $CHOKE_DMZ_IPADDR 53 -j ACCEPT
```

Bastion DNS client programs direct their client-to-server queries to the name server running on the choke machine:

```
# DNS local client-to-server request (53)
# -------------------------------------

ipchains -A output -i $BASTION_DMZ_INTERFACE -p udp \
        -s $BASTION_DMZ_IPADDR $UNPRIVPORTS \
        -d $CHOKE_DMZ_IPADDR 53 -j ACCEPT

ipchains -A input  -i $BASTION_DMZ_INTERFACE -p udp \
        -s $CHOKE_DMZ_IPADDR 53 \
        -d $BASTION_DMZ_IPADDR $UNPRIVPORTS -j ACCEPT

ipchains -A output -i $BASTION_DMZ_INTERFACE -p tcp \
        -s $BASTION_DMZ_IPADDR $UNPRIVPORTS \
        -d $CHOKE_DMZ_IPADDR 53 -j ACCEPT
```

```
ipchains -A input  -i $BASTION_DMZ_INTERFACE ! -y -p tcp \
        -s $CHOKE_DMZ_IPADDR 53 \
        -d $BASTION_DMZ_IPADDR $UNPRIVPORTS -j ACCEPT
```

Following these two sets of DNS rules are the regular DNS rules for the external interface and the external name servers. Table 3.3 in Chapter 3 shows the external DNS protocol table. The bastion name server is configured as a full DNS server, offering limited public DNS service. For local requests, it first attempts to forward the request to the ISP name server, if any:

```
# DNS caching & forwarding name server (53)
# ---------------------------------------

ipchains -A output -i $EXTERNAL_INTERFACE -p udp \
        -s $IPADDR 53 \
        -d $NAME_SERVER 53 -j ACCEPT

ipchains -A input  -i $EXTERNAL_INTERFACE -p udp \
        -s $NAME_SERVER 53 \
        -d $IPADDR 53 -j ACCEPT


# DNS local client-to-server request (53)
# ---------------------------------------

ipchains -A output -i $EXTERNAL_INTERFACE -p udp \
        -s $IPADDR $UNPRIVPORTS \
        -d $ANYWHERE 53 -j ACCEPT

ipchains -A input  -i $EXTERNAL_INTERFACE -p udp \
        -s $ANYWHERE 53 \
        -d $IPADDR $UNPRIVPORTS -j ACCEPT

ipchains -A output -i $EXTERNAL_INTERFACE -p tcp \
        -s $IPADDR $UNPRIVPORTS \
        -d $ANYWHERE 53 -j ACCEPT

ipchains -A input  -i $EXTERNAL_INTERFACE ! -y -p tcp \
        -s $ANYWHERE 53 \
        -d $IPADDR $UNPRIVPORTS -j ACCEPT

# DNS local server to remote client (53)
# ---------------------------------------

ipchains -A input  -i $EXTERNAL_INTERFACE -p udp \
        -s $ANYWHERE $UNPRIVPORTS \
        -d $IPADDR 53 -j ACCEPT

ipchains -A output -i $EXTERNAL_INTERFACE -p udp \
        -s $IPADDR 53 \
        -d $ANYWHERE $UNPRIVPORTS -j ACCEPT
```

```
ipchains -A input  -i $EXTERNAL_INTERFACE -p tcp \
        -s $ANYWHERE $UNPRIVPORTS \
        -d $IPADDR 53 -j ACCEPT

ipchains -A output -i $EXTERNAL_INTERFACE ! -y -p tcp \
        -s $IPADDR 53 \
        -d $ANYWHERE $UNPRIVPORTS -j ACCEPT
```

Choke DMZ Configuration as a Private Name Server

The choke hosts the private name server. LAN clients, including those running on the bastion, use the private name server. If the choke server can't service a query from its DNS cache, it forwards the request to the server running on the bastion.

Table 4.3 lists the DNS protocol used by the choke's DMZ interface.

Table 4.3   Choke DNS Protocol

Description	Protocol	Remote Address	Remote Port	In/Out	Local Address	Local Port	TCP Flag
Choke server query	UDP	BASTION_DMZ_IPADDR	53	Out	CHOKE_DMZ_IPADDR	53	—
Bastion server response	UDP	BASTION_DMZ_IPADDR	53	In	CHOKE_DMZ_IPADDR	53	—
Bastion client query	UDP	BASTION_DMZ_IPADDR	1024:65535	In	CHOKE_DMZ_IPADDR	53	—
Choke server response	UDP	BASTION_DMZ_IPADDR	1024:65535	Out	CHOKE_DMZ_IPADDR	53	—
Bastion client query	TCP	BASTION_DMZ_IPADDR	1024:65535	In	CHOKE_DMZ_IPADDR	53	Any
Choke server response	TCP	BASTION_DMZ_IPADDR	1024:65535	Out	CHOKE_DMZ_IPADDR	53	ACK

The choke firewall's DNS rules are the mirror image of the bastion's rules. The local DNS server forwards peer-to-peer server requests to the bastion's DNS server for requests the choke server can't resolve:

```
# DNS caching & forwarding name server (53)
# ------------------------------------

ipchains -A output -i $CHOKE_DMZ_INTERFACE -p udp \
        -s $CHOKE_DMZ_IPADDR 53 \
        -d $DMZ_ADDRESSES 53 -j ACCEPT

ipchains -A input  -i $CHOKE_DMZ_INTERFACE -p udp \
        -s $DMZ_ADDRESSES 53 \
        -d $CHOKE_DMZ_IPADDR 53 -j ACCEPT
```

The choke DNS server receives client queries from the client programs running on machines attached to the DMZ, including the bastion machine:

```
# DNS local server to client (53)
# ----------------------------

ipchains -A input  -i $CHOKE_DMZ_INTERFACE -p udp \
        -s $DMZ_ADDRESSES $UNPRIVPORTS \
        -d $CHOKE_DMZ_IPADDR 53 -j ACCEPT

ipchains -A output -i $CHOKE_DMZ_INTERFACE -p udp \
        -s $CHOKE_DMZ_IPADDR 53 \
        -d $DMZ_ADDRESSES $UNPRIVPORTS -j ACCEPT

ipchains -A input  -i $CHOKE_DMZ_INTERFACE -p tcp \
        -s $DMZ_ADDRESSES $UNPRIVPORTS \
        -d $CHOKE_DMZ_IPADDR 53 -j ACCEPT

ipchains -A output -i $CHOKE_DMZ_INTERFACE ! -y -p tcp \
        -s $CHOKE_DMZ_IPADDR 53 \
        -d $DMZ_ADDRESSES $UNPRIVPORTS -j ACCEPT
```

Filtering the AUTH User Identification Service (TCP Port 113)

The identd, or AUTH, user identification service is required for access to some Internet services. identd provides the username or ID associated with a connection. This is commonly requested by a remote mail server when you send email. You don't need to offer identd service, but you must account for incoming connection requests in some way to avoid lengthy timeouts.

Whether you've chosen to offer the IDENT user identification service on the external Internet interface or not, there is no reason not to offer the service locally. This means that AUTH must be enabled in /etc/inetd.conf on both firewall machines.

Bastion AUTH DMZ Configuration

Table 4.4 lists the complete client/server connection protocol for the AUTH service.

Table 4.4 *identd* **Protocol on the Bastions's DMZ Interface**

Description	Protocol	Remote Address	Remote Port	In/ Out	Local Address	Local Port	TCP Flag
Bastion client query	TCP	DMZ_ADDRESSES	113	Out	BASTION_DMZ_IPADDR	1024:65535	Any
DMZ server response	TCP	DMZ_ADDRESSES	113	In	BASTION_DMZ_IPADDR	1024:65535	ACK
DMZ client query	TCP	DMZ_ADDRESSES	1024:65535	In	BASTION_DMZ_IPADDR	113	Any
Bastion server response	TCP	DMZ_ADDRESSES	1024:65535	Out	BASTION_DMZ_IPADDR	113	ACK

Allowing Bastion's Outgoing AUTH Requests as a Client

Your machine would act as an AUTH client if you ran a mail or FTP server. There is
no reason not to allow your system to be an AUTH client:

```
ipchains -A output -i $BASTION_DMZ_INTERFACE -p tcp \
         -s $BASTION_DMZ_IPADDR $UNPRIVPORTS \
         -d $DMZ_ADDRESSES 113 -j ACCEPT

ipchains -A input -i $BASTION_DMZ_INTERFACE -p tcp ! -y \
         -s $DMZ_ADDRESSES 113 \
         -d $BASTION_DMZ_IPADDR $UNPRIVPORTS -j ACCEPT
```

Allowing Bastion's Incoming AUTH Requests as a Server

If you run the identd server out of /etc/inetd.conf, the following rules enable
incoming identd connection requests:

```
ipchains -A input  -i $BASTION_DMZ_INTERFACE -p tcp \
         -s $DMZ_ADDRESSES $UNPRIVPORTS \
         -d $BASTION_DMZ_IPADDR 113 -j ACCEPT

ipchains -A output -i $BASTION_DMZ_INTERFACE -p tcp ! -y \
         -s $BASTION_DMZ_IPADDR 113 \
         -d $DMZ_ADDRESSES $UNPRIVPORTS -j ACCEPT
```

Choke AUTH DMZ Configuration

Table 4.5 lists the complete client/server connection protocol for the AUTH service.

Table 4.5 *identd* **Protocol on the Choke's DMZ Interface**

Description	Protocol	Remote Address	Remote Port	In/Out	Local Address	Local Port	TCP Flag
DMZ client query	TCP	DMZ_ADDRESSES	1024:65535	In	CHOKE_DMZ_IPADDR	113	Any
Choke server response	TCP	DMZ_ADDRESSES	1024:65535	Out	CHOKE_DMZ_IPADDR	113	ACK
Choke client query	TCP	ANYWHERE	113	Out	CHOKE_DMZ_IPADDR	1024:65535	Any
Remote server response	TCP	ANYWHERE	113	In	CHOKE_DMZ_IPADDR	1024:65535	ACK

Allowing Choke's Incoming AUTH Requests as a Server

If you run the `identd` server out of `/etc/inetd.conf`, the following rules enable incoming `identd` connection requests:

```
ipchains -A input  -i $CHOKE_DMZ_INTERFACE -p tcp \
         -s $DMZ_ADDRESSES $UNPRIVPORTS \
         -d $CHOKE_DMZ_IPADDR 113 -j ACCEPT

ipchains -A output -i $CHOKE_DMZ_INTERFACE -p tcp ! -y \
         -s $CHOKE_DMZ_IPADDR 113 \
         -d $DMZ_ADDRESSES $UNPRIVPORTS -j ACCEPT
```

Allowing Choke's Outgoing AUTH Requests as a Client

Your machine would act as an AUTH client if you ran a mail or FTP server. There is no reason not to allow your system to be an AUTH client:

```
ipchains -A output -i $CHOKE_DMZ_INTERFACE -p tcp \
         -s $CHOKE_DMZ_IPADDR $UNPRIVPORTS \
         -d $ANYWHERE 113 -j ACCEPT

ipchains -A input  -i $CHOKE_DMZ_INTERFACE -p tcp ! -y \
         -s $ANYWHERE 113 \
         -d $CHOKE_DMZ_IPADDR $UNPRIVPORTS -j ACCEPT
```

Email (TCP SMTP Port 25, POP Port 110, IMAP Port 143)

Regardless of how mail is sent and received between the bastion and the Internet, internally, mail is typically handled by a central SMTP server. As a workable example, this section is based on the assumption that either the bastion or a machine in the DMZ is the local mail gateway and mail host. Local clients will retrieve incoming mail from the mail host using a local POP or IMAP server.

Four common approaches to client and server email combinations are described in this section:

- Sending mail through the SMTP bastion relay and receiving mail as a bastion POP client
- Sending mail through the SMTP bastion relay and receiving mail as a bastion IMAP client
- Sending mail through an SMTP DMZ relay and receiving mail as a DMZ POP client
- Sending mail through an SMTP DMZ relay and receiving mail as a DMZ IMAP client

The first two approaches are useful whether the bastion relays mail to either your ISP's SMTP server or to the final recipient destination. In either case, the DNS lookup is not performed by the local originating machine. The second two approaches use a mail gateway and host in the DMZ. Neither a POP nor an IMAP server runs on the bastion for local mail retrieval.

Relaying Outgoing Mail Through the Bastion's DMZ Interface (TCP Port 25)

When you relay outgoing mail through a remote gateway server, your client mail program sends all outgoing mail to your ISP's mail server. Your ISP acts as your mail gateway to the rest of the world. Your system doesn't need to know how to locate your mail destinations or the routes to them. The ISP mail gateway serves as your relay.

Alternatively, you can bypass your ISP's mail server and host your own. Your local server is responsible for collecting your outgoing mail, doing the DNS lookup on the destination hostname, and relaying the mail to its destination. Your client mail program points to your local SMTP server rather than to the ISP's server.

If you are relaying outgoing mail as an SMTP server and receiving mail as an SMTP client, you provide all your own mail services. Your local sendmail daemon is configured to relay outgoing mail to the remote destination hosts itself, as well as collect and deliver incoming mail.

Bastion SMTP Server DMZ Configuration

Table 4.6 lists the client/server connection protocol for SMTP.

Table 4.6   Bastion SMTP Mail Protocol DMZ Configuration

Description	Protocol	Remote Address	Remote Port	In/ Out	Local Address	Local Port	TCP Flag
Receiving incoming mail for relaying	TCP	DMZ_ADDRESSES	1024:65535	In	BASTION_DMZ_IPADDR	25	Any
Bastion server response	TCP	DMZ_ADDRESSES	1024:65535	Out	BASTION_DMZ_IPADDR	25	ACK

This ruleset allows you to relay outgoing mail for local machines:

```
ipchains -A input  -i $BASTION_DMZ_INTERFACE -p tcp \
         -s $DMZ_ADDRESSES $UNPRIVPORTS \
         -d $BASTION_DMZ_IPADDR 25 -j ACCEPT

ipchains -A output -i $BASTION_DMZ_INTERFACE -p tcp ! -y \
         -s $BASTION_DMZ_IPADDR 25 \
         -d $DMZ_ADDRESSES $UNPRIVPORTS -j ACCEPT
```

Choke SMTP Client DMZ Configuration

Table 4.7 lists the client/server connection protocol for SMTP.

Table 4.7   Choke SMTP Mail Protocol DMZ Configuration

Description	Protocol	Remote Address	Remote Port	In/ Out	Local Address	Local Port	TCP Flag
Send outgoing mail	TCP	BASTION_DMZ_IPADDR	25	Out	CHOKE_DMZ_IPADDR	1024:65535	Any
Bastion server response	TCP	BASTION_DMZ_IPADDR	25	In	CHOKE_DMZ_IPADDR	1024:65535	ACK

This ruleset allows you to send mail from local machines:

```
ipchains -A output -i $CHOKE_DMZ_INTERFACE -p tcp \
        -s $CHOKE_DMZ_IPADDR $UNPRIVPORTS \
        -d $BASTION_DMZ_IPADDR 25 -j ACCEPT

ipchains -A input -i $CHOKE_DMZ_INTERFACE -p tcp ! -y \
        -s $BASTION_DMZ_IPADDR 25 \
        -d $CHOKE_DMZ_IPADDR $UNPRIVPORTS -j ACCEPT
```

Retrieving Mail as a POP Client Through the Bastion's DMZ Interface (TCP Port 110)

How you receive mail depends on your situation. If you run your own local mail server, you can collect incoming mail directly on your Linux machine. If you retrieve your mail from your ISP account, you may or may not retrieve mail as a POP or IMAP client, depending on how you've configured your ISP email account, and depending on the mail delivery services the ISP offers.

Alternatively, if you'd rather keep your local email account relatively private and use your work or ISP email account as your public address, you could configure your work and ISP mail accounts to forward mail to your local server.

Connecting to a POP server is a very common means of retrieving mail from a remote mail host. The following example demonstrates the firewall rules necessary to retrieve mail from a POP server running on the bastion.

Bastion POP Server DMZ Configuration

Table 4.8 lists the bastion's server protocol for POP service.

Table 4.8 Bastion POP Mail Retrieval Protocol DMZ Configuration

Description	Protocol	Remote Address	Remote Port	In/Out	Local Address	Local Port	TCP Flag
Choke client query	TCP	CHOKE_DMZ_IPADDR	1024:65535	In	BASTION_DMZ_IPADDR	110	Any
Bastion server response	TCP	CHOKE_DMZ_IPADDR	1024:65535	Out	BASTION_DMZ_IPADDR	110	ACK

The bastion hosts a local POP server for the LAN. External access is not allowed on the external interface:

```
ipchains -A input  -i $BASTION_DMZ_INTERFACE -p tcp \
        -s $CHOKE_DMZ_IPADDR $UNPRIVPORTS \
        -d $BASTION_DMZ_IPADDR 110 -j ACCEPT

ipchains -A output -i $BASTION_DMZ_INTERFACE -p tcp ! -y \
        -s $BASTION_DMZ_IPADDR 110 \
        -d $CHOKE_DMZ_IPADDR $UNPRIVPORTS -j ACCEPT
```

Choke POP Client DMZ Configuration

Table 4.9 lists the choke's client protocol for POP service.

Table 4.9 Choke POP Mail Retrieval Protocol DMZ Configuration

Description	Protocol	Remote Address	Remote Port	In/Out	Local Address	Local Port	TCP Flag
Choke client query	TCP	BASTION_DMZ_IPADDR	110	Out	CHOKE_DMZ_IPADDR	1024:65535	Any
Bastion server response	TCP	BASTION_DMZ_IPADDR	110	In	CHOKE_DMZ_IPADDR	1024:65535	ACK

You retrieve mail from the POP server running on the bastion:

```
ipchains -A output -i $CHOKE_DMZ_INTERFACE -p tcp \
        -s $CHOKE_DMZ_IPADDR $UNPRIVPORTS \
        -d $BASTION_DMZ_IPADDR 110 -j ACCEPT

ipchains -A input  -i $CHOKE_DMZ_INTERFACE -p tcp ! -y \
        -s $BASTION_DMZ_IPADDR 110 \
        -d $CHOKE_DMZ_IPADDR $UNPRIVPORTS -j ACCEPT
```

Retrieving Mail as an IMAP Client Through the Bastion's DMZ Interface (TCP Port 143)

Connecting to an IMAP server is another common means of retrieving mail from a remote mail host. The following example demonstrates the firewall rules necessary to retrieve mail from an IMAP server running on the bastion.

Bastion IMAP Server DMZ Configuration

The bastion hosts a local IMAP server for the LAN. External access is not allowed on the external interface.

Table 4.10 lists the bastion's server protocol for IMAP.

Table 4.10   Bastion IMAP Mail Retrieval Protocol DMZ Configuration

Description	Protocol	Remote Address	Remote Port	In/ Out	Local Address	Local Port	TCP Flag
Choke client query	TCP	CHOKE_DMZ_IPADDR	1024:65535	In	BASTION_DMZ_IPADDR	143	Any
Bastion server response	TCP	CHOKE_DMZ_IPADDR	1024:65535	Out	BASTION_DMZ_IPADDR	143	ACK

The next ruleset allows incoming client connections from the choke machine:

```
ipchains -A input  -i $BASTION_DMZ_INTERFACE -p tcp \
        -s $CHOKE_DMZ_IPADDR $UNPRIVPORTS \
        -d $BASTION_DMZ_IPADDR 143 -j ACCEPT

ipchains -A output -i $BASTION_DMZ_INTERFACE -p tcp ! -y \
        -s $BASTION_DMZ_IPADDR 143 \
        -d $CHOKE_DMZ_IPADDR $UNPRIVPORTS -j ACCEPT
```

Choke IMAP Client DMZ Configuration

Table 4.11 lists the choke's client connection protocol for IMAP.

Table 4.11   Choke IMAP Mail Retrieval Protocol DMZ Configuration

Description	Protocol	Remote Address	Remote Port	In/ Out	Local Address	Local Port	TCP Flag
Choke client query	TCP	BASTION_DMZ_IPADDR	143	Out	CHOKE_DMZ_IPADDR	1024:65535	Any
Bastion server response	TCP	BASTION_DMZ_IPADDR	143	In	CHOKE_DMZ_IPADDR	1024:65535	ACK

You retrieve mail from the IMAP server running on the bastion:

```
ipchains -A output -i $CHOKE_DMZ_INTERFACE -p tcp \
        -s $CHOKE_DMZ_IPADDR $UNPRIVPORTS \
        -d $BASTION_DMZ_IPADDR 143 -j ACCEPT

ipchains -A input  -i $CHOKE_DMZ_INTERFACE -p tcp ! -y \
        -s $BASTION_DMZ_IPADDR 143 \
        -d $CHOKE_DMZ_IPADDR $UNPRIVPORTS -j ACCEPT
```

Relaying Outgoing Mail Through an SMTP Server in the DMZ (TCP Port 25)

There are potential security advantages to hosting local mail services from a machine in the DMZ, rather than from the bastion machine. Your local server is responsible for collecting your outgoing mail, doing the DNS lookup on the destination hostname, and relaying the mail to its destination. Your client mail program points to your local SMTP server.

If you are relaying outgoing mail as an SMTP server and receiving mail as an SMTP client, you provide all your own mail services. Your local `sendmail` daemon is configured to relay outgoing mail to the remote destination hosts itself, as well as collect and deliver incoming mail:

```
MAIL_DMZ_INTERFACE="eth0"
MAIL_SERVER_DMZ_IPADDR="192.168.1.4"
```

DMZ SMTP Server Configuration

Table 4.12 lists the complete client/server connection protocol for SMTP.

Table 4.12   SMTP Mail Protocol on a DMZ Server

Description	Protocol	Remote Address	Remote Port	In/Out	Local Address	Local Port	TCP Flag
Receiving incoming mail	TCP	ANYWHERE	1024:65535	In	MAIL_SERVER_DMZ_IPADDR	25	Any
DMZ server response	TCP	ANYWHERE	1024:65535	Out	MAIL_SERVER_DMZ_IPADDR	25	ACK
Send outgoing mail	TCP	ANYWHERE	25	Out	MAIL_SERVER_DMZ_IPADDR	1024:65535	Any
Remote server response	TCP	ANYWHERE	25	In	MAIL_SERVER_DMZ_IPADDR	1024:65535	ACK

The first DMZ mail server ruleset assumes that the bastion machine either runs a mail server that automatically relays incoming mail from the Internet to the DMZ mail host, or forwards incoming connections directly to the server in the DMZ. This allows you to receive incoming mail for local machines:

```
ipchains -A input  -i $MAIL_DMZ_INTERFACE -p tcp \
         -s $ANYWHERE $UNPRIVPORTS \
         -d $MAIL_SERVER_DMZ_IPADDR 25 -j ACCEPT

ipchains -A output -i $MAIL_DMZ_INTERFACE -p tcp ! -y \
         -s $MAIL_SERVER_DMZ_IPADDR 25 \
         -d $ANYWHERE $UNPRIVPORTS -j ACCEPT
```

The next ruleset allows the DMZ mail server to relay local mail to its remote destinations:

```
ipchains -A output -i $MAIL_DMZ_INTERFACE -p tcp \
         -s $MAIL_SERVER_DMZ_IPADDR $UNPRIVPORTS \
         -d $ANYWHERE 25 -j ACCEPT

ipchains -A input  -i $MAIL_DMZ_INTERFACE -p tcp ! -y \
         -s $ANYWHERE 25 \
         -d $MAIL_SERVER_DMZ_IPADDR $UNPRIVPORTS -j ACCEPT
```

The previous DMZ mail server rulesets also cover the case where the bastion machine is not running a mail relay server. Instead, the bastion uses `ipmasqadm portfw` to forward incoming mail connections to the DMZ server. This allows you to directly receive incoming mail for local machines:

```
ipchains -A input  -i $MAIL_DMZ_INTERFACE -p tcp \
         -s $ANYWHERE $UNPRIVPORTS \
         -d $MAIL_SERVER_DMZ_IPADDR 25 -j ACCEPT

ipchains -A output -i $MAIL_DMZ_INTERFACE -p tcp ! -y \
         -s $MAIL_SERVER_DMZ_IPADDR 25 \
         -d $ANYWHERE $UNPRIVPORTS -j ACCEPT
```

Choke SMTP Client DMZ Configuration

Table 4.13 lists the choke's client connection protocol for SMTP.

Table 4.13 Choke Client SMTP Mail Protocol to a DMZ Server

Description	Protocol	Remote Address	Remote Port	In/ Out	Local Address	Local Port	TCP Flag
Send outgoing mail	TCP	MAIL_SERVER_DMZ_IPADDR	25	Out	CHOKE_DMZ_IPADDR	1024:65535	Any
Remote server response	TCP	MAIL_SERVER_DMZ_IPADDR	25	In	CHOKE_DMZ_IPADDR	1024:65535	ACK

This allows you to send mail from local machines:

```
ipchains -A output -i $CHOKE_DMZ_INTERFACE -p tcp \
        -s $CHOKE_DMZ_IPADDR $UNPRIVPORTS \
        -d $MAIL_SERVER_DMZ_IPADDR 25 -j ACCEPT

ipchains -A input -i $CHOKE_DMZ_INTERFACE -p tcp ! -y \
        -s $MAIL_SERVER_DMZ_IPADDR 25 \
        -d $CHOKE_DMZ_IPADDR $UNPRIVPORTS -j ACCEPT
```

Bastion SMTP Conduit DMZ Configuration

Table 4.14 lists the client/server connection protocol for SMTP.

Table 4.14   Bastion SMTP Mail Protocol on a DMZ Conduit

Description	Protocol	Remote Address	Remote Port	In/ Out	Local Address	Local Port	TCP Flag
Receiving incoming mail	TCP	ANYWHERE	1024:65535	In	IPADDR	25	Any
DMZ server response	TCP	ANYWHERE	1024:65535	Out	IPADDR	25	ACK
Send outgoing mail	TCP	ANYWHERE	25	Out	IPADDR	1024:65535	Any
Remote server response	TCP	ANYWHERE	25	In	IPADDR	1024:65535	ACK

This section covers the case where the bastion machine is not running a mail relay server. Instead, the bastion uses `ipmasqadm ipportfw` to forward incoming mail connections to the DMZ server.

The first two rulesets allow incoming mail connections to the mail server running in the DMZ:

```
ipchains -A input  -i $EXTERNAL_INTERFACE -p tcp \
        -s $ANYWHERE $UNPRIVPORTS \
        -d $IPADDR 25 -j ACCEPT

ipchains -A output -i $EXTERNAL_INTERFACE -p tcp ! -y \
        -s $IPADDR 25 \
        -d $ANYWHERE $UNPRIVPORTS -j ACCEPT

ipchains -A output -i $BASTION_DMZ_INTERFACE -p tcp \
        -s $ANYWHERE $UNPRIVPORTS \
        -d $MAIL_SERVER_DMZ_IPADDR 25 -j ACCEPT
```

```
ipchains -A input  -i $BASTION_DMZ_INTERFACE -p tcp ! -y \
        -s $MAIL_SERVER_DMZ_IPADDR 25 \
        -d $ANYWHERE $UNPRIVPORTS -j ACCEPT

ipmasqadm portfw -a -P tcp -L $IPADDR 25 -R $MAIL_SERVER_DMZ_IPADDR 25
```

The next rulesets allow the DMZ mail server to relay local mail to its remote destinations:

```
ipchains -A input  -i $BASTION_DMZ_INTERFACE -p tcp \
        -s $MAIL_SERVER_DMZ_IPADDR $UNPRIVPORTS \
        -d $ANYWHERE 25 -j ACCEPT

ipchains -A output -i $BASTION_DMZ_INTERFACE -p tcp ! -y \
        -s $ANYWHERE 25 \
        -d $MAIL_SERVER_DMZ_IPADDR $UNPRIVPORTS -j ACCEPT

ipchains -A output -i $EXTERNAL_INTERFACE -p tcp \
        -s $IPADDR $UNPRIVPORTS \
        -d $ANYWHERE 25 -j ACCEPT

ipchains -A input  -i $EXTERNAL_INTERFACE -p tcp ! -y \
        -s $ANYWHERE 25 \
        -d $IPADDR $UNPRIVPORTS -j ACCEPT

ipmasqadm portfw -a -P tcp -L 192.168.1.4 25 -R $IPADDR 25
```

Retrieving Mail as a POP Client to a DMZ Server (TCP Port 110)

Connecting to a POP server is a very common means of retrieving mail from a remote mail host. The following example demonstrates the firewall rules necessary to retrieve mail from a POP server running on a machine in the DMZ.

Your local POP server runs on the same machine in the DMZ that hosts the local mail server:

```
POP_DMZ_INTERFACE="eth0"
POP_SERVER_DMZ_IPADDR="192.168.1.4"
```

DMZ POP Server Configuration

Table 4.15 lists the server connection protocol for a POP server.

Table 4.15 POP Server Protocol from a DMZ Server

Description	Protocol	Remote Address	Remote Port	In/Out	Local Address	Local Port	TCP Flag
Choke client query	TCP	CHOKE_DMZ_IPADDR	1024:65535	In	POP_SERVER_DMZ_IPADDR	110	Any
Local server response	TCP	CHOKE_DMZ_IPADDR	1024:65535	Out	POP_SERVER_DMZ_IPADDR	110	ACK

The mail server machine in the DMZ hosts a local POP server for the LAN. External access is not allowed on the external interface:

```
ipchains -A input  -i $POP_DMZ_INTERFACE -p tcp \
        -s $CHOKE_DMZ_IPADDR $UNPRIVPORTS \
        -d $POP_SERVER_DMZ_IPADDR 110 -j ACCEPT

ipchains -A output -i $POP_DMZ_INTERFACE -p tcp ! -y \
        -s $POP_SERVER_DMZ_IPADDR 110 \
        -d $CHOKE_DMZ_IPADDR $UNPRIVPORTS -j ACCEPT
```

Choke POP Client DMZ Configuration

Table 4.16 lists the client connection protocol for a POP server.

Table 4.16   Choke POP Mail Retrieval Protocol from a DMZ Server

Description	Protocol	Remote Address	Remote Port	In/Out	Local Address	Local Port	TCP Flag
Choke client query	TCP	POP_SERVER_DMZ_IPADDR	110	Out	CHOKE_DMZ_IPADDR	1024:65535	Any
DMZ server response	TCP	POP_SERVER_DMZ_IPADDR	110	In	CHOKE_DMZ_IPADDR	1024:65535	ACK

You retrieve mail from the POP server running on the server in the DMZ:

```
ipchains -A output -i $CHOKE_DMZ_INTERFACE -p tcp \
        -s $CHOKE_DMZ_IPADDR $UNPRIVPORTS \
        -d $POP_SERVER_DMZ_IPADDR 110 -j ACCEPT

ipchains -A input  -i $CHOKE_DMZ_INTERFACE -p tcp ! -y \
        -s $POP_SERVER_DMZ_IPADDR 110 \
        -d $CHOKE_DMZ_IPADDR $UNPRIVPORTS -j ACCEPT
```

Retrieving Mail as an IMAP Client to a DMZ Server (TCP Port 143)

Connecting to an IMAP server is a very common means of retrieving mail from a remote mail host. The following example demonstrates the firewall rules necessary to retrieve mail from an IMAP server running on a machine in the DMZ.

Your local IMAP server runs on the same machine in the DMZ that hosts the local mail server:

```
IMAP_DMZ_INTERFACE="eth0"
IMAP_SERVER_DMZ_IPADDR="192.168.1.4"
```

DMZ IMAP Server Configuration

Table 4.17 lists the DMZ server connection protocol for IMAP.

Table 4.17 IMAP Server Protocol from a DMZ Server

Description	Protocol	Remote Address	Remote Port	In/Out	Local Address	Local Port	TCP Flag
Choke client query	TCP	CHOKE_DMZ_IPADDR	1024:65535	In	IPMAP_SERVER_DMZ_IPADDR	143	Any
DMZ server response	TCP	CHOKE_DMZ_IPADDR	1024:65535	Out	IPMAP_SERVER_DMZ_IPADDR	143	ACK

The mail server machine in the DMZ hosts a local IMAP server for the LAN. External access is not allowed on the external interface:

```
ipchains -A input  -i $IMAP_DMZ_INTERFACE -p tcp \
        -s $CHOKE_DMZ_IPADDR $UNPRIVPORTS \
        -d $IMAP_SERVER_DMZ_IPADDR 143 -j ACCEPT

ipchains -A output -i $IMAP_DMZ_INTERFACE -p tcp ! -y \
        -s $IMAP_SERVER_DMZ_IPADDR 143 \
        -d $CHOKE_DMZ_IPADDR $UNPRIVPORTS -j ACCEPT
```

Choke IMAP Client DMZ Configuration

Table 4.18 lists the choke's client connection protocol for IMAP.

Table 4.18 Choke IMAP Mail Retrieval Protocol from a DMZ Server

Description	Protocol	Remote Address	Remote Port	In/Out	Local Address	Local Port	TCP Flag
Choke client query	TCP	IPMAP_SERVER_DMZ_IPADDR	143	Out	CHOKE_DMZ_IPADDR	1024:65535	Any
DMZ server response	TCP	IPMAP_SERVER_DMZ_IPADDR	143	In	CHOKE_DMZ_IPADDR	1024:65535	ACK

You retrieve mail from the IMAP server running on the server in the DMZ:

```
ipchains -A output -i $CHOKE_DMZ_INTERFACE -p tcp \
        -s $CHOKE_DMZ_IPADDR $UNPRIVPORTS \
        -d $IMAP_SERVER_DMZ_IPADDR 143 -j ACCEPT

ipchains -A input  -i $CHOKE_DMZ_INTERFACE -p tcp ! -y \
        -s $IMAP_SERVER_DMZ_IPADDR 143 \
        -d $CHOKE_DMZ_IPADDR $UNPRIVPORTS -j ACCEPT
```

Accessing Usenet News Services (TCP NNTP Port 119)

Usenet news is accessed over the NNTP protocol running on top of TCP through service port 119. Reading news and posting articles is handled by your local news client.

A non-ISP site isn't likely to host a news server for the outside world. Even hosting a local news server is unlikely for a small site. For the exception, the server rule should be configured to allow incoming connections from only a select set of external clients. A public server wouldn't normally be hosted on the external bastion machine. It's more likely that a news server would be running on a machine in the DMZ and the bastion would forward incoming NNTP connections to the internal server machine.

Bastion NNTP Conduit and Server DMZ Configurations

Table 4.19 lists the complete client/server connection protocol for the NNTP Usenet news service.

Table 4.19   Bastion NNTP Client/Server Conduit Protocol

Description	Protocol	Remote Address	Remote Port	In/Out	Local Address	Local Port	TCP Flag
DMZ client query	TCP	CHOKE_DMZ_IPADDR	1024:65535	In	NEWS_SERVER	119	Any
Remote server response	TCP	CHOKE_DMZ_IPADDR	1024:65535	Out	NEWS_SERVER	119	ACK
Remote client query	TCP	NEWS_SERVER_DMZ_IPADDR	119	Out	NNTP clients	1024:65535	Any
DMZ server response	TCP	NEWS_SERVER_DMZ_IPADDR	119	In	NNTP clients	1024:65535	ACK
Local server query	TCP	NEWS_SERVER_DMZ_IPADDR	1024:65535	In	NEWS_FEED	119	Any
Remote server response	TCP	NEWS_SERVER_DMZ_IPADDR	1024:65535	Out	NEWS_FEED	119	ACK

The server rules allow local connections to your ISP's news server. Both reading news and posting articles are handled by this ruleset:

```
ipchains -A input  -i $BASTION_DMZ_INTERFACE -p tcp \
        -s $CHOKE_DMZ_IPADDR $UNPRIVPORTS \
        -d $NEWS_SERVER 119 -j ACCEPT

ipchains -A output -i $BASTION_DMZ_INTERFACE -p tcp ! -y \
        -s $NEWS_SERVER 119 \
        -d $CHOKE_DMZ_IPADDR $UNPRIVPORTS -j ACCEPT
```

If a local news server is running on a machine in the DMZ, offering public service to select remote clients, a set of server rules allowing remote clients to connect to this machine's NNTP port is defined:

```
NEWS_SERVER_DMZ_IPADDR="192.168.1.6"

ipchains -A output -i $BASTION_DMZ_INTERFACE -p tcp \
         -s <my.news.clients> $UNPRIVPORTS \
         -d $NEWS_SERVER_DMZ_IPADDR 119 -j ACCEPT

ipchains -A input  -i $BASTION_DMZ_INTERFACE -p tcp ! -y \
         -s $NEWS_SERVER_DMZ_IPADDR 119 \
         -d $<my.news.clients> $UNPRIVPORTS -j ACCEPT
```

If the DMZ machines are assigned private class IP addresses, the port forwarding module is necessary:

```
ipmasqadm portfw -a -P tcp -L <my.news.clients> 119 \
                 -R $NEWS_SERVER_DMZ_IPADDR 119
```

If the local news server provides public Usenet newsgroups, as well as local newsgroups, the local server requires a news feed from a remote server. The following rules allow access to a remote news server acting as a news feed:

```
NEWS_FEED="<my.remote.news.feed>"

ipchains -A input  -i $BASTION_DMZ_INTERFACE -p tcp \
         -s $NEWS_SERVER_DMZ_IPADDR $UNPRIVPORTS \
         -d $NEWS_FEED 119 -j ACCEPT

ipchains -A output -i $BASTION_DMZ_INTERFACE -p tcp ! -y \
         -s $NEWS_FEED 119 \
         -d $NEWS_SERVER_DMZ_IPADDR $UNPRIVPORTS -j ACCEPT
```

Choke NNTP Client DMZ Configurations

Table 4.20 lists the complete client/server connection protocol for the NNTP Usenet news service.

Table 4.20   Choke NNTP Client Protocol

Description	Protocol	Remote Address	Remote Port	In/Out	Local Address	Local Port	TCP Flag
Choke client query	TCP	NEWS_SERVER	119	Out	CHOKE_DMZ_IPADDR	1024:65535	Any
Remote server response	TCP	NEWS_SERVER	119	In	CHOKE_DMZ_IPADDR	1024:65535	ACK
Choke client query	TCP	NEWS_SERVER_DMZ_IPADDR	119	Out	CHOKE_DMZ_IPADDR	1024:65535	Any
DMZ server response	TCP	NEWS_SERVER_DMZ_IPADDR	119	In	CHOKE_DMZ_IPADDR	1024:65535	ACK

The next two rules allow local clients to access remote news servers:

```
ipchains -A output -i $CHOKE_DMZ_INTERFACE -p tcp \
        -s $CHOKE_DMZ_IPADDR $UNPRIVPORTS\
        -d $NEWS_SERVER 119 -j ACCEPT

ipchains -A input  -i $CHOKE_DMZ_INTERFACE -p tcp ! -y \
        -s $NEWS_SERVER 119 \
        -d $CHOKE_DMZ_IPADDR $UNPRIVPORTS-j ACCEPT
```

The next two rules allow local clients to access a local news server in the DMZ:

```
ipchains -A output -i $CHOKE_DMZ_INTERFACE -p tcp \
        -s $CHOKE_DMZ_IPADDR $UNPRIVPORTS\
        -d $NEWS_SERVER_DMZ_IPADDR 119 -j ACCEPT

ipchains -A input  -i $CHOKE_DMZ_INTERFACE -p tcp ! -y \
        -s $NEWS_SERVER_DMZ_IPADDR 119 \
        -d $CHOKE_DMZ_IPADDR $UNPRIVPORTS-j ACCEPT
```

Telnet (TCP Port 23)

Depending on your level of trust, you will probably conclude that internal `telnet` service is perfectly acceptable. Depending on the other non–UNIX machine types on the LAN, `telnet` may be the only tool available.

The client and server rules here allow access to and from anywhere. If you use `telnet`, you might be able to limit the external addresses to a select subset. If that isn't practical, `telnet` should still be limited in `/etc/hosts.allow`.

Bastion Telnet DMZ Configuration

Table 4.21 lists the complete client/server connection protocol for the Telnet service.

Table 4.21 Bastion Telnet Protocol

Description	Protocol	Remote Address	Remote Port	In/Out	Local Address	Local Port	TCP Flag
Choke client request	TCP	CHOKE_DMZ_IPADDR	1024:65535	In	ANYWHERE	23	Any
Server response	TCP	CHOKE_DMZ_IPADDR	1024:65535	Out	ANYWHERE	23	ACK
Bastian client request	TCP	DMZ_ADDRESSES	23	Out	BASTION_DMZ_IPADDR	1024:65535	Any
DMZ server response	TCP	DMZ_ADDRESSES	23	In	BASTION_DMZ_IPADDR0	1024:65535	ACK

Note that incoming `telnet` connections from clients are allowed only from the choke firewall, as opposed to anywhere. `telnet` access from other machines in the DMZ is not allowed:

```
ipchains -A input  -i $BASTION_DMZ_INTERFACE -p tcp \
        -s $CHOKE_DMZ_IPADDR $UNPRIVPORTS \
        -d $ANYWHERE 23 -j ACCEPT

ipchains -A output -i $BASTION_DMZ_INTERFACE -p tcp ! -y \
        -s $ANYWHERE 23 \
        -d $CHOKE_DMZ_IPADDR $UNPRIVPORTS -j ACCEPT
```

The next two rules allow Telnet access from the bastion to any machine in the DMZ:

```
ipchains -A output -i $BASTION_DMZ_INTERFACE -p tcp \
        -s $BASTION_DMZ_IPADDR $UNPRIVPORTS \
        -d $DMZ_ADDRESSES 23 -j ACCEPT

ipchains -A input  -i $BASTION_DMZ_INTERFACE -p tcp ! -y \
        -s $DMZ_ADDRESSES 23 \
        -d $BASTION_DMZ_IPADDR $UNPRIVPORTS -j ACCEPT
```

Choke Telnet DMZ Configuration

Table 4.22 lists the complete client/server connection protocol for the Telnet service.

Table 4.22   Choke Telnet Protocol

Description	Protocol	Remote Address	Remote Port	In/Out	Local Address	Local Port	TCP Flag
Choke client request	TCP	ANYWHERE	23	Out	CHOKE_DMZ_IPADDR	1024:65535	Any
Remote server response	TCP	ANYWHERE	23	In	CHOKE_DMZ_IPADDR	1024:65535	ACK
Bastion client request	TCP	BASTION_DMZ_IPADDR	1024:65535	In	CHOKE_DMZ_IPADDR	23	Any
Choke server response	TCP	BASTION_DMZ_IPADDR	1024:65535	Out	CHOKE_DMZ_IPADDR	23	ACK

Note that outgoing `telnet` connections are allowed to anywhere, allowing for LAN clients that need to `telnet` to remote sites on the Internet:

```
ipchains -A output -i $CHOKE_DMZ_INTERFACE -p tcp \
        -s $CHOKE_DMZ_IPADDR $UNPRIVPORTS \
        -d $ANYWHERE 23 -j ACCEPT

ipchains -A input  -i $CHOKE_DMZ_INTERFACE -p tcp ! -y \
        -s $ANYWHERE 23 \
        -d $CHOKE_DMZ_IPADDR $UNPRIVPORTS -j ACCEPT
```

These rules allow `telnet` access from the bastion to the choke firewall machine. Incoming `telnet` access is not allowed from other machines in the DMZ:

```
ipchains -A input  -i $CHOKE_DMZ_INTERFACE -p tcp \
         -s $BASTION_DMZ_IPADDR $UNPRIVPORTS \
         -d $CHOKE_DMZ_IPADDR 23 -j ACCEPT

ipchains -A output -i $CHOKE_DMZ_INTERFACE -p tcp ! -y \
         -s $CHOKE_DMZ_IPADDR 23 \
         -d $BASTION_DMZ_IPADDR $UNPRIVPORTS -j ACCEPT
```

SSH (TCP Port 22)

The client and server rules here allow access to and from anywhere. In practice, a home-based site would probably limit the external addresses to a select subset, particularly since both ends of the connection must be configured to recognize each individual user account. Although it's not recommended to use `inetd` to start `sshd`, `sshd` can be compiled to honor the host access lists in `/etc/hosts.allow` and `/etc/hosts.deny`.

Bastion SSH Server and Conduit Protocol DMZ Configuration

Table 4.23 lists the server connection protocol for the SSH service.

Table 4.23   Bastion SSH Server Protocol

Description	Protocol	Remote Address	Remote Port	In/Out	Local Address	Local Port	TCP Flag
Choke cilent request	TCP	CHOKE_DMZ_IPADDR	1024:65535	In	ANYWHERE	22	Any
Server response	TCP	CHOKE_DMZ_IPADDR	1024:65535	Out	ANYWHERE	22	ACK
Choke client request	TCP	CHOKE_DMZ_IPADDR	513:1023	In	ANYWHERE	22	Any
Server response	TCP	CHOKE_DMZ_IPADDR	513:1023	Out	ANYWHERE	22	ACK

These rules allow local connections from the choke machine to both an `sshd` server running on the bastion and to external sites:

```
ipchains -A input  -i $BASTION_DMZ_INTERFACE -p tcp \
         -s $CHOKE_DMZ_IPADDR $UNPRIVPORTS \
         -d $ANYWHERE 22 -j ACCEPT

ipchains -A output -i $BASTION_DMZ_INTERFACE -p tcp ! -y \
         -s $ANYWHERE 22 \
         -d $CHOKE_DMZ_IPADDR $UNPRIVPORTS -j ACCEPT
```

```
ipchains -A input  -i $BASTION_DMZ_INTERFACE -p tcp \
        -s $CHOKE_DMZ_IPADDR $SSH_PORTS \
        -d $ANYWHERE 22 -j ACCEPT

ipchains -A output -i $BASTION_DMZ_INTERFACE -p tcp ! -y \
        -s $ANYWHERE 22 \
        -d $CHOKE_DMZ_IPADDR $SSH_PORTS -j ACCEPT
```

Bastion SSH Client Protocol DMZ Configuration

Table 4.24 lists the client connection protocol for the SSH service.

Table 4.24   Bastion SSH Client Protocol

Description	Protocol	Remote Address	Remote Port	In/ Out	Local Address	Local Port	TCP Flag
Bastion client request	TCP	DMZ_ADDRESSES	22	Out	BASTION_DMZ_IPADDR	1024:65535	Any
DMZ server response	TCP	DMZ_ADDRESSES	22	In	BASTION_DMZ_IPADDR	1024:65535	ACK
Bastion client request	TCP	DMZ_ADDRESSES	22	Out	BASTION_DMZ_IPADDR	513:1023	Any
DMZ server response	TCP	DMZ_ADDRESSES	22	In	BASTION_DMZ_IPADDR	513:1023	ACK

These rules allow the bastion to connect to all local machines in the DMZ:

```
ipchains -A output -i $BASTION_DMZ_INTERFACE -p tcp \
        -s $BASTION_DMZ_IPADDR $UNPRIVPORTS \
        -d $DMZ_ADDRESSES 22 -j ACCEPT

ipchains -A input  -i $BASTION_DMZ_INTERFACE -p tcp ! -y \
        -s $DMZ_ADDRESSES 22 \
        -d $BASTION_DMZ_IPADDR $UNPRIVPORTS -j ACCEPT

ipchains -A output -i $BASTION_DMZ_INTERFACE -p tcp \
        -s $BASTION_DMZ_IPADDR $SSH_PORTS \
        -d $DMZ_ADDRESSES 22 -j ACCEPT

ipchains -A input  -i $BASTION_DMZ_INTERFACE -p tcp ! -y \
        -s $DMZ_ADDRESSES 22 \
        -d $BASTION_DMZ_IPADDR $SSH_PORTS -j ACCEPT
```

Choke SSH Client Protocol DMZ Configuration

Table 4.25 lists the client connection protocol for the SSH service.

Table 4.25 Choke SSH Client Protocol

Description	Protocol	Remote Address	Remote Port	In/ Out	Local Address	Local Port	TCP Flag
Choke client request	TCP	ANYWHERE	22	Out	CHOKE_DMZ_IPADDR	1024:65535	Any
Remote server response	TCP	ANYWHERE	22	In	CHOKE_DMZ_IPADDR	1024:65535	ACK
Choke client request	TCP	ANYWHERE	22	Out	CHOKE_DMZ_IPADDR	513:1023	Any
Remote server response	TCP	ANYWHERE	22	In	CHOKE_DMZ_IPADDR	513:1023	ACK

These rules allow you to connect to remote sites using ssh:

```
ipchains -A output -i $CHOKE_DMZ_INTERFACE -p tcp \
        -s $CHOKE_DMZ_IPADDR $UNPRIVPORTS \
        -d $ANYWHERE 22 -j ACCEPT

ipchains -A input  -i $CHOKE_DMZ_INTERFACE -p tcp ! -y \
        -s $ANYWHERE 22 \
        -d $CHOKE_DMZ_IPADDR $UNPRIVPORTS -j ACCEPT

ipchains -A output -i $CHOKE_DMZ_INTERFACE -p tcp \
        -s $CHOKE_DMZ_IPADDR $SSH_PORTS \
        -d $ANYWHERE 22 -j ACCEPT

ipchains -A input  -i $CHOKE_DMZ_INTERFACE -p tcp ! -y \
        -s $ANYWHERE 22 \
        -d $CHOKE_DMZ_IPADDR $SSH_PORTS -j ACCEPT
```

Choke SSH Server Protocol DMZ Configuration

Table 4.26 lists the server connection protocol for the SSH service.

Table 4.26   Choke SSH Server Protocol

Description	Protocol	Remote Address	Remote Port	In/Out	Local Address	Local Port	TCP Flag
Bastion client request	TCP	BASTION_DMZ_IPADDR	1024:65535	In	CHOKE_DMZ_IPADDR	22	Any
Choke server response	TCP	BASTION_DMZ_IPADDR	1024:65535	Out	CHOKE_DMZ_IPADDR	22	ACK
Bastion client request	TCP	BASTION_DMZ_IPADDR	513:1023	In	CHOKE_DMZ_IPADDR	22	Any
Choke server response	TCP	BASTION_DMZ_IPADDR	513:1023	Out	CHOKE_DMZ_IPADDR	22	ACK

These rules allow incoming connections from the bastion to your sshd server:

```
ipchains -A input  -i $CHOKE_DMZ_INTERFACE -p tcp \
         -s $BASTION_FIREWALL $UNPRIVPORTS \
         -d $CHOKE_DMZ_IPADDR 22 -j ACCEPT

ipchains -A output -i $CHOKE_DMZ_INTERFACE -p tcp ! -y \
         -s $CHOKE_DMZ_IPADDR 22 \
         -d $BASTION_FIREWALL $UNPRIVPORTS -j ACCEPT

ipchains -A input  -i $CHOKE_DMZ_INTERFACE -p tcp \
         -s $BASTION_FIREWALL $SSH_PORTS \
         -d $CHOKE_DMZ_IPADDR 22 -j ACCEPT

ipchains -A output -i $CHOKE_DMZ_INTERFACE -p tcp ! -y \
         -s $CHOKE_DMZ_IPADDR 22 \
         -d $BASTION_FIREWALL $SSH_PORTS -j ACCEPT
```

FTP (TCP Ports 21 and 20)

FTP has two modes for exchanging data between a client and server, normal data channel port mode and passive data channel mode. Port mode is the default mechanism when using the ftp client program and connecting to a remote FTP site. Passive mode is the default mechanism when connecting to an FTP site through a Web browser. Occasionally, you might encounter an FTP site that supports only one mode or the other.

Three approaches to client and server FTP combinations are described in this section:

- The bastion is a gateway to remote FTP servers, as well as a possible local server; the choke machine is a client.
- The bastion is a client to internal servers; the choke machine is an FTP server.
- An FTP server runs in the DMZ; the bastion and choke machines are clients.

Bastion as FTP Server or Conduit, Choke as Client

It's almost a given that most sites will want FTP client access to remote file repositories. The first section allows internal hosts to connect to FTP servers both on the bastion and on remote hosts.

Incoming Local Client–to–Bastion Server Connections

Table 4.27 lists the server connection protocol for the FTP service.

Table 4.27 Bastion FTP Server Protocol

Description	Protocol	Remote Address	Remote Port	In/ Out	Local Address	Local Port	TCP Flag
Choke client request	TCP	CHOKE_DMZ_IPADDR	1024:65535	In	ANYWHERE	21	Any
Bastion server response	TCP	CHOKE_DMZ_IPADDR	1024:65535	Out	ANYWHERE	21	ACK
Bastion server port data channel request	TCP	CHOKE_DMZ_IPADDR	1024:65535	Out	ANYWHERE	20	Any
Choke client port data channel response	TCP	CHOKE_DMZ_IPADDR	1024:65535	In	ANYWHERE	20	ACK
Choke client passive data channel request	TCP	CHOKE_DMZ_IPADDR	1024:65535	In	ANYWHERE	1024:65535	Any
Bastion server passive data channel response	TCP	CHOKE_DMZ_IPADDR	1024:65535	Out	ANYWHERE	1024:65535	ACK

The following rules allow incoming `ftp` client connections from the choke machine, as well as from machines on the private LAN behind the choke firewall:

```
# Incoming FTP Client Request
# ------------------------

ipchains -A input  -i $BASTION_DMZ_INTERFACE -p tcp \
         -s $CHOKE_DMZ_IPADDR $UNPRIVPORTS \
         -d $ANYWHERE 21 -j ACCEPT

ipchains -A output -i $BASTION_DMZ_INTERFACE -p tcp ! -y \
         -s $ANYWHERE 21 \
         -d $CHOKE_DMZ_IPADDR $UNPRIVPORTS -j ACCEPT

# Port Mode Data Channel Responses
# ------------------------------------

ipchains -A output -i $BASTION_DMZ_INTERFACE -p tcp \
         -s $ANYWHERE 20 \
         -d $CHOKE_DMZ_IPADDR $UNPRIVPORTS -j ACCEPT

ipchains -A input  -i $BASTION_DMZ_INTERFACE -p tcp ! -y \
         -s $CHOKE_DMZ_IPADDR $UNPRIVPORTS \
         -d $ANYWHERE 20 -j ACCEPT

# Passive Mode Data Channel Responses
# --------------------------------

ipchains -A input  -i $BASTION_DMZ_INTERFACE -p tcp \
         -s $CHOKE_DMZ_IPADDR $UNPRIVPORTS \
         -d $ANYWHERE $UNPRIVPORTS -j ACCEPT

ipchains -A output -i $BASTION_DMZ_INTERFACE -p tcp ! -y \
         -s $ANYWHERE $UNPRIVPORTS \
         -d $CHOKE_DMZ_IPADDR $UNPRIVPORTS -j ACCEPT
```

Outgoing Choke–to–External Server Connections

Table 4.28 lists the client connection protocol for the FTP service.

Table 4.28   Choke FTP Client Protocol

Description	Protocol	Remote Address	Remote Port	In/ Out	Local Address	Local Port	TCP Flag
Choke client request	TCP	ANYWHERE	21	Out	CHOKE_DMZ_IPADDR	1024:65535	Any
Remote server response	TCP	ANYWHERE	21	In	CHOKE_DMZ_IPADDR	1024:65535	ACK
Remote server port data channel request	TCP	ANYWHERE	20	In	CHOKE_DMZ_IPADDR	1024:65535	Any
Choke client port data channel response	TCP	ANYWHERE	20	Out	CHOKE_DMZ_IPADDR	1024:65535	ACK
Choke client passive data channel request	TCP	ANYWHERE	1024:65535	Out	CHOKE_DMZ_IPADDR	1024:65535	Any
Remote server passive data channel response	TCP	ANYWHERE	1024:65535	In	CHOKE_DMZ_IPADDR	1024:65535	ACK

The following rules allow outgoing `ftp` client connections from the choke machine, as well as from machines on the private LAN behind the choke firewall:

```
# Outgoing FTP Client Request
# -------------------------

ipchains -A output -i $CHOKE_DMZ_INTERFACE -p tcp \
         -s $CHOKE_DMZ_IPADDR $UNPRIVPORTS \
         -d $ANYWHERE 21 -j ACCEPT

ipchains -A input  -i $CHOKE_DMZ_INTERFACE -p tcp ! -y \
         -s $ANYWHERE 21 \
         -d $CHOKE_DMZ_IPADDR $UNPRIVPORTS -j ACCEPT

# Port Mode Data Channel Responses
# ------------------------------------

ipchains -A input  -i $CHOKE_DMZ_INTERFACE -p tcp \
         -s $ANYWHERE 20 \
         -d $CHOKE_DMZ_IPADDR $UNPRIVPORTS -j ACCEPT
```

```
ipchains -A output -i $CHOKE_DMZ_INTERFACE -p tcp ! -y \
        -s $CHOKE_DMZ_IPADDR $UNPRIVPORTS \
        -d $ANYWHERE 20 -j ACCEPT

# Passive Mode Data Channel Responses
# -------------------------------------

ipchains -A output -i $CHOKE_DMZ_INTERFACE -p tcp \
        -s $CHOKE_DMZ_IPADDR $UNPRIVPORTS \
        -d $ANYWHERE $UNPRIVPORTS -j ACCEPT

ipchains -A input  -i $CHOKE_DMZ_INTERFACE -p tcp ! -y \
        -s $ANYWHERE $UNPRIVPORTS \
        -d $CHOKE_DMZ_IPADDR $UNPIRVPORTS -j ACCEPT
```

Bastion as Client, Choke as Internal FTP Server

It's often too convenient to ftp files between the bastion and internal machines. The following section is a special case. The bastion machine itself is allowed ftp access to the choke machine as a client. Client access from the bastion would not normally be allowed in a tightly secure environment.

Outgoing Bastion Client–to–Choke FTP Server Connections

Table 4.29 lists the client connection protocol for the FTP service.

Table 4.29   Bastion FTP Client Protocol

Description	Protocol	Remote Address	Remote Port	In/Out	Local Address	Local Port	TCP Flag
Bastion client request	TCP	CHOKE_DMZ_IPADDR	21	Out	BASTION_DMZ_IPADDR	1024:65535	Any
Choke server response	TCP	CHOKE_DMZ_IPADDR	21	In	BASTION_DMZ_IPADDR	1024:65535	ACK
Choke server port data channel request	TCP	CHOKE_DMZ_IPADDR	20	In	BASTION_DMZ_IPADDR	1024:65535	Any
Bastion client port data channel response	TCP	CHOKE_DMZ_IPADDR	20	Out	BASTION_DMZ_IPADDR	1024:65535	ACK
Bastion client passive data channel request	TCP	CHOKE_DMZ_IPADDR	1024:65535	Out	BASTION_DMZ_IPADDR	1024:65535	Any
Choke server passive data channel response	TCP	CHOKE_DMZ_IPADDR	1024:65535	In	BASTION_DMZ_IPADDR	1024:65535	ACK

The following rules allow outgoing `ftp` client connections from the bastion machine to the choke machine:

```
# Outgoing FTP Client Request
# -------------------------

ipchains -A output -i $BASTION_DMZ_INTERFACE -p tcp \
        -s $BASTION_DMZ_IPADDR $UNPRIVPORTS \
        -d $CHOKE_DMZ_IPADDR 21 -j ACCEPT

ipchains -A input  -i $BASTION_DMZ_INTERFACE -p tcp ! -y \
        -s $CHOKE_DMZ_IPADDR 21 \
        -d $BASTION_DMZ_IPADDR $UNPRIVPORTS -j ACCEPT

# Port Mode Data Channel Responses
# --------------------------------------

ipchains -A input  -i $BASTION_DMZ_INTERFACE -p tcp \
        -s $CHOKE_DMZ_IPADDR 20 \
        -d $BASTION_DMZ_IPADDR $UNPRIVPORTS -j ACCEPT

ipchains -A output -i $BASTION_DMZ_INTERFACE -p tcp ! -y \
        -s $BASTION_DMZ_IPADDR $UNPRIVPORTS \
        -d $CHOKE_DMZ_IPADDR 20 -j ACCEPT

# Passive Mode Data Channel Responses
# --------------------------------

ipchains -A output -i $BASTION_DMZ_INTERFACE -p tcp \
        -s $BASTION_DMZ_IPADDR $UNPRIVPORTS \
        -d $CHOKE_DMZ_IPADDR $UNPRIVPORTS -j ACCEPT

ipchains -A input  -i $BASTION_DMZ_INTERFACE -p tcp ! -y \
        -s $CHOKE_DMZ_IPADDR $UNPRIVPORTS \
        -d $BASTION_DMZ_IPADDR $UNPIRVPORTS -j ACCEPT
```

Incoming Bastion Client–to–Choke Server Connections

Table 4.30 lists the server connection protocol for the FTP service.

Table 4.30   Choke FTP Server Protocol

Description	Protocol	Remote Address	Remote Port	In/Out	Local Address	Local Port	TCP Flag
Bastion client request	TCP	BASTION_DMZ_IPADDR	1024:65535	In	CHOKE_DMZ_IPADDR	21	Any
Choke server response	TCP	BASTION_DMZ_IPADDR	1024:65535	Out	CHOKE_DMZ_IPADDR	21	ACK
Choke server port data channel request	TCP	BASTION_DMZ_IPADDR	1024:65535	Out	CHOKE_DMZ_IPADDR	20	Any
Bastion client port data channel response	TCP	BASTION_DMZ_IPADDR	1024:65535	In	CHOKE_DMZ_IPADDR	20	ACK
Bastion client passive data channel request	TCP	BASTION_DMZ_IPADDR	1024:65535	In	CHOKE_DMZ_IPADDR	1024:65535	Any
Choke server passive data channel response	TCP	BASTION_DMZ_IPADDR	1024:65535	Out	CHOKE_DMZ_IPADDR	1024:65535	ACK

The following rules allow incoming `ftp` client connections from the bastion machine to the choke machine:

```
# Incoming FTP Client Request
# --------------------------

ipchains -A input  -i $CHOKE_DMZ_INTERFACE -p tcp \
        -s $BASTION_DMZ_IPADDR $UNPRIVPORTS \
        -d $CHOKE_DMZ_IPADDR 21 -j ACCEPT

ipchains -A output -i $CHOKE_DMZ_INTERFACE -p tcp ! -y \
        -s $CHOKE_DMZ_IPADDR 21 \
        -d $BASTION_DMZ_IPADDR $UNPRIVPORTS -j ACCEPT

# Port Mode Data Channel Responses
# ------------------------------------

ipchains -A output -i $CHOKE_DMZ_INTERFACE -p tcp \
        -s $CHOKE_DMZ_IPADDR 20 \
        -d $BASTION_DMZ_IPADDR $UNPRIVPORTS -j ACCEPT

ipchains -A input  -i $CHOKE_DMZ_INTERFACE -p tcp ! -y \
        -s $BASTION_DMZ_IPADDR $UNPRIVPORTS \
        -d $CHOKE_DMZ_IPADDR 20 -j ACCEPT

# Passive Mode Data Channel Responses
# ---------------------------------
```

```
ipchains -A input  -i $CHOKE_DMZ_INTERFACE -p tcp \
        -s $BASTION_DMZ_IPADDR $UNPRIVPORTS \
        -d $CHOKE_DMZ_IPADDR $UNPRIVPORTS -j ACCEPT

ipchains -A output -i $CHOKE_DMZ_INTERFACE -p tcp ! -y \
        -s $CHOKE_DMZ_IPADDR $UNPRIVPORTS \
        -d $BASTION_DMZ_IPADDR $UNPRIVPORTS -j ACCEPT
```

FTP Server in DMZ, Bastion and Choke as Clients

Although similar to the earlier section allowing the bastion machine itself client access to the choke machine, the following section allows incoming client requests to a public FTP server in the DMZ.

FTP Server in the DMZ

Table 4.31 lists the server connection protocol for the FTP service running on a machine in the DMZ.

Table 4.31 DMZ FTP Server Protocol

Description	Protocol	Remote Address	Remote Port	In/Out	Local Address	Local Port	TCP Flag
Remote client request	TCP	DMZ_ADDRESSES	1024:65535	In	FTP_SERVER_DMZ_IPADDR	21	Any
DMZ server response	TCP	DMZ_ADDRESSES	1024:65535	Out	FTP_SERVER_DMZ_IPADDR	21	ACK
DMZ server port data channel request	TCP	DMZ_ADDRESSES	1024:65535	Out	FTP_SERVER_DMZ_IPADDR	20	Any
Remote client port data channel response	TCP	DMZ_ADDRESSES	1024:65535	In	FTP_SERVER_DMZ_IPADDR	20	ACK
Remote client passive data channel request	TCP	DMZ_ADDRESSES	1024:65535	In	FTP_SERVER_DMZ_IPADDR	1024:65535	Any
DMZ server passive data channel response	TCP	DMZ_ADDRESSES	1024:65535	Out	FTP_SERVER_DMZ_IPADDR	1024:65535	ACK

The following rules allow incoming `ftp` client connections from any machine in the DMZ network, including both the bastion and choke machines:

```
# Incoming FTP Client Request
# --------------------------

ipchains -A input  -i $DMZ_INTERFACE -p tcp \
        -s $DMZ_ADDRESSES $UNPRIVPORTS \
        -d $FTP_SERVER_DMZ_IPADDR 21 -j ACCEPT

ipchains -A output -i $DMZ_INTERFACE -p tcp ! -y \
        -s $FTP_SERVER_DMZ_IPADDR 21 \
        -d $DMZ_ADDRESSES $UNPRIVPORTS -j ACCEPT

# Port Mode Data Channel Responses
# ---------------------------------------

ipchains -A output -i $DMZ_INTERFACE -p tcp \
        -s $FTP_SERVER_DMZ_IPADDR 20 \
        -d $DMZ_ADDRESSES $UNPRIVPORTS -j ACCEPT

ipchains -A input  -i $DMZ_INTERFACE -p tcp ! -y \
        -s $DMZ_ADDRESSES $UNPRIVPORTS \
        -d $FTP_SERVER_DMZ_IPADDR 20 -j ACCEPT

# Passive Mode Data Channel Responses
# ---------------------------------

ipchains -A input  -i $DMZ_INTERFACE -p tcp \
        -s $DMZ_ADDRESSES $UNPRIVPORTS \
        -d $FTP_SERVER_DMZ_IPADDR $UNPRIVPORTS -j ACCEPT

ipchains -A output -i $DMZ_INTERFACE -p tcp ! -y \
        -s $FTP_SERVER_DMZ_IPADDR $UNPRIVPORTS \
        -d $DMZ_ADDRESSES $UNPRIVPORTS -j ACCEPT
```

Choke as Client to an FTP DMZ Server

Table 4.32 lists the client connection protocol for the FTP service.

Table 4.32 Choke FTP Client Protocol

Description	Protocol	Remote Address	Remote Port	In/Out	Local Address	Local Port	TCP Flag
Choke client request	TCP	FTP_SERVER_DMZ_IPADDR	21	Out	CHOKE_DMZ_IPADDR	1024:65535	Any
DMZ server response	TCP	FTP_SERVER_DMZ_IPADDR	21	In	CHOKE_DMZ_IPADDR	1024:65535	ACK
DMZ server port data channel request	TCP	FTP_SERVER_DMZ_IPADDR	20	In	CHOKE_DMZ_IPADDR	1024:65535	Any
Choke client port data channel response	TCP	FTP_SERVER_DMZ_IPADDR	20	Out	CHOKE_DMZ_IPADDR	1024:65535	ACK
Choke client passive data channel request	TCP	FTP_SERVER_DMZ_IPADDR	1024:65535	Out	CHOKE_DMZ_IPADDR	1024:65535	Any
DMZ server passive data channel response	TCP	FTP_SERVER_DMZ_IPADDR	1024:65535	In	CHOKE_DMZ_IPADDR	1024:65535	ACK

The following rules allow outgoing `ftp` client connections from the choke machine to an `ftp` server anywhere:

```
# Outgoing FTP Client Request
# --------------------------

ipchains -A output -i $CHOKE_DMZ_INTERFACE -p tcp \
        -s $CHOKE_DMZ_IPADDR $UNPRIVPORTS \
        -d $ANYWHERE 21 -j ACCEPT

ipchains -A input  -i $CHOKE_DMZ_INTERFACE -p tcp ! -y \
        -s $ANYWHERE 21 \
        -d $CHOKE_DMZ_IPADDR $UNPRIVPORTS -j ACCEPT

# Port Mode Data Channel Responses
# -------------------------------------

ipchains -A input  -i $CHOKE_DMZ_INTERFACE -p tcp \
        -s $ANYWHERE 20 \
        -d $CHOKE_DMZ_IPADDR $UNPRIVPORTS -j ACCEPT

ipchains -A output -i $CHOKE_DMZ_INTERFACE -p tcp ! -y \
        -s $CHOKE_DMZ_IPADDR $UNPRIVPORTS \
        -d $ANYWHERE 20 -j ACCEPT
```

```
# Passive Mode Data Channel Responses
# --------------------------------

ipchains -A output -i $CHOKE_DMZ_INTERFACE -p tcp \
        -s $CHOKE_DMZ_IPADDR $UNPRIVPORTS \
        -d $ANYWHERE $UNPRIVPORTS -j ACCEPT

ipchains -A input  -i $CHOKE_DMZ_INTERFACE -p tcp ! -y \
        -s $ANYWHERE $UNPRIVPORTS \
        -d $CHOKE_DMZ_IPADDR $UNPIRVPORTS -j ACCEPT
```

Web Services

Web services are generally based on the HTTP protocol. Several higher-level communication protocols are used for special purposes, including HTTPS for secure (SSL) access, and Web server proxy access.

Three approaches to client and server Web combinations are described in this section:

- The bastion is a server, or a gateway conduit to remote Web servers; the choke machine is a client.

- The bastion is a server, or a gateway conduit; a Web server runs in the DMZ; and the choke machine is a client.

- The bastion is a server, or a gateway conduit; the choke machine is a local Web proxy server.

Bastion as Web Server or Conduit, Choke as Client

It's almost inconceivable in today's world that a home-based site would not want to access the World Wide Web. The first section allows internal hosts to connect to Web servers both on the bastion and on remote hosts.

Incoming Internal Client Connections to Bastion Server

Table 4.33 lists the server connection protocol for the HTTP Web service.

Table 4.33   Bastion HTTP Server Protocol

Description	Protocol	Remote Address	Remote Port	In/ Out	Local Address	Local Port	TCP Flag
Choke client request	TCP	CHOKE_DMZ_IPADDR	1024:65535	In	ANYWHERE	80	Any
Server response	TCP	CHOKE_DMZ_IPADDR	1024:65535	Out	ANYWHERE	80	ACK

The following rules allow incoming HTTP client connections from the choke machine, as well as from machines on the private LAN behind the choke firewall:

```
ipchains -A input  -i $BASTION_DMZ_INTERFACE -p tcp \
        -s $CHOKE_DMZ_IPADDR $UNPRIVPORTS \
        -d $ANYWHERE 80 -j ACCEPT

ipchains -A output -i $BASTION_DMZ_INTERFACE -p tcp ! -y \
        -s $ANYWHERE 80 \
        -d $CHOKE_DMZ_IPADDR $UNPRIVPORTS -j ACCEPT
```

Table 4.34 lists the server connection protocol for the SSL service.

Table 4.34   Bastion SSL Server Protocol

Description	Protocol	Remote Address	Remote Port	In/ Out	Local Address	Local Port	TCP Flag
Choke client request	TCP	CHOKE_DMZ_IPADDR	1024:65535	In	ANYWHERE	443	Any
Server response	TCP	CHOKE_DMZ_IPADDR	1024:65535	Out	ANYWHERE	443	ACK

The following rules allow incoming SSL client connections from the choke machine, as well as from machines on the private LAN behind the choke firewall:

```
ipchains -A input  -i $BASTION_DMZ_INTERFACE -p tcp \
        -s $CHOKE_DMZ_IPADDR $UNPRIVPORTS \
        -d $ANYWHERE 443 -j ACCEPT

ipchains -A output -i $BASTION_DMZ_INTERFACE -p tcp ! -y \
        -s $ANYWHERE 443 \
        -d $CHOKE_DMZ_IPADDR $UNPRIVPORTS -j ACCEPT
```

Table 4.35 lists the server connection protocol for the Web proxy service.

Table 4.35   Bastion Web Proxy Server Protocol

Description	Protocol	Remote Address	Remote Port	In/ Out	Local Address	Local Port	TCP Flag
Choke client request	TCP	CHOKE_DMZ_IPADDR	1024:65535	In	WEB_PROXY_SERVER	WEB_PROXY_PORT	Any
Server response	TCP	CHOKE_DMZ_IPADDR	1024:65535	Out	WEB_PROXY_SERVER	WEB_PROXY_PORT	ACK

The following rules allow incoming Web proxy client connections from the choke machine, as well as from machines on the private LAN behind the choke firewall:

```
ipchains -A input  -i $BASTION_DMZ_INTERFACE -p tcp \
        -s $CHOKE_DMZ_IPADDR $UNPRIVPORTS \
        -d $WEB_PROXY_SERVER $WEB_PROXY_PORT -j ACCEPT

ipchains -A output -i $BASTION_DMZ_INTERFACE -p tcp ! -y \
        -s $WEB_PROXY_SERVER $WEB_PROXY_PORT \
        -d $CHOKE_DMZ_IPADDR $UNPRIVPORTS -j ACCEPT
```

Outgoing Choke Client Connections to External Servers

Table 4.36 lists the client connection protocol for the HTTP Web service.

Table 4.36   Choke HTTP Client Protocol

Description	Protocol	Remote Address	Remote Port	In/ Out	Local Address	Local Port	TCP Flag
Choke client request	TCP	ANYWHERE	80	Out	CHOKE_DMZ_IPADDR	1024:65535	Any
Remote server response	TCP	ANYWHERE	80	In	CHOKE_DMZ_IPADDR	1024:65535	ACK

This section allows local hosts to connect to Web servers both on the bastion and on remote hosts:

```
ipchains -A output -i $CHOKE_DMZ_INTERFACE -p tcp \
        -s $CHOKE_DMZ_IPADDR $UNPRIVPORTS \
        -d $ANYWHERE 80 -j ACCEPT

ipchains -A input  -i $CHOKE_DMZ_INTERFACE -p tcp ! -y \
        -s $ANYWHERE 80 \
        -d $CHOKE_DMZ_IPADDR $UNPRIVPORTS -j ACCEPT
```

Table 4.37 lists the client connection protocol for the SSL service.

Table 4.37   Choke SSL Client Protocol

Description	Protocol	Remote Address	Remote Port	In/ Out	Local Address	Local Port	TCP Flag
Choke client request	TCP	ANYWHERE	443	Out	CHOKE_DMZ_IPADDR	1024:65535	Any
Remote server response	TCP	ANYWHERE	443	In	CHOKE_DMZ_IPADDR	1024:65535	ACK

This section allows local hosts to connect to secure Web servers both on the bastion and on remote hosts:

```
ipchains -A output -i $CHOKE_DMZ_INTERFACE -p tcp \
        -s $CHOKE_DMZ_IPADDR $UNPRIVPORTS \
        -d $ANYWHERE 443 -j ACCEPT

ipchains -A input  -i $CHOKE_DMZ_INTERFACE -p tcp ! -y \
        -s $ANYWHERE 443 \
        -d $CHOKE_DMZ_IPADDR $UNPRIVPORTS -j ACCEPT
```

Table 4.38 lists the client connection protocol for the Web proxy service.

Table 4.38   Choke Web Proxy Client Protocol

Description	Protocol	Remote Address	Remote Port	In/ Out	Local Address	Local Port	TCP Flag
Choke client request	TCP	WEB_PROXY_SERVER	WEB_PROXY_PORT	Out	CHOKE_DMZ_IPADDR	1024:65535	Any
Remote server response	TCP	WEB_PROXY_SERVER	WEB_PROXY_PORT	In	CHOKE_DMZ_IPADDR	1024:65535	ACK

This section allows local hosts to connect to secure Web proxy servers both on the bastion and on remote hosts:

```
ipchains -A output -i $CHOKE_DMZ_INTERFACE -p tcp \
        -s $CHOKE_DMZ_IPADDR $UNPRIVPORTS \
        -d $WEB_PROXY_SERVER $WEB_PROXY_PORT -j ACCEPT

ipchains -A input  -i $CHOKE_DMZ_INTERFACE -p tcp ! -y \
        -s $WEB_PROXY_SERVER $WEB_PROXY_PORT \
        -d $CHOKE_DMZ_IPADDR $UNPRIVPORTS -j ACCEPT
```

Bastion as Conduit, Public Web Server in the DMZ, and Choke as Client

The bastion is a bidirectional conduit, a Web server runs in the DMZ, and the choke machine is a client.

Bastion Conduit to Remote and DMZ Web Servers

Table 4.39 lists the complete client/server connection protocol for the HTTP Web service.

Table 4.39 Bastion HTTP Client and Server Protocol

Description	Protocol	Remote Address	Remote Port	In/ Out	Local Address	Local Port	TCP Flag
DMZ client request	TCP	DMZ_ADDRESSES	1024:65535	In	ANYWHERE	80	Any
Remote server response	TCP	DMZ_ADDRESSES	1024:65535	Out	ANYWHERE	80	ACK
Remote client request	TCP	ANYWHERE	1024:65535	Out	WEB_SERVER_DMZ_IPADDR	80	Any
DMZ server response	TCP	ANYWHERE	1024:65535	In	WEB_SERVER_DMZ_IPADDR	80	ACK

This section allows local hosts to connect to Web servers both on the bastion and on remote hosts, and it allows remote clients to connect to a Web server in the DMZ:

```
ipchains -A input  -i $BASTION_DMZ_INTERFACE -p tcp \
        -s $DMZ_ADDRESSES $UNPRIVPORTS \
        -d $ANYWHERE 80 -j ACCEPT

ipchains -A output -i $BASTION_DMZ_INTERFACE -p tcp ! -y \
        -s $ANYWHERE 80 \
        -d $DMZ_ADDRESSES $UNPRIVPORTS -j ACCEPT

ipchains -A output -i $BASTION_DMZ_INTERFACE -p tcp \
        -s $ANYWHERE $UNPRIVPORTS \
        -d $WEB_SERVER_DMZ_IPADDR 80 -j ACCEPT

ipchains -A input  -i $BASTION_DMZ_INTERFACE -p tcp ! -y \
        -s $WEB_SERVER_DMZ_IPADDR 80 \
        -d $ANYWHERE $UNPRIVPORTS -j ACCEPT
```

Table 4.40 lists the complete client/server connection protocol for the SSL service.

Table 4.40 Bastion SSL Client and Server Protocol

Description	Protocol	Remote Address	Remote Port	In/ Out	Local Address	Local Port	TCP Flag
DMZ client request	TCP	DMZ_ADDRESSES	1024:65535	In	ANYWHERE	443	Any
Remote server response	TCP	DMZ_ADDRESSES	1024:65535	Out	ANYWHERE	443	ACK
Remote client request	TCP	ANYWHERE	1024:65535	Out	WEB_SERVER_DMZ_IPADDR	443	Any
DMZ server response	TCP	ANYWHERE	1024:65535	In	WEB_SERVER_DMZ_IPADDR	443	ACK

This section allows local hosts to connect to secure Web servers both on the bastion and on remote hosts, and it allows remote clients to connect to a secure Web server in the DMZ:

```
ipchains -A input  -i $BASTION_DMZ_INTERFACE -p tcp \
        -s $DMZ_ADDRESSES $UNPRIVPORTS \
        -d $ANYWHERE 443 -j ACCEPT

ipchains -A output -i $BASTION_DMZ_INTERFACE -p tcp ! -y \
        -s $ANYWHERE 443 \
        -d $DMZ_ADDRESSES $UNPRIVPORTS -j ACCEPT

ipchains -A output -i $BASTION_DMZ_INTERFACE -p tcp \
        -s $ANYWHERE $UNPRIVPORTS \
        -d $WEB_SERVER_DMZ_IPADDR 443 -j ACCEPT

ipchains -A input  -i $BASTION_DMZ_INTERFACE -p tcp ! -y \
        -s $WEB_SERVER_DMZ_IPADDR 443 \
        -d $ANYWHERE $UNPRIVPORTS -j ACCEPT
```

Table 4.41 lists the complete client/server connection protocol for the Web proxy service.

Table 4.41 Bastion Web Proxy Client and Server Protocol

Description	Protocol	Remote Address	Remote Port	In/Out	Local Address	Local Port	TCP Flag
Choke client request	TCP	CHOKE_DMZ_IPADDR	1024:65535	In	WEB_PROXY_SERVER	WEB_PROXY_PORT	Any
Remote server response	TCP	CHOKE_DMZ_IPADDR	1024:65535	Out	WEB_PROXY_SERVER	WEB_PROXY_PORT	ACK
Remote client request	TCP	ANYWHERE	1024:65535	Out	WEB_SERVER_DMZ_IPADDR	WEB_PROXY_PORT	Any
DMZ server response	TCP	ANYWHERE	1024:65535	In	WEB_SERVER_DMZ_IPADDR	1024:65535	ACK

This section allows local hosts to connect to Web proxy servers both on the bastion and on remote hosts, and it allows remote clients to connect to a Web proxy server in the DMZ:

```
ipchains -A input  -i $BASTION_DMZ_INTERFACE -p tcp \
        -s $CHOKE_DMZ_IPADDR $UNPRIVPORTS \
        -d $WEB_PROXY_SERVER $WEB_PROXY_PORT -j ACCEPT

ipchains -A output -i $BASTION_DMZ_INTERFACE -p tcp ! -y \
        -s $WEB_PROXY_SERVER $WEB_PROXY_PORT \
        -d $CHOKE_DMZ_IPADDR $UNPRIVPORTS -j ACCEPT

ipchains -A output -i $BASTION_DMZ_INTERFACE -p tcp \
        -s $ANYWHERE $UNPRIVPORTS \
        -d $WEB_SERVER_DMZ_IPADDR $WEB_PROXY_PORT -j ACCEPT
```

```
ipchains -A input  -i $BASTION_DMZ_INTERFACE -p tcp ! -y \
         -s $WEB_SERVER_DMZ_IPADDR $WEB_PROXY_PORT \
         -d $ANYWHERE $UNPRIVPORTS -j ACCEPT
```

Public Web Server in the DMZ

Two Web proxy packages included with Red Hat Release 6.0 are the proxy module included with the standard Apache server, and a separate package called Squid. Both packages allow you to define the service port. (Squid defaults to port 3130.)

Both the Apache proxy module and the Squid proxy server have been included in recent Red Hat releases. Prior to that, Apache source code had to be recompiled with the proxy module enabled. Squid was free, but was not yet part of the standard Red Hat distribution.

Table 4.42 lists the server connection protocol for the HTTP Web service.

Table 4.42 DMZ HTTP Server Protocol

Description	Protocol	Remote Address	Remote Port	In/ Out	Local Address	Local Port	TCP Flag
Choke client request	TCP	ANYWHERE	1024:65535	In	WEB_SERVER_DMZ_IPADDR	80	Any
DMZ server response	TCP	ANYWHERE	1024:65535	Out	WEB_SERVER_DMZ_IPADDR	80	ACK

The following rules allow incoming HTTP client connections from anywhere, including remote hosts as well as the bastion and choke machines:

```
WEB_DMZ_INTERFACE="etho"

ipchains -A input  -i $WEB_DMZ_INTERFACE -p tcp \
         -s $ANYWHERE $UNPRIVPORTS \
         -d $WEB_SERVER_DMZ_IPADDR 80 -j ACCEPT

ipchains -A output -i $WEB_DMZ_INTERFACE -p tcp ! -y \
         -s $WEB_SERVER_DMZ_IPADDR 80 \
         -d $ANYWHERE $UNPRIVPORTS -j ACCEPT
```

Table 4.43 lists the server connection protocol for the SSL service.

Table 4.43 DMZ SSL Server Protocol

Description	Protocol	Remote Address	Remote Port	In/ Out	Local Address	Local Port	TCP Flag
Remote client request	TCP	ANYWHERE	1024:65535	In	WEB_SERVER_DMZ_IPADDR	443	Any
DMZ server response	TCP	ANYWHERE	1024:65535	Out	WEB_SERVER_DMZ_IPADDR	443	ACK

The following rules allow incoming SSL secure Web client connections from any-where, including remote hosts as well as the bastion and choke machines:

```
WEB_DMZ_INTERFACE="etho"

ipchains -A input  -i $WEB_DMZ_INTERFACE -p tcp \
        -s $ANYWHERE $UNPRIVPORTS \
        -d $WEB_SERVER_DMZ_IPADDR 443 -j ACCEPT

ipchains -A output -i $WEB_DMZ_INTERFACE -p tcp ! -y \
        -s $WEB_SERVER_DMZ_IPADDR 443 \
        -d $ANYWHERE $UNPRIVPORTS -j ACCEPT
```

Table 4.44 lists the server connection protocol for the Web proxy service.

Table 4.44 DMZ Web Proxy Server Protocol

Description	Protocol	Remote Address	Remote Port	In/ Out	Local Address	Local Port	TCP Flag
Remote client request	TCP	proxy clients	1024:65535	In	WEB_SERVER_DMZ_IPADDR	WEB_PROXY_PORT	Any
DMZ server response	TCP	proxy clients	1024:65535	Out	WEB_SERVER_DMZ_IPADDR	WEB_PROXY_PORT	ACK

It's unlikely that a small system will have cause to offer Web proxy services over the Internet. More typically, a local proxy would run to provide a local cache, and possibly to proxy outgoing connections. A firewall rule isn't needed for a local proxy in this example. To the outside world, the proxy server appears as a normal Web client browser. For the exceptional cases, a sample firewall server rule would be:

```
WEB_DMZ_INTERFACE="etho"

ipchains -A input  -i $WEB_DMZ_INTERFACE -p tcp \
        -s <my.web.proxy_clients> $UNPRIVPORTS \
        -d $WEB_SERVER_DMZ_IPADDR $WEB_PROXY_PORT -j ACCEPT

ipchains -A output -i $WEB_DMZ_INTERFACE -p tcp ! -y \
        -s $WEB_SERVER_DMZ_IPADDR $WEB_PROXY_PORT \
        -d <my.web.proxy_clients> $UNPRIVPORTS -j ACCEPT
```

Choke as Client to Remote and DMZ Web Servers

Table 4.45 lists the client connection protocol for the HTTP Web service.

Table 4.45   Choke HTTP Client Protocol

Description	Protocol	Remote Address	Remote Port	In/Out	Local Address	Local Port	TCP Flag
Choke client request	TCP	ANYWHERE	80	Out	CHOKE_DMZ_IPADDR	1024:65535	Any
Remote server response	TCP	ANYWHERE	80	In	CHOKE_DMZ_IPADDR	1024:65535	ACK

The following rules allow outgoing HTTP client connections from the choke machine to a Web server to anywhere:

```
ipchains -A output -i $CHOKE_DMZ_INTERFACE -p tcp \
        -s $CHOKE_DMZ_IPADDR $UNPRIVPORTS \
        -d $ANYWHERE 80 -j ACCEPT

ipchains -A input  -i $CHOKE_DMZ_INTERFACE -p tcp ! -y \
        -s $ANYWHERE 80 \
        -d $CHOKE_DMZ_IPADDR $UNPRIVPORTS -j ACCEPT
```

Table 4.46 lists the client connection protocol for the SSL service.

Table 4.46   Choke SSL Client Protocol

Description	Protocol	Remote Address	Remote Port	In/Out	Local Address	Local Port	TCP Flag
Choke client request	TCP	ANYWHERE	443	Out	CHOKE_DMZ_IPADDR	1024:65535	Any
Remote server response	TCP	ANYWHERE	443	In	CHOKE_DMZ_IPADDR	1024:65535	ACK

The following rules allow outgoing SSL client connections from the choke machine to a secure Web server to anywhere:

```
ipchains -A output -i $CHOKE_DMZ_INTERFACE -p tcp \
        -s $CHOKE_DMZ_IPADDR $UNPRIVPORTS \
        -d $ANYWHERE 443 -j ACCEPT

ipchains -A input  -i $CHOKE_DMZ_INTERFACE -p tcp ! -y \
        -s $ANYWHERE 443 \
        -d $CHOKE_DMZ_IPADDR $UNPRIVPORTS -j ACCEPT
```

Table 4.47 lists the client connection protocol for the Web proxy service.

Table 4.47 Choke Web Proxy Client Protocol

Description	Protocol	Remote Address	Remote Port	In/Out	Local Address	Local Port	TCP Flag
Choke client request	TCP	WEB_PROXY_SERVER	WEB_PROXY_PORT	Out	CHOKE_DMZ_IPADDR	1024:65535	Any
Remote server response	TCP	WEB_PROXY_SERVER	WEB_PROXY_PORT	In	CHOKE_DMZ_IPADDR	1024:65535	ACK

The following rules allow outgoing client connections from the choke machine to Web proxy servers anywhere:

```
ipchains -A output -i $CHOKE_DMZ_INTERFACE -p tcp \
         -s $CHOKE_DMZ_IPADDR $UNPRIVPORTS \
         -d $WEB_PROXY_SERVER $WEB_PROXY_PORT -j ACCEPT

ipchains -A input  -i $CHOKE_DMZ_INTERFACE -p tcp ! -y \
         -s $WEB_PROXY_SERVER $WEB_PROXY_PORT \
         -d $CHOKE_DMZ_IPADDR $UNPRIVPORTS -j ACCEPT
```

Bastion as Web Server or Conduit, Choke as Local Web Proxy Server

Although it's possible to offer public Web service from a centralized internal server, it isn't usually done because of the greater potential for security breaches with misconfigured servers and CGI scripts, and the tendency to isolate private information from public information. That is, sites that host both a private, internal Web site and a public Web site usually run multiple Web servers on different machines in different LANs. More common scenarios would be to host the public Web site from either the bastion firewall or from a host on the perimeter network.

In the case of a small personal or business home site, one possibility is to run a public server on the bastion machine and a second, private proxy Web server on an internal machine, the choke firewall in this case. In this situation, the public server may or may not offer SSL service. The internal Web server offers proxy service. The private server isn't accessible from the bastion machine.

No additional rules are necessary in this case. From the bastion's perspective, the internal Web proxy appears to be a Web client. The only difference in this situation is that the Web proxy access rules given previously would not be necessary, unless your ISP requires you to use its Web proxy service.

No changes are required to either the bastion or the choke DMZ interface rules.

finger (TCP Port 79)

There's no harm in enabling outgoing access to remote finger servers. Offering internal finger service to the bastion machine is probably not overly useful. Offering internal finger service to the Internet is not only discouraged, in a masqueraded system, it's not possible without additional effort.

Bastion *finger* Conduit DMZ Configuration

Table 4.48 lists the complete client/server connection protocol for the finger service.

Table 4.48   Bastion *finger* Conduit Protocol

Description	Protocol	Remote Address	Remote Port	In/Out	Local Address	Local Port	TCP Flag
Choke client request	TCP	CHOKE_DMZ_IPADDR	1024:65535	In	ANYWHERE	79	Any
Remote server response	TCP	CHOKE_DMZ_IPADDR	1024:65535	Out	ANYWHERE	79	ACK
Remote client request	TCP	CHOKE_DMZ_IPADDR	79	Out	finger clients	1024:65535	Any
Choke server response	TCP	CHOKE_DMZ_IPADDR	79	In	finger clients	1024:65535	ACK

There's no harm in enabling outgoing access to remote finger servers, and these are the rules to do so:

```
ipchains -A input  -i $BASTION_DMZ_INTERFACE -p tcp \
        -s $CHOKE_DMZ_IPADDR $UNPRIVPORTS \
        -d $ANYWHERE 79 -j ACCEPT

ipchains -A output -i $BASTION_DMZ_INTERFACE -p tcp ! -y \
        -s $ANYWHERE 79 \
        -d $CHOKE_DMZ_IPADDR $UNPRIVPORTS -j ACCEPT
```

Server rules don't make much sense in a home-based site. A small ISP hosting user accounts would support internal finger servers:

```
ipchains -A output -i $BASTION_DMZ_INTERFACE -p tcp \
        -s $ANYWHERE $UNPRIVPORTS \
        -d $CHOKE_DMZ_IPADDR 79 -j ACCEPT

ipchains -A input  -i $BASTION_DMZ_INTERFACE -p tcp ! -y \
        -s $CHOKE_DMZ_IPADDR 79 \
        -d $ANYWHERE $UNPRIVPORTS -j ACCEPT
```

Choke *finger* Client and Server DMZ Configuration

Table 4.49 lists the complete client/server connection protocol for the finger service.

Table 4.49 Choke *finger* Protocol

Description	Protocol	Remote Address	Remote Port	In/ Out	Local Address	Local Port	TCP Flag
Choke client request	TCP	ANYWHERE	79	Out	CHOKE_DMZ_IPADDR	1024:65535	Any
Remote server response	TCP	ANYWHERE	79	In	CHOKE_DMZ_IPADDR	1024:65535	ACK
Remote client request	TCP	ANYWHERE	1024:65535	In	CHOKE_DMZ_IPADDR	79	Any
Choke server response	TCP	ANYWHERE	1024:65535	Out	CHOKE_DMZ_IPADDR	79	ACK

The following two rules enable outgoing client finger requests from the choke machine:

```
ipchains -A output -i $CHOKE_DMZ_INTERFACE -p tcp \
        -s $CHOKE_DMZ_IPADDR $UNPRIVPORTS  \
        -d $ANYWHERE 79 -j ACCEPT

ipchains -A input  -i $CHOKE_DMZ_INTERFACE -p tcp ! -y \
        -s $ANYWHERE 79 \
        -d $CHOKE_DMZ_IPADDR $UNPRIVPORTS -j ACCEPT
```

The following two rules enable incoming client finger requests to the choke machine:

```
ipchains -A input  -i $CHOKE_DMZ_INTERFACE -p tcp \
        -s $ANYWHERE $UNPRIVPORTS \
        -d $CHOKE_DMZ_IPADDR 79 -j ACCEPT

ipchains -A output -i $CHOKE_DMZ_INTERFACE -p tcp ! -y \
        -s $CHOKE_DMZ_IPADDR 79  \
        -d $ANYWHERE $UNPRIVPORTS -j ACCEPT
```

whois (TCP Port 43)

The whois program accesses the ARIN Registration Services database. It allows IP address and host and domain name lookups in human-readable form.

Bastion WHOIS Client Conduit DMZ Configuration

Table 4.50 lists the client connection protocol for the WHOIS service.

Table 4.50   Bastion WHOIS Client Protocol

Description	Protocol	Remote Address	Remote Port	In/Out	Local Address	Local Port	TCP Flag
Choke client request	TCP	CHOKE_DMZ_IPADDR	1024:65535	In	ANYWHERE	43	Any
Remote server response	TCP	CHOKE_DMZ_IPADDR	1024:65535	Out	ANYWHERE	43	ACK

The following rules allow incoming WHOIS client connections from the choke machine, as well as from machines on the private LAN behind the choke firewall:

```
ipchains -A input  -i $BASTION_DMZ_INTERFACE -p tcp \
         -s $CHOKE_FIREWALL $UNPRIVPORTS \
         -d $ANYWHERE 43 -j ACCEPT

ipchains -A output -i $BASTION_DMZ_INTERFACE -p tcp ! -y \
         -s $ANYWHERE 43 \
         -d $CHOKE_FIREWALL $UNPRIVPORTS -j ACCEPT
```

Choke WHOIS Client DMZ Configuration

Table 4.51 lists the client connection protocol for the WHOIS service.

Table 4.51   Choke WHOIS Client Protocol

Description	Protocol	Remote Address	Remote Port	In/Out	Local Address	Local Port	TCP Flag
Choke client request	TCP	ANYWHERE	43	Out	CHOKE_DMZ_IPADDR	1024:65535	Any
Remote server response	TCP	ANYWHERE	43	In	CHOKE_DMZ_IPADDR	1024:65535	ACK

The following rules allow outgoing WHOIS client connections from the choke machine, as well as from machines on the private LAN behind the choke firewall:

```
ipchains -A output -i $CHOKE_DMZ_INTERFACE -p tcp \
         -s $CHOKE_DMZ_IPADDR $UNPRIVPORTS \
         -d $ANYWHERE 43 -j ACCEPT
```

```
ipchains -A input  -i $CHOKE_DMZ_INTERFACE -p tcp ! -y \
        -s $ANYWHERE 43 \
        -d $CHOKE_DMZ_IPADDR $UNPRIVPORTS -j ACCEPT
```

gopher (TCP Port 70)

The Gopher information service is still available, but its use has largely been replaced by Web-based search engines. Netscape comes with built-in gopher client proxy support, however.

Bastion *gopher* Client Conduit DMZ Configuration

Table 4.52 lists the client connection protocol for the Gopher service.

Table 4.52   Bastion *gopher* Client Protocol

Description	Protocol	Remote Address	Remote Port	In/ Out	Local Address	Local Port	TCP Flag
Choke client request	TCP	CHOKE_DMZ_IPADDR	1024:65535	In	ANYWHERE	70	Any
Remote server response	TCP	CHOKE_DMZ_IPADDR	1024:65535	Out	ANYWHERE	70	ACK

The following rules allow incoming Gopher client connections from the choke machine, as well as from machines on the private LAN behind the choke firewall:

```
ipchains -A input  -i $BASTION_DMZ_INTERFACE -p tcp \
        -s $CHOKE_DMZ_IPADDR $UNPRIVPORTS \
        -d $ANYWHERE 70 -j ACCEPT

ipchains -A output -i $BASTION_DMZ_INTERFACE -p tcp ! -y \
        -s $ANYWHERE 70 \
        -d $CHOKE_DMZ_IPADDR $UNPRIVPORTS -j ACCEPT
```

Choke *gopher* Client DMZ Configuration

Table 4.53 lists the client connection protocol for the Gopher service.

Table 4.53   Choke *gopher* Client Protocol

Description	Protocol	Remote Address	Remote Port	In/ Out	Local Address	Local Port	TCP Flag
Choke client request	TCP	ANYWHERE	70	Out	CHOKE_DMZ_IPADDR	1024:65535	Any
Remote server response	TCP	ANYWHERE	70	In	CHOKE_DMZ_IPADDR	1024:65535	ACK

The next two rules enable outgoing client `gopher` requests from the choke machine:

```
ipchains -A output -i $CHOKE_DMZ_INTERFACE -p tcp \
         -s $CHOKE_DMZ_IPADDR $UNPRIVPORTS \
         -d $ANYWHERE 70 -j ACCEPT

ipchains -A input  -i $CHOKE_DMZ_INTERFACE -p tcp ! -y \
         -s $ANYWHERE 70 \
         -d $CHOKE_DMZ_IPADDR $UNPRIVPORTS -j ACCEPT
```

WAIS (TCP Port 210)

Wide Area Information Servers (WAIS) are now known as search engines. Web browsers typically provide a graphical front-end to the WAIS servers. Netscape contains the WAIS client code necessary to connect to WAIS servers.

Bastion WAIS Client Conduit DMZ Configuration

Table 4.54 lists the client connection protocol for the WAIS service.

Table 4.54 Bastion WAIS Client Protocol

Description	Protocol	Remote Address	Remote Port	In/Out	Local Address	Local Port	TCP Flag
Choke client request	TCP	CHOKE_DMZ_IPADDR	1024:65535	In	ANYWHERE	210	Any
Remote server response	TCP	CHOKE_DMZ_IPADDR	1024:65535	Out	ANYWHERE	210	ACK

The following two rules allow internal clients to access remote WAIS servers:

```
ipchains -A input  -i $BASTION_DMZ_INTERFACE -p tcp \
         -s $CHOKE_DMZ_IPADDR $UNPRIVPORTS \
         -d $ANYWHERE 210 -j ACCEPT

ipchains -A output -i $BASTION_DMZ_INTERFACE -p tcp ! -y \
         -s $ANYWHERE 210 \
         -d $CHOKE_DMZ_IPADDR $UNPRIVPORTS -j ACCEPT
```

Choke WAIS Client DMZ Configuration

Table 4.55 lists the client connection protocol for the WAIS service.

Table 4.55   Choke WAIS Client Protocol

Description	Protocol	Remote Address	Remote Port	In/ Out	Local Address	Local Port	TCP Flag
Choke client request	TCP	ANYWHERE	210	Out	CHOKE_DMZ_IPADDR	1024:65535	Any
Remote server response	TCP	ANYWHERE	210	In	CHOKE_DMZ_IPADDR	1024:65535	ACK

The following two rules allow client access to remote WAIS servers:

```
ipchains -A output -i $CHOKE_DMZ_INTERFACE -p tcp \
         -s $CHOKE_DMZ_IPADDR $UNPRIVPORTS \
         -d $ANYWHERE 210 -j ACCEPT

ipchains -A input  -i $CHOKE_DMZ_INTERFACE -p tcp ! -y \
         -s $ANYWHERE 210 \
         -d $CHOKE_DMZ_IPADDR $UNPRIVPORTS -j ACCEPT
```

RealAudio and QuickTime (554)

RealAudio and QuickTime both use the Real Time Streaming Protocol (RTSP) on TCP port 554, and the Real Time Transport Protocol (RTP) on either a TCP or UDP unprivileged port pair. RTSP provides the control stream. RTP provides the data stream.

The particular ports used for the unprivileged port pair are defined by the particular client software. For example, Apple's QuickTime uses ports 7070 and 7071 for the TCP data stream. It uses the first available port pair in the range from 6970 to 6999 for the UDP data stream.

Both services can be accessed over HTTP. In this case, special firewall rules are unnecessary. Both services can also be configured to use either a TCP or UDP data stream. HTTP and TCP offer more secure connections. UDP provides the best throughput.

The RealAudio proxy module included in the Red Hat distribution must be used both to accept incoming UDP datagrams, and to help protect UDP-based RealAudio and QuickTime network traffic. Additionally, the `ipmasqadm portfw` facility might be needed to forward incoming UDP packets to a masqueraded LAN machine.

Bastion RealAudio Client External Configuration

Table 4.56 lists the client connection protocol on the external Internet interface for the RealAudio service.

Table 4.56 Bastion RealAudio Client External Protocol

Description	Protocol	Remote Address	Remote Port	In/ Out	Local Address	Local Port	TCP Flag
Choke client request	TCP	ANYWHERE	554	Out	BASTION_EXTERNAL_IPADDR	1024:65535	Any
Remote server response	TCP	ANYWHERE	554	In	BASTION_EXTERNAL_IPADDR	1024:65535	ACK
Choke client request	TCP	ANYWHERE	1024:65535	Out	BASTION_EXTERNAL_IPADDR	7070:7071	Any
Remote server response	TCP	ANYWHERE	1024:65535	In	BASTION_EXTERNAL_IPADDR	7070:7071	ACK
Remote server response	UDP	ANYWHERE	1024:65535	In	BASTION_EXTERNAL_IPADDR	6970:6999	—
Choke client request	UDP	ANYWHERE	1024:65535	Out	BASTION_EXTERNAL_IPADDR	6970:6999	—

The following rules allow client control communication between the bastion machine and remote RealAudio servers:

```
ipchains -A output -i $BASTION_EXTERNAL_INTERFACE -p tcp \
        -s $BASTION_EXTERNAL_IPADDR $UNPRIVPORTS \
        -d $ANYWHERE 554 -j ACCEPT

ipchains -A input  -i $BASTION_EXTERNAL_INTERFACE -p tcp ! -y \
        -s $ANYWHERE 554 \
        -d $BASTION_EXTERNAL_IPADDR $UNPRIVPORTS -j ACCEPT
```

The following rules allow client data communication between the bastion machine and remote RealAudio servers using a TCP connection:

```
ipchains -A output -i $BASTION_EXTERNAL_INTERFACE -p tcp \
        -s $BASTION_EXTERNAL_IPADDR 7070:7071 \
        -d $ANYWHERE $UNPRIVPORTS -j ACCEPT

ipchains -A input  -i $BASTION_EXTERNAL_INTERFACE -p tcp ! -y \
        -s $ANYWHERE $UNPRIVPORTS \
        -d $BASTION_EXTERNAL_IPADDR 7070:7071 -j ACCEPT
```

The following rules allow client data communication between the bastion machine and remote RealAudio servers using UDP datagrams:

```
ipchains -A output -i $BASTION_EXTERNAL_INTERFACE -p udp \
         -s $BASTION_EXTERNAL_IPADDR 6970:6999 \
         -d $ANYWHERE $UNPRIVPORTS -j ACCEPT

ipchains -A input -i $BASTION_EXTERNAL_INTERFACE -p udp \
         -s $ANYWHERE $UNPRIVPORTS \
         -d $BASTION_EXTERNAL_IPADDR 6970:6999 -j ACCEPT
```

Bastion RealAudio Client Conduit DMZ Configuration

Table 4.57 lists the client conduit connection protocol for the RealAudio service.

Table 4.57 Bastion RealAudio Client Conduit Protocol

Description	Protocol	Remote Address	Remote Port	In/ Out	Local Address	Local Port	TCP Flag
Choke client request	TCP	CHOKE_DMZ_IPADDR	1024:65535	In	ANYWHERE	554	Any
Remote server response	TCP	CHOKE_DMZ_IPADDR	1024:65535	Out	ANYWHERE	554	ACK
Choke client request	TCP	CHOKE_DMZ_IPADDR	7070:7071	In	ANYWHERE	1024:65535	Any
Remote server response	TCP	CHOKE_DMZ_IPADDR	7070:7071	Out	ANYWHERE	1024:65535	ACK
Remote server response	UDP	CHOKE_DMZ_IPADDR	6970:6999	Out	ANYWHERE	1024:65535	—
Choke client request	UDP	CHOKE_DMZ_IPADDR	6970:6970	In	ANYWHERE	1024:65535	—

RealAudio / QuickTime in a Masqueraded Environment

If the LAN machines are masqueraded, the following lines are needed:

```
/sbin/modprobe ip_masq_raudio.o ports=7070, 7071,6970,6971
/usr/sbin/ipmasqadm portfw -f
/usr/sbin/ipmasqadm portfw -a -P udp -L $BASTION_EXTERNAL_IPADDR 6970 -R
➥$CHOKE_DMZ_IPADDR 6970
/usr/sbin/ipmasqadm portfw -a -P udp -L $BASTION_EXTERNAL_IPADDR 6971 -R
➥$CHOKE_DMZ_IPADDR 6971
```

The following rules allow a client on the choke machine to exchange control information with a remote RealAudio server:

```
ipchains -A input  -i $BASTION_DMZ_INTERFACE -p tcp \
        -s $CHOKE_DMZ_IPADDR $UNPRIVPORTS \
        -d $ANYWHERE 554 -j ACCEPT

ipchains -A output -i $BASTION_DMZ_INTERFACE -p tcp ! -y \
        -s $ANYWHERE 554 \
        -d $CHOKE_DMZ_IPADDR $UNPRIVPORTS -j ACCEPT
```

The following rules allow a client on the choke machine to exchange data communication with a remote RealAudio server using TCP connections:

```
ipchains -A input  -i $BASTION_DMZ_INTERFACE -p tcp \
        -s $CHOKE_DMZ_IPADDR 7070:7071 \
        -d $ANYWHERE $UNPRIVPORTS -j ACCEPT

ipchains -A output -i $BASTION_DMZ_INTERFACE -p tcp ! -y \
        -s $ANYWHERE $UNPRIVPORTS \
        -d $CHOKE_DMZ_IPADDR 7070:7071 -j ACCEPT
```

The following rules allow a client on the choke machine to exchange data communication with a remote RealAudio server using UDP datagrams:

```
ipchains -A input  -i $BASTION_DMZ_INTERFACE -p udp \
        -s $CHOKE_DMZ_IPADDR 6970:6999 \
        -d $ANYWHERE $UNPRIVPORTS -j ACCEPT

ipchains -A output -i $BASTION_DMZ_INTERFACE -p udp \
        -s $ANYWHERE $UNPRIVPORTS \
        -d $CHOKE_DMZ_IPADDR 6970:6999 -j ACCEPT
```

Choke RealAudio Client DMZ Configuration

Table 4.58 lists the client connection protocol for the RealAudio service.

Table 4.58 Choke RealAudio Client Protocol

Description	Protocol	Remote Address	Remote Port	In/Out	Local Address	Local Port	TCP Flag
Choke client request	TCP	ANYWHERE	554	Out	CHOKE_DMZ_IPADDR	1024:65535	Any
Remote server response	TCP	ANYWHERE	554	In	CHOKE_DMZ_IPADDR	1024:65535	ACK
Choke client request	TCP	ANYWHERE	1024:65535	Out	CHOKE_DMZ_IPADDR	7070:7071	Any
Remote server response	TCP	ANYWHERE	1024:65535	In	CHOKE_DMZ_IPADDR	7070:7071	ACK
Remote server response	UDP	ANYWHERE	1024:65535	In	CHOKE_DMZ_IPADDR	6970:6999	—
Choke client request	UDP	ANYWHERE	1024:65535	Out	CHOKE_DMZ_IPADDR	6970:6999	—

The following rules allow a local client to exchange control information with a remote server:

```
ipchains -A output -i $CHOKE_DMZ_INTERFACE -p tcp \
        -s $CHOKE_DMZ_IPADDR $UNPRIVPORTS \
        -d $ANYWHERE 554 -j ACCEPT

ipchains -A input  -i $CHOKE_DMZ_INTERFACE -p tcp ! -y \
        -s $ANYWHERE 554 \
        -d $CHOKE_DMZ_IPADDR $UNPRIVPORTS -j ACCEPT
```

The following rules allow a local client to exchange data communication with a remote RealAudio server using TCP connections:

```
ipchains -A output -i $CHOKE_DMZ_INTERFACE -p tcp \
        -s $CHOKE_DMZ_IPADDR 7070:7071 \
        -d $ANYWHERE $UNPRIVPORTS -j ACCEPT

ipchains -A input  -i $CHOKE_DMZ_INTERFACE -p tcp ! -y \
        -s $ANYWHERE $UNPRIVPORTS \
        -d $CHOKE_DMZ_IPADDR 7070:7071 -j ACCEPT
```

The following rules allow a local client to exchange data communication with a remote RealAudio server using UDP datagrams:

```
ipchains -A output -i $CHOKE_DMZ_INTERFACE -p udp \
        -s $CHOKE_DMZ_IPADDR 6970:6999 \
        -d $ANYWHERE $UNPRIVPORTS -j ACCEPT

ipchains -A input -i $CHOKE_DMZ_INTERFACE -p udp \
        -s $ANYWHERE $UNPRIVPORTS \
        -d $CHOKE_DMZ_IPADDR 6970:6999 -j ACCEPT
```

IRC (TCP Port 6667)

Port 6667 is the default IRC server port. Servers have the option of using a different port. If you access an IRC service provided over a different port, the rules must be modified accordingly.

The IRC proxy module supplied with the Linux distribution must be used because of the unprivileged-to-unprivileged port, client-to-client communication protocol, and to allow incoming connections from fellow remote clients. Business sites and commercial firewalls shouldn't allow IRC through the firewall because of the inherent security risks in the protocol.

Bastion IRC Client External Configuration

Table 4.59 lists the bastion's client connection protocol on the external Internet interface for the IRC service. Most people access an external Internet Relay Chat service. Therefore, a local server rule is not included here.

Table 4.59 Bastion IRC Client External Protocol

Description	Protocol	Remote Address	Remote Port	In/ Out	Local Address	Local Port	TCP Flag
Choke client request	TCP	ANYWHERE	6667	Out	BASTION_EXTERNAL_IPADDR	1024:65535	Any
Remote server response	TCP	ANYWHERE	6667	In	BASTION_EXTERNAL_IPADDR	1024:65535	ACK
Choke client to remote client request	TCP	ANYWHERE	1024:65535	Out	BASTION_EXTERNAL_IPADDR	1024:65535	Any
Remote client to Choke client response	TCP	ANYWHERE	1024:65535	In	BASTION_EXTERNAL_IPADDR	1024:65535	ACK
Remote client to Choke client request	TCP	ANYWHERE	1024:65535	In	BASTION_EXTERNAL_IPADDR	1024:65535	ACK
Choke client to remote client response	TCP	ANYWHERE	1024:65535	Out	BASTION_EXTERNAL_IPADDR	1024:65535	Any

The next set of rules allows client communication between local IRC clients and remote servers, as well as remote clients:

```
ipchains -A output -i $BASTION_EXTERNAL_INTERFACE -p tcp \
         -s $BASTION_EXTERNAL_IPADDR $UNPRIVPORTS \
         -d $ANYWHERE 6667 -j ACCEPT

ipchains -A input  -i $BASTION_EXTERNAL_INTERFACE -p tcp ! -y \
         -s $ANYWHERE 6667 \
         -d $BASTION_EXTERNAL_IPADDR $UNPRIVPORTS -j ACCEPT

ipchains -A output -i $BASTION_EXTERNAL_INTERFACE -p tcp \
         -s $BASTION_EXTERNAL_IPADDR $UNPRIVPORTS \
         -d $ANYWHERE $UNPRIVPORTS -j ACCEPT

ipchains -A input -i $BASTION_EXTERNAL_INTERFACE -p tcp ! -y \
         -s $ANYWHERE $UNPRIVPORTS \
         -d $BASTION_EXTERNAL_IPADDR $UNPRIVPORTS -j ACCEPT

ipchains -A input -i $BASTION_EXTERNAL_INTERFACE -p tcp \
         -s $ANYWHERE $UNPRIVPORTS \
         -d $BASTION_EXTERNAL_IPADDR $UNPRIVPORTS -j ACCEPT

ipchains -A output -i $BASTION_EXTERNAL_INTERFACE -p tcp ! -y \
         -s $BASTION_EXTERNAL_IPADDR $UNPRIVPORTS \
         -d $ANYWHERE $UNPRIVPORTS -j ACCEPT
```

Bastion IRC Client Conduit DMZ Configuration

Table 4.60 lists the client conduit connection protocol for the IRC service. Most people access an external Internet Relay Chat service. Therefore, a local server rule is not included here.

> **IRC in a Masqueraded Enviroment**
>
> If the LAN machines are masqueraded, the following line is needed:
>
> /sbin/modprobe ip_masq_irc.o

Table 4.60 Bastion IRC Client Conduit Protocol

Description	Protocol	Remote Address	Remote Port	In/Out	Local Address	Local Port	TCP Flag
Choke client request	TCP	CHOKE_DMZ_IPADDR	1024:65535	In	ANYWHERE	6667	Any
Remote server response	TCP	CHOKE_DMZ_IPADDR	1024:65535	Out	ANYWHERE	6667	ACK
Choke client to remote client request	TCP	CHOKE_DMZ_IPADDR	1024:65535	In	ANYWHERE	1024:65535	Any
Remote client to Choke client response	TCP	CHOKE_DMZ_IPADDR	1024:65535	Out	ANYWHERE	1024:65535	ACK
Remote client to Choke client request	TCP	CHOKE_DMZ_IPADDR	1024:65535	Out	ANYWHERE	1024:65535	ACK
Choke client to remote client response	TCP	CHOKE_DMZ_IPADDR	1024:65535	In	ANYWHERE	1024:65535	Any

The next set of rules allows client communication between local choke IRC clients and remote servers, as well as remote clients:

```
ipchains -A input  -i $BASTION_DMZ_INTERFACE -p tcp \
        -s $CHOKE_DMZ_IPADDR $UNPRIVPORTS \
        -d $ANYWHERE 6667 -j ACCEPT

ipchains -A output -i $BASTION_DMZ_INTERFACE -p tcp ! -y \
        -s $ANYWHERE 6667 \
        -d $CHOKE_DMZ_IPADDR $UNPRIVPORTS -j ACCEPT

ipchains -A input -i $BASTION_DMZ_INTERFACE -p tcp \
        -s $ANYWHERE $UNPRIVPORTS \
        -d $CHOKE_DMZ_IPADDR $UNPRIVPORTS -j ACCEPT

ipchains -A output -i $BASTION_DMZ_INTERFACE -p tcp ! -y \
        -s $CHOKE_DMZ_IPADDR $UNPRIVPORTS \
        -d $ANYWHERE $UNPRIVPORTS -j ACCEPT

ipchains -A output -i $BASTION_DMZ_INTERFACE -p tcp \
        -s $CHOKE_DMZ_IPADDR $UNPRIVPORTS \
        -d $ANYWHERE $UNPRIVPORTS -j ACCEPT

ipchains -A input -i $BASTION_DMZ_INTERFACE -p tcp ! -y \
        -s $ANYWHERE $UNPRIVPORTS \
        -d $CHOKE_DMZ_IPADDR $UNPRIVPORTS -j ACCEPT
```

Choke IRC Client DMZ Configuration

Table 4.61 lists the client connection protocol for the IRC service. Most people access an external Internet Relay Chat service. Therefore, a local server rule is not included here.

Table 4.61   Choke IRC Client Protocol

Description	Protocol	Remote Address	Remote Port	In/ Out	Local Address	Local Port	TCP Flag
Choke client request	TCP	ANYWHERE	6667	Out	CHOKE_DMZ_IPADDR	1024:65535	Any
Remote server response	TCP	ANYWHERE	6667	In	CHOKE_DMZ_IPADDR	1024:65535	ACK
Choke client to remote client request	TCP	ANYWHERE	1024:65535	Out	CHOKE_DMZ_IPADDR	1024:65535	Any
Remote client to Choke client response	TCP	ANYWHERE	1024:65535	In	CHOKE_DMZ_IPADDR	1024:65535	ACK
Remote client to Choke client request	TCP	ANYWHERE	1024:65535	In	CHOKE_DMZ_IPADDR	1024:65535	ACK
Choke client to remote client response	TCP	ANYWHERE	1024:65535	Out	CHOKE_DMZ_IPADDR	1024:65535	Any

The next set of rules allows client communication between local IRC clients and remote servers, as well as remote clients:

```
ipchains -A output -i $CHOKE_DMZ_INTERFACE -p tcp \
         -s $CHOKE_DMZ_IPADDR $UNPRIVPORTS \
         -d $ANYWHERE 6667 -j ACCEPT

ipchains -A input  -i $CHOKE_DMZ_INTERFACE -p tcp ! -y \
         -s $ANYWHERE 6667 \
         -d $CHOKE_DMZ_IPADDR $UNPRIVPORTS -j ACCEPT

ipchains -A output -i $CHOKE_DMZ_INTERFACE -p tcp \
         -s $CHOKE_DMZ_IPADDR $UNPRIVPORTS \
         -d $ANYWHERE $UNPRIVPORTS -j ACCEPT

ipchains -A input -i $CHOKE_DMZ_INTERFACE -p tcp ! -y \
         -s $ANYWHERE $UNPRIVPORTS \
         -d $CHOKE_DMZ_IPADDR $UNPRIVPORTS -j ACCEPT
```

```
ipchains -A input -i $CHOKE_DMZ_INTERFACE -p tcp \
        -s $ANYWHERE $UNPRIVPORTS \
        -d $CHOKE_DMZ_IPADDR $UNPRIVPORTS -j ACCEPT

ipchains -A output -i $CHOKE_DMZ_INTERFACE -p tcp ! -y \
        -s $CHOKE_DMZ_IPADDR $UNPRIVPORTS \
        -d $ANYWHERE $UNPRIVPORTS -j ACCEPT
```

CU-SeeMe (UDP Ports 7648, 7649, and 24032; TCP Ports 7648 and 7649)

Using CU-SeeMe requires access to a remote server. As such, a server rule is not included in the example.

Due to the inherent security problems in UDP, an explicit CU-SeeMe server should be specified. Also, the CU-SeeMe proxy module supplied in the Red Hat Linux distribution must be used for masqueraded clients.

Bastion CU-SeeMe Client External Configuration

Table 4.62 lists the client connection protocol on the external, Internet interface for the CU-SeeMe service.

Table 4.62 Bastion CU-SeeMe Client External Protocol

Description	Protocol	Remote Address	Remote Port	In/ Out	Local Address	Local Port	TCP Flag
Choke client request	UDP	CU-SeeMe server	7648:7649	Out	BASTION_EXTERNAL_IPADDR	1024:65535	—
Remote server response	UDP	CU-SeeMe server	7648:7649	In	BASTION_EXTERNAL_IPADDR	1024:65535	—
Choke client request	UDP	CU-SeeMe server	24032	Out	BASTION_EXTERNAL_IPADDR	1024:65535	—
Remote server response	UDP	CU-SeeMe server	24032	In	BASTION_EXTERNAL_IPADDR	1024:65535	—
Choke client request	TCP	CU-SeeMe server	7648:7649	Out	BASTION_EXTERNAL_IPADDR	1024:65535	Any
Remote server response	TCP	CU-SeeMe server	7648:7649	In	BASTION_EXTERNAL_IPADDR	1024:65535	ACK

> **CU-SeeMe**
>
> For more information on the firewall issues related to CU-SeeMe, refer to
> http://www.cu-seeme.com and http://www.wpine.com.

The next set of rules allows client communication between the bastion machine and remote servers:

```
ipchains -A output -i $BASTION_EXTERNAL_INTERFACE -p udp \
         -s $BASTION_EXTERNAL_IPADDR $UNPRIVPORTS \
         -d <cu-seeme.server> 7648:7649 -j ACCEPT

ipchains -A input -i $BASTION_EXTERNAL_INTERFACE -p udp \
         -s <cu-seeme.server> 7648:7649 \
         -d $BASTION_EXTERNAL_IPADDR $UNPRIVPORTS -j ACCEPT

ipchains -A output -i $BASTION_EXTERNAL_INTERFACE -p udp \
         -s $BASTION_EXTERNAL_IPADDR $UNPRIVPORTS \
         -d <cu-seeme.server> 24032 -j ACCEPT

ipchains -A input  -i $BASTION_EXTERNAL_INTERFACE -p udp \
         -s <cu-seeme.server> 24032 \
         -d $BASTION_EXTERNAL_IPADDR $UNPRIVPORTS -j ACCEPT

ipchains -A output -i $BASTION_EXTERNAL_INTERFACE -p tcp \
         -s $BASTION_EXTERNAL_IPADDR $UNPRIVPORTS \
         -d <cu-seeme.server> 7648:7649 -j ACCEPT

ipchains -A input -i $BASTION_EXTERNAL_INTERFACE -p tcp ! -y \
         -s <cu-seeme.server> 7648:7649 \
         -d $BASTION_EXTERNAL_IPADDR $UNPRIVPORTS -j ACCEPT
```

Bastion CU-SeeMe Client DMZ Configuration

Table 4.63 lists the client connection protocol on the bastion's DMZ interface for the CU-SeeMe service.

Table 4.63 Bastion CU–SeeMe Client Conduit Protocol

Description	Protocol	Remote Address	Remote Port	In/Out	Local Address	Local Port	TCP Flag
Choke client request	UDP	CHOKE_DMZ_IPADDR	1024:65535	In	CU-SeeMe server	7648:7649	—
Remote server response	UDP	CHOKE_DMZ_IPADDR	1024:65535	Out	CU-SeeMe server	7648:7649	—
Choke client request	UDP	CHOKE_DMZ_IPADDR	1024:65535	In	CU-SeeMe server	24032	—
Remote server response	UDP	CHOKE_DMZ_IPADDR	1024:65535	Out	CU-SeeMe server	24032	—
Choke client request	TCP	CHOKE_DMZ_IPADDR	1024:65535	In	CU-SeeMe server	7648:7649	Any
Remote server response	TCP	CHOKE_DMZ_IPADDR	1024:65535	Out	CU-SeeMe server	7648:7649	ACK

The next set of rules allows client communication between local CU-SeeMe clients and remote servers:

```
ipchains -A input  -i $BASTION_DMZ_INTERFACE -p udp \
         -s $CHOKE_DMZ_IPADDR $UNPRIVPORTS \
         -d <cu-seeme.server> 7648:7649 -j ACCEPT

ipchains -A output -i $BASTION_DMZ_INTERFACE -p udp \
         -s <cu-seeme.server> 7648:7649 \
         -d $CHOKE_DMZ_IPADDR $UNPRIVPORTS -j ACCEPT

ipchains -A input  -i $BASTION_DMZ_INTERFACE -p udp \
         -s $CHOKE_DMZ_IPADDR $UNPRIVPORTS \
         -d <cu-seeme.server> 24032 -j ACCEPT

ipchains -A output -i $BASTION_DMZ_INTERFACE -p udp \
         -s <cu-seeme.server> 24032 \
         -d $CHOKE_DMZ_IPADDR $UNPRIVPORTS -j ACCEPT

ipchains -A input  -i $BASTION_DMZ_INTERFACE -p tcp \
         -s $CHOKE_DMZ_IPADDR $UNPRIVPORTS \
         -d <cu-seeme.server> 7648:7649 -j ACCEPT

ipchains -A output -i $BASTION_DMZ_INTERFACE -p tcp ! -y \
         -s <cu-seeme.server> 7648:7649 \
         -d $CHOKE_DMZ_IPADDR $UNPRIVPORTS -j ACCEPT
```

Choke CU–SeeMe Client DMZ Configuration

Table 4.64 lists the client connection protocol for the CU–SeeMe service.

Table 4.64 Choke CU–SeeMe Client Protocol

Description	Protocol	Remote Address	Remote Port	In/ Out	Local Address	Local Port	TCP Flag
Choke client request	UDP	CU-SeeMe server	7648:7649	Out	CHOKE_DMZ_IPADDR	1024:65535	—
Remote server response	UDP	CU-SeeMe server	7648:7649	In	CHOKE_DMZ_IPADDR	1024:65535	—
Choke client request	UDP	CU-SeeMe server	24032	Out	CHOKE_DMZ_IPADDR	1024:65535	—
Remote server response	UDP	CU-SeeMe server	24032	In	CHOKE_DMZ_IPADDR	1024:65535	—
Choke client request	TCP	CU-SeeMe server	7648:7649	Out	CHOKE_DMZ_IPADDR	1024:65535	Any
Remote server response	TCP	CU-SeeMe server	7648:7649	In	CHOKE_DMZ_IPADDR	1024:65535	ACK

The next set of rules allows client communication between local CU–SeeMe clients and remote servers:

```
ipchains -A output -i $CHOKE_DMZ_INTERFACE -p udp \
        -s $CHOKE_DMZ_IPADDR $UNPRIVPORTS \
        -d <cu-seeme.server> 7648:7649 -j ACCEPT

ipchains -A input -i $CHOKE_DMZ_INTERFACE -p udp \
        -s <cu-seeme.server> 7648:7649 \
        -d $CHOKE_DMZ_IPADDR $UNPRIVPORTS -j ACCEPT

ipchains -A output -i $CHOKE_DMZ_INTERFACE -p udp \
        -s $CHOKE_DMZ_IPADDR $UNPRIVPORTS \
        -d <cu-seeme.server> 24032 -j ACCEPT

ipchains -A input  -i $CHOKE_DMZ_INTERFACE -p udp \
        -s <cu-seeme.server> 24032 \
        -d $CHOKE_DMZ_IPADDR $UNPRIVPORTS -j ACCEPT

ipchains -A output -i $CHOKE_DMZ_INTERFACE -p tcp \
        -s $CHOKE_DMZ_IPADDR $UNPRIVPORTS \
        -d <cu-seeme.server> 7648:7649 -j ACCEPT
```

```
ipchains -A input -i $CHOKE_DMZ_INTERFACE -p tcp ! -y \
         -s <cu-seeme.server> 7648:7649 \
         -d $CHOKE_DMZ_IPADDR $UNPRIVPORTS -j ACCEPT
```

Quake (UDP Ports 26000 and 1025 Through 1200)

By default, Quake servers listen for game connection requests on UDP port 26000.
When the server accepts a new player request, it returns the UDP port number it will
use to communicate with the player's client program. The server port for the ongoing,
private client/server exchange is usually a UDP port between 1025 and 1200.

Due to the inherent security problems in UDP, an explicit Quake server should be
specified. Also, the Quake proxy module supplied in the Red Hat Linux distribution
must be used to forward incoming UDP packets to masqueraded clients.

Bastion Quake Client External Configuration

Table 4.65 lists the bastion's client connection protocol on the external Internet interface for the Quake service.

Table 4.65   Bastion Quake Client External Protocol

Description	Protocol	Remote Address	Remote Port	In/Out	Local Address	Local Port	TCP Flag
Choke client connection request	UDP	Quake server	26000	Out	BASTION_EXTERNAL_IPADDR	1024:65535	—
Remote server connection response	UDP	Quake server	26000	In	BASTION_EXTERNAL_IPADDR	1024:65535	—
Choke client request	UDP	Quake server	1025:1200	Out	BASTION_EXTERNAL_IPADDR	1024:65535	—
Remote server response	UDP	Quake server	1025:1200	In	BASTION_EXTERNAL_IPADDR	1024:65535	—

Quake

For more information on the firewall issues related to Quake, refer to
http://www.gamers.org/dEngine/quake/spec.

The next set of rules allows client communication between the bastion machine and remote Quake servers:

```
ipchains -A output -i $BASTION_EXTERNAL_INTERFACE -p udp \
        -s $BASTION_EXTERNAL_IPADDR $UNPRIVPORTS \
        -d <quake.server> 26000 -j ACCEPT

ipchains -A input -i $BASTION_EXTERNAL_INTERFACE -p udp \
        -s <quake.server> 26000 \
        -d $BASTION_EXTERNAL_IPADDR $UNPRIVPORTS -j ACCEPT

ipchains -A output -i $BASTION_EXTERNAL_INTERFACE -p udp \
        -s $BASTION_EXTERNAL_IPADDR $UNPRIVPORTS \
        -d <quake.server> 1025:1200 -j ACCEPT

ipchains -A input   -i $BASTION_EXTERNAL_INTERFACE -p udp \
        -s <quake.server> 1025:1200 \
        -d $BASTION_EXTERNAL_IPADDR $UNPRIVPORTS -j ACCEPT
```

Bastion Quake Client DMZ Configuration

Table 4.66 lists the bastion's client conduit connection protocol for the Quake service.

Table 4.66   Bastion Quake Client Conduit Protocol

Description	Protocol	Remote Address	Remote Port	In/ Out	Local Address	Local Port	TCP Flag
Choke client connection request	UDP	CHOKE_DMZ_IPADDR	1024:65535	In	Quake server	26000	—
Remote server connection response	UDP	CHOKE_DMZ_IPADDR	1024:65535	Out	Quake server	26000	—
Choke client request	UDP	CHOKE_DMZ_IPADDR	1024:65535	In	Quake server	1025:1200	—
Remote server response	UDP	CHOKE_DMZ_IPADDR	1024:65535	Out	Quake server	1025:1200	—

The next set of rules allows client communication between local Quake clients and remote servers:

```
ipchains -A input   -i $BASTION_DMZ_INTERFACE -p udp \
        -s $CHOKE_DMZ_IPADDR $UNPRIVPORTS \
        -d <quake.server> 26000 -j ACCEPT
```

```
ipchains -A output -i $BASTION_DMZ_INTERFACE -p udp \
         -s <quake.server> 26000 \
         -d $CHOKE_DMZ_IPADDR $UNPRIVPORTS -j ACCEPT

ipchains -A input  -i $BASTION_DMZ_INTERFACE -p udp \
         -s $CHOKE_DMZ_IPADDR $UNPRIVPORTS \
         -d <quake.server> 1025:1200 -j ACCEPT

ipchains -A output -i $BASTION_DMZ_INTERFACE -p udp \
         -s <quake.server> 1025:1200 \
         -d $CHOKE_DMZ_IPADDR $UNPRIVPORTS -j ACCEPT
```

Bastion Quake Server Configuration

A Quake server can't be masqueraded and run from a machine in the DMZ. A Quake server must either run on the bastion machine or an internal public server with a registered IP address.

Table 4.67 lists the bastion's server connection protocol on the external Internet interface for remote Quake clients.

Table 4.67   Bastion Quake Server Protocol

Description	Protocol	Remote Address	Remote Port	In/ Out	Local Address	Local Port	TCP Flag
Choke client connection request	UDP	ANYWHERE	1024:65535	In	BASTION_EXTERNAL_IPADDR	26000	—
Remote server connection response	UDP	ANYWHERE	1024:65535	Out	BASTION_EXTERNAL_IPADDR	26000	—
Choke client request	UDP	ANYWHERE	1024:65535	In	BASTION_EXTERNAL_IPADDR	1025:1200	—
Bastion server response	UDP	ANYWHERE	1024:65535	Out	BASTION_EXTERNAL_IPADDR	1025:1200	—

The next set of rules allows client communication between local Quake clients and remote servers:

```
ipchains -A input  -i $BASTION_EXTERNAL_INTERFACE -p udp \
         -s $ANYWHERE $UNPRIVPORTS \
         -d $BASTION_EXTERNAL_IPADDR 26000 -j ACCEPT

ipchains -A output -i $BASTION_EXTERNAL_INTERFACE -p udp \
         -s $BASTION_EXTERNAL_IPADDR 26000 \
         -d $ANYWHERE  $UNPRIVPORTS -j ACCEPT
```

```
ipchains -A input  -i $BASTION_EXTERNAL_INTERFACE -p udp \
          -s $ANYWHERE  $UNPRIVPORTS \
          -d $BASTION_EXTERNAL_IPADDR 1025:1200 -j ACCEPT

ipchains -A output -i $BASTION_EXTERNAL_INTERFACE -p udp \
          -s $BASTION_EXTERNAL_IPADDR 1025:1200 \
          -d $ANYWHERE  $UNPRIVPORTS -j ACCEPT
```

Choke Quake Client DMZ Configuration

Table 4.68 lists the client connection protocol for the Quake service.

Table 4.68   Choke Quake Client Protocol

Description	Protocol	Remote Address	Remote Port	In/ Out	Local Address	Local Port	TCP Flag
Choke client connection request	UDP	Quake server	26000	Out	CHOKE_DMZ_IPADDR	1024:65535	—
Remote server connection response	UDP	Quake server	26000	In	CHOKE_DMZ_IPADDR	1024:65535	—
Choke client request	UDP	Quake server	1025:1200	Out	CHOKE_DMZ_IPADDR	1024:65535	—
Remote server response	UDP	Quake server	1025:1200	In	CHOKE_DMZ_IPADDR	1024:65535	—

The next set of rules allows client communication between local Quake clients and remote servers:

```
ipchains -A output -i $CHOKE_DMZ_INTERFACE -p udp \
          -s $CHOKE_DMZ_IPADDR $UNPRIVPORTS \
          -d <quake.server> 26000 -j ACCEPT

ipchains -A input -i $CHOKE_DMZ_INTERFACE -p udp \
          -s <quake.server> 26000 \
          -d $CHOKE_DMZ_IPADDR $UNPRIVPORTS -j ACCEPT

ipchains -A output -i $CHOKE_DMZ_INTERFACE -p udp \
          -s $CHOKE_DMZ_IPADDR $UNPRIVPORTS \
          -d <quake.server> 1025:1200 -j ACCEPT

ipchains -A input  -i $CHOKE_DMZ_INTERFACE -p udp \
          -s <quake.server> 1025:1200 \
          -d $CHOKE_DMZ_IPADDR $UNPRIVPORTS -j ACCEPT
```

Network Time Service (UDP Port 123)

Network time service (NTP) allows access to time providers. This is useful to maintain an accurate system clock, particularly if your internal clock tends to drift, and to establish the correct time and date at bootup or after a power loss. xntpd is also useful as an internal service to synchronize the clocks of all the local machines.

Enabling Private LAN Services

Chapter 1, "Preliminary Concepts Underlying Packet-Filtering Firewalls," introduces the idea that many common UNIX services are designed for internal LAN use. These services can present security risks and annoyances to your neighbors if external access to them is allowed or if they leak out unto the Internet. Chapter 3 talked about these services from a packet-filtering perspective and included redundant example rules to exemplify the kinds of things you don't want passing through the external interface to the Internet. Some of these services pose such potentially dangerous risks that they are often not run on the bastion machine, and some sites go so far as to remove the software from the bastion machine altogether.

Even though these services could be used on the bastion machine behind the protection of the firewall, the idea behind the bastion is that the external machine is secured and fortified to the greatest extent possible. A standalone system or a very small home LAN might have to make choices and compromises. The important thing is for the administrator to be aware of the risks and possible protections before making those choices.

Internally, these same services can be very useful. Your LAN may depend on them. They are a big part of what gives UNIX its power and flexibility. The addition of an internal choke firewall adds an extra layer of security and confidence when these services are offered for the LAN, whether from internal LAN servers or from the choke firewall host itself.

For the sake of example, the following ipchains rules are written from the perspective of the service being offered from the choke machine to internal clients.

Bastion as Local NTP Server DMZ Configuration

Table 4.69 lists the client and peer-to-peer server exchange protocol for the NTP service.

Table 4.69   Bastion NTP Server Protocols

Description	Protocol	Remote Address	Remote Port	In/Out	Local Address	Local Port
Choke client query	UDP	CHOKE_DMZ_IPADDR	1024:65535	In	BASTION_DMZ_IPADDR	123
Bastion server response	UDP	CHOKE_DMZ_IPADDR	1024:65535	Out	BASTION_DMZ_IPADDR	123
Choke server query	UDP	CHOKE_DMZ_IPADDR	123	In	BASTION_DMZ_IPADDR	123
Bastion peer-server response	UDP	CHOKE_DMZ_IPADDR	123	Out	BASTION_DMZ_IPADDR	123

As a client, the bastion machine periodically queries a public time service provider. The bastion machine runs xntpd as a local server to disseminate the time to internal machines.

The sample rules for accessing a remote server are covered in Chapter 3. The following are the server rules allowing DMZ clients access to the local bastion server:

```
ipchains -A input  -i $BASTION_DMZ_INTERFACE -p udp \
        -s $DMZ_LAN_ADDRESSES $UNPRIVPORTS \
        -d $BASTION_DMZ_IPADDR 123 -j ACCEPT

ipchains -A output -i $BASTION_DMZ_INTERFACE -p udp \
        -s $BASTION_DMZ_IPADDR 123 \
        -d $DMZ_LAN_ADDRESSES $UNPRIVPORTS -j ACCEPT
```

Peer-to-peer server exchanges are used between servers to synchronize their idea of the current time. A larger LAN might configure an additional internal machine to function as a secondary local time server, running xntpd on that machine, as well:

```
ipchains -A input  -i $BASTION_DMZ_INTERFACE -p udp \
        -s $CHOKE_DMZ_IPADDR 123 \
        -d $BASTION_DMZ_IPADDR 123 -j ACCEPT

ipchains -A output -i $BASTION_DMZ_INTERFACE -p udp \
        -s $BASTION_DMZ_IPADDR 123 \
        -d $CHOKE_DMZ_IPADDR 123 -j ACCEPT
```

Choke NTP Client and Peer-to-Peer Server DMZ Configuration

Table 4.70 lists the client and peer-to-peer server exchange protocol for the NTP service.

Table 4.70   Choke NTP Client and Server Protocols

Description	Protocol	Remote Address	Remote Port	In/ Out	Local Address	Local Port
Choke client query	UDP	BASTION_DMZ_IPADDR	123	Out	CHOKE_DMZ_IPADDR	1024:65535
Bastion server response	UDP	BASTION_DMZ_IPADDR	123	In	CHOKE_DMZ_IPADDR	1024:65535
Choke server query	UDP	BASTION_DMZ_IPADDR	123	Out	CHOKE_DMZ_IPADDR	123
Bastion peer-server response	UDP	BASTION_DMZ_IPADDR	123	In	CHOKE_DMZ_IPADDR	123

The following two rules allow client access to the bastion xntpd time server using the client program ntpdate:

```
ipchains -A output  -i $CHOKE_DMZ_INTERFACE -p udp \
         -s $CHOKE_DMZ_IPADDR $UNPRIVPORTS \
         -d $BASTION_DMZ_IPADDR 123 -j ACCEPT

ipchains -A input -i $CHOKE_DMZ_INTERFACE -p udp \
         -s $BASTION_DMZ_IPADDR 123 \
         -d $CHOKE_DMZ_IPADDR $UNPRIVPORTS -j ACCEPT
```

If the choke machine is configured as an internal server running xntpd, the peer-to-peer communication protocol must be supported with the following two rules:

```
ipchains -A output -i $CHOKE_DMZ_INTERFACE -p udp \
         -s $CHOKE_DMZ_IPADDR 123 \
         -d $BASTION_DMZ_IPADDR 123 -j ACCEPT

ipchains -A input  -i $CHOKE_DMZ_INTERFACE -p udp \
         -s $BASTION_DMZ_IPADDR 123 \
         -d $CHOKE_DMZ_IPADDR 123 -j ACCEPT
```

Remote System Logging (UDP Port 514)

System log files can be managed by a central log server machine. Central logging has some advantages in environments hosting many server machines. System log files and syslogd configuration is discussed in Chapter 6, "Verifying That the System Is Running as You Expect." Remote logging, specifically, is discussed in Chapter 7, "Issues At the UNIX System Administration Level."

For the purposes of illustration, the following example assumes a configuration where the bastion machine writes a copy of its system log entries to the `syslogd` server running on the choke machine.

Bastion as Local *syslog* Writer DMZ Configuration

Table 4.71 lists the writer's peer-to-peer server exchange protocol for the remote `syslog` service.

Table 4.71   Bastion *syslog* Writer Protocol

Description	Protocol	Remote Address	Remote Port	In/Out	Local Address	Local Port
Bastion server logging	UDP	CHOKE_DMZ_IPADDR	514	Out	BASTION_DMZ_IPADDR	514

The bastion's `/etc/syslog.conf` file contains an additional configuration line to write a copy of all log entries to the choke machine:

```
*.*             @choke
```

Peer-to-peer server exchanges are used between `syslogd` servers. The bastion system logs are copied to the choke machine's `syslogd` server:

```
ipchains -A output -i $BASTION_DMZ_INTERFACE -p udp \
        -s $BASTION_DMZ_IPADDR 514 \
        -d $CHOKE_DMZ_IPADDR 514 -j ACCEPT
```

Choke as Local *syslog* Reader DMZ Configuration

Table 4.72 lists the reader's peer-to-peer server exchange protocol for the remote `syslog` client.

Table 4.72   Choke *syslog* Reader Protocol

Description	Protocol	Remote Address	Remote Port	In/Out	Local Address	Local Port
Bastion server logging	UDP	BASTION_DMZ_IPADDR	514	In	CHOKE_DMZ_IPADDR	514

The choke's `/etc/rc.d/init.d/syslog` initialization script contains a modified startup line, adding the `-r` option to instruct the server to listen to the Internet domain socket on UDP port 514, as well as listen on its usual UNIX domain socket:

```
daemon syslogd -r
```

The following rule allows incoming log messages from the bastion `syslogd` server:

```
ipchains -A input -i $CHOKE_DMZ_INTERFACE -p udp \
         -s $BASTION_DMZ_IPADDR 514 \
         -d $CHOKE_DMZ_IPADDR 514 -j ACCEPT
```

Choke as a Local DHCP Server (UDP Ports 67 and 68)

Table 4.73 lists the server exchange protocol for the DHCP service.

Table 4.73   Choke DHCP Server Protocol

Description	Protocol	Remote Address	Local Port	In/ Out	Local Address	Remote Port
DHCPDISCOVER; DHCPREQUEST	UDP	0.0.0.0	68	In	255.255.255.255	67
DHCPOFFER	UDP	255.255.255.255	68	Out	0.0.0.0	67
DHCPOFFER	UDP	255.255.255.255	68	Out	CHOKE_LAN_IPADDR	67
DHCPREQUEST; DHCPDECLINE	UDP	0.0.0.0	68	In	CHOKE_LAN_IPADDR	67
DHCPACK; DHCPNAK	UDP	CHOKE_LAN_NETMASK	68	Out	CHOKE_LAN_IPADDR	67
DHCPACK	UDP	CHOKE_LAN_ ADDRESSES	68	Out	CHOKE_LAN_IPADDR	67
DHCPREQUEST; DHCPRELEASE	UDP	CHOKE_LAN_ ADDRESSES	68	In	CHOKE_LAN_IPADDR	67

Although you should never send DHCP server messages to the Internet, some people run a private DHCP server to assign IP addresses to local machines. DHCP can be useful not only for assigning IP addresses on a larger LAN with many machines, but also for very small personal home LANs. In fact, some people with a usually single standalone system sometimes run the `dhcpd` server locally if they carry a laptop computer between home and work. If the work environment assigns IP addresses dynamically, using DHCP at home makes transporting the laptop between networks easier.

For this example, the `dhcpd` server is running on the choke machine, providing dynamic IP address assignment for machines on the private LAN:

```
ipchains -A input  -i $CHOKE_LAN_INTERFACE -p udp \
         -s $BROADCAST_0 68 \
         -d $BROADCAST_1 67 -j ACCEPT

ipchains -A output -i $CHOKE_LAN_INTERFACE -p udp \
         -s $BROADCAST_0 67 \
         -d $BROADCAST_1 68 -j ACCEPT
```

```
ipchains -A output -i $CHOKE_LAN_INTERFACE -p udp \
        -s $CHOKE_LAN_IPADDR 67 \
        -d $BROADCAST_1 68 -j ACCEPT

ipchains -A input  -i $CHOKE_LAN_INTERFACE -p udp \
        -s $BROADCAST_0 68 \
        -d $CHOKE_LAN_IPADDR 67 -j ACCEPT

ipchains -A output -i $CHOKE_LAN_INTERFACE -p udp \
        -s $CHOKE_LAN_IPADDR 67 \
        -d $CHOKE_LAN_ADDRESSES/CHOKE_LAN_NETMASK 68 -j ACCEPT

ipchains -A output -i $CHOKE_LAN_INTERFACE -p udp \
        -s $CHOKE_LAN_IPADDR 67 \
        -d $CHOKE_LAN_ADDRESSES 68 -j ACCEPT

ipchains -A input  -i $CHOKE_LAN_INTERFACE -p udp \
        -s $CHOKE_LAN_ADDRESSES 68 \
        -d $CHOKE_LAN_IPADDR 67 -j ACCEPT
```

Enabling LAN Access to the Choke Firewall Machine

For a home or small business setup, there is probably little reason to limit direct access to the choke firewall machine from the internal LAN. This rule pair allows open communication between the choke machine and the private LAN:

```
ipchains -A input  -i $CHOKE_LAN_INTERFACE \
        -s $CHOKE_LAN_ADDRESSES -j ACCEPT

ipchains -A output -i $CHOKE_LAN_INTERFACE \
        -d $CHOKE_LAN_ADDRESSES -j ACCEPT
```

Enabling IP Masquerading

Masquerading traffic from the internal LAN isn't necessary. The bastion firewall is already masquerading all internal traffic from the DMZ crossing its external interface. For the sake of completeness, private LAN traffic is masqueraded on the DMZ by the choke firewall, as well, rather than simply being forwarded here. Depending on how specific the complementary rule on the bastion is, masquerading here can simplify the bastion's rule if it isn't expecting addresses from multiple internal networks. The following rule masquerades all traffic from the private LAN:

```
ipchains -A forward -i $CHOKE_DMZ_INTERFACE \
        -s $CHOKE_LAN_ADDRESSES -j MASQ
```

Alternatively, if you prefer more explicit masquerading rules, the following two rules enable masquerading for TCP and ICMP, but not for UDP:

```
ipchains -A forward -i $CHOKE_DMZ_INTERFACE -p tcp \
        -s $CHOKE_LAN_ADDRESSES -j MASQ
ipchains -A forward -i $CHOKE_DMZ_INTERFACE -p icmp \
        -s $CHOKE_LAN_ADDRESSES -j MASQ
```

Logging

Logging dropped packets on the internal interfaces might not be particularly useful in the relatively trusted environments this book is targeted at. Nevertheless, logging is a major tool in debugging firewall problems and understanding communication protocols. Because all traffic is allowed between the private LAN and the choke machine, logging would be enabled on a port-specific basis.

Summary

This chapter covers some of the firewall options available when protecting a LAN. Security policies are defined relative to the site's level of security needs, the importance of the data being protected, the cost of lost data or privacy. Starting with a simple home LAN and the firewall developed in Chapter 3, LAN and firewall setup options are discussed in increasingly complex configurations.

The major emphasis in this chapter is to use the firewall example from Chapter 3 as the basis to develop a formal, elaborate, textbook type of firewall. The bastion firewall has two network interfaces: one connected to the Internet, and one connected to a perimeter network, or DMZ. Public Internet services are offered from machines in the DMZ network. A second firewall, a choke firewall, is also connected to the DMZ network, separating the internal, private networks from the quasi-public server machines in the perimeter network. Private machines are protected behind the choke firewall on the internal LAN. The choke firewall protects the internal LAN from the compromised bastion machine and from any other machine in the perimeter network.

Some services, such as IRC or RealAudio, do not lend themselves to packet filtering, due to their application communication protocols, such as requiring incoming connections from the server, or multiple client/server exchanges over both TCP and UDP. These types of services require additional help, whether from kernel-supplied masquerade support modules or from application-level proxies. Firewall rulesets for several of these kinds of services are presented in this chapter, services that could not be easily protected by the firewall examples in Chapter 3.

5

Debugging the Firewall Rules

So NOW THE FIREWALL IS SET UP, INSTALLED, and activated. Nothing works! You're locked in—or worse yet, even X Window doesn't work. Who knows what's going on? Now what? Where do you even begin?

Firewall rules are notoriously difficult to get right. If you're developing by hand, bugs invariably crop up. Even if you produce a firewall script with an automatic firewall generation tool, your script will undoubtedly require customized tweaking eventually.

This chapter introduces additional reporting features of the ipchains tool and other system tools. The information is invaluable when debugging your firewall rules. This chapter explains what the information can tell you about your firewall. The tools are crude. The process is tedious. Be forewarned.

For additional information on ipchains reporting features, see the ipchains man page and the IPCHAINS-HOWTO.

General Firewall Development Tips

Tracking down a problem in the firewall is detailed and painstaking. There are no shortcuts to debugging the rules when something goes wrong. In general, the following tips can make the process a bit easier:

- Always execute the rules from a complete test script. Be sure the script flushes all existing rules and resets the default policies first. Otherwise, you can't be sure which rules are in effect or in which order.

- Don't execute new rules from the command line. Especially don't execute the default policy rules from the command line. You'll be cut off immediately if you're logged in using X Window or remotely from another system, including a system on the LAN.

- Execute the test script from the console. Don't try to debug from a remote machine. Working in X Window at the console may be more convenient, but the danger remains of losing access to X Window locally. Be prepared for the possibility of needing to switch over to a virtual console to regain control.

- When feasible, work on one service at a time. Add rules one at a time or as input and output rule pairs. Test as you go. This makes it much easier to isolate problem areas in the rules right away.

- Remember that the first matching rule wins. Order is important. Use the `ipchains` list commands as you go to get a feel for how the rules are ordered. Trace an imaginary packet through the list.

- Remember that there are at least two independent chains: input and output. If the input rules look right, the problem might be in the `output` chain, or vice versa.

- If the script appears to hang, chances are a rule is referencing a symbolic host-name rather than an IP address before the DNS rules have been enabled. Any rule using a hostname instead of an address must come after the DNS rules.

- Double-check the `ipchains` syntax. It's easy to mistype the rule's direction, to reverse the source and destination addresses or ports, or to switch upper- and lowercase-sensitive options.

- If a syntax error is encountered, the firewall script exits without installing subsequent rules. `ipchains` error messages are cryptic. If you're having difficulty identifying the problem rule, execute the script with the `-x` or `-v` shell option to list the rules as the script is executed—for example, `sh -v /etc/rc.d/rc.firewall`. The `-v` option prints the line in the script as it is read by the shell command interpreter. The `-x` option prints the line in the script as it is executed by the shell.

- When a service doesn't work, use the `ipchains` logging option, `-l`, to log all denied packets going in both directions. Do the log entries in `/var/log/messages` show anything being denied when you try the service?

- If you have Internet access from the firewall machine but not from the LAN, double-check that IP forwarding is enabled in `/etc/sysconfig/network`. Look for a line that reads `FORWARD_IPV4=yes`. IP forwarding can be permanently configured by hand in `/etc/sysconfig/network` or through the `control-panel` GUI interface. The IP forwarding option is found in the routing section of the `control-panel`'s network configuration dialogs. Neither of these configuration methods takes effect until the network is restarted. If IP forwarding wasn't enabled, you can enable it immediately by typing the following line as root:

  ```
  echo "1" > /proc/sys/net/ipv4/ip_forward
  ```

- If a service works on the LAN but not externally, turn on logging for accepted packets on the internal interface. Use the service *very* briefly to see which ports, addresses, flags, and so forth are in use in both directions. You won't want to log accepted packets for any length of time, or you'll have hundreds or thousands of log entries in `/var/log/messages`.

- If a service doesn't work at all, temporarily insert input and output rules at the beginning of the firewall script to accept everything in both directions and log all traffic with the `-l` option. Is the service available now? If so, check the log entries in `/var/log/messages` to see which ports are in use.

Listing the Firewall Rules

It's a good idea to list the rules you've defined to double-check that they are installed and in the order you expect. The `-L` option lists the actual rules for a given chain as they exist in the internal kernel table. Rules are listed in the order they are matched against a packet.

The basic format of the list command is:

```
ipchains -L input
ipchains -L output
ipchains -L forward
```

Unlike using `ipchains` to define actual rules, using `ipchains` to list existing rules can be done from the command line. The output goes to your terminal or can be redirected into a file.

The next sections use four sample rules on the `input` chain to illustrate the differences among the various listing format options available to you and to explain what the `output` fields mean. Using the different listing format options, the same four sample rules are listed with varying degrees of detail and readability. The listing format options are the same for the `input`, `output`, and `forward` chains.

ipchains -L input

Here is an abbreviated list of four rules from an `input` chain's table using the default listing options:

```
> ipchains -L input

1. Chain input (policy DENY):
2. target  prot  opt    source          destination     ports
3. DENY    all   ——l·   my.host.domain  anywhere        n/a
4. ACCEPT  icmp  ———     anywhere        my.host.domain  echo-reply
5. ACCEPT  all   ———     anywhere        anywhere        n/a
6. ACCEPT  tcp   !y——    anywhere        my.host.domain  www -> 1024:65535
```

Line 1 identifies the listing as being for the input chain. The input chain's default policy is DENY.

Line 2 contains these column headings:

- target refers to the target disposition of a packet matching the rule—ACCEPT, DENY, or REJECT.

- prot is abbreviated for protocol, which can be all, tcp, udp, or icmp.

- opt stands for the packet's options, or flag bits. The four most common flags you'll see will be none, l (log a packet matching the rule), y (SYN must be set), and !y (ACK must be set).

- source is the address the packet originates from.

- destination is the packet's destination address.

- ports lists both the source and destination ports, the ICMP message type, or n/a if no ports are specified in the rule.

Line 3 is the basic IP spoofing rule, denying incoming packets claiming to be from your machine, with logging enabled.

Line 4 accepts incoming ping replies to your outgoing ping requests.

Line 5 illustrates how the simple -L list command, without qualifying arguments, lacks some important detail. The rule appears to accept all incoming packets—tcp, udp, and icmp—from anywhere. The missing detail in this case is the interface, lo. This is the rule accepting all input on the loopback interface.

Line 6 accepts packets from remote Web servers you've contacted. The protocol is tcp. Incoming server responses to your browser requests must have the ACK bit set (!y). The Web server's source port is port 80, www. Your browser, as the client program, will have contacted the server from one of the unprivileged ports, 1024–65535.

ipchains -L input -n

The -n option reports all fields as numeric values rather than as symbolic names. This option can save time if your rules use a lot of symbolic hostnames that otherwise would require DNS lookups before being listed. Additionally, a port range is more informative if it is listed as 23:79 rather than as telnet:finger.

The line numbers in the listings throughout this chapter are not part of the output, but have been added for ease of discussion.

Using the same four sample rules from the input chain, the following shows what the listing output looks like using the -n numeric option:

```
> ipchains -L input -n

1. Chain input (policy DENY):
2. target     prot opt    source        destination     ports
3. DENY       all  ----l- 192.168.10.30 0.0.0.0/0       n/a
4. ACCEPT     icmp ------ 0.0.0.0/0     192.168.10.30   0 -> *
5. ACCEPT     all  ------ 0.0.0.0/0     0.0.0.0/0       n/a
6. ACCEPT     tcp  !y---- 0.0.0.0/0     192.168.10.30   80 -> 1024:65535
```

Line 1 identifies the listing as being for the input chain. The input chain's default policy is DENY.

Line 2 contains these column headings:

- target refers to the target disposition of a packet matching the rule—ACCEPT, DENY, or REJECT.

- prot is abbreviated for protocol, which can be all, tcp, udp, or icmp.

- opt stands for the packet's options, or flag bits. The four most common flags you'll see will be none, l (log a packet matching the rule), y (SYN must be set), and !y (ACK must be set).

- source is the address the packet originates from.

- destination is the packet's destination address.

- ports lists both the source and destination ports, the ICMP message type, or n/a if no ports are specified in the rule.

Line 3 is the basic IP spoofing rule, denying incoming packets claiming to be from your machine at IP address 192.168.10.30, with logging enabled.

Line 4 accepts incoming ping replies to your outgoing ping requests.

Line 5 illustrates how the simple -L list command, without qualifying arguments, lacks some important detail. The rule appears to accept all incoming packets—tcp, udp, and icmp—from anywhere. The missing detail in this case is the interface, lo. This is the rule accepting all input on the loopback interface.

Line 6 accepts packets from remote Web servers you've contacted. The protocol is tcp. Incoming server responses to your browser requests must have the ACK bit set (!y). The Web server's source port is port 80, www. Your browser, as the client program, will have contacted the server from one of the unprivileged ports, 1024–65535.

ipchains -L input -v

The -v option produces more verbose output, including the interface name. Reporting the interface name is especially helpful when the machine has more than one network interface.

Using the same four sample rules from the input chain, the following shows what the listing output looks like using the -v verbose option:

```
> ipchains -L input -v

1. Chain input (policy DENY: 60018 packets, 4120591 bytes):
2.  pkts bytes target prot opt    tosa tosx ifname * source        destination
ports
3.    0     0 DENY   all  ----l- 0xFF 0x00 eth0      my.host.domain anywhere
n/a
4.    0     0 ACCEPT icmp ------ 0xFF 0x00 eth0      anywhere       my.host.domain
echo-reply
5. 61004 5987K ACCEPT all  ------ 0xFF 0x00 lo        anywhere       anywhere
n/a
6.  2332 1597K ACCEPT tcp  !y---- 0xFF 0x00 eth0      anywhere       my.host.domain
www -> 1024:65535
```

Line 1 identifies the listing as being for the input chain. The input chain's default policy is DENY. 60018 packets have passed through the input chain's rules, accounting for 4120591 bytes of network traffic.

Line 2 contains the following column headings:

- pkts is the number of packets that have matched the rule.

- bytes is the number of bytes contained in the packets matching the rule.

- target refers to the target disposition of a packet matching the rule—ACCEPT, DENY, or REJECT.

- prot stands for protocol, and can be all, tcp, udp, or icmp.

- opt stands for the packet's options, or flag bits. The four most common flags you'll see will be none, l (log a packet matching the rule), y (SYN must be set), and !y (ACK must be set).

- The Type of Service (TOS) masks, tosa and tosx, are and and xor masks, respectively. Four of the bits correspond to four different ways of handling packet delivery priority: Minimum Delay, Maximum Throughput, Maximum Reliability, and Minimum Cost. You specify one of the service priority bits to be set in the and mask to select the bit. The result of the and operation is xor'ed with the xor mask to set or clear the flag.

Type of Service (TOS) Flags

TOS bits in the IP packet header aren't used generally. At best, you can use them as a hint or indication of preference. The recipient probably won't honor the TOS bits. If this is all gibberish to you, ignore it. Most people won't use the TOS masks.

The TOS flags are an official part of the IP protocol standard. Space was reserved for them in anticipation of the day when they would be used. Instead, IP evolved into a simple, best-effort protocol. Current router standards proposals are suggesting reusing these bits for new router QoS (quality of service) information.

- `ifname` is the network interface name—such as `eth0`, `eth1`, `lo`, or `ppp0`—this rule applies to. Only packets on this specific network interface will match the rule. This field becomes important if you have a LAN with separate firewall rules for the different interfaces.

- `*` is a placeholder for two unused fields included in the output. I've replaced the fields, `mark` and `outsize`, to save space:

  - `mark` is not used or well documented yet.

  - `outsize` is not documented.

- `source` is the address the packet originates from.

- `destination` is the packet's destination address.

- `ports` lists both the source and destination ports, the ICMP message type, or `n/a` if no ports are specified in the rule.

Line 3 is the basic IP spoofing rule, denying incoming packets claiming to be from your machine, with logging enabled.

Line 4 accepts incoming `ping` replies to your outgoing `ping` requests.

Line 5 illustrates how the simple `-L` list command, with the verbose option, provides some clarifying detail when the rules refer to multiple interfaces. With the `-v` option, it's clear that the rule refers to the loopback interface, `lo`. This is the rule accepting all input on the loopback interface.

Line 6 accepts packets from remote Web servers you've contacted. The protocol is `tcp`. Incoming server responses to your browser requests must have the `ACK` bit set (`!y`). The Web server's source port is port `80`, `www`. Your browser, as the client program, will have contacted the Web server from one of the unprivileged ports, `1024–65535`.

Unused Fields—Mark and Outsize

`mark` and `outsize` are placeholders for functionality that isn't implemented yet. "marking" a packet has to do with QoS (quality of service). The TOS bits aren't used, and development companies and standards committees are looking to reuse the TOS field with new QoS bits, which is called *packet marking.* QoS will give service providers the ability to offer different tiers of service quality throughput to their business customers, as well as distinguish between the needs of, say, a low bandwidth `telnet` session and a high bandwidth, real-time video stream.

ipchains -L input -nv

Using the same four sample rules from the `input` chain, the following shows what the listing output looks like using the `-n` numeric and `-v` verbose options together:

```
> ipchains -L input -nv

1. Chain input (policy DENY: 60018 packets, 4120591 bytes):
2.  pkts bytes target prot opt    tosa tosx ifname * source          destination
ports
3.    0     0 DENY   all  ----1- 0xFF 0x00 eth0     192.168.10.30 0.0.0.0/0
n/a
4.    0     0 ACCEPT icmp ------ 0xFF 0x00 eth0     0.0.0.0/0     192.168.10.30 0
-> *
5. 61004 5987K ACCEPT all  ------ 0xFF 0x00 lo      0.0.0.0/0     0.0.0.0/0
n/a
6.  2332 1597K ACCEPT tcp  !y---- 0xFF 0x00 eth0     0.0.0.0/0     192.168.10.30
80 -> 1024:65535
```

Line 1 identifies the listing as being for the `input` chain. The `input` chain's default policy is `DENY`. `60018` packets have passed through the `input` chain's rules, accounting for `4120591` bytes of network traffic.

Line 2 contains the following column headings:

- `pkts` is the number of packets that have matched the rule.

- `bytes` is the number of bytes contained in the packets matching the rule.

- `target` refers to the target disposition of a packet matching the rule—`ACCEPT`, `DENY`, or `REJECT`.

- `prot` stands for protocol, and can be `all`, `tcp`, `udp`, or `icmp`.

- `opt` stands for the packet's options, or flag bits. The four most common flags you'll see will be none, `l` (log a packet matching the rule), `y` (`SYN` must be set), and `!y` (`ACK` must be set).

- The Type of Service (TOS) masks, `tosa` and `tosx`, are and and xor masks, respectively. Four of the bits correspond to four different ways of handling packet delivery priority: Minimum Delay, Maximum Throughput, Maximum Reliability, and Minimum Cost. You specify one of the service priority bits to be set in the and mask to select the bit. The result of the and operation is xor'ed with the xor mask to set or clear the flag.

- `ifname` is the network interface name—such as `eth0`, `eth1`, `lo`, or `ppp0`—this rule applies to. Only packets on this specific network interface will match the rule. This field becomes important if you have a LAN with separate firewall rules for the different interfaces.

- `*` is a placeholder for two unused fields included in the output. I've replaced the fields, `mark` and `outsize`, to save space.

  - `mark` is not used or well documented yet.

  - `outsize` is not documented.

- **source** is the address the packet originates from.

- **destination** is the packet's destination address.

- **ports** lists both the source and destination ports, the ICMP message type, or **n/a** if no ports are specified in the rule.

Line 3 is the basic IP spoofing rule, denying incoming packets claiming to be from your machine, with logging enabled.

Line 4 accepts incoming **ping** replies to your outgoing **ping** requests.

Line 5 illustrates how the simple **-L** list command, with the verbose option, provides some clarifying detail when the rules refer to multiple interfaces. With the **-v** option, it's clear that the rule refers to the loopback interface, **lo**. This is the rule accepting all input on the loopback interface.

Line 6 accepts packets from remote Web servers you've contacted. The protocol is **tcp**. Incoming server responses to your browser requests must have the **ACK** bit set (**!y**). The Web server's source port is port **80**, **www**. Your browser, as the client program, will have contacted the Web server from one of the unprivileged ports, **1024–65535**.

Checking the Input, Output, and Forwarding Rules

Now that you've seen what a firewall chain listing looks like and the formatting options available, we'll go through brief lists of input, output, and forwarding rules. The sample rules are representative of some of the rules you'll most likely use yourself.

Checking the Input Rules

Your input rules are mostly **ACCEPT** rules when the default policy is **DENY**. Everything is denied by default and you explicitly define what will be accepted. The following example contains a representative sample of input acceptance rules:

```
> ipchains -L input

  Chain input (policy DENY):
  target prot opt    source          destination     ports

1. ACCEPT icmp ------ anywhere        my.host.domain
   destination-unreachable
2. ACCEPT icmp ------ anywhere        my.host.domain source-quench
3. ACCEPT icmp ------ anywhere        my.host.domain time-exceeded
4. ACCEPT icmp ------ anywhere        my.host.domain parameter-problem
5. ACCEPT udp  ------ isp.name.server my.host.domain domain -> domain
6. ACCEPT udp  ------ isp.name.server my.host.domain domain ->
   1024:65535
7. ACCEPT tcp  !y---- isp.name.server my.host.domain domain ->
   1024:65535
8. REJECT tcp  ------ anywhere        my.host.domain 1024:65535 -> auth
```

```
 9.  ACCEPT tcp  !y---- anywhere          my.host.domain auth -> 1024:65535
10.  ACCEPT tcp  ------ anywhere          my.host.domain 1024:65535 -> www
11.  ACCEPT tcp  !y---- anywhere          my.host.domain www -> 1024:65535
12.  ACCEPT tcp  !y---- isp.news.server my.host.domain nntp -> 1024:65535
13.  ACCEPT tcp  ------ anywhere          my.host.domain 1024:65535 -> smtp
14.  ACCEPT tcp  !y---- anywhere          my.host.domain smtp -> 1024:65535
```

The default policy for incoming packets is DENY. Denied packets are simply dropped without any notification being returned to the source address. There are 14 rules on the chain:

- Line 1—Incoming ICMP Destination Unreachable error messages are accepted from anywhere.

- Line 2—Incoming ICMP Source Quench flow control messages are accepted from anywhere.

- Line 3—Incoming ICMP Time Exceeded error messages are accepted from anywhere.

- Line 4—Incoming ICMP Parameter Problem error messages are accepted from anywhere.

- Line 5—A UDP packet with your ISP's name server source address is accepted if the source and destination ports are both the domain service port 53. This packet type would be a server-to-server communication, where your local name server forwarded a lookup request to your ISP's name server, and this packet contains the response to your request.

- Line 6—A UDP packet with your ISP's name server source address is accepted if the source port is the domain service port 53, addressed to this interface and an unprivileged destination port. This packet type would be a server-to-client UDP response containing DNS lookup information that a client on your machine requested.

- Line 7—A TCP packet with your ISP's name server source address is accepted if the source port is the domain service port 53, the ACK bit is set in the packet's flag field, and the destination port is in the unprivileged range. If your machine is configured as a DNS client, this packet type would typically be a server-to-client TCP response containing DNS lookup information that a client on your machine requested after an initial UDP request failed.

- Line 8—All incoming TCP packets destined for the local identd server at auth service port 113 are rejected. An ICMP error notification type 3, Service Unavailable, will be returned to the source address.

- Line 9—All incoming TCP packets coming from the auth service port 113 and targeted to an unprivileged destination port are accepted, provided the ACK bit is set. These packets contain responses to auth requests one of your clients initiated.

- Line 10—Incoming TCP packets from any source address with an unprivileged source port are accepted if they are targeted to your Web server's service port 80. Packets with either the SYN or ACK flags are accepted.

- Line 11—Incoming TCP response packets from any source address and source port 80 are accepted if they are targeted to a local unprivileged port and the ACK bit is set. These packets are incoming responses from remote Web servers you've contacted through your Web browser.

- Line 12—Incoming TCP response packets from your ISP's news server source address and the nntp source port 119 are accepted if they are targeted to a local unprivileged port and the ACK bit is set. These packets are incoming responses from your ISP's news server when you are reading Usenet news.

- Line 13—Incoming TCP packets from any source address with an unprivileged source port are accepted if they are targeted to your mail server's smtp service port 25. Packets with either the SYN or ACK flags are accepted to allow incoming connections to your server to accept incoming mail.

- Line 14—Incoming TCP response packets from any source address and smtp source port 25 are accepted if they are targeted to a local unprivileged port and the ACK bit is set. These packets are incoming responses from remote mail servers you've contacted to send outgoing mail.

Checking the Output Rules

Your output rules are mostly ACCEPT rules when the default policy is REJECT or DENY. Everything is blocked by default. You explicitly define what will be accepted. The following example contains a representative sample of output acceptance rules:

```
> ipchains -L output

    Chain output (policy REJECT):
    target prot opt    source          destination       ports

1.  ACCEPT icmp ------ my.host.domain anywhere          destination-unreachable
2.  ACCEPT icmp ------ my.host.domain anywhere          source-quench
3.  ACCEPT icmp ------ my.host.domain isp.address.range time-exceeded
4.  ACCEPT icmp ------ my.host.domain anywhere          parameter-problem
5.  ACCEPT udp  ------ my.host.domain isp.name.server   domain -> domain
6.  ACCEPT udp  ------ my.host.domain isp.name.server   1024:65535-> domain
7.  ACCEPT tcp  ------ my.host.domain isp.name.server   1024:65535-> domain
8.  ACCEPT tcp  ------ my.host.domain anywhere          1024:65535 -> auth
9.  ACCEPT tcp  !y---- my.host.domain anywhere          www -> 1024:65535
10. ACCEPT tcp  ------ my.host.domain anywhere          1024:65535 -> www
11. ACCEPT tcp  ------ my.host.domain isp.news.server   1024:65535 -> nntp
12. ACCEPT tcp  !y---- my.host.domain anywhere          smtp -> 1024:65535
13. ACCEPT tcp  ------ my.host.domain anywhere          1024:65535 -> smtp
```

The default policy for the `output` chain is `REJECT`. Your local programs will receive an error notice immediately if a connection isn't allowed. There are 13 rules on the chain:

- Line 1—Outgoing ICMP type 3 error messages are allowed to go anywhere. Although the message is identified as a Destination Unreachable message, it is in fact a general error type message. The message contains a field specifying the specific type of error code.

- Line 2—ICMP Source Quench flow control messages are allowed to go anywhere.

- Line 3—ICMP Time Exceeded messages can be sent only to your ISP's machines. This rule limits responses to remote `traceroute` requests to only your ISP.

- Line 4—ICMP Parameter Problem error messages are allowed to go anywhere.

- Line 5—A UDP packet with your ISP's name server destination address is accepted if the source and destination ports are both the `domain` service port 53. This packet type would be a server-to-server communication, where your local name server is forwarding a lookup request to your ISP's name server after a local cache miss.

- Line 6—A UDP packet with your ISP's name server destination address is accepted if the source port is an unprivileged port and the destination port is the `domain` service port 53. This packet type would be a client-to-server UDP request for DNS lookup information from a client on your machine to the remote server.

- Line 7—A TCP packet with your ISP's name server destination address is accepted if the source port is an unprivileged port, the destination port is the `domain` service port 53, and either the `SYN` or `ACK` flags are set in the packet's flag field. If your machine is configured as a DNS client, this packet type would typically be a client-to-server TCP request for DNS lookup information from a client on your machine after an initial UDP request failed.

- Line 8—All outgoing TCP packets coming from an unprivileged source port and targeted to the `auth` destination service port 113 are accepted. These packets contain requests to an `auth identd` server one of your clients initiated.

- Line 9—Outgoing TCP response packets to any destination address with an unprivileged destination service port are accepted if they originate at your Web server's service port 80. The `ACK` bit must be set, because these packets are your Web server's responses to incoming requests.

- Line 10—Outgoing TCP request packets targeted to anywhere and destination port 80 are accepted if they originate from a local unprivileged port. These packets are outgoing requests and ongoing connections with remote Web servers you've contacted through your Web browser.

- Line 11—Outgoing TCP request packets targeted to your ISP's news server's IP address and the nntp destination port 119 are accepted if they originate from a local unprivileged port. These packets are outgoing requests and ongoing connections with your ISP's news server when you are reading Usenet news.

- Line 12—Outgoing TCP packets from your mail server's smtp service source port 25 are accepted if they are targeted to an unprivileged destination port and the ACK bit is set. These packets are outgoing responses to remote mail clients who have contacted you to deliver incoming mail.

- Line 13—Outgoing TCP packets from an unprivileged port are accepted if they are targeted to smtp destination port 25. These packets are outgoing connection requests and ongoing connections with remote mail servers you've contacted to send outgoing mail.

Checking the Forwarding Rules

The forwarding rules logically fall between the input rules and the output rules. An incoming packet must first be accepted on the input chain. If the packet's destination address is something other than the address of the interface the packet arrived on, the packet is passed on to the forward chain. If the packet matches a forwarding rule, the packet is passed on the next interface's output chain. If the packet is accepted on the output chain, it is ultimately sent out on its way.

For the purposes of illustration, the firewall rule shown next forwards and masquerades only TCP traffic from the internal network interface. UDP traffic is not routed. General ICMP traffic is not routed.

This section is based on a representative sample forwarding rule. As you can see, an elaborate set of forwarding rules isn't necessary in a small home setup:

```
ipchains -A forward -i $EXTERNAL_INTERFACE -p tcp -s $INTERNAL_LAN_ADDRESSES -j
MASQ

> ipchains -L forward -v

Chain forward (policy REJECT: 0 packets, 0 bytes):
 pkts bytes target prot opt    tosa tosx ifname source destination ports
   80  4130 MASQ   tcp  ------ 0xFF 0x00 eth0   choke  anywhere    any->any
```

ICMP Masquerading in Linux

Until recently, ICMP messages other than error messages were not masqueraded unless a special ICMP masquerade service was explicitly compiled into the kernel. The service was not enabled by default. As of Red Hat Release 6.0, general ICMP masquerading is enabled by default. This means that it's possible for an internal machine to ping a remote host or run traceroute without recompiling the kernel.

The default policy is REJECT, so no packets will be forwarded without an explicit rule.

In this case the -v option is helpful again. The rule says that packets arriving from the internal LAN, $INTERNAL_LAN_ADDRESSES, are forwarded on to the external interface, eth0. They are forwarded to the external interface only in the case where their destination address is a remote address. The internal LAN interface can't be explicitly defined under ipchains semantics. The interface is implied by the LAN source address in the packet. A packet with a LAN source address, arriving on the internal network interface, does not belong to the same network as the external network interface. If the packet's destination address is not the internal network interface's address on this machine, the destination address is necessarily a remote address, relative to the internal interface.

Notice that these packets would be rejected at the external interface if masquerading were not enabled. The masquerading rules are applied when the packet leaves the internal interface's input queue, before transferring the packet to the external interface's output queue. Assuming your firewall rejects outgoing packets with private network source addresses, packets from your LAN would be dropped at the external interface if masquerading were not enabled in the forwarding rule.

The next point of interest is that only the TCP protocol is masqueraded. Neither UDP packets nor ICMP control messages will be forwarded out through the external interface. Again, even if these packets are allowed out from the firewall machine, they are not allowed out on behalf of the internal machine because these packets are not specified in the forward/masquerade rule.

A small site could just as comfortably use the following more general rule to masquerade all internal traffic destined for remote addresses, rather than just TCP packets. Any traffic allowed out by the output rules for the external interface would be allowed out for the internal machine as well:

```
ipchains -A forward -i $EXTERNAL_INTERFACE -s $INTERNAL_LAN_ADDRESSES
    -j MASQ
```

Testing an Individual Packet Against the Firewall Rules

Individual packet types can be tested against the firewall rules with the -C option. ipchains will report on stdout whether the packet would be accepted, denied, rejected, masqueraded, etc. based on the rules currently in effect.

Using the -C option, rather than a -I insert or -A append option, tells ipchains that you are constructing a packet description. You want to know how the currently installed firewall rules will handle this packet type.

There are some ipchains syntax differences between defining actual rules and defining test packet descriptions. The -C syntax is relentlessly unforgiving. The differences can be confusing because illegalities under -C are perfectly legal when defining an actual rule.

ipchains doesn't have implied default values when using the -C option. Exact command-line argument values must be specified. The test packet descriptions must use
the -i option to specify an interface. Individual, explicit source and destination ports
must be specified. Ranges aren't allowed. So in the following examples, $UNPRIVPORTS
is replaced with port **5000**, a single port from that range. Because source and destination ports must be specified, source and destination addresses must be specified, as
well. The negation operator, !, isn't allowed. You can use the -y option, but you can't
use ! -y. Both numeric identifiers and symbolic names are allowed for the source and
destination addresses and ports.

The following ipchains -C examples assume you have a firewall installed, as
described in Chapter 3, "Building and Installing a Firewall."

A packet matching the next description is denied, even if you are hosting a Web
server. The recommended rules against IP address spoofing don't allow incoming
packets claiming to be from your source address:

```
> ipchains -C input -i eth0 -p tcp -y \
          -s <my.host.domain> 5000 \
          -d <my.host.domain> 80
```

denied

A packet matching this description is accepted if you are hosting a Web server. This
type of packet is expected as part of the ongoing connection between your server and
a remote Web client:

```
> ipchains -C output -i eth0 -p tcp \
          -s <my.host.domain> 80 \
          -d any/0 5000
```

accepted

An outgoing packet matching this description is rejected rather than denied. The
firewall examples in this book deny incoming packets and reject outgoing packets.
The -y option says the SYN flag must be set, which means the connection is being
requested by your Web server. Your Web server cannot initiate a connection to a
remote client:

```
> ipchains -C output -i eth0 -p tcp -y \
          -s <my.host.domain> 80 \
          -d any/0 5000
```

rejected

A packet matching this description is masqueraded. Any packet coming from a
machine on the LAN and destined for an unresolvable address (i.e., a remote address)
is masqueraded and forwarded out through the external interface:

```
> ipchains -C forward -i eth0 -p tcp \
          -s <my.lan.ip.address> 5000 \
          -d any/0 80
```

masqueraded

The masquerade example shows another difference between regular `ipchains` rule syntax and `-C` rule syntax. `-j MASQ` is not allowed. Only the `forward` chain can be specified.

Checking for Open Ports

Listing your firewall rules with `ipchains -L` is the main tool available for checking for open ports. Open ports are defined to be open by your `ACCEPT` rules. The Red Hat Linux distribution doesn't include any other related tools besides `netstat` for identifying open ports. Many third-party tools are available on the Internet, though.

`netstat` has several uses. In the next section, we'll use it to check for active ports so we can double-check that the TCP and UDP ports in use are the ports the firewall rules are accounting for. `netstat` returns in Chapter 6, "Verifying That the System Is Running as You Expect," where it is used for a slightly different purpose.

Following this, two third-party port scanning tools—`strobe` and `nmap`—are introduced.

netstat -a [-n -p -A inet]

`netstat` reports a variety of network status information. Quite a few command-line options are documented to select what information `netstat` reports. The following options are useful for identifying open ports, reporting whether they are in active use and by whom, and reporting which programs and which specific processes are listening on the ports:

- `-a` lists all ports that are either in active use or being listened to by local servers.

- `-n` displays the hostnames and port identifiers in numeric format. Without the `-n` option, the hostnames and port identifiers are displayed as symbolic names, as much as will fit in 80 columns. Using `-n` avoids a potentially long wait while remote hostnames are looked up. Not using `-n` produces a more readable listing.

- `-p` lists the name of the program listening on the socket. You must be logged in as `root` to use the `-p` option.

- `-A inet` specifies the address family reported. The listing includes the ports in use as they are associated with your network interface cards. Local UNIX address family socket connections aren't reported, including local network-based connections in use by programs, such as any X Window program you might have running.

> ### Types of Sockets—TCP/IP and UNIX
>
> Linux was inspired by BSD UNIX. Sockets were introduced in BSD 4.3 UNIX in 1986. Two main socket types were the Internet domain, AF_INET, and the UNIX domain, AF_UNIX, sockets. AF_INET is the TCP/IP socket used across a network. AF_UNIX is a socket type local to the kernel. The UNIX domain socket type is used for interprocess communication on the same computer. It is more efficient than using TCP/IP for local sockets. Nothing goes out on the network.

The following `netstat` output is limited to the `INET` domain sockets. The listing reports all ports being listened to by network services, including the program name and the specific process ID of the listening program:

```
> netstat -a -p -A inet

1.   Active Internet connections (servers and established)
2.   Proto Recv-Q Send-Q Local Address    Foreign Address State   PID/
     Program name

3.   tcp      0   143 internal:telnet    macintosh:62360 ESTABLISHED
     15392/in.telnetd
4.   tcp      0     0 *:smtp             *:*             LISTEN
     3674/sendmail: acce
5.   tcp      0     0 my.host.domain:www *:*             LISTEN  638/httpd
6.   tcp      0     0 internal:domain    *:*             LISTEN  588/named
7.   tcp      0     0 localhost:domain   *:*             LISTEN  588/named
8.   tcp      0     0 *:auth             *:*             LISTEN  574/inetd
9.   tcp      0     0 *:pop-3            *:*             LISTEN  574/inetd
10.  tcp      0     0 *:telnet           *:*             LISTEN  574/inetd
11.  tcp      0     0 *:ftp              *:*             LISTEN  574/inetd
12.  udp      0     0 *:domain           *:*                     588/named
13.  udp      0     0 internal:domain    *:*                     588/named
14.  udp      0     0 localhost:domain   *:*                     588/named
```

Line 1 identifies the listing as including local servers and active Internet connections. This selection was indicated with the `-A inet` option to `netstat`.

Line 2 contains these column headings:

- `Proto` refers to the transport protocol the service runs over, TCP or UDP.
- `Recv-Q` is the number of bytes received from the remote host but not yet delivered to the local program.
- `Send-Q` is the number of bytes sent from the local program that haven't been acknowledged by the remote host yet.
- `Local Address` is the local socket, the network interface and service port pair.
- `Foreign Address` is the remote socket, the remote network interface, and service port pair.
- `State` is the local socket's connection state for sockets using the TCP protocol, `ESTABLISHED` connection, `LISTEN`ing for a connection request, as well as a number of intermediate connection establishment and shutdown states.
- `PID/Program name` is the process ID (PID) and program name that owns the local socket.

Line 3 shows that a `telnet` connection is established over the internal LAN network interface from a Macintosh. The `netstat` command was typed from this connection.

Line 4 shows that `sendmail` listening for incoming mail on the SMTP port associated with all network interfaces, including the external interface connected to the Internet, the internal LAN interface, and the loopback, localhost interface.

Line 5 shows that a local Web server is listening for connections on the external interface to the Internet.

Line 6 shows that the name server is listening on the internal LAN interface for DNS lookup connection requests from local machines over TCP.

Line 7 shows that the name server is listening on the loopback interface for DNS lookup connection requests from clients on this machine over TCP.

Line 8 shows that `inetd` is listening for connections on the `auth` port associated with all interfaces on behalf of `identd`.

Line 9 shows that `inetd` is listening for connections on the `pop-3` port associated with all interfaces on behalf of `popd`. (`inetd` is listening on all interfaces for incoming POP connections. If a connection request arrives, `inetd` starts a `popd` server to service the request.) Both the firewall and higher-level security mechanisms at the `tcp_wrapper` level and the `popd` configuration level limit incoming connections to the LAN machines.

Line 10 shows that `inetd` is listening for connections on the `telnet` port associated with all interfaces on behalf of `telnetd`. (`inetd` is listening on all interfaces for incoming `telnet` connections. If a connection request arrives, `inetd` starts a `telnetd` server to service the request.) Both the firewall and higher-level security mechanisms at the `tcp_wrapper` level limit incoming connections to the LAN machines.

Line 11 shows that `inetd` is listening for connections on the `ftp` port associated with all interfaces on behalf of `ftpd`. (`inetd` is listening on all interfaces for incoming `ftp` connections. If a connection request arrives, `inetd` starts an `ftpd` server to service the request.) Both the firewall and higher-level security mechanisms at the `tcp_wrapper` level and the `ftpd` server configuration level limit incoming connections to the LAN machines.

Line 12 shows that the name server is listening on all interfaces for DNS server-to-server communications and accepting local lookup requests over UDP.

Line 13 shows that the name server is listening on the internal LAN network interface for DNS server-to-server communications and lookup requests over UDP.

Line 14 shows that the name server is listening on the loopback interface for DNS lookup requests from local clients on this machine over UDP.

netstat **Output Reporting Conventions**

In `netstat` output, the local and foreign (that is, remote) addresses are listed as `<address:port>`. Under the `Local Address` column, the address is the name or IP address of one of your network interface cards. When the address is listed as `*`, it means that the server is listening on all network interfaces, rather than on just a single interface. The port is either the symbolic or numeric service port identifier the server is using. Under the `Foreign Address` column, the address is the name or IP address of the remote client currently participating in a connection. The `*.*` is printed when the port is idle. The port is the remote client's port on its end.

Idle servers listening over the TCP protocol are reported as LISTENing for a connection request. Idle servers listening over the UDP protocol are reported as blank. UDP has no state. The netstat output is simply making a distinction between stateful TCP and stateless UDP.

The next two sections describe two third-party tools available from the Internet, strobe and nmap.

strobe

strobe is a simple TCP port scanner. Use it to report which TCP ports are open on your network interfaces. strobe is available at http://metalab.unc.edu/pub/Linux/system/network/admin.

The following sample strobe output reports the TCP ports strobe has found servers listening on. strobe's default output includes the scanned hostname and the entry from /etc/services describing the port. With a firewall installed, there could be additional servers running on the machine, as well, hidden behind publicly blocked ports:

```
> strobe firewall

strobe 1.02 (c) 1995 Julian Assange -Proff- (proff@suburbia.apana.org.au).
firewall      ssh        22/tcp                # SSH Remote Login Protocol
firewall      smtp       25/tcp mail
firewall      domain     53/tcp nameserver     # name-domain server
firewall      www        80/tcp http           # WorldWideWeb HTTP
firewall      auth       113/tcp authentication tap ident
```

nmap

nmap is a fairly new network security auditing tool that includes many of the newer scanning techniques in use today. You should check your system security with nmap. It's a given that other people will. nmap is available at http://metalab.unc.edu/pub/Linux/system/network/admin/.

The following sample nmap output reports the state of all TCP and UDP ports. Because the verbose option isn't used, nmap reports only the ports that are open, that have servers listening on them. nmap output includes the scanned hostname, IP address, port, open or closed state, transport protocol in use on that port, and symbolic service port name from /etc/services. Because sebastion is an internal host, additional telnet and X11 ports are open for internal LAN access:

```
> nmap -sT -sU sebastion

WARNING:  -sU is now UDP scan — for TCP FIN scan use -sF

Starting nmap V. 2.12 by Fyodor (fyodor@dhp.com, www.insecure.org/nmap/)
Interesting ports on sebastion.firewall.lan (192.168.1.2):
```

```
Port    State     Protocol    Service
21      open      tcp         ftp
22      open      tcp         ssh
23      open      tcp         telnet
25      open      tcp         smtp
53      open      udp         domain
53      open      tcp         domain
113     open      tcp         auth
123     open      udp         ntp
6000    open      tcp         X11

nmap run completed — 1 IP address (1 host up) scanned in 3 seconds
```

Debugging SSH—A Real-Life Example

Early on, a friend impressed upon me the importance of using ssh rather than telnet. I hadn't yet discovered the joys and wonders of my firewall bible, *Building Internet Firewalls* by D. Brent Chapman and Elizabeth D. Zwicky (O'Reilly & Associates, 1995), nor had I discovered the pleasure of reading the RFC (Request for Comment) standards at www.ietf.cnri.reston.va.us/rfc.html. If a firewall rule example didn't exist in the Linux HOWTOs, I had to figure out the protocol the hard way, by using the system tools available and enabling firewall logging. The SSH protocol was one of the first.

I had downloaded, compiled, and installed ssh. I'd set up the authentication keys locally and at one of my ISPs. Outgoing ssh connections to the ISP worked without a problem. Incoming ssh connections from the ISP worked without a problem. Everything was great.

It didn't take long to discover that incoming ssh connections from my employer didn't work. Trying to ssh to my home machine from work, I'd get the password challenge. It was accepted. I'd get the local login banner and a shell prompt under my login account. Then nothing. The keyboard didn't respond. If instead, I used ssh to connect to my ISP from work, and then used ssh to log into my home computer from the ISP machine, everything worked as expected. I could log in from my ISP. I could log in to my ISP from work. But I couldn't log in directly from work.

The only option was to ssh into my ISP, and from there to ssh into the local machine, and use the system tools, ps and netstat, to see what was different between using ssh from the ISP and using ssh from work.

I didn't understand the SSH protocol, so I didn't understand what I was seeing. In fact, I completely misinterpreted what I was seeing but came up with workable firewall rules in spite of myself.

My first thought was that the local sshd server was crashing. Using ps -ax, there were three copies of the sshd server running. One was the master server daemon. One was the server that had been forked off to handle the ongoing connection from the ISP. One was the server that had been forked off to handle the ongoing connection from work, the incoming connection that was hung. Okay. The servers were running.

The next step was to use `netstat -a -A inet` to look at the connection states. The master `sshd` server was listening for new connections on port 22, as expected. The server handling the ongoing connection from my ISP was listening on port 22, and the remote ISP client was using an unprivileged port, again as expected. The server handling the ongoing connection from work was listening on port 22, but the remote work client was using the privileged port, 1023! This was confusing. The work client was using a privileged port, and the ISP client was using an unprivileged port.

So what's the deal with SSH? Looking at `/etc/services`, SSH appears to be a standard TCP service using port 22. If it were, the following I/O server ruleset for incoming SSH connections would work:

```
ipchains -A input   -i $EXTERNAL_INTERFACE -p tcp  \
         -s $ANYWHERE $UNPRIVPORTS \
         -d $IPADDR 22 -j ACCEPT

ipchains -A output -i $EXTERNAL_INTERFACE -p tcp ! -y \
         -s $IPADDR 22 \
         -d $ANYWHERE $UNPRIVPORTS -j ACCEPT
```

In fact, these rules did work for the ISP connection. The rules were correct, but `ssh` would hang from work after logging in. As it turns out, these two rules were also what allowed me to get as far as the password prompt, the login banner, and the shell prompt from work. These two rules weren't enough to cover all of the SSH protocol.

To double-check what I was seeing, I enabled logging for all incoming and outgoing traffic related to port 22, both accepted and denied. The firewall packet logs verified the situation. All outgoing packets from port 22 were being accepted. Outgoing packets from port 22 to the unprivileged port were being accepted. Outgoing packets from port 22 to the privileged port were being accepted. Incoming packets from the unprivileged port to port 22 were being accepted. Incoming packets from the privileged port, 1023, were being denied. In the end, this explained why the `ssh` login from work got so far as echoing back the login banner and shell prompt.

At that point, my firewall rules were pretty primitive. The firewall used a deny-everything-in-by-default policy and an allow-everything-out-by-default policy. Far more was allowed out than is today. The standard TCP protocol rules were sufficient for the connection from the ISP. The combination of the deny-everything-in with the allow-everything-out default policies confused the issue for the connection from work. My firewall at the time allowed the server's outgoing packets on the privileged ports, but wouldn't allow the remote client's incoming packets. The server was able to send the banner and shell prompt. The client couldn't reply to the server.

Because I never tried to have more than one or two incoming SSH connections at a time, I was under the impression that `sshd` made the connection between an unprivileged port and port 22, and then shunted it off to an ongoing connection with the forked copy of itself between port 1022 or 1023 and 22—when connected to work. Of course, the server doesn't choose the client's port. The client side chooses the port, unprivileged or privileged.

It wasn't until later that I read the ssh source code. Depending on local configuration parameters, the ssh client starts at port 1023 and searches down to port 513, assigning the connection to the first free port it finds. With other configuration parameters, the client uses an unprivileged port. The server accepts ongoing connections from either:

```
ipchains -A input  -i $EXTERNAL_INTERFACE -p tcp  \
        -s $ANYWHERE 1022:1023 \
        -d $IPADDR 22 -j ACCEPT

ipchains -A output -i $EXTERNAL_INTERFACE -p tcp ! -y \
        -s $IPADDR 22 \
        -d $ANYWHERE 1022:1023 -j ACCEPT
```

In this case, logging all packets to and from port 22, both accepted and denied, was enough to diagnose the problem, at least in terms of the firewall rules. It took longer to understand what the rules were actually accounting for.

Summary

This chapter introduced the ipchains rule listing mechanism, Linux port and network daemon information available via netstat, as well as a few of the third-party tools available for verifying that the firewall rules are installed and ordered as you expect. The ipchains packet-matching option for testing individual packet types against the installed firewall rules was demonstrated.

This chapter emphasizes the firewall rules and the ports they protect. The next chapter shifts the focus slightly to emphasize which server programs are using these ports, as well as the firewall, system, and server information generated in the system log files.

III

System Level Security and Monitoring

6

Verifying that the System Is Running as You Expect

CHAPTER 5, "DEBUGGING THE FIREWALL RULES," emphasizes how `ipchains` can be used as a diagnostic tool to validate and test the firewall rules and the service ports they protect—to determine that the rules are in place and functioning correctly. This chapter focuses on which server programs are using these ports. You need to determine that the only programs and services running are the ones you expect. After you have verified which programs and ports are in use, you next need to determine what these programs and the firewall are telling you when they report status and error messages in the system log files. This chapter introduces additional administration tools and log file information you can use.

You can never be 100% certain that your UNIX system is running correctly. You can have only a reasonable degree of confidence based on the fact that the system is running as you expect it to be—as you intend it to be. UNIX systems are too complex, the configuration issues cross too many boundaries, to ever be absolutely certain that everything is running correctly. The system logs help you verify that your system is running as you expect it to be and inform you of events and states that diverge from the expected.

Checking the Network Interfaces with *ifconfig*

`ifconfig`'s primary job is to configure and activate the network interfaces. It is executed from a network startup script managed by the runlevel manager when the system boots. Later, ifconfig is useful as a debugging tool for reporting the status of the network interfaces.

ifconfig alone, without any options, reports the status of all active network interfaces. With the -a option, ifconfig reports the status of all network interfaces, active or not. When all the interfaces are up, the two report options produce identical output.

If an interface is unexpectedly down, that's usually a sign of a network configuration problem. Check the interface configurations through the control-panel or linuxconf programs.

The following output is for a machine with a single network interface card. ifconfig reports the status of the physical interface, eth0, and the loopback interface, lo:

```
> ifconfig

eth0      Link encap:Ethernet  HWaddr 00:A0:CC:40:9B:A8
          inet addr:192.168.1.2  Bcast:192.168.1.255  Mask:255.255.255.0
          UP BROADCAST RUNNING MULTICAST  MTU:1500  Metric:1
          RX packets:266027 errors:0 dropped:0 overruns:0 frame:0
          TX packets:202290 errors:0 dropped:0 overruns:0 carrier:0
          collisions:17805 txqueuelen:100
          Interrupt:9 Base address:0xec00

lo        Link encap:Local Loopback
          inet addr:127.0.0.1  Mask:255.0.0.0
          UP LOOPBACK RUNNING  MTU:3924  Metric:1
          RX packets:51997 errors:0 dropped:0 overruns:0 frame:0
          TX packets:51997 errors:0 dropped:0 overruns:0 carrier:0
          collisions:0 txqueuelen:0
```

When there's a problem, the main thing you want to know is whether the interface is up. The third line of each interface's report indicates the interface's status and configuration. eth0 is active, UP, in this example.

Notice that ifconfig reports other status information you might be interested in at some point. The MAC hardware Ethernet address, Hwaddr, the IP address, inet addr, the broadcast address, Bcast, and the network mask, Mask, are reported. Other generally less useful information, such as the default maximum frame size, MTU, number of packets received, RX, and number of packets transmitted, TX, is also reported.

Maximum Transmission Unit (MTU) and Fragmentation

It is best to leave MTU set to 1500, the system default value. Most networks today are Ethernet networks. The Ethernet MTU is 1500 bytes. Other link layer protocols (for example, ATM or token ring) have larger recommended MTU sizes. Setting the MTU to something larger than 1500 bytes guarantees packet fragmentation somewhere along the line when the packet crosses network boundaries. TCP connections negotiate their MTU when the connection is first established.

Bandwidth isn't as much of a problem on today's network backbones as fragmentation is. The processing time required for fragmentation is an important performance factor. You get better performance with more, smaller packets than with fewer, larger packets that must be fragmented along the way.

Checking the Network Connection with *ping*

For testing basic network connectivity, ping is the tool of choice. If the external network interface is up but you can't connect to a remote host, ping can indicate whether packets are passing through the interface. ping traffic must be enabled in the firewall rules, of course. A negative ping response doesn't prove that a remote site is down. The site might not be honoring Echo Request ICMP messages. A positive ping response proves that packets are being transmitted and the remote host is responding.

With only a hostname or an IP address as an argument, ping sends packets indefinitely until you kill the process, at which point ping reports its final summary statistics:

```
> ping <smtp.my.isp.domain>

PING smtp.my.isp.domain (10.10.22.85): 56 data bytes
64 bytes from 10.10.22.85: icmp_seq=0 ttl=253 time=4.2 ms
64 bytes from 10.10.22.85: icmp_seq=1 ttl=253 time=4.4 ms
64 bytes from 10.10.22.85: icmp_seq=2 ttl=253 time=4.1 ms
64 bytes from 10.10.22.85: icmp_seq=3 ttl=253 time=5.4 ms
64 bytes from 10.10.22.85: icmp_seq=4 ttl=253 time=3.9 ms

> ^C

--- smtp.my.isp.domain ping statistics ---
5 packets transmitted, 5 packets received, 0% packet loss
round-trip min/avg/max = 3.9/4.4/5.4 ms
```

pinging a machine doesn't mean that the services on that machine are running or are available for your use. It simply means that a ping packet has traversed the network and a reply has found its way back. If a particular network service isn't available, or a particular remote host isn't responding, you at least know that your network is up and running if some host somewhere responds.

In this example, you know that your ISP's mail server machine is running. You don't know whether the mail server program itself is running. That is, if your mail service is hanging and you run ping against your ISP's mail server machine, the previous output tells you that the server machine is online. It's possible that the mail server program itself is not running.

Honoring *ping* Requests

Notice that the remote host might not respond to ping's Echo Request messages from a remote Internet site, even if the host is up. For as basic and simple a tool as ping is, ping also has a long history of use as a hacker's denial-of-service tool. As such, the firewall examples in this book honor ping requests from only the ISP's server machines, out of courtesy to the ISP's need for internal network analysis.

Checking Network Processes with *netstat*

In Chapter 5, we used `netstat -a -p -A inet` to check which programs were running and listening on which network interfaces, over which transport protocols (TCP or UDP), and on which service ports. The `-A inet` option limited the report to services and ports related to remote network communications. Without the `-A` option, `netstat` reports on both INET and UNIX domain sockets.

`netstat -a -p -A unix` prints the same information for the active UNIX domain sockets, notably those sockets used by local services. You should be able to explain every entry in the report:

```
> netstat -a -p

1.  Active UNIX domain sockets (servers and established)
2.  Proto RefCnt Flags    Type   State      I-Node PID/Program name Path

3.  unix  1      [ ]      STREAM CONNECTED 938     588/named       @0000007b
4.  unix  0      [ ACC ]  STREAM LISTENING 500119 521/syslogd      /dev/log
5.  unix  1      [ ]      STREAM CONNECTED 864     532/klogd       @00000075
6.  unix  0      [ ACC ]  STREAM LISTENING 1083   661/xfs
/tmp/.font-unix/fs-1
7.  unix  0      [ ACC ]  STREAM LISTENING 939     588/named
/var/run/ndc
8.  unix  1      [ ]      STREAM CONNECTED 492327 3674/sendmail @00000722
9.  unix  0      [ ]      STREAM CONNECTED 129     1/init          @00000016
10. unix  1      [ ]      STREAM CONNECTED 1349   893/sshd         @0000008a
11. unix  1      [ ]      STREAM CONNECTED 549784 521/syslogd      /dev/log
12. unix  1      [ ]      STREAM CONNECTED 492328 521/syslogd      /dev/log
13. unix  1      [ ]      STREAM CONNECTED 1350   521/syslogd      /dev/log
14. unix  1      [ ]      STREAM CONNECTED 953     521/syslogd      /dev/log
15. unix  1      [ ]      STREAM CONNECTED 865     521/syslogd      /dev/log
```

Line 1 identifies the report as listing UNIX domain sockets used by local servers and active connections.

Line 2 contains these column headings:

- `Proto` refers to the transport protocol the service runs over, `unix` in this case.

- `RefCnt` is the number of processes attached to this socket.

- `Flags` is `ACC` or blank. `ACC` indicates that a process is waiting to accept an incoming connection request.

- `Type` is the kind of socket the service is using. `STREAM` indicates a connection, analogous to a TCP connection. A `DGRAM` socket would be analogous to a UDP, connectionless protocol.

- `State` is the local socket's connection state, established connection (`ESTABLISHED`), listening for a connection request (`LISTEN`), as well as a number of intermediate connection establishment and shutdown states (e.g., `SYN SENT`, `SYN RECV`, `FIN WAIT`, `FIN SENT`).

- I-Node is the inode number of the file system object the program used to attach to the socket. An inode is the system's way of defining and identifying a file.

- PID/Program name is the process ID (PID) and program name that owns the local socket.

- Path is the pathname of the object the program used to attach to the socket.

Line 3 shows that the name server, named, is currently connected to a second internal name server.

Lines 4 and 11–15 show that the system logging daemon, syslogd, is listening or connected to 6 sockets. This particular machine is configured to produce 6 separate syslog output files. The netstat output isn't sufficient to know which socket is associated with which log. syslog configuration is covered later in this chapter.

Line 5 shows that the kernel logging daemon, klogd, is listening for messages from the kernel message buffers and available through /proc/kmsg. klogd works in conjunction with syslogd.

Line 6 shows that xfs is listening for local X Window font requests.

Line 7 shows that named is listening for local lookup and server requests.

Line 8 shows that sendmail is connected to send, relay, and receive mail.

Line 9 shows that init, the parent of all UNIX processes, is listening to restart terminal sessions and accept runlevel change commands.

Line 10 shows that sshd is connected to accept local ssh sessions and fork off individual servers for each connection.

This system is running as expected. init must be running. syslogd and klogd should be running. The remaining optional servers—named, xfs, sendmail, and sshd—are all intended to be running on this machine.

Checking All Processes with *ps -ax*

ps reports on process status. The -a option selects all processes with controlling terminals, usually user programs running interactively in the foreground. The -x option selects processes without controlling terminals, usually permanent system daemons running automatically in the background. The two options together report all UNIX processes, including their process ID, controlling tty, run status, system time used, and the program name. Adding the -u option produces additional, user-oriented information, including the user login name.

ps -ax lists all processes on your UNIX system. As with netstat, you should be familiar with every program running on your system and why the program is running. With the exception of a few special UNIX system daemons—notably init, kflushd, kpiod, kswapd, mdrecoveryd, and mingetty—all other daemons should be services you've explicitly enabled under the runlevel manager, /etc/inetd.conf, or /etc/rc.d/rc.local. Any other programs should be user programs you can identify. Most importantly, ps -ax shouldn't report any processes you don't expect to see.

The following is typical sample output from ps -ax:

```
> ps -ax
```

```
1.    PID  TTY    STAT   TIME   COMMAND
2.      1  ?      S      0:03   init
3.      2  ?      SW     0:02   [kflushd]
4.      3  ?      SW     0:00   [kpiod]
5.      4  ?      SW     0:01   [kswapd]
6.      5  ?      SW<    0:00   [mdrecoveryd]
7.    202  ?      S      0:00   /sbin/dhcpcd
         -c /etc/sysconfig/network-scripts/ifdhcp
8.    521  ?      S      0:03   syslogd -m 0
9.    532  ?      S      0:00   klogd
10.   546  ?      S      0:00   /usr/sbin/atd
11.   560  ?      S      0:01   crond
12.   574  ?      S      0:01   inetd
13.   588  ?      S      0:10   named
14.   638  ?      S      0:02   httpd
15.   661  ?      S      0:01   xfs
16.   893  ?      S      0:07   /usr/local/sbin/sshd
17.   928  tty2   S      0:00   /sbin/mingetty tty2
18.   930  ?      S      0:04   update (bdflush)
19.  1428  tty1   S      0:00   /sbin/mingetty tty1
20.  3674  ?      S      0:00   sendmail: accepting connections on port 25
21. 17531  ?      S      0:00   in.telnetd -n
22. 17532  pts/1  S      0:00   login -- bob
23. 17533  pts/1  S      0:00   -ksh
24. 17542  pts/1  R      0:00   ps -ax
```

Line 1 contains these column headings:

- PID is the unique process ID.
- TTY is the process's controlling terminal, if it has one.
- STAT is the process run state. In the listing, ps is running, Runnable. The other processes are Sleeping, that is, not on a run queue because they are waiting for some event to handle or respond to.
- TIME is the amount of CPU time the process has consumed.
- COMMAND is the process's program name.

Line 2 shows that init is running, the parent of all other processes. It always runs. Most flavors of UNIX crash if init dies.

Line 3 shows that kflushd is running. kflushd is not a process. It is a kernel thread that periodically flushes modified file system buffers back to disk.

Line 4 shows that kpiod is running. kpiod is not a process. It is a kernel thread that manages demand paging.

Line 5 shows that kswapd is running. kswapd is not a process. It is a kernel thread that selects physical memory pages for swapping from memory to swap space on disk to free memory for other processes.

Line 6 shows that `mdrecoveryd` is running. `mdrecoveryd` is not a process. It is a kernel driver thread that manages multiple disk devices as a single unit, i.e., RAID.

Line 7 shows that `dhcpcd` is running, the DHCP client that receives a dynamic IP address assignment from a DHCP server.

Line 8 shows that `syslogd` is running, the system message logger. It collects messages from system programs and writes them to the specified log files, the console, terminals, and so on.

Line 9 shows that `klogd` is running, the kernel message logger. It collects messages from the kernel message buffers and writes them to the specified log files and console in cooperation with `syslogd`.

Line 10 shows that `atd` is running, the daemon that schedules user programs to run at predefined times. `atd` is the user-level equivalent of `crond`.

Line 11 shows that `crond` is running, the daemon that runs system and administrative programs at predefined times.

Line 12 shows that `inetd` is running, the network service superserver that listens for connections on behalf of other services so that the individual service daemons don't need to run in the background when there is no active service request.

Line 13 shows that `named` is running, the DNS name server.

Line 14 shows that `httpd` is running, the Apache Web server. The server is not managed by `inetd`, so the process runs permanently in the background.

Line 15 shows that `xfs` is running, the X Window font server.

Line 16 shows that `sshd` is running, the SSH server. SSH is not managed by `inetd`, so the process runs permanently in the background.

Line 17 shows that `mingetty` (`tty2`) is running. `mingetty` is started from `/etc/inittab` to listen for logins on terminal lines. In this case, `tty2` is a virtual console.

Line 18 shows that `update` (`bdflush`) is running. `update` is the user space component of `kflushd` for writing modified file system buffers back to disk.

Line 19 shows that `mingetty` (`tty1`) is running. `mingetty` is started from `/etc/inittab` to listen for logins on terminal lines. In this case, `tty1` is the physical console.

Line 20 shows that `sendmail` is running, the mail server.

Line 21 shows that `in.telnetd` is running. `in.telnetd` was started by `inetd` when I telnet-ed into the system to generate the previous `ps` output.

Line 22 shows that `login` is running. `login` is the login session created after I logged into the system to general the `ps` output.

Line 23 shows that `ksh` is running, the shell program the login session is running under.

Line 24 shows that `ps` is running, the instantiation of `ps` that created the output.

If you see unfamiliar or unexpected processes, someone might have gained access to your machine. Chapter 8, "Intrusion Detection and Incident Reporting," discusses the steps to take in that event.

Interpreting the System Logs

syslogd is the service daemon that logs system events. syslogd's main system log file is /var/log/messages. Many programs use syslogd's standard logging services. Other programs, such as the Apache Web server, maintain their own separate log files.

What Gets Logged Where

By default, system log files are written in the /var/log directory. Which files are written and what is written into them are defined in the syslog configuration file, /etc/syslog.conf. UNIX distributions and releases vary. The Linux distribution is certainly preconfigured to write messages to at least the messages file. Red Hat 6.0 is preconfigured to write system log information into four separate files—messages, secure, maillog, and spooler:

- /var/log/messages is the system catchall file. It may, in fact, be the only log file used. It contains a copy of whatever messages are written to the console, any operating system messages written to the kernel's internal log buffer, and any messages produced by programs that use the syslog() system call, such as named, sendmail, and login.

- /var/log/secure contains reports of root logins, user logins and su attempts to other users. Reports of connections from other systems and root login failures at the system daemon level are also written here. Each login is recorded.

- /var/log/maillog contains a record of incoming and outgoing mail traffic and server status.

- /var/log/spooler won't be used by most systems. The file contains error messages from the uucp and news server (innd) daemons.

syslog Configuration

Not all log messages are equally important, or even interesting. This is where /etc/syslog.conf comes in. You can tailor the log output to meet your own needs and convenience. The configuration file /etc/syslog.conf allows you to tailor the log output to meet your own needs.

Defining Nondefault System Log Files
You can redirect or duplicate system messages to other log files to categorize them by topic or importance.

Messages are categorized by the subsystem that produces them. In the man pages, these categories are called *facilities* (see Table 6.1).

Table 6.1 *syslog* **Log Facility Categories**

Facility	Message Category
auth or security	Security/authorization
authpriv	Private security/authorization
cron	cron daemon messages
daemon	System daemon–generated messages
ftp	FTP server messages
kern	Kernel messages
lpr	Printer subsystem
mail	Mail subsystem
news	Network news subsystem
syslog	syslogd-generated messages
user	User program–generated messages
uucp	UUCP subsystem

Within any given facility category, log messages are divided into *priority* types. The priorities, in increasing order of importance, are listed in Table 6.2.

Table 6.2 *syslog* **Log Message Priorities**

Priority	Message Type
debug	Debug messages
info	Informational status messages
notice	Normal but important conditions
warning or warn	Warning messages
err or error	Error messages
crit	Critical conditions
alert	Immediate attention required
emerg or panic	System is unusable

An entry in syslog.conf specifies a logging facility, its priority, and where to write the messages. Not obvious is that the priority is inclusive. It's taken to mean all messages at that priority and higher. If you specify messages at the error priority, for example, all messages at priority error and higher are included.

Logs can be written to devices, such as the console, to files, and to remote machines.

These two entries write all kernel messages to both the console and to `/var/log/messages`. Messages can be duplicated to multiple destinations:

```
kern.*                                  /dev/console
kern.*                                  /var/log/messages
```

This entry writes panic messages to all default locations, including `/var/log/messages`, the console, and all user terminal sessions:

```
*.emerg                                 *
```

The next two entries write authentication information related to `root` privilege and connections to `/var/log/secure`, and user authorization information to `/var/log/auth`. With the priority defined at the `info` level, `debug` messages won't be written:

```
authpriv.info                           /var/log/secure
auth.info                               /var/log/auth
```

The next two entries write general daemon information to `/var/log/daemon`, and mail traffic information to `/var/log/maillog`:

```
daemon.notice                           /var/log/daemon
mail.info                               /var/log/maillog
```

Daemon messages at the `debug` and `info` priorities and mail messages at the `debug` priority are not logged (author's preference). `named` and systematic mail checking produce uninteresting informational messages on a regular basis.

The final entry logs all message categories of priority `info` or higher to `/var/log/messages`, with the exception of `auth`, `authpriv`, `daemon`, and `mail`. In this case, the latter four message facilities are set to `none`, because their messages are directed to their own, dedicated log files:

```
*.info;auth,authpriv,daemon,mail.none   /var/log/messages
```

Tips About Log Files in /var/log

`syslogd` doesn't create files. It only writes to existing files. If a log file doesn't exist, you can create it with the `touch` command and then make sure it is owned by `root`. For security purposes, log files are often not readable by general users. The security log file, `/var/log/secure`, in particular, is readable by `root` alone.

More Information About syslog Configuration

For a more complete description of `syslog` configuration options and example configurations, see the man pages for `syslog.conf(5)` and `sysklogd(8)`.

Firewall Log Messages: What Do They Mean?

To generate firewall logs, the kernel must be compiled with firewall logging enabled. Red Hat 6.0 has firewall logging enabled by default. Prior versions require you to recompile the kernel.

Individually matched packets are logged as `kern.info` messages for firewall rules that have the `-l` option set. Most of the IP packet header fields are reported when a packet matches a rule with logging enabled. Firewall log messages are written to `/var/log/messages` and the console by default.

You could duplicate the firewall log messages to a different file by creating a new log file and adding a line to `/etc/syslog.conf`:

```
kern.info                                    /var/log/fwlog
```

All kernel messages are directed to the console and to `/var/log/messages`, as well. When booted, the kernel doesn't generate many informational messages other than firewall log messages.

As an example, this rule denying access to the `portmap/sunrpc` port 111 would produce the following message in `/var/log/messages`:

```
ipchains -A input -p udp -i $EXTERNAL_INTERFACE \
        -d $IPADDR 111 -j DENY -l

  (1)    (2)     (3)           (4)          (5)  (6)  (7)     (8)
Jun  9 14:07:01 firewall kernel: Packet log: input DENY eth0 PROTO=17

            (9)      (10)      (11)      (12)
       10.10.22.85:14386 192.168.10.30:111

       (13)   (14)     (15)     (16)     (17)
       L=316 S=0x00 I=14393 F=0x0000 T=52
```

The log message fields are numbered for the purposes of discussion:

- Field 1 is the date, `Jun 9`.
- Field 2 is the time the log was written, `14:07:01`.
- Field 3 is the computer's hostname, `firewall`.
- Field 4 is the log facility generating the message, `kernel`. The IPFW logging routine appends `Packet log` to the facility name.
- Field 5 is the firewall chain the rule is attached to, `input`. The built-in chains include `input`, `output`, and `forward`.
- Field 6 is the action taken with regard to this packet, `DENY`. Options include `ACCEPT`, `REJECT`, `DENY`, `MASQ`, `REDIRECT`, and `RETURN`.
- Field 7 is the network interface the packet was arriving on or leaving from, `eth0`.
- Field 8 is the message protocol type contained in the packet, `PROTO=17`. Field values include `6` (`TCP`), `17` (`UDP`), `1` (`ICMP/<code>`), and `PROTO=<number>` for other protocol types.

- Field 9 is the packet's source address, `10.10.22.85`.
- Field 10 is the packet's source port, `14386`.
- Field 11 is the packet's destination address, `192.168.10.30`.
- Field 12 is the packet's destination port, `111`.

The remaining fields are not especially interesting from a logging perspective:

- Field 13 is the packet's total length in bytes, `L=316`, including both the packet header and its data.
- Field 14 is the type of service (TOS) field, `S=0x00`.
- Field 15 is the packet's datagram ID, `I=14393`. The datagram ID is either the packet ID or the segment this TCP fragment belongs to.
- Field 16 is the fragment byte offset, `F=0x0000`. If this packet contains a TCP fragment, the fragment offset indicates where in the reconstructed segment this fragment belongs.
- Field 17 is the packet's time-to-live (TTL) field, `T=52`. Time-to-live is the maximum number of hops (that is, routers visited) remaining before the packet expires.

When interpreting the log, the most interesting fields are

```
Jun  9 14:07:01 input DENY eth0 PROTO=17 10.10.22.85:14386 192.168.10.30:111
```

This says the denied packet is a UDP packet coming in on the external interface, `eth0`, from an unprivileged port at `10.10.22.85`. It was targeted to this machine's (`192.168.10.30`) port `111`, the `sunrpc/portmap` port. (This can be a frequently seen message, because `portmap` is one of the most commonly targeted services.)

Commonly Probed Ports

If you log the packets your firewall denies, you will find that only a small subset of the entire 65536 port range is probed, typically. (The newer stealth probes won't generate a log message, even if logging is enabled for the port.) Often, only a single service port of particular interest to the prober is tested.

Hostility Ratings in Table 6.3

Hostility ratings are general estimates. Any probe can be motivated by innocent curiosity. At best, the ratings are subjective estimates based on a combination of the potential danger to the system if port access were allowed, the likelihood of being hostile if that port was the only port probed as an isolated incident, and the port's use historically as a potential target. In the end, you must decide on a probe's importance for yourself, based on the case-by-case circumstances. Nevertheless, there's a big difference between someone using `ping` or traceroute on your system, or looking for an `ftp` or Web server, versus probing for an open `pop`, `imap`, or `portmap` daemon.

Of all the possible ports, Table 6.3 lists the ports more commonly probed. The ports in Table 6.3 are associated with services that are inherently insecure LAN services, that are associated with services known to harbor security flaws historically, that are the targets of specific kinds of attacks, or are part of the signature of particular hacking tools. The ports in Table 6.3 are the ports most frequently discussed in CERT advisories and the ports I personally have seen probed most often over the last few years, and include many of the same ports warned against by Cheswick and Bellovin in their book, *Firewalls and Internet Security—Repelling the Wily Hacker* (Addison-Wesley).

Table 6.3 Commonly Probed Ports

Service	Port	Protocol	Hostility	Explanation
reserved	0	TCP/UDP	High	Source or destination—no legitmate use
	0–5	TCP	High	sscan signature
echo	7	TCP/UDP	High	UDP attack
systat	11	TCP	High	User process (ps) information
netstat	15	TCP	High	Network status: open connections, routing tables, and so on
chargen	19	TCP/UDP	High	UDP attack
ftp	21, 20	TCP	Low–High	FTP service
ssh	22	TCP	Medium–High	SSH service
ssh	22	UDP	Low	Old version of PC Anywhere
telnet	23	TCP	High	telnet service
smtp	25	TCP	High	Looking for SPAM relay or old vulnerabilities
domain	53	TCP	High	TCP zone transfers, DNS spoofing
bootps	67	UDP	Low	Probable mistake
tftpd	69	UDP	Medium–High	Insecure FTP alternative
finger	79	TCP	Low	User information
link	87	TCP	High	tty link—commonly used by intruders
pop-3	110, 109	TCP	High	One of three most exploited ports

continues

Table 6.3 Continued

Service	Port	Protocol	Hostility	Explanation
sunrpc	111	TCP/UDP	High	Most exploited port
nntp	119	TCP	Medium–High	Public news feed or SPAM relay
ntp	123	UDP	Low	Network time synchronization; okay, but impolite
netbios-ns	137	TCP/UDP	Low–High	Harmless to UNIX
netbios-dgm	138	TCP/UDP	Low–High	Harmless to UNIX
netbios-ssn	139	TCP	Low–High	Harmless to UNIX
imap	143	TCP	High	One of three most exploited ports
NeWS	144	TCP	High	Window management system
snmp	161, 162	UDP	Medium	Remote network administration and queries
xdmcp	177	UDP	High	X Display Login Manager
exec	512	TCP	High	Intranet only
biff	512	UDP	High	Intranet only
login	513	TCP	High	Intranet only
who	513	UDP	High	Intranet only
shell	514	TCP	High	Intranet only
syslog	514	UDP	High	Intranet only
printer	515	TCP	High	Intranet only
talk	517	UDP	Medium	Intranet only
ntalk	518	UDP	Medium	Intranet only
route	520	UDP	High	Routing tables
uucp	540	TCP	Medium	UUCP service
mount	635	UDP	High	mountd exploit
socks	1080	TCP	High	SPAM relay; proxy server exploit
SQL	1114	TCP	High	sscan signature
openwin	2000	TCP	High	OpenWindows
NFS	2049	TCP/UDP	High	Remote file access
pcanywhere	5632	UDP	Low	PC Anywhere
X11	6000+n	TCP	High	X Window system

Service	Port	Protocol	Hostility	Explanation
NetBus	12345, 12346, 20034	TCP	High	Harmless to UNIX
BackOrifice	31337	UDP	High	Harmless to UNIX
traceroute	33434-33523	UDP	Low	Incoming traceroute
ping	8	ICMP	Low–High	Incoming ping
redirect	5	ICMP	High	Redirect bomb
traceroute	11	ICMP	Low	Outgoing traceroute response
UNIX OS probe	0	TCP/UDP	High	Broadcasts to destination address 0.0.0.0

Common Port Scan Log Examples

Of the commonly probed ports, the log messages you'll see most often are listed here. If firewall log output is old hat to you, skip ahead to the next section. If you haven't seen a firewall log entry before, these are what you'll see most often. The log entries are abridged to avoid line wrap across the page:

- 22/UDP—PC Anywhere (old version):
    ```
    input DENY eth0 PROTO=17 10.10.22.85:14386 192.168.10.30:22
    ```
- 23/TCP—telnet:
    ```
    input DENY eth0 PROTO=6 10.10.22.85:14386 192.168.10.30:23
    ```
- 25/TCP—smtp:
    ```
    input DENY eth0 PROTO=6 10.10.22.85:14386 192.168.10.30:25
    ```
- 79/TCP—finger:
    ```
    input DENY eth0 PROTO=6 10.10.22.85:14386 192.168.10.30:79
    ```
- 110/TCP—pop-3:
    ```
    input DENY eth0 PROTO=6 10.10.22.85:14386 192.168.10.30:110
    ```
- 111/UDP—sunrpc:
    ```
    input DENY eth0 PROTO=17 10.10.22.85:14386 192.168.10.30:111
    ```
- 119/TCP—nntp:
    ```
    input DENY eth0 PROTO=6 10.10.22.85:14386 192.168.10.30:119
    ```
- 123/UDP—ntp:
    ```
    input DENY eth0 PROTO=17 10.10.22.85:14386 192.168.10.30:123
    ```
- 143/TCP—imap:
    ```
    input DENY eth0 PROTO=6 10.10.22.85:14386 192.168.10.30:143
    ```

- 161/UDP —snmp :
  ```
  input DENY eth0 PROTO=17 10.10.22.85:14386 192.168.10.30:161
  ```
- 520/UDP—route:
  ```
  input DENY eth0 PROTO=17 10.10.22.85:14386 192.168.10.30:520
  ```
- 635/UDP—mount:
  ```
  input DENY eth0 PROTO=17 10.10.22.85:14386 192.168.10.30:635
  ```
- 1080/TCP—socks:
  ```
  input DENY eth0 PROTO=6 10.10.22.85:14386 192.168.10.30:1080
  ```
- 2049/UDP—nfs:
  ```
  input DENY eth0 PROTO=17 10.10.22.85:14386 192.168.10.30:2049
  ```
- 5632/UDP—PC Anywhere:
  ```
  input DENY eth0 PROTO=17 10.10.22.85:14386 192.168.10.30:5632
  ```
- 12345/TCP—NetBus:
  ```
  input DENY eth0 PROTO=6 10.10.22.85:14386 192.168.10.30:12345
  ```
- 31337/UDP—BackOrifice:
  ```
  input DENY eth0 PROTO=17 10.10.22.85:14386 192.168.10.30:31337
  ```
- 33434:33523/UDP—traceroute:
  ```
  input DENY eth0 PROTO=17 10.10.22.85:14386 192.168.10.30:33434
  ```
- 8/ICMP—ping echo_request:
  ```
  input DENY eth0 PROTO=1 10.10.22.85:8 192.168.10.30:0
  ```

Automated Log Analysis Packages

Log analysis packages are tools that monitor what's written to the system logs, reporting on anomalous entries or taking some kind of predefined action. These tools can run continually in the background, be run periodically by crond, or be run manually. The packages identify potential security problems and notify you when questionable log entries appear.

Red Hat Linux is distributed with a log analysis tool, swatch. Third-party log analysis tools are also available on the Web. Three packages—autobuse, logcheck, and swatch—stand out as either particularly useful or easy to find. All are configurable and can send mail notifications of unusual events.

autobuse

autobuse periodically examines new log entries to identify common probes. Questionable results are sent in email. autobuse is copyright 1998 by Grant Taylor and can be found at http://www.picante.com/~gtaylor/download/autobuse/.

logcheck

logcheck periodically examines new log entries for security violations and unusual activity. Questionable results are sent in email. logcheck is a clone of a similar package from the TIS Gauntlet firewall package. logcheck comes preconfigured to recognize many different log entry patterns. (I use logcheck myself. It's a great package.) logcheck is written by Craig H. Rowland (crowland@psionic.com) and can be found at http://www.psionic.com.

swatch

swatch, the simple watcher program, is an easily configured log file filter and monitor. swatch monitors log files and acts to selectively take one or more user-specified actions based on matched patterns found in the log entries. It can be run periodically by crond or it can continually run in the background as a real-time log monitor. swatch is included as part of the Red Hat distribution.

Summary

This chapter focuses on verifying that the programs and services you've selected are running, and verifying which service ports the programs are listening on. Helpful tools are ifconfig, ping, netstat, and ps. Server programs and the kernel report status and error messages in the system log files under /var/log. The system logging daemon configuration file, /etc/syslog.conf, is introduced as a prelude to explaining what the firewall log entries indicate. The most frequently probed ports are described. These are the ports that will be referenced in the firewall log most frequently. Finally, the log monitoring and analysis tool supplied with the Linux distribution, along with two additional third-party tools, are described. Log monitoring tools can be configured to notify you or take some other kind of action in response to patterns found in the log files.

Now that you have an understanding of which services are running, the ports they are using, and what the firewall log messages are indicating, Chapter 7, "Issues At the UNIX System Administration Level," leaves these lower-level issues behind and takes a look at higher-level security measures. The packet-filtering firewall isn't a complete security solution. At the system administration level, each service can be further protected at the application configuration level. Although the packet-filtering level focuses on connection access to specific ports, the application level focuses on specific host and user access control to the programs running on these ports.

7

Issues at the UNIX System Administration Level

THIS CHAPTER LEAVES THE LOWER-LEVEL firewall issues behind and takes a look at some of the higher-level security measures you can take. A packet-filtering firewall isn't a complete security solution. At the system administration level, each service can be further protected at the application configuration level. The packet-filtering level focuses on connection access between IP addresses and service ports, and the application level focuses on specific network, host, and user access control to the individual programs running on these ports, and the individual files these programs access.

Authentication: Verifying Identity

The IP network layer does not provide for authentication. The only identifying information available is the source address in the IP packet header. As you've seen, source addresses can be forged. Authentication—determining that the source is who or what it claims to be—is handled at higher levels. In the TCP/IP reference model, authentication is handled by the application layer.

UNIX user authentication is ultimately provided through the use of secret passwords known only to the individual user that owns the account. Derivative LAN mechanisms based on the host the user is connecting from, and centrally managed account databases, are built on top of the basic password mechanism. User authentication is one of the core bases of UNIX security. As with all evolving systems, the UNIX password authentication system has required security enhancements from time to time. This section looks at two of those enhancements: shadow passwords and MD5 hashing. Two of the most common LAN authentication mechanisms, built on top of the password mechanism, rhost authentication and NIS management, are discussed in terms of what they are and how they are dangerously insecure in an Internet environment.

Shadow Passwords

By default, UNIX passwords are encrypted and stored in /etc/passwd. /etc/passwd is world-readable (i.e., any account or program on the system can read the file) because it contains user account information necessary to various programs, including the user ID, user group ID, password, username, fields for physical location and phone number, the user's home directory, and the user's preferred, default shell.

Because the file is world-readable, a hacker can apply brute-force methods to break the passwords by trying all combinations of up to 8 characters and matching the encrypted result against the encrypted password. This brute-force method used to be prohibitively expensive on the average computer. As computers have become more powerful, it's now a simple matter to run a password-cracking tool as a background task and break the passwords fairly quickly.

Shadow passwords are one attempt to circumvent this vulnerability by moving the encrypted password to a shadow password file created for this purpose. The user account information remains in the world-readable /etc/passwd file. The actual password is stored in /etc/shadow, a file that is readable by root alone.

Red Hat Linux has provided some level of support for shadow passwords for a long time. As of release 6.0, support for shadow passwords is integrated into the installation and configuration GUI interfaces. You can enable shadow passwords by simply selecting the option in a check box. Earlier Linux versions required you to manually convert to shadow passwords by using the pwconv program.

Remote Access to the Password File

Because /etc/passwd is readable by anyone, remote users can obtain a copy of the file in unanticipated ways. A misconfigured FTP server is a well-known access point. A remotely accessible NFS-mounted root file system is another access point. Remote access to the NIS database is a freebie. Spoofed access through the rhost authentication mechanism is another possibility. Clandestine access via the shell though the sendmail server port is another mechanism. Each of these possibilities is discussed in this chapter.

MD5 Password Hashing

Shadow passwords are an attempt to help solve the vulnerability caused by a world-readable password file. MD5 password hashing is an attempt to help solve the vulnerability caused by the relative ease with which 8-character passwords can be cracked today.

MD5 hashed passwords have a maximum length of 256 characters. The result of MD5 hashing of any object is a 128-bit value. This value is thought to be computationally impossible to reproduce, or at least as computationally impossible today as the standard 8-character, DES encrypted passwords were 10 and 15 years ago.

As of Red Hat release 6.0, MD5 library support is included. Support for MD5 encrypted passwords is integrated into the installation program and the configuration GUI interfaces `linuxconf` and `control-panel`. You can enable MD5 password encryption by simply selecting the option in a check box.

Berkeley *rhost* Authentication: *hosts.equiv* and *.rhosts*

The idea behind host-based authentication is that once a user has been authenticated on a system, that user can be authenticated on all locally networked computers by association. On a systemwide level, those associations are defined by the system administrator who adds the hostnames to a file, `/etc/hosts.equiv`. Individual users can customize their own list of associations by adding the hostnames to their own file, `~/.rhosts`.

The `rhost` authentication method was introduced in BSD 4.2. In conjunction with the Berkeley remote commands `rlogin` and `rsh`, once a user logged in to a computer, he or she had convenient access to his or her accounts on all computers on the LAN. What was often done in loose environments, by system administrator and user alike, was the most convenient—rather than list each individual hostname, a one-character wild card, +, was used to allow access among all machines the user had an account on. This was especially convenient for the `root` account. The system administrator had accounts on all machines.

Obviously, `rhost` authentication is a LAN service, not an Internet service. The identities of local networked machines are implicitly trusted based on their hostnames. On the Internet, both IP source addresses and DNS database tables can be forged—hence, the ongoing warnings throughout the book about disabling the Berkeley remote services on a firewall machine.

`rhost` authentication is a great convenience in a LAN environment where users have accounts on multiple machines. The point is that `rhost` authentication must be disabled on a machine accessible from the Internet. Firewall machines, in particular, must have `rhost` authentication disabled by removing all `.rhost` files from the system, as well as by disabling access to the Berkeley r commands.

Shared Access to Central Authentication: Network Information Service

The Network Information Service (NIS) is a LAN service for centrally managing user and host authentication. NIS is included in the Red Hat Linux distributions and can be enabled in the installation and configuration GUI interfaces, along with shadow passwords and MD5 encryption. As with rhost authentication and the Berkeley remote commands, NIS should not be enabled on a firewall machine.

An NIS server provides host, user, password, and group membership lookup services to client hosts. Clients can query other clients, asking who their NIS server is. Clients can query clients and servers in other domains. Without configurable restrictions based on IP source address, the NIS server answers all who ask, provided they know the server's domain name. Users can see the encrypted passwords. Users can change their password-related information remotely.

NIS is a UDP service accessed through the portmap daemon. As with any portmapped service, the service remains open even if the firewall denies access to service port 111, portmap. A general port scan can locate the actual port the NIS server is bound to.

From an external network security point of view, NIS incorporates the worst of all worlds: remotely readable password files for user authentication and remotely readable /etc/hosts tables for host authentication—and packet filtering can't protect the service unless access to all nondedicated UDP ports is disabled.

Authorization: Defining Access Rights to Identities

When the identity of the user is verified, after the user is authenticated to be who or what it claims to be, the next issue concerns what computer resources that user is authorized to access. On a global system level, authorization issues center around who and what is allowed access to root-privileged resources, who and what is allowed to assume the identity of another account, which remote systems are allowed access to which local network services, and which services have read, write, and execute access to which files and directories on the system.

root Account Access

By definition, the superuser root account is authorized to do and access anything. Obviously, access to the root account must be strongly authenticated. Consequently, root should not be allowed to log in from a remote host, nor should other authenticated services, such as ftp, allow remote root access.

Where root logins may originate is controlled in /etc/securetty. By default, root logins are confined to the physical console terminal and any virtual consoles configured for that terminal, tty devices. Do not add pseudoterminals, ttyp network devices, to /etc/securetty.

Limiting Account Access to *su*

su allows a user to switch between user accounts, assuming the user and group identity of a different account on the system. Even though su requires the user to provide the password for the switched account, some system administrators prefer to limit who can use the su program.

In Linux, the mechanism for controlling who can execute this type of program is controlled through group memberships. The wheel group exists to control access to su and other programs viewed as system administration programs. This layered approach to access control is part of the security-through-depth philosophy. Just as users must know the target password to use su, users can't use most system administration programs to start with, because general users don't have write permission for the system resources involved. Controlling execution access to these programs is an extra layer of protection.

To limit access to the su program to a few selected users, the general scheme is to add the selected users to the wheel group in /etc/group. Then change the su program's group membership and access permissions:

1. Add selected users to the wheel group in /etc/group.

2. Change su's group ownership to the wheel group:

   ```
   chgrp wheel /bin/su
   ```

3. Change su's access permission bits to set the user ID (the purpose of su). Give the su program's owner, root, read, write, and execute permission. Give members of su's group, wheel, read and execute permission. Disallow any other access by anyone:

   ```
   chmod 4750 /bin/su
   ```

tcp_wrappers

The TCP wrapper program, tcpd, provides the ability to define access control lists for specific local services, allowing or denying access from specific networks, systems, or users. As such, tcp_wrappers allows you to define exactly which remote systems are and are not allowed access to each individual network service offered from the system. tcpd is a wrapper program. This means that inetd is configured to execute tcpd rather than the specific server program requested. tcpd performs various authorization checks and then executes the service itself. Because tcpd is a filter program that executes only briefly between inetd and the requested server program, tcpd is not a continually running system daemon. The entire authorization mechanism is usually referred to as tcp_wrappers. tcp_wrappers is both a host authentication tool and an authorization tool.

In Red Hat Linux, /etc/inetd.conf is preconfigured to use tcp_wrappers around applicable services. Major applicable services include ftp, telnet, pop-3 remote mail access, imap remote mail access, finger, and the in.identd auth service.

Not all services can be TCP-wrapped. Generally, the service must be managed by inetd. This means that an individual instantiation of the program must be executed by inetd for each incoming TCP connection or UDP datagram request. It's possible to manage servers, such as the Apache Web server and the third-party SSH server, under inetd, but these servers are usually run continually as daemons. httpd is run in stand-alone mode for performance reasons. sshd is run in standalone mode because the inetd connection can time out on slower systems when stronger encryption is used. sshd, however, has the option of honoring the hosts_access files on its own.

tcp_wrappers provides much stronger levels of authorization checking for TCP-based services than it does for UDP-based services.

For TCP services, if the client machine offers identd service, tcpd will perform username lookups to log the username along with the hostname and service name. Some degree of source IP address and DNS hostname spoofing protection is offered via reverse hostname lookups. The hostname DNS returns from an IP address-to-hostname lookup must match the IP address DNS returns from a subsequent hostname-to-address lookup. Source-routed socket connection options are not allowed.

For UDP services, only basic access control based on hostname or address is available, including the reverse DNS lookups for protection against source address and DNS hostname spoofing. Access control isn't as thorough for UDP services, however. inetd can be configured to start UDP servers with a wait option, telling the server to wait for a few minutes after receiving the last datagram. The purpose is to avoid the overhead of restarting the server if another request is received shortly after. If new requests arrive from some host while the server is waiting, tcp_wrappers will have no effect on the subsequent client/server exchanges.

As with the firewall rules, the first matching tcp_wrappers rule wins, and access control defaults to accept. The allow list is always processed before the deny list. The following is the order the access lists are applied in:

1. If an incoming request matches an entry in /etc/hosts.allow, access is allowed.

2. If an incoming request has not matched an allow rule, then if it matches an entry in /etc/hosts.deny, access is denied.

3. If an incoming request has not matched either an allow or a deny rule, access is allowed.

When setting up hosts.allow and hosts.deny, the goal is the same as with the firewall rules. You want a deny-everything-by-default policy, with accept rules for the explicit exceptions you want to allow.

The primary fields in an access control list are a server name and a client list, separated by a colon.

Access control lists can match on wildcards. The two most commonly used wildcards are ALL and LOCAL.

ALL is self-explanatory. If it is used in the server field, all tcp_wrappered services are included. If it is used in the client list field, all clients are included.

LOCAL refers to the loopback interface and to unqualified hostnames, that is, hosts without a dot in their name, or hostnames without a domain name. Unqualified host-names refer to machines that share the same domain as the local machine. Note, however, that tcpd matches on the first name in /etc/hosts. LOCAL does not match on the following alias fields that are optionally available in /etc/hosts. For home machines without their own local domain name, the firewall machine will have a domain name assigned by the ISP. Internal LAN machines will not be LOCAL. They will belong to an internal, private domain.

PARANOID matches any host whose name doesn't match its address. tcpd's default mode is to be compiled with PARANOID checking turned on all the time. This means that nonmatching hosts are denied access to tcp_wrapped services before the access control lists are consulted. If tcpd is recompiled with PARANOID turned off, the PARANOID wildcard can be used to selectively apply PARANOID checking to individual services.

Access control lists can match on patterns. The two most common patterns are a dot followed by a domain name and a network address ending in a dot. Both patterns match any host in the matched domain or network.

The following is a sample /etc/hosts.allow file:

```
1. ALL: LOCAL .internal.lan
2. in.ftpd: friend@trusted.host.net
3. sshd : 10.30.27.
4. ipop3d: 10.30.27.45 EXCEPT PARANOID
```

Line 1 allows access to all TCP-wrapped services from the local machine and from all hosts on the internal LAN.

Line 2 additionally allows access to the FTP server from a specific remote user account. Specifying a username won't work if the remote site isn't running the IDENT service. Specifying a username won't work if the remote machine is a personal com-puter, a PC or a Macintosh.

Line 3 additionally allows access to the SSH server from any host on the remote 10.30.27.0 network.

Line 4 additionally allows access to the POP server from a specific remote IP address. If you had recompiled tcpd without the PARANOID functionality enabled glob-ally, the PARANOID exception would enable the PARANOID functionality for this access rule. Line 4 is saying that connections to the POP server from IP address 10.30.27.45 are allowed, but only after determining that the IP address and hostname match after cross-checking with a reverse address-to-name lookup.

This is a sample /etc/hosts.deny file:

```
ALL: ALL
```

All tcp_wrapped services are denied access from all clients. Because the rules in hosts.deny are applied after the rules in hosts.allow, this entry effectively defines a deny-everything-by-default policy. The rules in hosts.allow define the exceptions to the policy.

For more information on `tcp_wrappers`, refer to the following man pages: `tcpd(8)`, `hosts_access(5)`, `hosts_options(5)`, `tcpdchk(8)`, `tcpdmatch(8)`, `inetd(8)`, and `inetd.conf(5)`.

File and Directory Permissions

Along with user authentication and general service authorization is the underlying concept of who has access to objects in the file system. UNIX file access permissions are controlled at the read, write, and execute levels for the file's owner and group membership, and globally for any user. Who has write access to a given file or directory is the most obvious issue. Access issues become more subtle when speaking of services that run with system privileges on behalf of the user. UNIX has the capability of limiting the access permissions of the servers themselves, as well as limiting the server's view of the underlying file system.

World-Writable Files

No file requires write access by everyone. Files requiring multiple writers can be handled by including all concerned users in a single group created for the purpose of sharing that resource. You can find the world-writable files on your system by running find with the following arguments:

```
find / -perm -0002 -fstype ext2 -type f -print
```

Depending on what you've installed from the Linux distribution, you will find a few world-writable files. Game score files under `/var/lib/games` are often world-writable. This is a security flaw in current Red Hat Linux distributions. Occasionally, you'll find world-writable source files or documentation files. The open file access permissions on these files are a security oversight on the part of the maintainer.

> **RPC and** *tcp_wrappers*
>
> RPC-based services cannot be started by `tcpd`, but the RPC `portmap` daemon honors the access control lists in `/etc/hosts.allow` and `/etc/hosts.deny` on its own. The access list service name is *portmap*, regardless of the actual name of the `portmap` daemon. (Sometimes the daemon is named or referred to as `rpcbind`.)
>
> The access control lists are only a partial solution for RPC services, however, because a port scan will identify the open RPC ports anyway. A hacker could bypass both the `portmap` daemon and the access control lists.
>
> For more information on using `hosts.allow` and `hosts.deny` with the `portmap` daemon, refer to the man pages, `portmap(8)`.

World-Writable Directories

Very few directories require write access by everyone. Ideally, /tmp should be the only world-writable directory on your system. In reality, a few more globally writable directories exist for LAN services designed to share files, such as SAMBA. You can find the world-writable directories on your system by running find with the following arguments:

```
find / -perm -0002 -fstype ext2 -type d -print
```

Depending on what you've installed from the Linux distribution, you will find a few more world-writable directories. With the possible exception of a few directories under /var, any other directories should not have global write access.

setuid and *setgid* Programs

setuid and setgid programs are programs that run under the effective user ID or group ID of some other account. The program accesses or modifies system resources as a privileged process on behalf of the user executing the setuid program.

For example, user programs, such as login, passwd, and su, all need to access privileged system account services available only to the root account. sendmail needs to write to user mail box files owned by the individual users. Mailbox files are normally readable and writable only by the owning user and by the mail system group. The Berkeley remote programs rcp, rsh, and rlogin all need to establish connections using privileged service ports accessible only to the root account.

setuid programs have a long history of security exploits. One of the first things successful hackers do is install Trojan setuid binaries to give themselves root system privileges.

One of the most dangerous mistakes is to create setuid shell scripts. A shell script is a human-readable executable file. With a little determination, it's possible for an unprivileged user to find a way to modify a system shell script, or to duplicate a setuid shell script and then rewrite the commands. Today's standard directory permissions make this much more difficult to do than it was when UNIX was young.

System integrity checking software, discussed in Chapter 8, "Intrusion Detection and Incident Reporting," regularly check for unexpected setuid and setgid programs. You can find the setuid and setguid programs on your system by running find with the following arguments:

```
find / \( -perm -4000 -o -perm -2000 \) -fstype ext2 -type f -print
```

chroot Services

Publicly accessible services that read or write to part of the file system can have their file system access limited to a specific directory tree. chroot changes a process' view of the system by defining a particular directory to appear to be the root file system for that process. The process is not allowed to see anything above that point. Defining a limited, virtual view of the file system is an additional security protection on top of whatever server-specific access limitations are defined.

Services running in `chroot` environments can require duplication of other pieces of the file system that are now outside the `chroot` environment. For example, `ftp` uses the `ls` program to allow users to see a directory listing of the current `ftp` directory. In a `chroot` environment, these binaries are outside the `chroot` directory, so the binaries must be duplicated within the `chroot` directory structure. System configuration files, shared libraries, and server log files may also need to be duplicated within the `chroot` directory structure. For more information on the `chroot` program, see the online man page, `chroot(1)`.

Server-Specific Configuration

One of the best ways to protect yourself, with or without a firewall, is to run only the services you need. If you do not need a service, turn it off. If you do need a particular service, pay attention to the server's configuration settings.

This section looks at individual server configuration options from a security perspective.

Telnet Configuration Issues

Telnet service shouldn't be offered to remote sites, nor should you use it to access remote sites, unless you have no other option. SSH is far preferable to Telnet. `telnetd` is enabled from `/etc/inetd.conf`. As distributed by Red Hat, `telnetd` is a `tcp_wrapped` service. Limit outside access to your `telnetd` server to specific external hosts through both the firewall configuration and the `/etc/hosts.allow` configuration.

When a `telnet` session is initiated, the contents of `/etc/issue.net` are printed on the client's terminal before the login prompt is sent. `/etc/issue.net` contains system identification information you might not want to be publicly available to anyone that probes your open `telnet` port. The specifics of `/etc/issue.net` are discussed later in this chapter.

In terms of `telnet`, specifically, the server can be configured to not print system information at all, ignoring `/etc/issue.net` and simply printing a `login` prompt. By starting the server with the `-h` option, `/etc/issue.net` is ignored. The `telnet` server can be configured to do this by editing `/etc/inetd.conf` and changing the `telnet` entry to read:

```
telnet  stream  tcp    nowait  root    /usr/sbin/tcpd  in.telnetd -h
```

SSH Configuration Issues

SSH is a third-party replacement for programs such as `telnet` and `rlogin`. Not only are SSH sessions encrypted, but encryption begins with initial connection establishment, before the user is prompted for a password. SSH is available as both a freeware software package for noncommercial use and as a fuller-featured commercial product. Information on SSH can be found at SSH Communications Security in Finland. Its Web site is at http://www.ssh.fi/. The noncommercial version of SSH is distributed as source code you must compile on your system. The official source code repository is at ftp://ftp.cs.hut.fi/pub/ssh. Both the original version 1 and a new version 2 are available.

The sshd daemon is normally started as a standalone background process, rather than started as needed by inetd. SSH Communications Security explains that for host encryption key sizes larger than 512 bits (768 bits is the default host key size), RSA host encryption key exchange can take longer than inetd's timeout period. Because servers are normally tcp_wrapped from /etc/inetd.conf, SSH is written with built-in support for tcp_wrappers.

The way to compile and install either the original SSH1 version 1.2.26 source code or the newer, rewritten SSH2 version 2.0.13 source code is the following:

```
./configure —with-libwrap
make all
make install
```

For SSH1, edit the server configuration file, /etc/sshd_config, and the client configuration file, /etc/ssh_config, to suit your site's needs. Create RSA keys for domains containing hosts you anticipate sharing connections with:

```
make-ssh-known-hosts <domainname>
```

Then, to start the sshd daemon automatically at boot time, edit /etc/rc.d/rc.local and add the following line:

```
/usr/local/sbin/sshd
```

For SSH2, edit the server configuration file, /etc/ssh2/sshd2_config, and the client configuration file, /etc/ssh2/ssh2_config, to suit your site's needs. RSA keys were automatically created for you during the installation process.

Then, to start the sshd2 daemon automatically at boot time, edit /etc/rc.d/rc.local and add the following line:

```
/usr/local/sbin/sshd2
```

For more information on ssh usage, see the online man pages ssh(1), sshd(8), ssh-keygen(1), and make-ssh-known-hosts(1), or ssh2(1), sshd2(8), and ssh-keygen2(1).

SMTP Configuration Issues

Mail servers have a long history of vulnerability exploits, both smtp and sendmail, as well as mail delivery agents pop and imap. Carefully controlling remote access to these servers can go a long way towards securing these services. Much work has been done to make the current mail server, sendmail, as secure as possible. Red Hat Linux 6.0 is distributed with sendmail version 8.9.3, one of the most recent versions of sendmail.

Nevertheless, much of the potential problem with `sendmail` lies in its local configuration and which remote hosts are allowed to relay mail through the local server. Fortunately for us, `sendmail`'s default Linux configuration is secure. A single-system site will need to do nothing with the `sendmail` configuration.

A system providing mail service for a LAN will need to enable relaying for the LAN hosts. Otherwise, your mail server won't accept outgoing mail from your local machines. Relaying is enabled for specific hosts in one of two files, `/etc/mail/access` or `/etc/mail/relay-domains`. An example of `/etc/mail/access` for a small LAN might contain:

```
localhost.localdomain      RELAY
localhost                  RELAY
windows.private.lan        RELAY
linux2.private.lan         RELAY
macintosh.private.lan      RELAY
```

The configuration files in `/etc/mail` are pairs of files, an ASCII file and a hashed database file created from the ASCII file. After editing one of the ASCII files, its hashed counterpart needs to be updated. The following command updates the `/etc/mail/access` hash table, `/etc/mail/access.db`:

```
makemap hash /etc/mail/access < /etc/mail/access
```

Additional information on `sendmail` configuration can be found in the `man` pages: `sendmail(8)`, `aliases(5)`, and `newaliases(1)`. Definitive information for the current release can be found under the `/usr/doc/sendmail` directory. The most current information can be found at `http://www.sendmail.org/`.

Ensure that you are up-to-date with the current `sendmail` and are using `smrsh`, the secure shell specifically designed to work with `sendmail`.

smrsh

Users can direct `sendmail` to execute commands on their behalf. The `vacation` program is an example, automatically generating mail responses to incoming mail. The result is that users can execute any program on the system, but running the program with system level privileges rather than their own. `smrsh` is a restricted shell for `sendmail`. By replacing `/bin/sh` with `/usr/sbin/smrsh` in the `sendmail` configuration file, `/etc/sendmail.cf`, users are limited to which programs can be executed by `sendmail`. `smrsh` executes only programs you've installed or created links to in `/etc/smrsh/`. The directory is empty by default. Specifically, do not put any of the shells, `sed`, `awk`, `perl`, or any other interpreter program in `/etc/smrsh/`. Most small sites won't need to put anything in `/etc/smrsh/`.

Testing Your Mail Server for Relay Capability

A third-party program, `rlytest`, tests a mail server for remote relay capability. A public service to test your mail server remotely is available from `http://maps.vix.com/tsi/ar-test.html`.

The `rlytest` program is available at `http://www.unicom.com/sw/#rlytest`.

To replace the standard shell with `smrsh`, edit `/etc/sendmail.cf` and change the line that begins with:

```
Mlocal,     P=/bin/sh,
```

to

```
Mlocal,     P=/usr/sbin/smrsh,
```

DNS Configuration Issues

DNS, implemented as the Berkeley Internet Name Domain (BIND) service on Linux, is not an inherently insecure service. Other than the potential problems with any UDP-based service, the remaining potential problems center around the TCP-based aspects of DNS. Security issues center around the configuration parameters affecting the server's relationship with other servers, and the information the server can provide to clients. DNS becomes potentially insecure in terms of privacy and denial-of-service exploits involving DNS-spoofing or DNS cache poisoning. Privacy is a question of what information you store in your name server database and who you allow to query that database. Denial-of-service exploits are a question of who you allow to copy your local name server database, who you copy zone information from, and who you allow to update your database.

For more information on DNS and BIND, refer to the `man` pages `named(8)`, `resolver(5)`, and `hostname(7)`; the official Bind 8 documentation in `/usr/doc/bind-8.2/html/index.html`; *DNS & BIND* by Albitz and Liu (O'Reilly); and the `DNS-HOWTO`.

/etc/resolv.conf

The resolver is the client component of DNS. Rather than being a specific client program, the resolver is part of the C libraries compiled into any program requiring network access. The resolver code is what actually sends the DNS query to some name server. `/etc/resolv.conf` is the resolver's configuration file.

For a system without a local `named` running, two directives are important: `domain` and `nameserver`. `domain` is the local domain name. Up to three `nameserver` directives can be listed, each pointing to a specific name server host. In this situation, a third directive, `option rotate`, can be used to query name servers in round-robin fashion, rather than trying the first name server first each time. An example of `resolv.conf` might contain your ISP's domain name and pointers to three of the ISP's name servers:

```
domain my.isp.net
nameserver 192.168.47.81
nameserver 192.168.60.7
nameserver 192.168.60.8
option rotate
```

For a system running a local `named` name server, a single `nameserver` directive points to the local machine. An example of `resolv.conf` might contain:

```
domain my.isp.net
nameserver 127.0.0.1
```

For a system running a local `named` for a LAN, a third directive, `search`, could be used in place of the `domain` directive. The `search` directive takes a list of domains from which to query name servers. An example of `resolv.conf` might contain:

```
search my.local.lan my.isp.net
nameserver 127.0.0.1
```

Resource Records in the BIND Master Files

If `named` is running, it may be authoritative for a zone or piece of the domain space. A master zone file defines characteristics of a zone the name server is authoritative for. The file contains control information for the zone and resource records describing the address–to–name mapping for hosts within the zone. In the case of a standalone system or a system running `named` configured as a forwarding name server, `named` would be authoritative for the `localhost`.

Zone files are stored in `/var/named/`. The files can have arbitrary names. Red Hat Linux's `caching-nameserver` package provides a `named.local` file for the mandatory `localhost` zone, which is almost identical to the following example. The following is an example of a zone file for `localhost`, `/var/named/named.127.0.0`, which every name server must have in order to serve local lookups for itself:

```
1. 0.0.127.in-addr.arpa.   IN    SOA    localhost.    root.localhost. (
2.                          1              ; serial
3.                          28800          ; refresh
4.                          14400          ; retry
5.                          3600000        ; expire
6.                          604800         ; default_ttl
7.                 )
8.        IN     NS     localhost.
9. 1      IN     PTR    localhost.
```

Lines 1–7 contain the zone's control information. Lines 8 and 9 are resource records:

- Line 1 begins an SOA (Start of Authority) control record for the zone. `0.0.127.in-addr.arpa.` is the origin of the zone. Because the origin and the domain are the same, the origin could be symbolized as `@`. `IN` indicates the data in this record belongs to the Internet data class (as opposed to, for example, the hesiod data class). `SOA` indicates that this resource record is a Start of Authority record. `localhost.` is the name of the domain. `root.localhost.` indicates the email address of the contact person who is responsible for the zone information. The opening parenthesis indicates the beginning of a multiline record.

- Line 2 is a serial number. If you served secondary name servers, a change in the serial number would indicate that the zone data had changed and they would need to update their local copies of the zone database.

- Line 3 is the refresh rate, in seconds, indicating how often secondary servers should check the zone data's serial number. In this case, any secondaries would check the serial number every 8 hours.

- Line 4 is the retry rate, in seconds, indicating how long between attempts a secondary server should wait if the attempt to contact the primary server at refresh time failed. In this case, a secondary server would continue trying to contact the server every 4 hours.

- Line 5 is the expiration time, in seconds, indicating at which point a secondary will purge the zone's information from its cache if it failed to contact the primary server for this length of time. In this case, the secondary expires the zone data if it hasn't been able to contact the primary server for the last 41 days.

- Line 6 is the time-to-live interval, in seconds, indicating how long remote servers may cache information returned in response to a query. There won't be any queries to `localhost` from remote servers, but if there were, the time-to-live interval is one week in this case.

- Line 7 contains the closing parenthesis for the multiline SOA record.

- Line 8 is a name server (`NS`) resource record, indicating that the `localhost` is the name server for this domain. For records following the SOA record, origin, `@`, `0.0.127.in-addr.arpa.` is implied as the value for the first field.

- Line 9 is a pointer (`PTR`) resource record, indicating that the address-to-name mapping for address `127.0.0.1` is to hostname `localhost`. The leading `1` in the record indicates that this record defines the address-to-name mapping for address `127.0.0.1`. Because the origin in expressed as an old-style arpanet domain beginning with the IP domain address in reverse dot quad format, the leading `1` is shorthand for `1.0.0.127.in-addr.arpa.`.

/etc/named.conf

`named` is the server component of DNS. The server either finds the requested information in its local cache, or it sends the DNS query to some other name server. `/etc/named.conf` is the `named` daemon's configuration file.

The `/etc/named.conf` filename and format are new with BIND 8.2, which is the version of BIND shipping with Red Hat Linux 6.0.

> **Upgrading** *named.boot* **to** *named.conf*
> Prior versions of BIND used `/etc/named.boot` as their server configuration file. A Perl script, `/usr/doc/bind-8.2/named-bootconf/Grot/named-bootconf.pl`, will convert an existing `named.boot` file to the new `named.conf` format:
>
> ```
> cd /usr/doc/bind-8.2/named-bootconf/Grot
> perl ./named-bootconf.pl < /etc/named.boot > /tmp/named.conf
> ```

named.conf takes many possible configuration statements. Refer to /usr/doc/ bind-8.2/html/config.html for a full list and descriptions. Only the statements used in the following sections on configuring specific server setups are described here.

Configuring a Local Caching-Only, Forwarding Name Server

Chapter 3, "Building and Installing a Firewall," describes a DNS server configuration where the firewall machine hosts a forwarding name server for local use. The server does not provide DNS service to remote hosts on the Internet. It is not authoritative for any public domain. The forwarding server merely caches lookup information locally after initially forwarding unresolved requests to one of the ISP's name servers. This section presents examples of /etc/resolv.conf, /var/named/ database, and /etc/named.conf configuration files for a local forwarding name server.

Local Forwarding Name Server Host Configuration

Local DNS clients point to their local host as the name server to query. /etc/resolv.conf contains:

```
domain my.isp.net
nameserver 127.0.0.1
```

The localhost zone database file, /var/named/named.127.0.0, is the only zone information file needed.

The local named server configuration file, /etc/named.conf, contains the following:

```
 1. options {
 2.          directory "/var/named";
 3.          forward only;
 4. //       forward first;
 5.          forwarders {
 6.                     my.name.server.1;
 7.                     my.name.server.2;
 8.                     my.name.server.3;
 9.          };

10.          query-source address * port 53;

11.          allow-query {
12.                  127.0.0.1;
13. //               192.168.1/24;
14.          };
15.          listen-on port 53 {
16.                  127.0.0.1;
17. //               192.168.1.1;
18.          };
19. };

20. zone "0.0.127.in-addr.arpa" {
21.          type master;
22.          notify no;
23.          file "named.127.0.0";
```

```
24. };

25. zone "." {
26.         type hint;
27.         file "root.cache";
28. };
```

The /etc/name.conf file contains two kinds of records in this example, the options record and the zone record. Options may be defined for the server overall in the options record, and the individual option settings may be defined in the individual zone records to apply to only that zone. Lines 1–19 define an options record:

- Line 1 declares the record type to be an options record and opens the multiline record with a left brace.
- Line 2 defines the name server's working directory, /var/named/, where zone master files are kept.
- Line 3 instructs the server to function as a forward only name server. That is, the server will direct unresolved queries to only the hosts listed in the forwarders record.
- Line 4 is a commented-out, alternate form of the forward option. It instructs the server to function as a forward first name server. That is, the server will first direct unresolved queries to the hosts listed in the forwarders record. If those hosts are unable to resolve the query, or are not responding, the server will attempt to resolve the query itself, functioning as a regular name server.
- Line 5 opens a multiline forwarders record, indicated by the left brace. The forwarders record contains a list of servers to forward queries to.
- Lines 6–8 list individual name servers to forward requests to. Up to three servers may be listed.
- Line 9 closes the forwarders record, indicated by the right brace.
- Line 10 is needed when a firewall stands between the local server and the Internet. The line defines the server's source port to be port 53 when it sends peer-to-peer lookup requests to other servers. That is, the server uses UDP port 53 as both the source and destination port for server-to-server queries.
- Line 11 opens a multiline allow-query record, indicated by the left brace. The allow-query record contains a list of network IP addresses to accept queries from.
- Line 12 instructs the server to accept queries from the localhost.
- Line 13 is a commented out, additional network to accept queries from. If a LAN is attached to an internal network interface, you might want to accept queries from hosts on the LAN.
- Line 14 closes the allow-query record, indicated by the right brace.

- Line 15 opens a multiline `listen-on` record, indicated by the left brace. The `listen-on` record defines the port the server listens for queries from clients on. The record contains a list of local network interfaces to listen on.

- Line 16 instructs the server to listen for queries arriving on the `loopback` interface.

- Line 17 is a commented out, additional network interface to listen on for queries. If a LAN is attached to an internal network interface, you would specify the address of the internal interface's IP address.

- Line 18 closes the `listen-on` record, indicated by the right brace.

- Line 19 closes the `options` record, indicated by the right brace.

- Line 20 opens a multiline `zone` record for the loopback network. Zone domain names are specified as ARPANET domains, so the `loopback` network address, `127.0.0`, is specified in reverse dot quad order as ARPANET domain `0.0.127.in-addr.arpa`.

- Line 21 declares the zone data described by this record to be the master copy. This name server is the authoritative server for this zone.

- Line 22 indicates that no other servers need be notified if the zone data is changed.

- Line 23 provides the name of the zone database file. Because `named.127.0.0` is a relative pathname, it is assumed to be located relative to `/var/named/`, specified as the `directory` setting in the `options` record.

- Line 24 closes the `zone` record, indicated by the right brace.

- Line 25 opens a multiline `zone` record for the `root` domain cache, giving the location of the Internet's `root` domain servers. A `forward only` name server does not need the `root` zone, because all queries are forwarded to the specific hosts declared in the `forwarders` record. A `forward first` name server, as well as a regular name server, needs this `zone` record as a hint of where to start looking for authoritative name servers.

- Line 26 declares the zone data described by this record to be a hint. That is, it's only a place to start.

- Line 27 provides the name of the zone database file. Because `root.cache` is a relative pathname, it is assumed to be located relative to `/var/named/`, specified as the `directory` setting in the `options` record.

- Line 28 closes the `zone` record, indicated by the right brace.

Naming Conventions and Authoritative Sources for *root.cache*

Red Hat distributes a copy of the `root` name server cache file as `/var/named/named.ca`. That file is renamed here as `root.cache`, the name used in the DNS-HOWTO. Copies can also be downloaded from `ftp.rs.internic.net` as `/domain/named.root`.

DNS LAN Client Configuration

Client machines on a small internal LAN needn't run their own name servers. Instead, they can simply point to the local name server host as the name server to query. Their `/etc/resolv.conf` contains:

```
domain my.private.lan
nameserver 192.168.1.1
```

This is all a local client machine requires to make DNS lookup requests.

If you need to run name servers on LAN machines, alternate configuration possibilities include forwarding local requests to the master name server only, forwarding local requests to the ISP name servers (just as the master does), or forwarding to the other local name servers first.

The next section describes yet another configuration possibility when running a local name server on an internal machine. In this case, the public name server will be a dummy server claiming to be authoritative. The internal server will be the true authoritative server for the internal, private LAN, invisible to the Internet.

Configuring a Classic Public and Private Name Server Set

Chapter 4, "LAN Issues, Multiple Firewalls, and Perimeter Networks," describes a DNS server configuration where the firewall machine hosts a public DNS server and an internal machine hosts a local, private server. The public server claims to be authoritative for the domain, but in fact knows nothing about the LAN machines. Its true purpose is to serve as the firewall conduit to external DNS servers and to provide a mechanism to hide local DNS information. The private server is, in fact, authoritative for the private LAN domain and performs local lookup services for machines on the LAN.

This section presents examples of `/etc/resolv.conf`, `/var/named/` database, and `/etc/named.conf` configuration files for both the public and private name server machines.

Public Name Server Configuration

The public name server claims to be authoritative for the local domain, when, in fact, it has little or no information about the internal LAN. The fact that the server claims to be authoritative is meaningless in a home setting where the firewall machine is connected to a consumer-ISP network. There is little reason to configure the server to answer queries from remote hosts. A small business setup with multiple public IP addresses could conceivably have reason to provide some amount of local information to remote hosts. For the purposes of illustration, the public server accepts remote queries.

Because the public server knows nothing about the LAN, the machine's local DNS clients don't use the name server running on their machine. Instead, local clients use the private name server running on an internal machine. For the purposes of example, the internal machine is the choke firewall described in Chapter 4. `/etc/resolv.conf` contains:

```
search my.local.lan my.isp.net
nameserver 192.168.11.2
```

The localhost zone database file, /var/named/named.127.0.0, is always needed by the name server.

For the purposes of illustration, assume the site owns the block of addresses in the 192.168.10.0 and 192.168.11.0 networks, that the firewall machine's external IP address is 192.168.10.30, and that the DMZ network is in the 192.168.11.0 address space.

Besides the local host file, two more zone files are stored in /var/named/. The first is the public server's address-to-name mapping file, named.public:

```
1. 10.168.192.in-addr.arpa.  IN  SOA  my.domain.com.  postmaster.my.domain.com. (
2.                                1999072701 ; Serial
3.                                28800      ; Refresh after 8 hours
4.                                14400      ; Retry 4 hours
5.                                3600000    ; Expire after 41 days
6.                                86400 )    ; Minimum

7.        IN     NS      bastion.my.domain.com.
8.        IN     MX      10 bastion.my.domain.com.

9. 30     IN     PTR     bastion.my.domain.com.
```

Lines 1–6 contain the zone's control information. Lines 7, 8, and 9 are resource records:

- Line 1 begins an SOA control record for the zone. 10.168.192.in-addr.arpa. is the origin of the zone. IN indicates the data in this record belongs to the Internet data class. SOA indicates that this resource record is the Start of Authority record. my.domain.com. is the name of the domain. postmaster.my.domain.com. indicates the email address of the contact person who is responsible for the zone information. The opening parenthesis indicates the beginning of a multiline record.

- Line 2 is a serial number. If you served secondary name servers, a change in the serial number would indicate that the zone data had changed and they would need to update their local copies of the zone database. In this case, the serial number is expressed in the common convention of year, month, day, and number of times the database was changed on that date: YYYYMMDDNN.

- Line 3 is the refresh rate, in seconds, indicating how often secondary servers should check the zone data's serial number. In this case, any secondaries would check the serial number ever 8 hours.

- Line 4 is the retry rate, in seconds, indicating how long between attempts a secondary server should wait if the attempt to contact the primary server at refresh time failed. In this case, a secondary server would continue trying to contact the server every 4 hours.

- Line 5 is the expiration time in seconds, indicating at which point a secondary will purge the zone's information from its cache if it failed to contact the primary server for this length of time. In this case, the secondary expires the zone data if it hasn't been able to contact the primary server for the last TTL (time-to-live) seconds. In this case, the secondary would expire the zone data after approximately 41 days.

- Line 6 is the time-to-live interval, indicating how long remote servers may cache information returned in response to a query. The time-to-live interval for information supplied to remote queries is one week in this case.

- Line 7 is an NS, name server, resource record, indicating that bastion.my.domain.com., the public firewall machine, is the name server for this domain.

- Line 8 is an MX, mail exchanger, resource record, indicating that bastion.my.domain.com. is the host that is either the mail host or the mail forwarder for this domain. The 10 value, the exchanger preference ranking, has no purpose in this example. For sites with multiple mail exchangers, each host can be given a preference priority rank ranging from 0 to 65535. Incoming mail delivery is attempted to each host in turn, lowest rank to highest, until delivery succeeds.

- Line 9 is a PTR, pointer, resource record, indicating the address-to-name mapping for hostname bastion.my.domain.com.. The leading 30 in the record indicates that this record defines the address-to-name mapping for address 192.168.10.30.

A second zone file is needed for reverse name-to-address lookups. The file is /var/named/named.public.reverse. The first eight lines are identical to the address-to-name zone file, including the SOA record, the NS record, and the MX record. The PTR record is replaced with a new record type, the A, address, record:

```
1. 10.168.192.in-addr.arpa.  IN  SOA  my.domain.com.
   postmaster.my.domain.com. (
2.                                   1999072701 ; Serial
3.                                   28800      ; Refresh after 8 hours
4.                                   14400      ; Retry 4 hours
5.                                   3600000    ; Expire after 41 days
6.                                   86400 )    ; Minimum

7.          IN     NS      bastion.my.domain.com.
8.          IN     MX      10 bastion.my.domain.com.

9. bastion.my.domain.com.  IN   A    192.168.10.30
```

Line 9 is an A, address, resource record, indicating that the name-to-address mapping for hostname bastion.my.domain.com. is address 192.168.10.30.

The local named server configuration file, /etc/named.conf, contains the following:

```
1. options {
2.      directory "/var/named";
```

```
 3.             forward first;
 4.             forwarders {
 5.                     my.name.server.1;
 6.                     my.name.server.2;
 7.                     my.name.server.3;
 8.             };

 9.             query-source address * port 53;

10.             allow-query {
11.                     ! 127/8;
12.                     192.168.11.2;
13.                     ! 192.168.11/24;
14.                     *;
15.             };

16.             allow-transfer { ! *; };
17.             allow-update { ! *; };

18.             listen-on port 53 {
19.                     192.168.10.30;
20.                     192.168.11.1;
21.             };
22. };

23. zone "0.0.127.in-addr.arpa" {
24.             type master;
25.             notify no;
26.             file "named.127.0.0";
27. };

28. zone "my.domain.com" {
29.             type master;
30.             notify no;
31.             file "named.public.reverse";
32. };

33. zone "10.168.192.in-addr.arpa" {
34.             type master;
35.             notify no;
36.             file "named.public";
37. };

38. zone "." {
39.             type hint;
40.             file "root.cache";
41. };
```

The /etc/name.conf file contains two kinds of records in this example, the options record and the zone record. Options may be defined for the server overall in the options record, and the individual option settings may be defined in the individual zone records to apply to only that zone. Lines 1–22 define the options record:

- Line 1 declares the record type to be an `options` record and opens the multiline record with a left brace.

- Line 2 defines the name server's working directory, `/var/named/`, where zone master files are kept.

- Line 3 instructs the server to function as a `forward first` name server. That is, the server will first direct unresolved queries to the hosts listed in the `forwarders` record. If those hosts are unable to resolve the query, or are not responding, the server will attempt to resolve the query itself, functioning as a regular name server.

- Line 4 opens a multiline `forwarders` record, indicated by the left brace. The `forwarders` record contains a list of servers to forward queries to.

- Lines 5–7 list individual name servers to forward requests to. Up to three servers may be listed.

- Line 8 closes the `forwarders` record, indicated by the right brace.

- Line 9 is needed when a firewall stands between the local server and the Internet. The line defines the server's source port to be `port 53` when it sends peer-to-peer lookup requests to other servers. That is, the server uses UDP port 53 as both the source and destination port for server-to-server queries.

- Line 10 opens a multiline `allow-query` record, indicated by the left brace. The `allow-query` record contains a list of network IP addresses to accept and deny queries from. The order of the addresses is important. The address list is checked for a match in the order the list is defined. The first matching rule wins.

- Line 11 instructs the server to deny queries from the `localhost`. Local queries are sent to the private, internal name server.

- Line 12 instructs the server to accept queries from the internal name server at `192.168.11.2`. If the public server doesn't have the information in its local cache, it will forward the query to the remote name servers.

- Line 13 instructs the server to deny queries from any other host on the internal LAN. Internal queries are directed to the private, internal name server.

- Line 14 instructs the server to accept queries from anywhere. Because the wild-card acceptance rule follows the denied addresses, queries coming from any address other than those in the denied lists are accepted.

- Line 15 closes the `allow-query` record, indicated by the right brace.

- Line 16 contains a single-line `allow-transfer` record. The `allow-transfer` record uses the negation operator, `!`, to deny zone transfer requests from any-where. By default, zone transfers are allowed to anywhere.

- Line 17 contains a single-line `allow-update` record. The `allow-update` record uses the negation operator, `!`, to deny zone database update instructions from anywhere. By default, zone updates are denied. Including the option explicitly provides a form of documentation, as well as a backup rule in case of error.

- Line 18 opens a multiline `listen-on` record, indicated by the left brace. The `listen-on` record defines the port on which the server listens for queries from clients. The record contains a list of local network interfaces to listen on.

- Line 19 instructs the server to listen for queries arriving on the external, Internet interface, `192.168.10.30`.

- Line 20 instructs the server to listen for queries arriving on the internal, LAN interface, `192.168.11.1`.

- Line 21 closes the `listen-on` record, indicated by the right brace.

- Line 22 closes the `options` record, indicated by the right brace.

- Line 23 opens a multiline `zone` record for the loopback network. Zone domain names are specified as ARPANET domains, so the `loopback` network address, `127.0.0`, is specified in reverse dot quad order as ARPANET domain `0.0.127.in-addr.arpa`.

- Line 24 declares the zone data described by this record to be the master copy. This name server is the authoritative server for this zone.

- Line 25 indicates that no other servers need be notified if the zone data is changed.

- Line 26 provides the name of the zone database file. Because `named.127.0.0` is a relative pathname, it is assumed to be located relative to `/var/named/`, specified as the `directory` setting in the `options` record.

- Line 27 closes the `zone` record, indicated by the right brace.

- Line 28 opens a multiline `zone` record for the public domain, `my.domain.com`. The zone information in this file is used for reverse name-to-address lookups.

- Line 29 declares the zone data described by this record to be the master copy. This name server is the authoritative server for this zone.

- Line 30 indicates that no other servers need be notified if the zone data is changed.

- Line 31 provides the name of the zone database file. Because `named.public.reverse` is a relative pathname, it is assumed to be located relative to `/var/named/`, specified as the `directory` setting in the `options` record.

- Line 32 closes the `zone` record, indicated by the right brace.

- Line 33 opens a multiline `zone` record for the public domain, `10.168.192.in-addr.arpa`, used for address-to-name lookups.

- Line 34 declares the zone data described by this record to be the master copy. This name server is the authoritative server for this zone.

- Line 35 indicates that no other servers need be notified if the zone data is changed.

- Line 36 provides the name of the zone database file. Because `named.public` is a relative pathname, it is assumed to be located relative to `/var/named/`, specified as the `directory` setting in the `options` record.

- Line 37 closes the `zone` record, indicated by the right brace.

- Line 38 opens a multiline `zone` record for the `root` domain cache, giving the location of the Internet's `root` domain servers. The `forward first` name server, as well as a regular name server, needs this `zone` record as a hint of where to start looking for authoritative name servers.

- Line 39 declares the zone data described by this record to be a hint. That is, it's only a place to start.

- Line 40 provides the name of the zone database file. Because `root.cache` is a relative pathname, it is assumed to be located relative to `/var/named/`, specified as the `directory` setting in the `options` record.

- Line 41 closes the `zone` record, indicated by the right brace.

Private Name Server Configuration

The private name server is authoritative for two local domains: the internal, private LAN, `my.local.lan`, and the DMZ LAN between the bastion and choke firewalls, `my.firewall.lan`. Local clients, both LAN clients and local clients on the public bastion firewall machine, use the private name server running on an internal machine. For the purposes of example, the internal choke machine is the choke firewall described in Chapter 4. Its `/etc/resolv.conf` contains:

```
search my.local.lan my.firewall.lan
nameserver 127.0.0.1
```

The `localhost` database zone file, `/var/named/named.127.0.0`, is always needed by the name server.

For the purposes of illustration, assume the site owns the blocks of addresses in the `192.168.10.0` and `192.168.11.0` networks, and that the bastion firewall machine's external IP address is `192.168.10.30`. The `192.168.11.0` network is used for the DMZ. The bastion's internal interface uses IP address `192.168.11.1`. The choke's external interface uses IP address `192.168.11.2`.

Two more pairs of zone files are stored in `/var/named/`. The first pair is the DMZ's address-to-name and name-to-address mapping files. The second pair is the private LAN's address-to-name and name-to-address mapping files.

The DMZ address-to-name database zone file is `/var/named/named.dmz`. It contains:

```
1. 11.168.192.in-addr.arpa.  IN  SOA  my.dmz.lan.
   postmaster.my.dmz.lan. (
2.                           1999072701 ; Serial
3.                           28800      ; Refresh after 8 hours
4.                           14400      ; Retry 4 hours
5.                           3600000    ; Expire after 41 days
6.                           86400  )   ; Minimum
```

```
7.        IN    NS    choke.my.dmz.lan.
8.        IN    MX    10 bastion.my.dmz.lan.

9.  1     IN    PTR   bastion.my.dmz.lan.
10. 2     IN    PTR   choke.my.dmz.lan.
```

Lines 1–6 contain the zone's control information. Lines 7–10 are resource records:

- Line 1 begins an SOA control record for the zone. `11.168.192.in-addr.arpa.` is the origin of the zone. `IN` indicates the data in this record belongs to the Internet data class. `SOA` indicates that this resource record is the Start of Authority record. `my.dmz.lan.` is the name of the domain. `postmaster.my.dmz.lan.` indicates the email address of the contact person who is responsible for the zone information. The opening parenthesis indicates the beginning of a multiline record.

- Line 2 is a serial number. If you served secondary name servers, a change in the serial number would indicate that the zone data had changed and they would need to update their local copies of the zone database. In this case, the serial number is expressed in the common convention of year, month, day, and number of times the database was changed on that date: `YYYYMMDDNN`.

- Line 3 is the refresh rate, in seconds, indicating how often secondary servers should check the zone data's serial number. In this case, any secondaries would check the serial number ever 8 hours.

- Line 4 is the retry rate, in seconds, indicating how long between attempts a secondary server should wait if the attempt to contact the primary server at refresh time failed. In this case, a secondary server would continue trying to contact the server every 4 hours.

- Line 5 is the expiration time, in seconds, indicating at which point a secondary will purge the zone's information from its cache if it failed to contact the primary server for this length of time. In this case, the secondary expires the zone data if it hasn't been able to contact the primary server for the last TTL seconds. In this case, the secondary would expire the zone data after approximately 41 days.

- Line 6 is the time-to-live interval, indicating how long remote servers may cache information returned in response to a query. There won't be any queries to `localhost` from remote servers, but if there were, the time-to-live interval is one week in this case.

- Line 7 is an `NS`, name server, resource record, indicating that `choke.my.dmz.lan.`, the internal firewall machine, is the name server for this domain.

- Line 8 is an `MX`, mail exchanger, resource record, indicating that `bastion.my.dmz.lan.` is the host that is either the mail host or the mail forwarder for this domain. The `10` value, the exchanger preference ranking, has no purpose in this example. For sites with multiple mail exchangers, each host can be given a preference priority rank ranging from 0 to 65535. Incoming mail delivery is attempted to each host in turn, lowest rank to highest, until delivery succeeds.

- Line 9 is a PTR, pointer, resource record, indicating the address-to-name mapping for hostname bastion.my.dmz.lan.. The leading 1 in the record indicates that this record defines the address-to-name mapping for address 192.168.11.1.

- Line 10 is a PTR, pointer, resource record, indicating the address-to-name mapping for hostname choke.my.dmz.lan.. The leading 2 in the record indicates that this record defines the address-to-name mapping for address 192.168.11.2.

The DMZ name-to-address database zone file is /var/named/named.dmz.reverse. The first eight lines are identical to the address-to-name zone file, including the SOA record, the NS record, and the MX record. The PTR records are replaced with the A, address, record:

```
1. 11.168.192.in-addr.arpa.  IN  SOA  my.dmz.lan.
   postmaster.my.dmz.lan. (
2.                                   1999072701 ; Serial
3.                                   28800      ; Refresh after 8 hours
4.                                   14400      ; Retry 4 hours
5.                                   3600000    ; Expire after 41 days
6.                                   86400 )    ; Minimum

7.           IN      NS      choke.my.dmz.lan.
8.           IN      MX      10 bastion.my.dmz.lan.

9. bastion.my.dmz.lan.    IN   A    192.168.11.1
10. choke.my.dmz.lan.     IN   A    192.168.11.2
```

Line 9 is an A, address, resource record, indicating that the name-to-address mapping for hostname bastion.my.dmz.lan. is address 192.168.11.1.

Line 10 is an A, address, resource record, indicating that the name-to-address mapping for hostname choke.my.dmz.lan. is address 192.168.11.2.

The internal, private LAN address-to-name database zone file is /var/named/named.local.lan. It contains:

```
1. 1.168.192.in-addr.arpa.  IN  SOA  my.local.lan.
   postmaster.my.local.lan. (
2.                                   1999072701 ; Serial
3.                                   28800      ; Refresh after 8 hours
4.                                   14400      ; Retry 4 hours
5.                                   3600000    ; Expire after 41 days
6.                                   86400 )    ; Minimum

7.           IN      NS      choke.my.local.lan.
8.           IN      MX      10 bastion.my.dmz.lan.

9. 1         IN      PTR     choke.my.local.lan.
10. 2        IN      PTR     macintosh.my.local.lan.
11. 3        IN      PTR     bsd.my.local.lan.
```

Lines 1–6 contain the zone's control information. Lines 7–11 are resource records:

- Line 1 begins an SOA control record for the zone. `1.168.192.in-addr.arpa.` is the origin of the zone. `IN` indicates the data in this record belongs to the Internet data class. `SOA` indicates that this resource record is the Start of Authority record. `my.local.lan.` is the name of the domain. `postmaster.my.local.lan.` indicates the email address of the contact person who is responsible for the zone information. The opening parenthesis indicates the beginning of a multiline record.

- Line 2 is a serial number. If you served secondary name servers, a change in the serial number would indicate that the zone data had changed and they would need to update their local copies of the zone database. In this case, the serial number is expressed in the common convention of year, month, day, and number of times the database was changed on that date: `YYYYMMDDNN`.

- Line 3 is the refresh rate, in seconds, indicating how often secondary servers should check the zone data's serial number. In this case, any secondaries would check the serial number ever 8 hours.

- Line 4 is the retry rate, in seconds, indicating how long between attempts a secondary server should wait if the attempt to contact the primary server at refresh time failed. In this case, a secondary server would continue trying to contact the server every 4 hours.

- Line 5 is the expiration time, in seconds, indicating at which point a secondary will purge the zone's information from its cache if it failed to contact the primary server for this length of time. In this case, the secondary expires the zone data if it hasn't been able to contact the primary server for the last 3600000 seconds. In this case, the secondary would expire the zone data after approximately 41 days.

- Line 6 is the time-to-live interval, indicating how long remote servers may cache information returned in response to a query. There won't be any queries to `localhost` from remote servers, but if there were, the time-to-live interval is one week in this case.

- Line 7 is an `NS`, name server, resource record, indicating that `choke.my.local.lan.`, the internal firewall machine's internal network interface, is the name server for this domain.

- Line 8 is an `MX`, mail exchanger, resource record, indicating that `bastion.my.dmz.lan.` is the host that is either the mail host or the mail forwarder for this domain. The mail exchanger is not required to be in the same network. The `10` value, the exchanger preference ranking, has no purpose in this example. For sites with multiple mail exchangers, each host can be given a preference priority rank ranging from 0 to 65535. Incoming mail delivery is attempted to each host in turn, lowest rank to highest, until delivery succeeds.

- Line 9 is a PTR, pointer, resource record, indicating the address-to-name mapping for hostname choke.my.local.lan..The leading 1 in the record indicates that this record defines the address-to-name mapping for address 192.168.1.1.

- Line 10 is a PTR, pointer, resource record, indicating the address-to-name mapping for hostname macintosh.my.local.lan..The leading 2 in the record indicates that this record defines the address-to-name mapping for address 192.168.1.2.

- Line 11 is a PTR, pointer, resource record, indicating the address-to-name mapping for hostname bsd.my.local.lan..The leading 3 in the record indicates that this record defines the address-to-name mapping for address 192.168.1.3.

The internal, private LAN name-to-address database zone file is /var/named/named.local.lan.reverse. The first eight lines are identical to the address-to-name zone file, including the SOA record, the NS record, and the MX record. The PTR records are replaced with the A, address, record:

```
1. 1.168.192.in-addr.arpa.  IN  SOA  my.local.lan.
   postmaster.my.local.lan. (
2.                                 1999072701 ; Serial
3.                                 28800      ; Refresh after 8 hours
4.                                 14400      ; Retry 4 hours
5.                                 3600000    ; Expire after 41 days
6.                                 86400 )    ; Minimum

7.        IN      NS      choke.my.local.lan.
8.        IN      MX      10 bastion.my.dmz.lan.

9. choke.my.local.lan.      IN   A   192.168.1.1
10. macintosh.my.local.lan. IN   A   192.168.1.2
11. bsd.my.local.lan.       IN   A   192.168.1.3
```

Line 9 is an A, address, resource record, indicating that the name-to-address mapping for hostname choke.my.local.lan. is address 192.168.1.1.

Line 10 is an A, address, resource record, indicating that the name-to-address mapping for hostname macintosh.my.local.lan. is address 192.168.1.2.

Line 11 is an A, address, .resource record, indicating that the name-to-address mapping for hostname bsd.my.local.lan. is address 192.168.1.3.

The local named server configuration file, /etc/named.conf, contains the following:

```
1. options {
2.        directory "/var/named";
3.        forward only;
4.        forwarders {
5.                192.168.11.1;
6.        };

7.        query-source address * port 53;

8.        allow-query {
```

```
 9.                     127/8;
10.                     192.168.11.1;
11.                     ! 192.168.11/24;
12.                     192.168.1/24;
13.            };

14.            allow-transfer { ! *; };
15.            allow-update { ! *; };

16.            listen-on port 53 { *; };
17. };

18. zone "0.0.127.in-addr.arpa" {
19.            type master;
20.            notify no;
21.            file "named.127.0.0";
22. };

23. zone "my.dmz.lan" {
24.            type master;
25.            notify no;
26.            file "named.dmz.reverse";
27. };

28. zone "11.168.192.in-addr.arpa" {
29.            type master;
30.            notify no;
31.            file "named.dmz";
32. };

33. zone "my.local.lan" {
34.            type master;
35.            notify no;
36.            file "named.local.lan.reverse";
37. };

38. zone "1.168.192.in-addr.arpa" {
39.            type master;
40.            notify no;
41.            file "named.local.lan";
42. };

43. zone "." {
44.            type hint;
45.            file "root.cache";
46. };
```

The /etc/name.conf file contains two kinds of records in this example, the options record and the zone record. Options may be defined for the server overall in the options record, and the individual option settings may be defined in the individual zone records to apply to only that zone. Lines 1–17 define the options record:

- Line 1 declares the record type to be an `options` record and opens the multiline record with a left brace.

- Line 2 defines the name server's working directory, `/var/named/`, where zone master files are kept.

- Line 3 instructs the server to function as a `forward only` name server. That is, the server will direct unresolved queries only to the hosts listed in the `forwarders` record. The only server the choke's name server will forward to is the name server running on the bastion firewall machine.

- Line 4 opens a multiline `forwarders` record, indicated by the left brace. The `forwarders` record contains a list of servers to forward queries to.

- Line 5 lists bastion firewall's internal interface IP address.

- Line 6 closes the `forwarders` record, indicated by the right brace.

- Line 7 is needed when a firewall stands between the local server and the external network. The line defines the server's source port to be `port 53` when it sends peer-to-peer lookup requests to other servers. That is, the server uses UDP port 53 as both the source and destination port for server-to-server queries.

- Line 8 opens a multiline `allow-query` record, indicated by the left brace. The `allow-query` record contains a list of network IP addresses to accept and deny queries from. The order of the addresses is important. The address list is checked for a match in the order the list is defined. The first matching rule wins.

- Line 9 instructs the server to accept queries from the `localhost`.

- Line 10 instructs the server to accept queries from clients on the public name server at `192.168.11.1`. If the private server doesn't have the information in its local cache, it will forward the query to the public name server, which may or not forward the query to remote name servers.

- Line 11 instructs the server to deny queries from any other hosts on the DMZ LAN. In this case, it's expected that any hosts on the DMZ network direct their queries to the public, external name server.

- Line 12 instructs the server to accept queries from any machine on the internal, private LAN.

- Line 13 closes the `allow-query` record, indicated by the right brace.

- Line 14 contains a single-line `allow-transfer` record. The `allow-transfer` record uses the negation operator, `!`, to deny zone transfer requests from anywhere. By default, zone transfers are allowed to anywhere.

- Line 15 contains a single-line `allow-update` record. The `allow-update` record uses the negation operator, `!`, to deny zone database update instructions from anywhere. By default, zone updates are denied. Including the option explicitly provides a form of documentation, as well as a backup rule in case of error.

- Line 16 contains a single-line `listen-on` record. The `listen-on` record defines the port the server listens for queries from clients on. The record contains a list of local network interfaces to listen on. The internal name server listens on all interfaces.

- Line 17 closes the `options` record, indicated by the right brace.

- Line 18 opens a multiline `zone` record for the loopback network. Zone domain names are specified as ARPANET domains, so the `loopback` network address, `127.0.0`, is specified in reverse dot quad order as ARPANET domain `0.0.127.in-addr.arpa`.

- Line 19 declares the zone data described by this record to be the master copy. This name server is the authoritative server for this zone.

- Line 20 indicates that no other servers need be notified if the zone data is changed.

- Line 21 provides the name of the zone database file. Because `named.127.0.0` is a relative pathname, it is assumed to be located relative to `/var/named/`, specified as the `directory` setting in the `options` record.

- Line 22 closes the `zone` record, indicated by the right brace.

- Line 23 opens a multiline `zone` record for the internal DMZ domain, `my.dmz.lan`. The zone information in this file is used for reverse name-to-address lookups.

- Line 24 declares the zone data described by this record to be the master copy. This name server is the authoritative server for this zone.

- Line 25 indicates that no other servers need be notified if the zone data is changed.

- Line 26 provides the name of the zone database file. Because `named.dnz.reverse` is a relative pathname, it is assumed to be located relative to `/var/named/`, specified as the `directory` setting in the `options` record.

- Line 27 closes the `zone` record, indicated by the right brace.

- Line 28 opens a multiline `zone` record for the internal DMZ domain, `11.168.192.in-addr.arpa`, used for address-to-name lookups.

- Line 29 declares the zone data described by this record to be the master copy. This name server is the authoritative server for this zone.

- Line 30 indicates that no other servers need be notified if the zone data is changed.

- Line 31 provides the name of the zone database file. Because `named.dmz` is a relative pathname, it is assumed to be located relative to `/var/named/`, specified as the `directory` setting in the `options` record.

- Line 32 closes the `zone` record, indicated by the right brace.

- Line 33 opens a multiline `zone` record for the internal local domain, `my.local.lan`. The zone information in this file is used for reverse name-to-address lookups.

- Line 34 declares the zone data described by this record to be the master copy. This name server is the authoritative server for this zone.

- Line 35 indicates that no other servers need be notified if the zone data is changed.

- Line 36 provides the name of the zone database file. Because `named.local.lan.reverse` is a relative pathname, it is assumed to be located relative to `/var/named/`, specified as the `directory` setting in the `options` record.

- Line 37 closes the `zone` record, indicated by the right brace.

- Line 38 opens a multiline `zone` record for the internal local domain, `1.168.192.in-addr.arpa`, used for address-to-name lookups.

- Line 39 declares the zone data described by this record to be the master copy. This name server is the authoritative server for this zone.

- Line 40 indicates that no other servers need be notified if the zone data is changed.

- Line 41 provides the name of the zone database file. Because `named.local.lan` is a relative pathname, it is assumed to be located relative to `/var/named/`, specified as the `directory` setting in the `options` record.

- Line 42 closes the `zone` record, indicated by the right brace.

- Line 43 opens a multiline `zone` record for the `root` domain cache, giving the location of the Internet's `root` domain servers. The `forward first` name server, as well as a regular name server, needs this `zone` record as a hint of where to start looking for authoritative name servers.

- Line 44 declares the zone data described by this record to be a hint. That is, it's only a place to start.

- Line 45 provides the name of the zone database file. Because `root.cache` is a relative pathname, it is assumed to be located relative to `/var/named/`, specified as the `directory` setting in the `options` record.

- Line 46 closes the `zone` record, indicated by the right brace.

Controlling Access to Zone Data

With the exception of DNS cache poisoning based on IP address spoofing, allowing incoming DNS client queries from remote hosts does not pose a great security risk, provided the local master zone databases don't contain information you don't want to make public. (Large organizations sometimes use the DNS database as a central repository for private information, such as the names, phone numbers, and addresses of all their employees.) As shown earlier, the name server's `allow-query` option can be used to limit who can query the name server.

The greater potential risk when running a name server involves read access to the entire zone database over a TCP connection. As shown in the previous examples, outgoing zone transfers to remote hosts are allowed by default. Access to the complete zone database must be limited to only the official secondary name servers, if any. The `allow-transfer` option is necessary to limit which hosts have zone transfer authority. Allowing access to the entire database allows remote access to your entire LAN topology.

The greatest potential risk involves allowing write access to the zone database. As shown in the previous examples, incoming zone database updates from remote hosts are denied by default. Write access to secondary servers' database must be limited to only the official primary name server. The `allow-update` option is necessary to allow hosts to have zone update authority. Allowing write access to the database allows remote sites to spoof or rewrite your entire domain's idea of itself.

FTP Configuration Issues

FTP has a long history of security exploits. Although the currently known problems have been fixed, new problems are sure to crop up over time. Regardless of any potential security weaknesses in the server software itself, the greatest potential security problem, the local configuration, remains. The two areas for concern are the settings in `ftp`'s configuration files in `/etc`, and the directory and file permissions and contents in the public, anonymous `ftp` area, `/home/ftp`.

By default, authenticated access to the `ftp` server is enabled in `/etc/inetd.conf`. If the anonymous `ftp` package is installed, anonymous `ftp` access is enabled, as well. `ftpd` is protected by `tcp_wrappers`. The `ftpd` server is started by `inetd` and passed two command-line options, `-l` and `-a`. The `-l` option turns on logging. All `ftp` sessions are logged by `syslogd`. The `-a` option tells `ftpd` to use its access configuration file, `/etc/ftpaccess`. If you host a public anonymous `ftp` service, two more options are recommended, `-i` and `-o`. The `-i` option logs all incoming file transfers in `/var/log/xferlog`. The `-o` option logs all outgoing file copies to `/var/log/xferlog`.

> **For More Information: FTP Configuration**
>
> For more information on `ftp` configuration, see the man pages `ftpd(8)`, `ftpaccess(5)`, `ftpconversions(5)`, and `xfer-log(5)`. For more information on anonymous `ftp` configuration, see the documents "Anonymous FTP Configuration Guidelines," available at `ftp://ftp.cert.org/pub/tech_tips/anonymous_ftp_config`, "UNIX Configuration Guidelines," available at `http://www.cert.org/ftp/tech_tips/UNIX_configuration_guidelines`, and "UNIX Computer Security Checklist," available at `http://www.cert.org/ftp/tech_tips/AUSCERT checklist1.1`. For more information on `ftp` security problems, see the documents "Anonymous FTP Abuses," available at `http://www.cert.org/ftp/tech_tips/anonymous_ftp_abuses`, and "Problems With The FTP PORT Command" available at `http://www.cert.org/ftp/tech_tips/ FTP_PORT_attacks`.

Authenticated FTP and General Configuration Files in /etc

FTP has five configuration files in /etc:

- /etc/ftpaccess is the main configuration file for the ftpd server.
- /etc/ftpconversions contains a list of conversion specifications for compressed, gziped, and tared files.
- /etc/ftpgroups contains a list of user groups and the ftp area the server should chroot into for each group. For example, separate groups might be defined for different software development groups.
- /etc/ftphosts contains a list of users allowed to access the system as authenticated ftp users, and the hosts they may connect from.
- /etc/ftpusers contains a list of valid local accounts that are not granted authenticated ftp access. The root and other system accounts should be listed in ftpusers.

The configuration files you will probably want to customize are ftphosts and ftpaccess. You may never need to modify ftpconversions, ftpgroups, or ftpusers. An example of an /etc/ftphosts file is:

```
allow bob 192.168.1.*
allow jake 10.10.47.112
```

The bob account is allowed authenticated access from any host on the private LAN. The jake account is allowed authenticated access from the single remote host at 10.10.47.112.

Because ftpd is protected by tcp_wrappers, the following entry in /etc/hosts.allow would enable these incoming connections to the ftp server:

```
in.ftpd: LOCAL 192.168.1. 10.10.47.112
```

Authenticated ftp access requires the users to have local accounts on the system, valid passwords in /etc/passwd, and a standard shell defined in /etc/passwd.

/etc/ftpaccess is the main server configuration file. ftpd can take many configuration options. The following is an example of a configuration file:

```
1. class    friends    real  192.168.1.*
2. class    friends    real  10.10.47.112
3. # class  other      anonymous  *

4. deny !nameserved .no_name_server

5. greeting brief
6. # banner /home/ftp/banner

7. message /welcome.msg           login
8. message .message               cwd=*

9. email root@localhost
```

```
10. loginfails 5
11. limit-time anonymous 30
12. anonymous-root /home/ftp
13. defaultserver private

14. compress        yes     friends
15. tar             yes     friends
16. chmod           no      friends
17. delete          yes     friends
18. overwrite       yes     friends
19. rename          yes     friends

20. noretrieve passwd shadow group gshadow core

21. upload  /home/ftp *               no
22. upload  /home/ftp /incoming yes  bob   bob  0622 dirs
23. upload  /home/ftp /incoming yes  jake  jake 0622 nodirs

24. log transfers   anonymous       inbound,outbound
25. log security    anonymous

26. passwd-check rfc822 enforce
```

The /etc/ftpaccess file contains access group definitions and permissions, pointers to login banners directory information files, and the location of log files:

- Line 1 defines a class of authenticated users, friends, who are allowed access from any host on the local 192.168.1 network.

- Line 2 adds another member to the friends class to include access from the remote host at 10.10.47.112.

- Line 3 defines a class of anonymous users, other, who are allowed access from any host. The line is commented out.

- Line 4 denies access to sites whose address doesn't resolve. The contents of the file, /home/ftp/.no_name_server, are displayed to the user.

- Line 5 defines how much information is displayed before the remote user logs in. brief displays only your hostname. By default, both the hostname and the ftpd version are displayed.

- Line 6 defines a file containing a message to be displayed before the user logs in. The line is commented out.

- Line 7 defines a file containing a message to be displayed after the user logs in.

- Line 8 defines a file containing a message to be displayed whenever the user changes directories.

- Line 9 specifies the email address of the owner of the ftp area.

- Line 10 specifies the number of failed login attempts a user may make before the connection is ended.

- Line 11 defines the length of time, in minutes, an anonymous session may last. In this case, if the user remained connected and walked away from his or her computer, the ftp session would be terminated after 30 minutes.

- Line 12 specifies the top of the anonymous ftp directory tree.

- Line 13 is another way to deny anonymous access.

- Lines 14–19 defines functions members of a class are authorized for. In this example, authenticated users are not allowed to change a file's read-write access permissions.

- Line 20 specifies files that may not be transferred by anyone.

- Line 21 denies incoming file transfers to the anonymous ftp area.

- Line 22 allows the authenticated bob account to upload files into the incoming directory, and to create additional directories under /home/ftp/incoming.

- Line 23 allows the authenticated jake account to upload files into the incoming directory, but not to create any additional subdirectories.

- Line 24 logs all anonymous file transfers, both incoming and outgoing.

- Line 25 logs any attempts by anonymous users to access secured files or to perform illegal functions.

- Line 26 enables strict password checking and terminates the session if the user does not supply a compliant password.

Anonymous FTP and */home/ftp*

If you install the anonymous ftp package, anonymous ftp will be available as soon as you boot the system and enable networking. Anonymous ftp access requires there be an ftp account in /etc/passwd. The ftp account entry in /etc/passwd should have a disabled password, indicated by an * in the password field. Its home directory should be /home/ftp. Its login shell should be /bin/false.

Anonymous users run as the anonymous user account, ftp. The ftpd server automatically performs a chroot to the anonymous ftp area, /home/ftp, when inetd starts the server for the current connection and the user requests an anonymous session.

In addition to general server configuration issues, the contents, ownership, and access permissions of the /home/ftp directory tree must be carefully defined. Misconfigurations of the anonymous area's access permissions are one of the main reasons ftp sites can be compromised.

/home/ftp and its subdirectories should not be owned by the anonymous user, ftp, nor should they be in the ftp user group. The directories should be owned by root or some other account. Only the directory's owner, root, should have write access to /home/ftp or any of its subdirectories.

The anonymous `ftp` area contains four subdirectories by default, `bin`, `etc`, `lib`, and `pub`. Because anonymous `ftp` runs in a `chroot`-ed environment, files normally found in `/bin`, `/etc`, and `/lib` that `ftpd` uses must be duplicated in directories with the same names and paths, relative to the `chroot root` directory, `/home/ftp`. Each of these directories requires slightly different group memberships and access permissions:

- `/home/ftp/bin` contains copies of the executable programs `ftp` uses to provide the `ls` function, `cd` function, and file compression. `bin` and its contents should have the directory or execute access bits set for all, and read and write access should be denied to all. That is, `bin` and all files under `bin` should be `chmod 0111`.

- `/home/ftp/etc` contains a local copy of the cache file containing information about dynamically loaded libraries, `ld.so.cache`. This file must be writable by `root` and readable by all. `etc` also contains dummy copies of `/etc/passwd` and `/etc/group`. These two files should contain minimal account information for owners of files in the anonymous `ftp` area. Owners will normally be the `root` and `ftp` accounts. The `/home/ftp/etc/passwd` file should not, under any circumstances, contain any passwords. The password entries should be disabled by having an `*` in the password field. `group` and `passwd` must be readable by all. They should not be writable by anyone. The sole purpose of the `group` and `passwd` files is to provide the owner and group membership names for the `ls` command. The `etc` directory should have the directory or execute access bits set for all, and read and write access should be denied to all. That is, the `etc` directory itself should be `chmod 0111`.

Caution: Contents of the FTP Password File

It is especially important that `/home/ftp/etc/passwd` contains no passwords. A common misconfiguration is using a copy of the system password file containing encrypted passwords. It's a simple matter for anonymous users to copy the `passwd` file, get the names of user accounts, crack the passwords, and gain regular remote `login` access.

- /home/ftp/lib contains copies of the few dynamically loadable libraries ftp needs. lib and its contents should have the directory or execute access bits, and the read access bits, set for all. Write access should be denied to all. That is, lib and all files under lib should be chmod 0555.

- /home/ftp/pub is the top of the public ftp directory tree. pub and any subdirectories contain the files your anonymous ftp server is making available. pub and its subdirectories should have the directory or execute access bits, and the read access bits, set for all. Write access should be denied to all. That is, pub and all directories under pub should be chmod 0555. All files under pub should be readable by all. That is, files under pub should be chmod 0444.

Caution: User and Group Ownership of the FTP *pub* Directory

As of the Red Hat 6.0 default installation, the pub directory is owned by root and is a member of the ftp group. pub and all directories under pub are setgid to the ftp group. This isn't an immediate security problem because none of the directories allow write access. However, if write access were allowed to one of these directories, and anonymous ftp service was offered, this default configuration would open your site to one of the most common ftp security exploits. A remote, anonymous user would be able to write files to your system and modify existing files. That is, the remote user could establish an illegal, hidden WAREZ site in your ftp area, mount a denial-of-service attack by filling your file system, or, depending on the local services you have enabled, gain shell login access through the ftp account. Note also that if the chmod function was enabled for anonymous users in /etc/ftpaccess, the remote user could modify file and directory permissions, as well.

POP Server Configuration Issues

POP mail retrieval service, if used, would generally be configured as a private local service in a small site. Local users would use POP to retrieve their mail to local workstations from a central mail server machine. If you need to offer POP service to remote sites, special care must be taken to ensure as secure a configuration as possible, such as requiring the connections be made over SSH.

As a private, local service, the popd server is enabled in /etc/inetd.conf. If all available tcp_wrappered services are available to local machines in /etc/hosts.allow, a specific ipop3d entry is not necessary, and all external service access is denied by default in /etc/hosts.deny. Security is further increased by the packet-filtering firewall, because incoming remote connections to the POP server are denied by default. There are no firewall rules allowing remote access to the local server.

To configure the ipop3d server, each mail user account name must be added to the popusers group in /etc/group. The system configuration program, linuxconf, provides a GUI interface to edit the /etc/group file.

The POP server configuration files are housed in the /etc/ppp directory. Two files, options and pap-secrets, are of interest. (Because most sites use PAP authentication, rather than CHAP authentication, the third file, chap-secrets, will not be modified.)

The following is an example of an /etc/ppp/options configuration file with accompanying explanations:

```
1. usehostname
2. noipdefault
3. auth
4. login
5. require-pap
```

Line 1, usehostname, requires that the server's hostname be specified as part of the authentication process.

Line 2, noipdefault, requires that the client specify the server's IP address as part of the authentication process.

Line 3, auth, requires that the client authenticate itself before the actual mail retrieval connection is established.

Line 4, login, tells the POP server to use the password in /etc/passwd to authenticate the user, rather than needing to specify a password in ASCII clear text in the pap-secrets file. (The login option should not be used for dialin POP accounts.)

Line 5, require-pap, requires PAP authentication to be used.

The following is an example of an /etc/ppp/pap-secrets configuration file with accompanying explanations that contains an entry for each individual user account with POP mail access authorization:

```
1. # user   server        secret  IP addresses
2. name     192.168.1.1   ""      192.168.1.3 host.local.lan
```

Line 1 is a comment labeling the required fields in the configuration file.

Line 2 contains a sample user account entry:

- name is the user account's login name.

- 192.168.1.1 is the server's IP address, which in this case is the IP address of the internal network interface.

- "" is the user's password field. The field contains a blank string because the /etc/ppp/options file enables the login option to verify the POP account password against the system password file.

- 192.168.1.3 host.local.lan is a list of IP addresses and hostnames the user is allowed to connect from.

Alternatively, the following is an example of an /etc/ppp/pap-secrets configuration file with accompanying explanations that contains a global entry allowing all regular user accounts POP mail access authorization:

```
1. # user  server      secret  IP addresses
2. *        192.168.1.1  " "
3. root     192.168.1.1  "*"     .
4. bin      192.168.1.1  "*"     .
5. mail     192.168.1.1  "*"     .
6. games    192.168.1.1  "*"     .
7. nobody   192.168.1.1  "*"     .
```

Line 1 is a comment labeling the required fields in the configuration file.
Line 2 contains a global user account entry:

- * indicates any valid user account's login name. Remember to include all users in popusers group in /etc/group.

- 192.168.1.1 is the server's IP address, which in this case is the IP address of the internal network interface.

- "" is the user's password field. The field contains a blank string because the /etc/ppp/options file enables the login option to verify the POP account password against the system password file.

- The IP addresses field is empty, indicating that the users' connections may be made from anywhere.

Lines 3–7 contain sample user account entries that are not authorized to access the POP server. Because this configuration example allows access from all users in the /etc/passwd file, disallowed user accounts must be listed individually:

- The user field contains the account name to deny access to.

- 192.168.1.1 is the server's IP address, which in this case is the IP address of the internal network interface.

- "*" is the user's password field. The field contains an asterisk string indicating that the user password is invalid.

- The IP addresses field contains a hyphen, indicating that no IP source addresses are allowed.

As a limited, public service, two additional configuration steps must be taken to enhance security. First, each allowed remote IP address or hostname must be listed as a client to the ipop3d server in /etc/hosts.allow. Second, individual firewall rules need to be defined to allow each of these remote hosts access to the local POP server.

DHCP Server Configuration Issues

Running a local DHCP server, dhcpd, on the firewall machine is dangerous. If network neighbors on your ISP's subnet are DHCP clients, they can confuse your server with the ISP's DHCP server. Running a misconfigured DHCP server is a sure way to get your ISP account terminated until you've fixed the problem.

Nevertheless, running a local server for internal LAN use has advantages in some situations. One situation is a small home site, possibly a site comprised of a single dual-homed Linux machine and a notebook computer used both at work and at home. Another situation is a small business site with more computers than can be conveniently managed by hand.

For a small site with a single internal LAN, configuring the dhcpd server on the firewall machine requires special care before invoking the server to ensure the LAN is served and the Internet is not. The firewall rules must meticulously ensure that local server messages are allowed to pass through only the internal network interface to the LAN. Alternatively, if one of the machines on the LAN is a second Linux machine, the internal machine could host the DHCP service for other machines on the LAN. The firewall rules must ensure that DHCP messages from the LAN are not forwarded through the external network interface.

For larger sites with a DMZ network and a second internal choke firewall, the dhcpd server could be hosted from the internal firewall machine. Both the external firewall and the internal firewall would ensure that local DHCP traffic remains within the confines of the LAN.

Limiting DHCP server traffic to a specific network interface in a multihomed machine is not difficult. The issue is simply that the specific network interface must be defined for dhcpd before the server is first executed. To assign your dhcpd server to a particular interface, edit the /etc/rc.d/init.d/dhcpd startup script. By default, the server is invoked as:

```
daemon /usr/sbin/dhcpd
```

Assuming your external interface is eth0 and your internal interface is eth1, edit the line to read:

```
daemon /usr/sbin/dhcpd eth1
```

If the daemon is running on the firewall machine, rather than on an internal machine, you might need to add a routing table entry for the internal network interface. If so, add the following line to /etc/rc.d/rc.local:

```
route add -host 255.255.255.0 dev eth1
```

dhcpd's server configuration file is /etc/dhcpd.conf. The file may contain global parameters. The file must contain a declaration record for each subnet attached to the server machine. A simple example for a private, dynamically changing LAN is as follows:

```
 1. option domain-name "local.lan";
 2. option domain-name-servers 192.168.1.1;
 3. option subnet-mask 255.255.255.0;

 4. subnet 192.168.1.0 netmask 255.255.255.0 {
 5.         range 192.168.1.2 192.168.1.254;
 6.         default-lease-time 86400;
 7.         max-lease-time 2592000;
 8.         option broadcast-address 192.168.1.255;
 9.         option routers 192.168.1.1;
10. }
```

Line 1 is a global parameter specifying the domain-name.

Line 2 is a global parameter specifying the domain-name-servers.

Line 3 is a global parameter specifying the subnet-mask. Any IP address matching on the first 24 bits, the network address, is a member of the subnet network address space.

Line 4 begins the subnet record for the particular network interface. The subnet's network address is 192.168.1.0 and its network mask is 255.255.255.0. Any IP address matching on the first 24 bits, the network address, is a member of the local network address space.

Line 5 defines the dynamic IP address pool range by the first and last address in the range.

Line 6 defines the default-lease-time in seconds. There are 86,400 seconds in a day, so the default lease time is one day.

Line 7 defines the max-lease-time in seconds. There are 2,592,000 seconds in 30 days, so the maximum lease time is one month.

Line 8 spells out the LAN's broadcast-address.

Line 9 specifies the LAN's gateway router.

Line 10 closes the subnet record for the particular network interface.

For more information on dhcpd configuration, see the online man pages dhcpd(8) and dhcpd.conf(5).

NTP Configuration Issues

The Network Time Protocol (NTP) is used to synchronize your local computers' system times with that of an authoritative remote time server. Typically, sites run the NTP client, ntpdate, on a single machine to retrieve the current time from several remote servers. (NTP works best with at least three remote servers to query.) ntpdate makes a best-guess estimate of the current time, based on the servers' reported authority level and precision and on the range of differences among the answers it receives from the various servers, and updates the local system time accordingly. To reduce redundant Internet traffic, this same machine also runs a local NTP server, xntpd, to disseminate the current time to other machines on the LAN. If the site is large, this local server might be configured as a master, authoritative server for the site. Additional internal machines might be configured to run their own xntpd servers as secondary peer servers to distribute the time to multiple internal machines, thereby reducing the load on the master server.

For the purposes of a small LAN, an example is given consisting of a single host that runs the clock setting client program, ntpdate, at boot time to initialize the system time from several remote servers. Then the host starts xntpd to offer local time service to the other machines on the LAN. The other machines run xntpd as a client to periodically query the local server.

The server machine is configured to execute the /etc/rc.d/init.d/xntpd startup script at boot time. If the configuration file, /etc/ntp/step-tickers, exists, ntpdate reads the names of the remote time servers to query from this file. Then the startup script executes the xntpd daemon.

xntpd's configuration file is /etc/ntp.conf. The following is a sample ntp.conf configuration file with accompanying explanation for the LAN's main server machine:

```
1. restrict default nomodify
2. server  127.0.0.1
3. restrict 127.0.0.1
```

Line 1 defines our default level of trust in remote hosts. By default, remote hosts are trusted for the time, but they aren't allowed to make modification to the local server's configuration. Remote servers are not contacted by the local xntpd server in this configuration, however.

Line 2 declares the local machine as a time server.

Line 3 removes the default restrictions from the local server so that the server's configuration can be modified locally at run time.

The client machine is also configured to execute the /etc/rc.d/init.d/xntpd startup script at boot time. If the configuration file, /etc/ntp/step-tickers, exists, ntpdate reads the names of the remote time servers to query from this file. Then the startup script executes the xntpd daemon.

Caveat: Interactions Between *ntpdate* and *xntpd*

ntpdate won't query for time if xntpd is currently running. In the configuration here, xntpd doesn't periodically query remote hosts for the current time. To periodically update the time from a remote server, the following shell script could be run as a cron job to stop the xntpd daemon, use ntpdate to get the current time, and then restart xntpd:

```
#!/bin/sh
sh /etc/rc.d/init.d/xntpd restart
```

xntpd's configuration file is `/etc/ntp.conf`. The following is a sample `ntp.conf` configuration file with accompanying explanation for the internal LAN machines:

```
1. restrict  192.168.11.1 nomodify
2. server 192.168.11.1
3. server  127.0.0.1
4. restrict 127.0.0.1
```

Line 1 defines the default level of trust in remote hosts. By default, remote hosts are trusted for the time, but they aren't allowed to make modification to the local server's configuration.

Line 2 declares the remote server to be the firewall machine's internal network interface. The minimum and maximum polling intervals are not specified, for the purposes of illustration. The default `minpoll` value is 6, which amounts to approximately 1 minute. The default `maxpoll` value is 10, which amounts to approximately 15 minutes.

Line 3 declares the local machine as a time server.

Line 4 removes the default restrictions from the local server so that the server's configuration can be modified locally at runtime.

HTTP CGI Script Configuration Issues

CGI scripts and programs are executed by the Web server to perform special functions beyond the capabilities of the Web server. The scripts usually execute local system programs to perform their functions. They have as much authorization to system resources as the account the script is `setuided` to or that the Web server itself has. The exact actions the scripts take are usually based on arbitrary, user-supplied data.

For More Information: Official NTP Servers

Running as a public primary server requires that you receive your official time via a radio or satellite receiver or modem. There are currently around 50 public primary servers in the world, supported by approximately 100 public secondary servers, which in turn are supported by thousands of higher stratum public servers. NTP server sites typically prefer to serve a particular geographic area or network address block. Information on public secondary servers near you is available from `http://www.eecis.udel.edu/~mills/ntp/servers.html`. Additional information on the NTP protocol, software, and documentation is available from the same site at `http://www.eecis.udel.edu/~mills/ntp/`.

CGI scripts are especially vulnerable to security exploits unless special precautions are taken. If the script or program requires special system account privileges to perform its function, the author may define the script's setuid or setgid bits to run as a privileged user. In this case, the script is executing with special system privileges. Web server processes should run under an unprivileged account such as user nobody. If the Web server parent daemon, which runs with root privileges, is misconfigured, it can fork child server processes off with root privileges as well, rather than with the recommended minimal privileges of user nobody. In this case, the CGI script runs with root privileges. These potential aspects of the script's authorization level have lead to serious, successful exploits when the remote user was able to gain root access to the system by supplying the script with unexpected data.

In addition to the CGI security precautions recommended in the Apache Web server documentation, available from www.apache.org, two other common additional safeguards can be taken. The first is to run an intermediate server, cgiwrap, which protects CGI scripts much as tcp_wrappers protects services managed by inetd. The second is to carefully check user input before accessing system resources on the remote user's behalf.

cgiwrap doesn't limit remote access to CGI scripts. Instead, cgiwrap ensures that the script runs with the intended permissions, and not those of the server, even if the server is mistakenly running with root privileges. The cgiwrap source code package and documentation is available from ftp://ftp.cc.umr.edu/pub/cgi/cgiwrap.

Carefully controlling the contents of user input to the scripts is more difficult, because the expected input for any given program is unique. A paper available from CERT, "How To Remove Meta-characters From User-Supplied Data In CGI Scripts," at http://www.cert.org/tech_tips/cgi_metacharacters.html describes a general approach to error checking code and supplies examples in Perl script and C source code. The general idea is that all user input must be checked. User-supplied data streams longer than some maximum expected value must be discarded. This step alone protects the script from buffer overflow exploits. Rather than attempting to write code to anticipate every undefined and unexpected possible user input, the paper recommends defining exactly which ASCII characters are legal and tossing any input that includes illegal characters.

SOCKS: An Application-Level Proxy Firewall

SOCKS is a circuit gateway proxy package. (SOCKS was the development project's internal name, standing for sockets. After release, the development name stuck and the software continues to be called SOCKS.) In a LAN environment, SOCKS' purpose is to function as an application-level proxy firewall. Client programs on the LAN are allowed access only to the local SOCKS server machine. Only the SOCKS server is allowed access to the Internet. SOCKS is a transparent proxy. To the user, the client program appears to connect directly to the remote service. Because the SOCKS client programs are modified to communicate only with the SOCKS server, the client programs connect to the local server instead. The server authenticates the user and establishes a connection to the remote service on the client's behalf. When the connection is established, the SOCKS server relays data between the local client and the remote server. Because the server is a proxy for the LAN clients, the LAN machines are invisible to the Internet, just as they are with packet-level IP address masquerading.

SOCKS version 4 supports proxying TCP services. The current version 5 additionally supports proxying UDP and multicast services, provides for strong user authentication and DNS lookup services for the client, and includes the client code as shared libraries, removing the need to recompile the client programs in some cases.

The new UDP relaying is an especially attractive feature to take advantage of in a multitiered security scheme. Packet-level filtering cannot adequately enforce proper UDP exchanges. The UDP relay feature creates a host and port association between the client and server processes, ensuring that the client receives datagrams from only the intended remote server. For multiprotocol services, such as RealAudio, that use a TCP connection as a control channel and UDP for the data stream, SOCKS associates the remote host end of the TCP connection with the expected source of the incoming UDP datagrams.

SOCKS' ability to enforce correct use of application-level protocols is also attractive for TCP callback services, such as FTP, in port data channel mode. SOCKS ensures that the incoming data channel connection from TCP port 20 originates from the remote host the client connected to when establishing the command channel on TCP port 21.

All in all, SOCKS is an attractive alternative to the IP masquerading modules supplied with Linux, provided your client programs are all SOCKS-aware. Although the Linux-supplied masquerade modules support a handful of popular services, SOCKS offers support for any network service.

In a SOCKS proxy environment, you would block your LAN from access to the Internet, instead allowing LAN access only to the internal network interface. It is particularly important to block incoming connection attempts from the Internet to the SOCKS server on TCP port 1080. The server should never accept connections from remote sites.

As a proxy service, SOCKS effectively performs IP masquerading for the LAN clients. With SOCKS providing the only conduit between the LAN and the Internet, packet level-IP masquerading is not needed.

SOCKS is available as both a free and a commercial product. The top level SOCKS Web site is at `http://www.socks.nec.com/`. The noncommercial reference release of SOCKS version 5 is available from `http://www.socks.nec.com/socks5.html`.

Miscellaneous System Accounts
in */etc/passwd* and */etc/group*

The user authentication files, /etc/passwd and /etc/group, contain a number of special system account entries. The entries allow the services they are associated with to run without root privileges and to more tightly control access to programs and file system areas reserved for these services. Depending on your installation, most of these system accounts will be unused because you won't run the services the accounts are associated with.

As distributed from Red Hat, the system account entries' passwords are disabled in /etc/passwd. They contain an * in the password field. This means that logins as these users are not allowed. Instead, system processes are started with reduced authorization levels rather than starting with root privilege.

Although logins to these system accounts are not allowed by default due to the disabled password fields, two further security precautions are to define /bin/false as the login shell for needed accounts that don't have a shell or program, and to remove the remaining accounts from /etc/passwd and /etc/group altogether. A minimal set of system accounts in /etc/passwd consists of the following entries:

```
root:x:0:0:root:/root:/bin/bash
bin:x:1:1:bin:/bin:/bin/false
adm:x:3:4:adm:/var/adm:/bin/false
sync:x:5:0:sync:/sbin:/bin/sync
shutdown:x:6:0:shutdown:/sbin:/sbin/shutdown
halt:x:7:0:halt:/sbin:/sbin/halt
mail:x:8:12:mail:/var/spool/mail:/bin/false
nobody:x:99:99:Nobody:/:/bin/false
```

The remaining default system accounts are special purpose accounts. You can remove any of the accounts in Table 7.1 that you don't need from both the password and group files.

Don't Over-Prune the System Groups

/etc/group contains additional system groups beyond the groups associated with the special purpose system accounts. Do not remove other system group names from /etc/group. These additional groups serve as access control mechanisms for software subsystems, such as the man page directories, and for certain devices, such as the console, kernel and physical memory, the disk drives, and physical terminals.

Table 7.1   Special-Purpose System Accounts

Account	Associated Server or Subsystem
daemon	PPP and POP servers
lp	Printing subsystem
news	News server subsystem
uucp	UUCP servers
operator	System Administration alias
games	Various game programs
gopher	Gopher server
ftp	FTP server
xfs	X Window font server
gdm	Gnome display manager
postgres	SQL database server
squid	squid Web proxy server

Setting Your *PATH* Variable

The shell PATH environment variable defines the directories your shell searches for executable programs when you run a program. The shell searches the directories in the order you've defined them in the PATH variable.

The directory search order introduces a potential security problem, especially on multiuser systems. It's often convenient to add the current directory, ., to the PATH. If the dot is used in user account PATHs, the dot should be the final directory listed. It should never precede the system binary directories. Otherwise, someone could place a Trojan program with the same name as ls, for example, in a directory you would be likely to list. The dot should not be used in root's PATH at all. The shell's directory search for root should be limited to the standard system binary directories. The root account should execute programs in other directories by explicitly supplying the full pathname on the command line.

Individual PATH variables are defined in the user's shell initialization file. Depending on the shell used, the file is named .profile, .login, .cshrc, .kshrc, .bashrc, and so forth. A standard sh-style PATH for root could be: PATH=/bin:/sbin:/usr/bin:/usr/sbin.

A standard PATH for a regular user who runs X Window could be:

PATH=/bin:/usr/bin:/usr/X11R6/bin:/usr/local/bin:.

/etc/issue.net

`/etc/issue.net` contains the `login` banner displayed when someone attempts a remote `login`. The banner is displayed, followed by the prompts for username and password. `/etc/issue` contains the same information for local `logins`.

One of the problems with offering `telnet` service is that the `login` banner is displayed before the user authentication process begins. Anyone can open a `telnet` connection to your machine and read the banner information. By default, most UNIX systems, Linux included, display the operating system name and release version, as well as the computer's CPU type. For example, the Red Hat Linux Release 6.0 `issue.net` displays:

```
Red Hat Linux release 6.0 (Hedwig)
Kernel 2.2.5-15 on an i686
```

This is exactly the kind of information the port scan programs are trying to ascertain. The remote `login` banner gives the information to them for free if `telnet` service is open to the Internet.

Both `/etc/issue` and `/etc/issue.net` are created every time the system boots. The files are created by the `/etc/rc.d/rc.local` shell script. If you need to offer remote `telnet` service, you should edit `/etc/rc.d/rc.local` to either write more limited information into `/etc/issue.net` or remove the code from `rc.local` and create your own `/etc/issue.net` by hand.

For example, you could create a simple remote `login` banner by placing the following lines in `/etc/issue.net`:

```
Welcome to Bastion

%d
```

The following would be displayed when someone attempted a remote `telnet` connection to your machine:

```
Welcome to Bastion

13:45 on Saturday, 24 July 1999
```

Remote Logging

`syslogd`, the system logging daemon, can be configured to write the system logs to a remote machine. The average home user probably doesn't have a need for this added level of complexity and system administration overhead. A site that uses a networked server configuration similar to the example in Chapter 4, with services offered from internal machines in the DMZ, might want to keep a remote copy of the system logs. Maintaining a remote copy offers two advantages: Log files are consolidated on a single machine, making it easier for a system administrator to monitor the logs, and the information is protected if one of the server machines is ever compromised.

Chapter 8 discusses the importance system logs play during recovery if a system is ever compromised. One of the first things a hacker does after successfully gaining `root` access to a compromised machine is to either erase the system logs or install Trojan programs that won't log his or her activities. The system log files are either gone or untrustworthy at exactly the time when you need them most. Maintaining a remote copy of the logs helps protect this information, at least up to the point when the hacker replaces the daemons writing the log file information.

To log system information remotely, both the local logging configuration and the remote logging configuration require slight modifications.

On the remote machine collecting the system logs, edit the boot time configuration script, `/etc/rc.d/init.d/syslog`, and add the `-r` option to the `syslogd` invocation. The `-r` option tells `syslogd` to listen on the UDP syslog service port 514 for incoming log information from remote systems.

On the local machine producing the system logs, edit `syslogd`'s configuration file, `/etc/syslog.conf`, and add lines specifying what log facilities and priorities you want written to a remote host. For example, the following copies all log information to *hostname*:

```
*.*                          @hostname
```

Keeping Current with Software Upgrades

One of the most important security precautions you can take is to keep your system software up-to-date, particularly network services and the kernel itself. This precaution is especially critical for open-source systems such as Linux, where developers and hackers alike have equal access to the source code.

Getting Errata Updates from Red Hat

Security patches and upgrades to Red Hat Linux are available from `www.redhat.com` under the Support page's Errata section. Web links change as Web sites are reorganized. The current URL for Red Hat's Errata area is `http://www.redhat.com/corp/support/errata/`. I'd recommend checking the Errata area weekly for recent security upgrades.

An Example: *mountd* Exploit

A buffer overflow vulnerability was discovered in the NFS `mountd` daemon in the fall of 1998, allowing a hacker to gain `root` access to the system. This version of `mountd` was released in Red Hat version 5.1 shortly before the vulnerability was discovered. When the hacker community discovered the security hole, programs to take advantage of the flaw were quickly disseminated across the Internet. Red Hat, along with the other Linux vendors, published a security patch almost immediately. For more information on the `mountd` exploit, see CERT advisory `http://www.cert.org/advisories/CA-98.12.mountd.html`.

Nearly everyone I've spoken with who ran `mountd` and wasn't protected by a firewall was hacked before they upgraded to the patched version.

The `mountd` exploit is an example of:

- The need to keep current with security upgrades and patches.
- Buffer overflow vulnerabilities.
- Running servers publicly not intended for the Internet. Even if NFS file systems were not mounted, or not publicly exported, the vulnerability was in `mountd` itself.
- The need to block external access to LAN services and daemons.

Summary

Even with a packet-filtering firewall in place, a UNIX system can easily be compromised if security considerations and precautions are not taken at the system administration level. No single security layer or mechanism offers complete protection against system compromise. This chapter explains various system administration and server configuration options you should use to help secure the system.

A number of areas requiring the system administrator's attention are presented, including authentication and how shadow passwords and MD5 password hashing are better than the default UNIX password mechanism. After authentication, system administration issues centering around authorization are presented. The TCP wrapper mechanism is explained. The danger of world-writable files and directories is discussed, along with tools to help locate world-writable objects in the file system. Security configuration issues and mechanisms specific to a number of common Internet services are covered, including services such as `telnet`, `smtp`, `ftp`, `pop`, and DNS.

8

Intrusion Detection and Incident Reporting

A PROPERLY CONFIGURED UNIX SYSTEM can be quite secure. For all the inherent dangers associated with a system as complicated as UNIX, UNIX security issues tend to be better understood than those of other operating systems because UNIX has been in use and evolving in the real world for 20 years. It's been the basis of the Internet.

Nevertheless, configuration mistakes are going to be made. Software bugs will crop up forever. In a less-than-ideal world, security compromises have to be made. Security developers and hackers are in a continual race to keep one step ahead of each other. What is secure today might not be secure tomorrow. It's practically a given that some piece of software you're running securely today won't be secure tomorrow.

Chapter 7, "Issues At the UNIX System Administration Level," spoke of the importance of keeping your system software up-to-date. It described how quickly after Red Hat 5.1 was released, a buffer overflow vulnerability in Linux's mountd daemon was found and exploited. A security upgrade was released almost immediately. This was, by far, not the first time such a thing has happened, and it won't be the last.

As hacking technology grows more sophisticated and a vulnerability is found in a piece of software, it's not the case that the software goes from being secure to becoming categorically insecure and then never used again. The vulnerability is fixed and the software lives on. It's secure again, for now. Hackers are continually looking for new vulnerabilties and new approaches. So one day, a new security hole might be discovered in that same piece of software. The process cycles again.

I'd like to say that if you follow every suggestion and procedure in this book, your system will never be broken into—but that's not true. There are no guarantees. System security is an ongoing process, a system of vigilance and keeping up-to-date, keeping one step ahead of the hackers. The danger is always there.

A final precaution you should take, and take regularly, is running system-integrity checkers. This chapter introduces a number of free, third-party system-integrity checkers, or intrusion detection tools. This chapter concludes with some common symptoms of system compromise, makes some suggestions about what to do if the unthinkable happens and your system is ever broken into, and looks at the factors behind making a decision to report an incident.

System-Integrity Checkers

System-integrity checkers specialize in a number of analyses, audits, and vulnerability checks. Some of them serve as security-analysis tools to help you fine-tune your system's configuration. Some of them actively probe for known vulnerabilities. Some of them compare the current system to a known prior state, checking for unauthorized or suspicious changes. The tools are readily available from Linux software repositories, Web and ftp security sites, DARPA-funded university security projects, and government security sites.

COPS

The Computer Oracle and Password System (COPS) by Dan Farmer is a suite of programs that together check for a large set of potential security vulnerability areas on a UNIX system. cops is intended to be run periodically as a cron job. Results are written to a report file and optionally mailed to a specific user, usually the root account.

Among the tests cops performs are file and directory access permissions, password quality, ftp configuration, checksums of key executable files, tftp access, sendmail configuration, inetd.conf setup, and the state of various, assorted configuration files in /etc.

The COPS package is widely available. Two sources are ftp://info.cert.org/pub/tools/cops/cops.1.04.tar.gz and http://metalab.unc.edu/pub/Linux/system/security/cops_104_linux.tgz.

Because COPS is intended as a security-analysis tool for UNIX systems generally, the COPS configuration files and executables need customization for any given flavor and release of Linux.

Crack

Crack is a standalone password-guessing program. Similar functionality is built into some of the other system-integrity–checking software, as well. The tool is designed to help system administrators identify user accounts with weak, easily crackable passwords. It uses a combination of general and specialized dictionaries and various heuristic algorithms to test for different pattern combinations. Crack has built-in support for merging the passwd and shadow files if shadow passwords are used. Crack uses the DES encryption scheme that UNIX passwords have historically been based on. During installation, the Red Hat Linux 6.0 distribution offers the option of using MD5-based passwords. Crack doesn't support MD5 without modification at this time.

Crack is available from `ftp://info.cert.org/pub/tools/crack/crack5.0.tar.gz`.

ifstatus

ifstatus checks the system's network interface configurations. Any interface in debug or promiscuous mode is reported. Network interfaces in these modes might be a sign that an intruder has gained access and is using a packet sniffer locally, usually to read clear text passwords, such as those that telnet passes over a network.

ifstatus is available from `ftp://coast.cs.purdue.edu/pub/tools/unix/ifstatus`.

Additional information on packet-sniffing issues can be found in "Ongoing Network Monitoring Attacks" from `http://www.cert.org/advisories/CA-94.01.ongoing.network.monitoring.attacks.html`.

MD5

MD5 is a cryptographic checksum algorithm used to ensure data integrity. MD5 reads a string or file and produces a 128-bit checksum. Red Hat Linux is now supplied with an MD5 checksum program and C programming support libraries. Some of the system-integrity packages presented here come with their own MD5 libraries to create checksum databases of selected system files.

SATAN

The Security Administrator Tool for Analyzing Networks (SATAN), by Wietse Venema and Dan Farmer, is a tool to help identify security vulnerabilities in network service configurations. SATAN checks for common problems related to NFS, NIS, tftp, ftp, and the BSD remote commands, as well as performing port scans to identify open ports. It produces lengthy reports and tutorials describing the problems found and possible solutions to them. SATAN takes quite a bit of work to get running on a Linux system, but the quality and breadth of the reports make the effort worthwhile. SATAN's user interface has been reworked as a Web browser interface.

For further information on SATAN, see `ftp://ftp.porcupine.org/pub/security/index.html`. SATAN is available from many sites, including `ftp://ftp.porcupine.org/pub/security/satan-1.1.1.tar.Z`, `ftp://ftp.net.ohio-state.edu/pub/security/satan/`, and `ftp://sunsite.unc.edu/pub/packages/security/Satan-for-Linux/`.

tiger

tiger is a collection of scripts and C programs designed to check for security vulnerabilities that could allow someone to gain unauthorized root access. tiger checks system configuration settings for such things as PATH variables, inetd.conf, NFS exported file systems, unusual filenames, file and directory permissions, and .rhost files. tiger maintains a database of digital signatures for key system files to check for tampering. tiger is widely available, including from http://metalab.unc.edu/pub/Linux/ system/security/tiger-2.2.4.tgz and http://www.net.tamu.edu/ftp/security/ TAMU/tiger-2.2.4p1.tar.gz.

tripwire

tripwire builds and maintains a database of MD5 digital signatures for all or a set of files and directories on the system. Its purpose is to detect unauthorized additions, deletions, or changes to files. The last public version of tripwire, 1.2, is widely available from sites such as http://www.cert.org/ftp/tools/tripwire/ tripwire-1.2.tar.Z and ftp://ftp.auscert.org.au/pub/coast/COAST/Tripwire/ tripwire-1.2.tar.Z.

tripwire is now a commercial product available from Tripwire Security Systems, Inc. at http://www.tripwiresecurity.com/. Commercial version Tripwire 2.0 is free for Red Hat Linux.

Symptoms Suggesting That the System Might be Compromised

Unexpected changes in reports from the auditing tools mentioned in the last section, particularly digital signature mismatches and changes to file and directory permissions, are strong indications that the system might be compromised. Often, the successful hacker will try to hide his or her tracks. The hacker doesn't want you to detect his or her presence. Your computer is the hacker's new base of operations. Fortunately, the hacker is on a new system, and hackers make mistakes, too. Nevertheless, continual vigilance is the name of the game. The hacker might be far more skillful at hiding his or her tracks than you are at tracking down anomalous system states.

UNIX systems are too diverse, customizable, and complicated to define an ironclad, fully comprehensive list of definitive symptoms proving the system is compromised. As with any kind of detective or diagnostic work, you have to look for clues where you can—as systematically as you can. RFC 2196, "Site Security Handbook," provides a list of signs to check for. The "Intruder Detection Checklist," available from CERT at http://www.cert.org/ftp/tech_tips/intruder_detection_checklist, provides another list of anomalies to check for. "Steps for Recovering from a UNIX Root Compromise," also available from CERT at http://www.cert.org/tech_tips/ root_compromise.html, provides a third list of items to check for.

The following sections incorporate all three lists, including all or most of their points in one form or another. I've roughly categorized system anomalies into the following: indications related to the system logs; changes to the system configuration; changes related to the file system, file contents, file access permissions, and file size; changes to user accounts, passwords, and user access; problems indicated in the security audit reports; and unexpected performance degradation. The anomalous indications often cross category boundaries.

System Log Indications

System log indications include unusual error and status messages in the logs, truncated log files, deleted log files, and emailed status reports:

- System log files—Unexplained entries in the system log files, shrinking log files, and missing log files all suggest something is wrong. /var/log/auth contains a record of all account accesses. /var/log/secure contains privileged account accesses. /var/log/maillog records all mail connections. /var/log/xferlog records ftp and uucp file transfers, if configured. /var/log/messages contains the majority of the system log information.

- System daemon status reports—Instead of, or in addition to, writing to the log files, some daemons such as crond send status reports in email. Unusual or missing reports suggests something is not right.

- Anomalous console and terminal messages—Unexplained messages, possibly meant to announce the hacker's presence, during a login session are obviously suspicious.

- Repeated access attempts—Ongoing login attempts or illegal file access attempts through ftp or a Web server, particularly attempts to subvert CGI scripts, are suspicious when the attempts are persistent, even if the attempts appear to end in repeated failure.

The automatic log-monitoring programs presented in Chapter 5, "Debugging the Firewall Rules," are helpful to put up an alert or take some other action in real-time.

System Configuration Indications

System configuration indications include modified configuration files and system scripts, unintended processes running inexplicably, unexpected service port usage and assignments, and changes in network device operational status:

- cron jobs—Check the cron configuration scripts and executables for modification.

- Altered system configuration files—A digital signature check would indicate changed configuration files in /etc. These files are critical to proper system functioning. Any change to a file (such as /etc/inetd.conf, /etc/named.conf and its related DNS database files in /var/named, /etc/passwd, /etc/group, /etc/hosts.equiv, or any network file system export configuration file) is important to check.

- Unexplained services and processes as shown by ps—Unexpectedly running programs are a bad sign.

- Unexpected connection and unexpected port usage as shown by netstat—Unexpected network traffic is a very bad sign.

- System crashes and missing processes—System crashes, as well as unexpected server crashes, might be suspect.

- Changes in device configuration—Reconfiguring a network interface to be in promiscuous or debug mode is a sign that a packet sniffer is installed.

File System Indications

File system indications include new files and directories, missing files and directories, altered file contents, MD5 digitial signature mismatches, new setuid programs, and rapidly growing or overflowing file systems:

- New files and directories—Besides files with suddenly bad digital signatures, you might discover new files and directories. Especially suspicious are filenames starting with one or more dots and legitimate sounding filenames appearing in unlikely places.

- setuid and setgid programs—New setuid files, and newly set setuid files, are a good place to start looking under the hood for problems.

- Missing files—Missing files, particularly log files, indicate a problem of some kind.

- Rapidly changing file system sizes as shown by df—If the machine is compromised, rapidly growing file systems might be a sign of a hacker monitoring program producing large log files.

- Modified public file archives—Check the contents of your Web and ftp areas for new or modified files.

- New files in /dev—CERT warns especially to check for the presence of new ASCII files in /dev, which are typically Trojan programs' configuration files.

User Account Indications

User account indications include new user accounts, changes to the `passwd` file, unusual activity in the user process accounting reports or missing process accounting reports, changes to user files—especially environmental files—and loss of account access:

- New and modified user accounts—New accounts in `/etc/passwd` and processes running under new or unexpected user IDs as shown by `ps` are indications of new accounts. Accounts with suddenly missing passwords indicate an open account.

- User accounting records—Unusual user accounting reports, inexplicable logins, missing or edited log files (such as `/var/log/lastlog`, `/var/log/pacct`, or `/var/log/usracct`), and irregular user activity are signs of trouble.

- Changes to `root` or user accounts—A serious sign is if a user's login environment is modified, or damaged to the point that the account is inaccessible. Of particular concern are changes to users' `.rhost` and `.forward` files, and changes to their `PATH` environment variable.

- Loss of account access—Similar to changes to a user's login environment is intentional access denial, whether by changing the account password, removing the account, or for regular users, by changing the runlevel to single-user mode.

Security Audit Tool Indications

Security audit tool indications include digital signature mismatches, file size changes, changes to file permission mode bits, and new `setuid` and `setgid` programs.

Files with mismatched digital signatures can be files that are new, files whose lengths or creation or modification dates have changed, and files whose access modes are altered. Of particular concern are newly installed Trojan horse programs. Frequent targets for replacement are programs run from `/etc/inetd.conf`, `ls`, `ps`, `netstat`, `ifconfig`, `telnet`, `login`, `su`, `ftp`, `inetd`, `syslogd`, `du`, `df`, `sync`, and `libc`.

System Performance Indications

System performance indications include unusually high load averages and heavy disk access.

Unexplained, poor system performance could be caused by unusual process activity, unusually high run load averages, excessive network traffic, or heavy file system access.

If your system shows signs of a successful compromise, don't panic. Don't reboot the system. Important information could be lost. Simply physically disconnect the system from the Internet.

What To Do If Your System Is Compromised

Both the paper "Steps for Recovering from a UNIX Root Compromise," available from CERT at `http://www.cert.org/tech_tips/root_compromise.html`, and RFC 2196, "Site Security Handbook," discuss procedures to follow in the event of a successful security breach. These documents present more formal procedures that a business, government office, or university might follow. The procedures assume some amount of spare storage space for taking snapshots of the system, assume available staff to analyze and diagnose the security problem, and discuss situations where the victim site might want to initiate formal legal action.

For small sites with Internet access provided through a public, consumer-oriented ISP, the following usually happens: a site is compromised without the system owner's awareness, the site is used as a new base of operations to launch attacks against other sites, someone complains to the ISP, and the customer learns of the compromise when the ISP calls and disconnects the customer's Internet service. When the customer convinces the ISP that the system has been compromised and has fixed the problem, the ISP usually restores the customer's service. Weeks can pass in the interim.

If worse comes to worst, what do you do if you learn your system has been broken into? Again, first, disconnect the machine from the Internet.

Don't reboot the system right away. If the hacker installed or started programs by hand, rebooting destroys the system state information.

If storage space is available, take a snapshot of the entire system in its current state for later analysis. If that isn't an option for you, at least snapshot the system logs under /var/log and the system configuration files under the /etc directory.

Keep a log. Write everything down. Documenting what you do and what you find is not only for reporting the incident to a response team, your ISP, or a lawyer. Documenting also helps to keep a record of what you've examined and what remains to be done.

The steps you might take to determine whether the system is compromised are the same steps to take in analyzing the compromised system:

1. Check the system logs, what processes are running, and what ports are bound to. Check the contents of the system configuration files. Verify the contents and access modes of all your files and directories by checking their digital signatures. Check for new setuid programs. Compare configuration and user files against clean backup copies.

   It's very likely that the hacker installed Trojan horse programs in place of the very system tools you're using to analyze the system.

2. Take stock of any volatile information, such as which processes are running and which ports are in use.

3. Boot off a boot floppy or a backup copy of the system. Examine the system using the clean tools from the unaffected system.

4. Determine how the hacker succeeded in gaining entry, and what was done to your system.

5. Completely reinstall the system from the original Linux distribution media.

6. Correct the security vulnerability, whether by making a more careful selection of services to run, reconfiguring servers more securely, defining access lists at the tcp_wrapper level and at the individual server level, installing a packet-filtering firewall, or installing application proxy servers.

7. Enable all logging.

8. Restore user and special configuration files known to be untainted.

9. Install any new security upgrades from your Linux vendor. Install and configure system-integrity packages. Create MD5 checksums for the newly installed binaries and store the checksum database on a floppy or some other system.

10. Monitor the system for recurring access attempts by the hacker.

Most people I've spoken with feel guilty and foolish after their system has been compromised. Remember, security is an ongoing, ever-escalating battle of wits between the hackers and the systems administrators. You didn't invite the hacker in. He or she made a conscious effort, probably a very determined effort, to discover your system's vulnerabilities and to take advantage of them. Don't blame the victim. You're not alone. Many, many systems are compromised. Just try to be more alert to what the bad guys are trying to do for the next time.

Incident Reporting

An *incident* can be a number of things; you need to define it for yourself. In the most general terms, an incident is any anomalous access attempt from the Internet. In the strictest terms, an incident is a successful anomalous login access, successful denial-of-service attack, successful server vulnerability exploit, and/or successful usurping of your system's resources and services.

As the administrator for an Internet-connected machine, you should monitor your system log files, system-integrity reports, and system-accounting reports as a matter of habit. Even with minimal logging enabled, sooner or later you'll see something you believe is important enough to report. With full logging enabled, you'll have plenty of log entries to ponder 24 hours a day.

Some access attempts are more serious than others. Some will annoy you personally more than others.

The following sections start by discussing reasons why you might want to report an incident, and considerations concerning which types of incidents you might report. These are individual decisions. In the event you choose to report something, the remaining sections focus on the various reporting groups available to choose from and the kinds of information you need to supply them.

Why Report an Incident?

You might want to report an incident even if the hacker's attempt was unsuccessful. These are some of the reasons:

- To end the probes—Your firewall ensures that most probes remain harmless. Even harmless probes are annoying if they occur repeatedly. Persistent, repeated, ongoing scans fill your log files. Depending on how you've defined the notification triggers in any log-monitoring software you run, repeated probes can pester you with continual email notifications.

- To help protect other sites—Automated probes and scans are generally building a database of all vulnerable hosts in a large IP address block. When identified as potentially vulnerable to specific exploits, these hosts are targeted for selective attacks. Today's sophisticated hacking tools can compromise a vulnerable system and hide its tracks in seconds. Reporting an incident might put a stop to the scans before someone, somewhere, gets hurt.

- To inform the system or network administrator—Attacking sites are quite often compromised systems, host a compromised user account, have misconfigured software, are being spoofed, or have an individual troublemaker. System administrators are usually responsive to an incident report. ISPs tend to stop their troublemaking customers before other customers start complaining that remote sites have blocked access from their address block and they can't exchange email with a friend or family at a remote site.

- To receive confirmation of the attack—Sometimes you might simply want confirmation as to whether what you're seeing in the logs is a problem or not. Sometimes you might want confirmation that a remote site was indeed leaking packets unintentionally due to a faulty configuration. The remote site is often glad for the heads-up, too, that its network isn't behaving as it had intended.

- To increase awareness and monitoring by all involved parties—If you report the incident to the attacking site, the site will hopefully monitor its configurations and user activities more carefully. If you report the incident to an abuse center, the abuse staff can contact the remote site with more clout than an individual carries, keep an eye out for continued activity and better help customers who have been compromised. If you report the incident to a security newsgroup, other people can get a better idea of what to watch out for.

What Kinds of Incidents Might You Report?

Which incidents you report is completely dependent on your tolerance, how serious you consider different probes to be, and how much time you care to devote against what is a global, exponentially growing infestation. It comes down to how you define the term "incident." In different people's minds, incidents can range anywhere from simple port scans, to attempts to access your private files or system resources, to denial-of-service attacks, to crashing your servers or your entire system, to gaining root login access to your system:

- Denial-of-service attacks—Any kind of denial-of-service attack is blatantly hostile. It's difficult not to take such an attack personally. These attacks are the electronic form of vandalism, obstruction, harrassment, and theft of service. Because some forms of denial-of-service attacks are possible due to the inherent nature of networked devices, there is little or nothing you can do about some forms of attack other than to report the incidents and block the attacker's entire address block.

- Attempts to reconfigure your system—A hacker can't reconfigure your servers without a `root` login account on your machine, but he or she could conceivably modify your system's in-memory, network-related tables—or try, at least. Exploits to consider include:

  - Unauthorized DNS zone transfers, to or from your machine, over TCP. For more information on zone transfers, see *DNS & BIND* by Albitz and Liu (O'Reilly).

  - Changes to your dynamic routing tables via ICMP Redirect or probes to UDP port 520 for `routed` or `gated`. (Remember, a firewall machine should not support dynamic routing.) For more information on routing table exploits, see *Firewalls and Internet Security: Repelling the Wily Hacker* by Cheswick and Bellovin (Addison-Wesley).

  - Attempts to reconfigure your network interfaces or routing tables via probes to UDP port 161 for `snmpd`.

- Attempts to gain local configuration and network topology information— Network information requests are mostly directed to UDP port 161 for `snmpd`. DNS queries over TCP port 53 provide network topology information, as do routing queries to UDP port 520 for `routed` or `gated`.

- Attempts to gain login account access—Probes to `telnet` TCP port 23 and `ssh` TCP port 22 are obvious. Less obvious are probes to ports associated with servers known to be exploitable, either historically or currently. Buffer overflow exploits are generally intended, ultimately, to execute commands and gain shell access. The `mountd` exploit is an example of this.

- Attempts to access nonpublic files—Attempts to access private files, such as the `/etc/passwd` file, configuration files, or proprietary files, show up in your FTP log (`/var/log/xferlog` or `/var/log/messages`) and in your Web server access log (`/var/log/httpd/error_log`).

- Attempts to use private services—By definition, any service you haven't made available to the Internet is private. I'm referring to private services potentially available through your public servers, such as attempting to relay mail through your mail server. Chances are people are up to no good if they're trying to use your machine instead of their own or their ISP's. Relay attempts show up in your mail log file (`/var/log/maillog`).

- Attempts to store files on your disk—If you host an improperly configured anonymous FTP site, it's possible for someone to set up a repository of stolen software (`WAREZ`) on your machine. Attempts to upload files are recorded in your FTP log (`/var/log/xferlog`) if `ftpd` is configured to log file uploads.

- Attempts to crash your system or individual servers—Buffer overflow attempts against CGI scripts available through your Web site are possibly the easiest to identify by error messages written in the CGI script's log files. Other reports of erroneous data would appear in your general `syslog` file (`/var/log/messages`), your general daemon log (`/var/log/daemon`), your mail log (`/var/log/maillog`), your FTP log (`/var/log/xferlog`), or your secure access log (`/var/log/secure`).

- Attempts to exploit specific, known, currently exploitable vulnerabilities—Hackers find new vulnerabilities with each new software release. Keep up-to-date with the newest advisories from `www.cert.org` and your Linux software vendor. In the last year or so, the most widely exploited services have been `sunrpc/mount`, `pop3`, `imap`, `socks`, `ftp`, CGI script vulnerabilties, `smtp` mail relaying, and the BSD remote commands.

To Whom Do You Report an Incident?

You have a number of options in terms of whom you report an incident to:

- `root`, `postmaster`, or `abuse` at the offending site—The obvious place to lodge a complaint is with the administrator of the offending site. Informing the system administrator is often all that's required to take care of a problem. This isn't always possible, though. Many probes originate from spoofed, nonexistent IP addresses. An `nslookup` on the source address returns a message that the host or domain is nonexistent.

- Network coordinator—If the IP address doesn't resolve, contacting the coordinator for the network address block is often helpful. The coordinator can contact the administrator at the offending site or else put you in direct contact. If the IP address doesn't resolve through `nslookup`, you can almost always find the network coordinator by supplying the address to the `whois` databases. The `whois` command is hard-wired into the ARIN database. All four databases are available through the Web:

  - ARIN—The American Registry for Internet Numbers maintains the IP address database for the Western hemisphere, the Americas. ARIN is located at `http://whois.arin.net/whois/arinwhois.html`.

- APNIC—The Asia Pacific Network Information Centre maintains the IP address database for Asia. APNIC is located at `http://www.apnic.net/reg.html`.

- RIPE—The Réseaux IP Européens maintains the IP address database for Europe. RIPE is located at `http://www.ripe.net/db/whois.html`.

- NIRPNET—The Department of Defense Whois Database maintains the IP address database for military networks. NIRPNET is located at `http://nic.mil/cgi-bin/whois`.

- Your ISP abuse center—If scans are originating from within your ISP's address space, your abuse center is the place to contact. Your ISP can be helpful with scans originating elsewhere, too, by contacting the offending site on your behalf. Chances are good your machine isn't the only machine being probed on the ISP's network.

- CERT—The CERT Coordination Center is unlikely to have the resources to respond to general, run-of-the-mill incidents. CERT's priorities are more likely aimed at global issues, large institutions, and Internet security emergencies. Nevertheless, CERT welcomes incident report information for its tracking and statistical reporting efforts. CERT can be contacted at `http://www.cert.org/contact_cert/contactinfo.html` or by email at `cert@cert.org`.

- Your Linux vendor—If your system is compromised due to a software vulnerability in its distribution, your vendor will want to know so that a security upgrade can be developed and released.

What Information Do You Supply?

An incident report must contain enough information to help the incident response team track down the problem. When contacting the site the attack originated from, remember that your contact person might be the individual who intentionally launched the attack. What you include out of the following list depends on who you are contacting and how comfortable you are including the information:

- Your email address
- Your phone number, if appropriate
- Your IP address, hostname, and domain name
- The IP addresses and hostnames, if available, involved in the attack
- The date and time of the incident (include your time zone relative to GMT)
- A description of the attack
- How you detected the attack

- Representative log file entries showing the incident
- A description of the log file format
- References to advisories and security notices describing the nature and significance of the attack
- What you want the person to do (e.g., fix it, confirm it, explain it, monitor it, be informed of it)

Where Do You Find More Information?

As network security comes increasingly into the public's mind, the number of security-related Web sites is growing quickly. CERT and COAST remain the granddaddy repositories for security information and tools. Various departments in the federal government also provide enormous amounts of security information over the Web. The following is a list of some of the most well-known, largest, longest-established, and official security Web sites available:

- http://www.cert.org—CERT Coordination Center: Carnegie-Mellon Software Engineering Institute. CERT maintains advisories, notices, mailing lists, security documents, security related software repositories, and annual and long-term reports of Internet hacking activity.
- http://www.first.org—FIRST: Forum of Incident Response and Security Teams. FIRST maintains lists of incident response team members for companies, universities, and the government.
- http://www.cerias.purdue.edu—CERIAS: Center for Education and Research in Information Assurance and Security. CERIAS is incorporating the COAST project (http://www.cs.purdue.edu/coast). COAST hosts security-related software tools, papers, guidelines, reports, and standards.
- http://ciac.llnl.gov—CIAC: Computer Incident Advisory Capability. CIAC provides technical assistance and incident response services to Department of Energy (DOE) sites. However, CIAC also hosts security bulletins, tutorials, security software tools, and links to other security-related sites.
- http://csrc.nist.gov—NIST: National Institute of Standards and Technology. NIST hosts a Computer Security Resource Clearinghouse, which includes numerous security-related publications.
- http://www.fedcirc.gov—FedCIRC: The Federal Computer Incident Response Capability provides technical assistance and incident response services to federal government computer sites. However, FedCIRC also hosts advisories, vulnerability notices, security documents, links to related sites, and security software tools.

Summary

This chapter focuses on monitoring system integrity and intrusion detection. Third-party analysis tools, available from many Web and `ftp` security sites, are presented, including tools such as COPS, `Crack`, SATAN, `tiger`, and `tripwire`. The importance of digital signatures, such as those produced by MD5 and `tripwire`, is shown. For the case where you suspect the system might be compromised, a list of potential problem indications is presented. If you see some of these indications and conclude the system is compromised, a list of recovery steps is discussed. Finally, incident-reporting considerations are discussed, along with pointers to whom you might report an incident.

IV

Appendixes

A

Security Resources

THIS APPENDIX LISTS THE MOST COMMON SOURCES of security-related notices, information, tools, updates, and patches currently on the Internet. Many more sites exist, and new sites pop up every day, so consider this list a starting point, not a complete list.

Information Sources

Security information of all kinds, notices and alerts, white papers, tutorials, and so on can be found in the following sources:

- CERT Coordination Center:
  `http://www.cert.org/`
- CIAC (Computer Incident Advisory Capability):
  `http://ciac.llnl.gov/ciac/`
- COAST Internet Firewalls—Resources:
  `http://www.cs.purdue.edu/coast/firewalls/`
- COAST Security Archive:
  `ftp://coast.cs.purdue.edu/pub/`
- Dave Dittrich's Security Page:
  `http://www.washington.edu/People/dad/`

- Firewall Wizards Mailing List Archive:
  `http://www.nfr.net/firewall-wizards/fwsearch.html`
- Internet Engineering Task Force (IETF):
  `http://www.ietf.cnri.reston.va.us/home.html`
- Linux Firewall and Security Site:
  `http://linux-firewall-tools.com/linux`
- Linux Security Resources:
  `http://www.linux-security.org/`
- Matt's UNIX Security:
  `http://www.deter.com/unix/`
- NIH Computer Security Information:
  `http://www.alw.nih.gov/Security/`
- Red Hat Security Page:
  `http://www.redhat.com/LinuxIndex/Administration/Security/`
- SANS Institute:
  `http://www.sans.org/`

Software Collections

The following sites specialize in maintaining repositories of security-related software of all kinds:

- CERT Archive:
  `http://www.cert.org/ftp/tools/`
- COAST Security Tools:
  `http://www.cs.purdue.edu/coast/coast-tools.html`
- FreeFire Security Tools:
  `http://sites.inka.de/sites/lina/freefire-1/tools.html`
- Linux Router Project:
  `http://www.linuxrouter.org/`
- Linuxberg Software:
  `http://idirect.Linuxberg.com/software.html`
- Masquerading Applications:
  `http://www.tsmservices.com/masq`
- Sunsite Security Area:
  `ftp://sunsite.unc.edu/pub/Linux/system/security/`

Security Tools

Security software tools are mirrored at many sites. These are some of the most common tools, with pointers to where to find them:

- argus:
  ftp://ftp.sei.cmu.edu/pub/argus/
- COPS:
  ftp://sunsite.unc.edu/pub/Linux/system/security/cops_104_linux.tgz
  ftp://coast.cs.purdue.edu/pub/tools/unix/cops
  http://www.cert.org/ftp/tools/cops/
- crack:
  http://www.cert.org/ftp/tools/crack/
  http://www.cert.org/ftp/tools/cracklib/
  ftp://coast.cs.purdue.edu/pub/tools/unix/crack
  ftp://coast.cs.purdue.edu/pub/tools/unix/cracklib/
- dig:
  ftp://coast.cs.purdue.edu/pub/tools/unix/dig/
- icmpinfo:
  ftp://coast.cs.purdue.edu/pub/tools/unix/netmon/icmpinfo/
  http://www.deter.com/unix/software/icmpinfo-1.10.tar.gz
- ifstatus:
  ftp://coast.cs.purdue.edu/pub/tools/unix/ifstatus/
- IPSec:
  http://www.xs4all.nl/~freeswan/
- ISS:
  http://www.deter.com/unix/software/iss13.tar.gz
- Linux IP Firewalling Chains:
  http://www.rustcorp.com/linux/ipchains/
- Linux IPFW Firewall Design Tool:
  http://linux-firewall-tools.com/linux/firewall/
- logcheck:
  ftp://coast.cs.purdue.edu/pub/tools/unix/logcheck/
- lsof:
  ftp://coast.cs.purdue.edu/pub/tools/unix/lsof/
- md5:
  http://www.cert.org/ftp/tools/md5/
  ftp://coast.cs.purdue.edu/pub/tools/unix/md5/
- netcat:
  ftp://coast.cs.purdue.edu/pub/tools/unix/netcat/

- nmap:
  ftp://coast.cs.purdue.edu/pub/tools/unix/nmap/
- SATAN:
  ftp://coast.cs.purdue.edu/pub/tools/unix/satan/satan/satan-1.1.1.tar.Z
  http://www.fish.com/~zen/satan/satan.html
- sbscan:
  ftp://sunsite.unc.edu/pub/Linux/system/security/sbscan-0.04.tar.gz
- SINUS Firewall Page:
  http://www.ifi.unizh.ch/ikm/SINUS/firewall/
- SOCKS:
  http://www.socks.nec.com
- SSH:
  http://www.ssh.fi/sshprotocols2/
- SSL:
  http://psych.psy.uq.oz.au/~ftp/Crypto/
- strobe:
  ftp://coast.cs.purdue.edu/pub/tools/unix/strobe/
- tiger (Linux):
  ftp://sunsite.unc.edu/pub/Linux/system/security/tiger-2.2.4.tgz
  http://www.net.tamu.edu/ftp/security/TAMU/tiger-2.2.4.tgz
- TIS Firewall Toolkit:
  http://www.tis.com/research/software/
- tripwire:
  http://www.tripwiresecurity.com/
  ftp://coast.cs.purdue.edu/pub/tools/unix/Tripwire/
  http://www.cert.org/ftp/tools/tripwire/

Firewall Tools

- Firewall Design Tool:
  http://linux-firewall-tools.com/linux/firewall/
- FWCONFIG:
  http://www.mindstorm.com/~sparlin/fwconfig.shtml
- IP Filter:
  http://cheops.anu.edu.au/~avalon/
- ipfwadm Dotfile Module:
  http://www.wolfenet.com/~jhardin/ipfwadm.html

- Isinglass PPP Firewall:
  `http://www.tummy.com/isinglass/`
- Mason:
  `http://www.pobox.com/~wstearns/mason/`
- SINUS Firewall:
  `http://www.ifi.unizh.ch/ikm/SINUS/firewall/`
- TIS Firewall Toolkit:
  `ftp://ftp.tis.com/pub/firewalls/toolkit/`

Reference Papers and FAQs

Most of the reference papers listed in the following topic-oriented sections are maintained at CERT. They are mirrored by many sites.

UNIX Security

- Anonymous FTP Abuses:
  `http://www.cert.org/ftp/tech_tips/anonymous_ftp_abuses`
- ANONYMOUS FTP CONFIGURATION GUIDELINES:
  `http://www.cert.org/ftp/tech_tips/anonymous_ftp_config`
- Denial of Service Attacks:
  `http://www.cert.org/ftp/tech_tips/denial_of_service`
- Intruder Detection Checklist:
  `http://www.cert.org/ftp/tech_tips/intruder_detection_checklist`
- Problems with the FTP PORT Command:
  `http://www.cert.org/ftp/tech_tips/FTP_PORT_attacks`
- Protecting Yourself from Password File Attacks:
  `http://www.cert.org/ftp/tech_tips/passwd_file_protection`
- Steps for Recovering from a UNIX Root Compromise:
  `http://www.cert.org/tech_tips/root_compromise.html`
- UNIX Computer Security Checklist:
  `http://www.cert.org/ftp/tech_tips/AUSCERT_checklist1.1`
- UNIX Configuration Guidelines:
  `http://www.cert.org/ftp/tech_tips/UNIX_configuration_guidelines`

Firewall Issues

- Defeating Denial of Service Attacks Which Employ IP Source Address Spoofing:
  `http://www.ietf.cnri.reston.va.us/rfc/rfc2267.txt`
- Firewall Policy Guide (ICSA):
  `http://www.icsa.net/services/consortia/firewalls/fwpg.shtml`
- Internet Firewalls Frequently Asked Questions:
  `http://www.clark.net/pub/mjr/pubs/fwfaq/`
- IP Masquerade for Linux
  `http://www.tor.shaw.wave.ca/~ambrose/`
- Linux Firewall & LAN Security FAQ:
  `http://linux-firewall-tools.com/linux/faq/`
- Linux firewall facilities for kernel-level packet screening:
  `http://www.xos.nl/linux/ipfwadm/paper/`
- Linux IP Masquerading Web Site:
  `http://www.indyramp.com/masq/`
- Packet Filtering for Firewall Systems:
  `http://www.cert.org/ftp/tech_tips/packet_filtering`
- Port Forwarding:
  `http://www.ox.compsoc.org.uk/~steve/portforwarding.html`
- PORTUS Firewall Tutorial:
  `http://www.lsli.com/tutorial.html`
- TCP SYN Flooding and IP Spoofing Attacks (CERT Advisory CA-96.21):
  `http://www.cert.org/advisories/CA-96.21.tcp_syn_flooding.html`
- TCP/UDP Service Port Numbers (IANA):
  `http://www.isi.edu/in-notes/iana/assignments/port-numbers`

Web Server Issues

- Apache Web Server Security Tips:
  `http://www.apache.org/docs/misc/security_tips.html`
- How To Remove Meta-characters From User-Supplied Data In CGI Scripts:
  `http://www.cert.org/ftp/tech_tips/cgi_metacharacters`
- The World Wide Web Security FAQ:
  `http://www.w3.org/Security/Faq/www-security-faq.html`

Online Documentation

Linux is distributed with a full set of documentation in several formats. The HTML documents listed here are especially relevant to network security issues:

- Firewalling and Proxy Server HOWTO:
  `/usr/doc/HOWTO/other-formats/html/Firewall-HOWTO.html`
- HOWTOs:
  `/usr/doc/HOWTO/other-formats/html/HOWTO-INDEX.html`
- Linux IP Masquerade mini HOWTO:
  `/usr/doc/HOWTO/other-formats/html/mini/IP-Masquerade.html`
- Linux IPCHAINS-HOWTO:
  `/usr/doc/HOWTO/other-formats/html/IPCHAINS-HOWTO.html`
- Linux Security HOWTO:
  `/usr/doc/HOWTO/other-formats/html/Security-HOWTO.html`
- Network Administrator's Guide (NAG):
  `/usr/doc/LDP/nag/nag.html`
- System Administrators' Guide (SAG):
  `/usr/doc/LDP/sag/sag.html`

General Web Sites

Both informational and software Linux sites abound; the following are some of the best starting places for both:

- CableModem Info:
  `http://www.cablemodeminfo.com/`
- FreshMeat:
  `http://freshmeat.net/`
- Generic Linux links:
  `http://www.emuse.net/`
- Linux Applications and Utilities:
  `http://www.xnet.com/~blatura/linapps.shtml`
- Linux Apps:
  `http://www.linuxapps.com/`
- Linux Documentation Project:
  `http://metalab.unc.edu/LDP/`
- Linux Powered:
  `http://www.linuxpowered.com/html/linux_links/netw.html`
- Linux Start:
  `http://linuxstart.com/`

- Linux Today:
  `http://linuxtoday.com/`
- Linux World:
  `http://www.linuxworld.com/`
- Red Hat:
  `http://www.redhat.com/`
- SlashDot:
  `http://slashdot.org/`
- SUNET (Swedish University Network):
  `http://ftp.sunet.se/pub/os/Linux/`
- Sunsite:
  `http://metalab.unc.edu/pub/Linux/`

Books

Apache Server for Dummies, by Ken A. L. Coar. Foster City, CA: IDG Books Worldwide, Inc., 1998.

Building Internet Firewalls, by D. Brent Chapman and Elizabeth D. Zwicky. Sebastopol, CA: O'Reilly & Associates, Inc., 1995.

Firewalls and Internet Security: Repelling the Wily Hacker, by William R. Cheswick and Steven M. Bellovin. Reading, MA: Addison-Wesley, 1994.

Linux Network Toolkit, by Paul G. Sery. Foster City, CA: IDG Books Worldwide, Inc., 1998.

B

Firewall Examples and Support Scripts

A FIREWALL FOR A STANDALONE SYSTEM, or for protecting a home LAN, is described in Chapter 3, "Building and Installing a Firewall." The standalone example is extended in Chapter 4, "LAN Issues, Multiple Firewalls, and Perimeter Networks," to function as a bastion firewall with a full set of firewall rules applied to both the external Internet interface and to the internal LAN interface. The same standalone firewall from Chapter 3 is also refurbished to function as a secondary choke firewall. The bastion serves as the gateway to both the Internet and to a DMZ network containing public servers. The choke serves as the gateway between a private LAN and either the DMZ or the bastion firewall, depending on how the DMZ is designed.

The sample firewall is presented piecemeal in Chapter 3. This appendix presents the same firewall example as it would appear in a firewall script, both in `ipchains` semantics and in `ipfwadm` semantics. Again, the example is not optimized. The `ipchains` and `ipfwadm` versions are presented with an almost one-to-one correspondence.

Rule optimization isn't discussed in the book. Some simple optimizations are shown here using both `ipchains` and `ipfwadm` based on a simple firewall script for a single home computer.

Finally, a few support scripts are shown. UNIX systems don't lend themselves well to having dynamically assigned IP addresses. DNS, in particular, expects a stable view of its host address. Many systems are dependent on DHCP for dynamically assigned IP addresses, especially home systems with 24/7 Internet connections. Both DNS and the firewall script require some help, both when an IP address is first assigned, and later if a new IP address is assigned dynamically while the machine is online.

ipchains rc.firewall for an Individual System or Home LAN from Chapter 3

Chapter 3 covers the application protocols and firewall rules for the types of services most likely to be used on an individual, standalone Linux box. If a small LAN of personal, client computers were attached to an internal LAN, the firewall forwards and masquerades all traffic between the LAN and the Internet. As an example, Chapter 3 demonstrates numerous safeguards and logging events that aren't strictly necessary in a fully functional firewall. Additionally, both client and server rules are presented for services not everyone will use. The complete firewall script, as it would appear in /etc/rc.d/rc.firewall, and built upon ipchains, follows:

```
#!/bin/sh

echo "Starting firewalling... "

# Some definitions for easy maintenance.

# ---------------------------------------------------------------------
# EDIT THESE TO SUIT YOUR SYSTEM AND ISP.

EXTERNAL_INTERFACE="eth0"              # Internet-connected interface
LOOPBACK_INTERFACE="lo"               # or your local naming convention
LAN_INTERFACE_1="eth1"                # internal LAN interface

IPADDR="my.ip.address"                # your IP address
LAN_1="192.168.1.0/24"                # whatever (private) range you use
LAN_IPADDR_1="192.168.1.1"            # your internal interface address

ANYWHERE="any/0"                      # match any IP address

DHCP_SERVER="my.dhcp.server"          # if you use one
MY_ISP="my.isp.address.range"         # ISP & NOC address range
NAMESERVER_1="my.name.server.1"       # everyone must have at least one

SMTP_SERVER="any/0"                   # external mail server
SMTP_GATEWAY="my.isp.server"          # external mail relay
POP_SERVER="my.pop.server"            # external pop server, if any
IMAP_SERVER="my.isp.imap.server"      # external imap server, if any
NEWS_SERVER="my.news.server"          # external news server, if any
WEB_PROXY_SERVER="my.www.proxy"       # ISP Web proxy server, if any
WEB_PROXY_PORT="www.proxy.port"       # ISP Web proxy port, if any
                                      # typically 8008 or 8080
```

```
LOOPBACK="127.0.0.0/8"                   # reserved loopback address range
CLASS_A="10.0.0.0/8"                     # class A private networks
CLASS_B="172.16.0.0/12"                  # class B private networks
CLASS_C="192.168.0.0/16"                 # class C private networks
CLASS_D_MULTICAST="224.0.0.0/4"          # class D multicast addresses
CLASS_E_RESERVED_NET="240.0.0.0/5"       # class E reserved addresses
BROADCAST_SRC="0.0.0.0"                  # broadcast source address
BROADCAST_DEST="255.255.255.255"         # broadcast destination address
PRIVPORTS="0:1023"                       # well-known, privileged port range
UNPRIVPORTS="1024:65535"                 # unprivileged port range

TRACEROUTE_SRC_PORTS="32769:65535"
TRACEROUTE_DEST_PORTS="33434:33523"


# --------------------------------------------------------------------

# If your IP address is dynamically assigned by a DHCP server,
# name servers are found in /etc/dhcpc/resolv.conf.  If used, the
# sample ifdhcpc-done script updates these automatically and
# appends them to /etc/dhcpc/hostinfo-$EXTERNAL_INTERFACE or
# /etc/dhcpc/dhcpcd-$EXTERNAL_INTERFACE.info.

# If using the sample ifdhcpc-done script, the following NAMESERVER
# definitions (one per server, up to 3) will be overridden correctly
# here.

#   The IP address, $IPADDR, is defined by DHCP.

if [ -f /etc/dhcpc/hostinfo-$EXTERNAL_INTERFACE ]; then
    . /etc/dhcpc/hostinfo-$EXTERNAL_INTERFACE
elif [ -f /etc/dhcpc/dhcpcd-$EXTERNAL_INTERFACE.info ]; then
    . /etc/dhcpc/dhcpcd-$EXTERNAL_INTERFACE.info
    DHCP_SERVER=$DHCPSIADDR
else
    echo "rc.firewall:  DHCP is not configured."
    ipchains -F
    ipchains -P input  DENY
    ipchains -P output DENY
    ipchains -A input   -i $LOOPBACK_INTERFACE -j ACCEPT
    ipchains -A output -i $LOOPBACK_INTERFACE -j ACCEPT
    ipchains -A input   -i $LAN_INTERFACE -j ACCEPT
    ipchains -A output -i $LAN_INTERFACE -j ACCEPT
    exit 1
fi

# If using the sample ifdhcpc-done script, any previous definitions of
# IPADDR and NAMESERVER will be overridden correctly here.
```

```
# ------------------------------------------------------------------
# EDIT THESE TO MATCH THE NUMBER OF SERVERS OR CONNECTIONS
# YOU SUPPORT.

# X Window port allocation begins at 6000 and increments
# for each additional server running from 6000 to 6063.

XWINDOW_PORTS="6000"                    # (TCP) X Window

# SSH starts at 1023 and works down to 513 for
# each additional simultaneous incoming connection.

SSH_PORTS="1020:1023"                   # simultaneous connections

# ------------------------------------------------------------------

SOCKS_PORT="1080"                       # (TCP) socks
OPENWINDOWS_PORT="2000"                 # (TCP) openwindows
NFS_PORT="2049"                         # (TCP/UDP) NFS

# ------------------------------------------------------------------

# Flush any existing rules from all chains.
ipchains -F

# Set the default policy to deny.
ipchains -P input   DENY
ipchains -P output  REJECT
ipchains -P forward REJECT

# Set masquerade timeout to 10 hours for TCP connections.
ipchains -M -S 36000 0 0

# Disallow Fragmented Packets
ipchains -A input -f -i LAN_INTERFACE_1 -j DENY

# Enable TCP SYN Cookie Protection
echo 1 >/proc/sys/net/ipv4/tcp_syncookies

# Enable IP spoofing protection
# turn on Source Address Verification
for f in /proc/sys/net/ipv4/conf/*/rp_filter; do
    echo 1 > $f
done

# Disable ICMP Redirect Acceptance
for f in /proc/sys/net/ipv4/conf/*/accept_redirects; do
    echo 0 > $f
done
```

```
# Disable Source-Routed Packets
for f in /proc/sys/net/ipv4/conf/*/accept_source_route; do
    echo 0 > $f
done

# These modules are necessary to masquerade
# their respective services.
#/sbin/modprobe ip_masq_ftp.o
#/sbin/modprobe ip_masq_raudio.o
#/sbin/modprobe ip_masq_irc.o
#/sbin/modprobe/ip_masq_vdolive.o
#/sbin/modprobe/ip_masq_cuseeme.o
#/sbin/modprobe/ip_masq_quake.o


# ---------------------------------------------------------------------
# LOOPBACK

# Unlimited traffic on the loopback interface
ipchains -A input  -i $LOOPBACK_INTERFACE -j ACCEPT
ipchains -A output -i $LOOPBACK_INTERFACE -j ACCEPT


# ---------------------------------------------------------------------
# Refuse any connections from problem sites.

# /etc/rc.d/rc.firewall.blocked contains a list of
# ipchains -A input -i $EXTERNAL_INTERFACE -s <address/mask> -j DENY
# rules to block all access.

# Refuse packets claiming to be from the banned list.
if [ -f /etc/rc.d/rc.firewall.blocked ]; then
    . /etc/rc.d/rc.firewall.blocked
fi


# ---------------------------------------------------------------------
# SPOOFING & BAD ADDRESSES
# Refuse spoofed packets.
# Ignore blatantly illegal source addresses.
# Protect yourself from sending to bad addresses.

# Refuse spoofed packets pretending to be from
# the external interface's IP address.
ipchains -A input  -i $EXTERNAL_INTERFACE -s $IPADDR -j DENY -l

# Refuse packets claiming to be to or from a Class A private network.
ipchains -A input  -i $EXTERNAL_INTERFACE -s $CLASS_A -j DENY
ipchains -A input  -i $EXTERNAL_INTERFACE -d $CLASS_A -j DENY
ipchains -A output -i $EXTERNAL_INTERFACE -s $CLASS_A -j DENY -l
ipchains -A output -i $EXTERNAL_INTERFACE -d $CLASS_A -j DENY -l

# Refuse packets claiming to be to or from a Class B private network.
ipchains -A input  -i $EXTERNAL_INTERFACE -s $CLASS_B -j DENY
```

```
ipchains -A input  -i $EXTERNAL_INTERFACE -d $CLASS_B -j DENY
ipchains -A output -i $EXTERNAL_INTERFACE -s $CLASS_B -j DENY -l
ipchains -A output -i $EXTERNAL_INTERFACE -d $CLASS_B -j DENY -l

# Refuse packets claiming to be to or from a Class C private network.
ipchains -A input  -i $EXTERNAL_INTERFACE -s $CLASS_C -j DENY
ipchains -A input  -i $EXTERNAL_INTERFACE -d $CLASS_C -j DENY
ipchains -A output -i $EXTERNAL_INTERFACE -s $CLASS_C -j DENY -l
ipchains -A output -i $EXTERNAL_INTERFACE -d $CLASS_C -j DENY -l

# Refuse packets claiming to be from the loopback interface.
ipchains -A input  -i $EXTERNAL_INTERFACE -s $LOOPBACK -j DENY
ipchains -A output -i $EXTERNAL_INTERFACE -s $LOOPBACK -j DENY -l

# Refuse malformed broadcast packets.
ipchains -A input  -i $EXTERNAL_INTERFACE -s $BROADCAST_DEST -j DENY -l
ipchains -A input  -i $EXTERNAL_INTERFACE -d $BROADCAST_SRC  -j DENY -l
ipchains -A output -i $EXTERNAL_INTERFACE -s $BROADCAST_DEST -j DENY -l
ipchains -A output -i $EXTERNAL_INTERFACE -d $BROADCAST_SRC  -j DENY -l

# Refuse Class D multicast addresses.
# Multicast is only illegal as a source address.
# Multicast uses UDP.
ipchains -A input  -i $EXTERNAL_INTERFACE -s $CLASS_D_MULTICAST \
         -j DENY -l
ipchains -A output -i $EXTERNAL_INTERFACE -s $CLASS_D_MULTICAST \
         -j REJECT -l

# Refuse Class E reserved IP addresses.
ipchains -A input  -i $EXTERNAL_INTERFACE -s $CLASS_E_RESERVED_NET \
         -j DENY -l
ipchains -A output -i $EXTERNAL_INTERFACE -d $CLASS_E_RESERVED_NET \
         -j REJECT

# Refuse addresses defined as reserved by the IANA.
# 0.*.*.*, 1.*.*.*, 2.*.*.*, 5.*.*.*, 7.*.*.*, 23.*.*.*, 27.*.*.*
# 31.*.*.*, 37.*.*.*, 39.*.*.*, 41.*.*.*, 42.*.*.*, 58-60.*.*.*

ipchains -A input -i $EXTERNAL_INTERFACE -s 1.0.0.0/8 -j DENY -l
ipchains -A input -i $EXTERNAL_INTERFACE -s 2.0.0.0/8 -j DENY -l
ipchains -A input -i $EXTERNAL_INTERFACE -s 5.0.0.0/8 -j DENY -l
ipchains -A input -i $EXTERNAL_INTERFACE -s 7.0.0.0/8 -j DENY -l
ipchains -A input -i $EXTERNAL_INTERFACE -s 23.0.0.0/8 -j DENY -l
ipchains -A input -i $EXTERNAL_INTERFACE -s 27.0.0.0/8 -j DENY -l
ipchains -A input -i $EXTERNAL_INTERFACE -s 31.0.0.0/8 -j DENY -l
ipchains -A input -i $EXTERNAL_INTERFACE -s 37.0.0.0/8 -j DENY -l
ipchains -A input -i $EXTERNAL_INTERFACE -s 39.0.0.0/8 -j DENY -l
ipchains -A input -i $EXTERNAL_INTERFACE -s 41.0.0.0/8 -j DENY -l
ipchains -A input -i $EXTERNAL_INTERFACE -s 42.0.0.0/8 -j DENY -l
ipchains -A input -i $EXTERNAL_INTERFACE -s 58.0.0.0/7 -j DENY -l
ipchains -A input -i $EXTERNAL_INTERFACE -s 60.0.0.0/8 -j DENY -l
```

```
# 65: 01000001    - /3 includes 64 - need 65-79 spelled out
ipchains -A input -i $EXTERNAL_INTERFACE -s 65.0.0.0/8 -j DENY -l
ipchains -A input -i $EXTERNAL_INTERFACE -s 66.0.0.0/8 -j DENY -l
ipchains -A input -i $EXTERNAL_INTERFACE -s 67.0.0.0/8 -j DENY -l
ipchains -A input -i $EXTERNAL_INTERFACE -s 68.0.0.0/8 -j DENY -l
ipchains -A input -i $EXTERNAL_INTERFACE -s 69.0.0.0/8 -j DENY -l
ipchains -A input -i $EXTERNAL_INTERFACE -s 70.0.0.0/8 -j DENY -l
ipchains -A input -i $EXTERNAL_INTERFACE -s 71.0.0.0/8 -j DENY -l
ipchains -A input -i $EXTERNAL_INTERFACE -s 72.0.0.0/8 -j DENY -l
ipchains -A input -i $EXTERNAL_INTERFACE -s 73.0.0.0/8 -j DENY -l
ipchains -A input -i $EXTERNAL_INTERFACE -s 74.0.0.0/8 -j DENY -l
ipchains -A input -i $EXTERNAL_INTERFACE -s 75.0.0.0/8 -j DENY -l
ipchains -A input -i $EXTERNAL_INTERFACE -s 76.0.0.0/8 -j DENY -l
ipchains -A input -i $EXTERNAL_INTERFACE -s 77.0.0.0/8 -j DENY -l
ipchains -A input -i $EXTERNAL_INTERFACE -s 78.0.0.0/8 -j DENY -l
ipchains -A input -i $EXTERNAL_INTERFACE -s 79.0.0.0/8 -j DENY -l

# 80: 01010000    - /4 masks 80-95
ipchains -A input -i $EXTERNAL_INTERFACE -s 80.0.0.0/4 -j DENY -l

# 96: 01100000    - /4 masks 96-111
ipchains -A input -i $EXTERNAL_INTERFACE -s 96.0.0.0/4 -j DENY -l

# 126: 01111110    - /3 includes 127 - need 112-126 spelled out
ipchains -A input -i $EXTERNAL_INTERFACE -s 112.0.0.0/8 -j DENY -l
ipchains -A input -i $EXTERNAL_INTERFACE -s 113.0.0.0/8 -j DENY -l
ipchains -A input -i $EXTERNAL_INTERFACE -s 114.0.0.0/8 -j DENY -l
ipchains -A input -i $EXTERNAL_INTERFACE -s 115.0.0.0/8 -j DENY -l
ipchains -A input -i $EXTERNAL_INTERFACE -s 116.0.0.0/8 -j DENY -l
ipchains -A input -i $EXTERNAL_INTERFACE -s 117.0.0.0/8 -j DENY -l
ipchains -A input -i $EXTERNAL_INTERFACE -s 118.0.0.0/8 -j DENY -l
ipchains -A input -i $EXTERNAL_INTERFACE -s 119.0.0.0/8 -j DENY -l
ipchains -A input -i $EXTERNAL_INTERFACE -s 120.0.0.0/8 -j DENY -l
ipchains -A input -i $EXTERNAL_INTERFACE -s 121.0.0.0/8 -j DENY -l
ipchains -A input -i $EXTERNAL_INTERFACE -s 122.0.0.0/8 -j DENY -l
ipchains -A input -i $EXTERNAL_INTERFACE -s 123.0.0.0/8 -j DENY -l
ipchains -A input -i $EXTERNAL_INTERFACE -s 124.0.0.0/8 -j DENY -l
ipchains -A input -i $EXTERNAL_INTERFACE -s 125.0.0.0/8 -j DENY -l
ipchains -A input -i $EXTERNAL_INTERFACE -s 126.0.0.0/8 -j DENY -l

# 217: 11011001    - /5 includes 216 - need 217-219 spelled out
ipchains -A input -i $EXTERNAL_INTERFACE -s 217.0.0.0/8 -j DENY -l
ipchains -A input -i $EXTERNAL_INTERFACE -s 218.0.0.0/8 -j DENY -l
ipchains -A input -i $EXTERNAL_INTERFACE -s 219.0.0.0/8 -j DENY -l

# 223: 11011111    - /6 masks 220-223
ipchains -A input -i $EXTERNAL_INTERFACE -s 220.0.0.0/6 -j DENY -l
# ------------------------------------------------------------------
# ICMP
```

```
# (4)  Source_Quench
#      Incoming & outgoing requests to slow down (flow control)

ipchains -A input  -i $EXTERNAL_INTERFACE -p icmp \
        -s $ANYWHERE 4 -d $IPADDR -j ACCEPT

ipchains -A output -i $EXTERNAL_INTERFACE -p icmp \
        -s $IPADDR 4 -d $ANYWHERE -j ACCEPT

# (12) Parameter_Problem
#      Incoming & outgoing error messages

ipchains -A input  -i $EXTERNAL_INTERFACE -p icmp \
        -s $ANYWHERE 12 -d $IPADDR -j ACCEPT

ipchains -A output -i $EXTERNAL_INTERFACE -p icmp \
        -s $IPADDR 12 -d $ANYWHERE -j ACCEPT

# (3)  Dest_Unreachable, Service_Unavailable
#      Incoming & outgoing size negotiation, service or
#      destination unavailability, final traceroute response

ipchains -A input  -i $EXTERNAL_INTERFACE -p icmp \
        -s $ANYWHERE 3 -d $IPADDR -j ACCEPT

ipchains -A output -i $EXTERNAL_INTERFACE -p icmp \
        -s $IPADDR 3 -d $MY_ISP -j ACCEPT

ipchains -A output -i $EXTERNAL_INTERFACE -p icmp \
        -s $IPADDR fragmentation-needed -d $ANYWHERE -j ACCEPT

# (11) Time_Exceeded
#      Incoming & outgoing timeout conditions,
#      also intermediate TTL response to traceroutes

ipchains -A input  -i $EXTERNAL_INTERFACE -p icmp \
        -s $ANYWHERE 11 -d $IPADDR -j ACCEPT

ipchains -A output -i $EXTERNAL_INTERFACE -p icmp \
        -s $IPADDR 11 -d $MY_ISP -j ACCEPT

# Allow outgoing pings to anywhere.

ipchains -A output -i $EXTERNAL_INTERFACE -p icmp \
        -s $IPADDR 8 -d $ANYWHERE -j ACCEPT

ipchains -A input  -i $EXTERNAL_INTERFACE -p icmp \
        -s $ANYWHERE 0 -d $IPADDR -j ACCEPT

# Allow incoming pings from trusted hosts.
```

```
ipchains -A input  -i $EXTERNAL_INTERFACE -p icmp \
         -s $MY_ISP 8 -d $IPADDR -j ACCEPT

ipchains -A output -i $EXTERNAL_INTERFACE -p icmp \
         -s $IPADDR 0 -d $MY_ISP -j ACCEPT

# -------------------------------------------------------------------
# UNPRIVILEGED PORTS
# Avoid ports subject to protocol and system administration problems.

# OpenWindows: establishing a connection
ipchains -A output -i $EXTERNAL_INTERFACE -p tcp -y \
         -s $IPADDR \
         -d $ANYWHERE $OPENWINDOWS_PORT -j REJECT

# OpenWindows incoming connection
ipchains -A input -i $EXTERNAL_INTERFACE -p tcp -y \
         -d $IPADDR $OPENWINDOWS_PORT -j DENY

# X Window: establishing a remote connection
ipchains -A output -i $EXTERNAL_INTERFACE -p tcp -y \
         -s $IPADDR \
         -d $ANYWHERE $XWINDOW_PORTS -j REJECT

# X Window: incoming connection attempt
ipchains -A input -i $EXTERNAL_INTERFACE -p tcp -y \
         -d $IPADDR $XWINDOW_PORTS -j DENY -l

# SOCKS: establishing a connection
ipchains -A output -i $EXTERNAL_INTERFACE -p tcp -y \
         -s $IPADDR \
         -d $ANYWHERE $SOCKS_PORT -j REJECT -l

# SOCKS incoming connection
ipchains -A input -i $EXTERNAL_INTERFACE -p tcp -y \
         -d $IPADDR $SOCKS_PORT -j DENY

# NFS: TCP connections
ipchains -A input -i $EXTERNAL_INTERFACE -p tcp -y \
         -d $IPADDR $NFS_PORT -j DENY -l

ipchains -A output -i $EXTERNAL_INTERFACE -p tcp -y \
         -d $ANYWHERE $NFS_PORT -j REJECT -l

# NFS: UDP connections
ipchains -A input -i $EXTERNAL_INTERFACE -p udp \
         -d $IPADDR $NFS_PORT -j DENY -l

# NFS incoming request  (normal UDP mode)
ipchains -A output -i $EXTERNAL_INTERFACE -p udp \
         -d $ANYWHERE $NFS_PORT -j REJECT -l
```

```
# -----------------------------------------------------------------------
# NOTE:
#      The symbolic names used in /etc/services for the port numbers
#      vary by supplier. Using them is less error-prone and more
#      meaningful.

# -----------------------------------------------------------------------
# Required Services

# DNS client modes (53)
# ---------------------

ipchains -A output -i $EXTERNAL_INTERFACE -p udp \
        -s $IPADDR $UNPRIVPORTS \
        -d $NAMESERVER_1 53 -j ACCEPT

ipchains -A input  -i $EXTERNAL_INTERFACE -p udp \
        -s $NAMESERVER_1 53 \
        -d $IPADDR $UNPRIVPORTS -j ACCEPT

# TCP client-to-server requests are allowed by the protocol
# if UDP requests fail. This is rarely seen. Usually, clients
# use TCP as a secondary name server for zone transfers from
# their primary name servers, and as hackers.

ipchains -A output -i $EXTERNAL_INTERFACE -p tcp \
        -s $IPADDR $UNPRIVPORTS \
        -d <my.dns.primary> 53 -j ACCEPT

ipchains -A input -i $EXTERNAL_INTERFACE -p tcp ! -y \
        -s <my.dns.primary> 53 \
        -d $IPADDR $UNPRIVPORTS -j ACCEPT


# DNS server modes (53)
# ---------------------

# DNS caching & forwarding name server
# ------------------------------------

# Server-to-server query or response
# Caching only name server uses UDP, not TCP

ipchains -A output -i $EXTERNAL_INTERFACE -p udp \
        -s $IPADDR 53 \
        -d $NAMESERVER_1 53 -j ACCEPT

ipchains -A input  -i $EXTERNAL_INTERFACE -p udp \
        -s $NAMESERVER_1 53 \
        -d $IPADDR 53 -j ACCEPT
```

```
# DNS full name server
# --------------------

# Client-to-server DNS transaction
ipchains -A input  -i $EXTERNAL_INTERFACE -p udp \
        -s <my.dns.clients> $UNPRIVPORTS \
        -d $IPADDR 53 -j ACCEPT

ipchains -A output -i $EXTERNAL_INTERFACE -p udp \
        -s $IPADDR 53 \
        -d <my.dns.clients> $UNPRIVPORTS -j ACCEPT

# Peer-to-peer server DNS transaction
ipchains -A input  -i $EXTERNAL_INTERFACE -p udp \
        -s <my.dns.clients> 53 \
        -d $IPADDR 53 -j ACCEPT

ipchains -A output -i $EXTERNAL_INTERFACE -p udp \
        -s $IPADDR 53 \
        -d <my.dns.clients> 53 -j ACCEPT

# Zone Transfers
# due to the potential danger of zone transfers,
# allow TCP traffic to only specific secondaries.

ipchains -A input  -i $EXTERNAL_INTERFACE -p tcp \
        -s <my.dns.secondaries> $UNPRIVPORTS \
        -d $IPADDR 53 -j ACCEPT

ipchains -A output -i $EXTERNAL_INTERFACE -p tcp ! -y \
        -s $IPADDR 53 \
        -d <my.dns.secondaries> $UNPRIVPORTS -j ACCEPT

# ----------------------------------------------------------------------

# AUTH (113) - Allowing Your Outgoing AUTH Requests as a Client
# ------------------------------------------------------------

ipchains -A output -i $EXTERNAL_INTERFACE -p tcp \
        -s $IPADDR $UNPRIVPORTS \
        -d $ANYWHERE 113 -j ACCEPT

ipchains -A input -i $EXTERNAL_INTERFACE -p tcp ! -y \
        -s $ANYWHERE 113 \
        -d $IPADDR $UNPRIVPORTS -j ACCEPT

# AUTH server (113)
# -----------------
# Accepting Incoming AUTH Requests
```

```
ipchains -A input  -i $EXTERNAL_INTERFACE -p tcp \
        -s $ANYWHERE $UNPRIVPORTS \
        -d $IPADDR 113 -j ACCEPT

ipchains -A output -i $EXTERNAL_INTERFACE -p tcp ! -y \
        -s $IPADDR 113 \
        -d $ANYWHERE $UNPRIVPORTS -j ACCEPT

# OR

# Rejecting Incoming AUTH Requests

ipchains -A input  -i $EXTERNAL_INTERFACE -p tcp \
        -d $IPADDR 113 -j REJECT

# ----------------------------------------------------------------------
# TCP services on selected ports

# Sending Mail through a remote SMTP gateway (25)
# --------------------------------------------------

# SMTP client to an ISP account without a local server

ipchains -A output -i $EXTERNAL_INTERFACE -p tcp \
        -s $IPADDR $UNPRIVPORTS \
        -d $ SMTP_GATEWAY 25 -j ACCEPT

ipchains -A input  -i $EXTERNAL_INTERFACE -p tcp ! -y \
        -s $ SMTP_GATEWAY 25 \
        -d $IPADDR $UNPRIVPORTS -j ACCEPT

# OR
# Sending Mail through a local SMTP server

ipchains -A output -i $EXTERNAL_INTERFACE -p tcp \
        -s $IPADDR $UNPRIVPORTS \
        -d $ANYWHERE 25 -j ACCEPT

ipchains -A input  -i $EXTERNAL_INTERFACE -p tcp ! -y \
        -s $ANYWHERE 25 \
        -d $IPADDR $UNPRIVPORTS -j ACCEPT

# Receiving Mail as a Local SMTP server (25)
# --------------------------------------------

ipchains -A input  -i $EXTERNAL_INTERFACE -p tcp \
        -s $ANYWHERE $UNPRIVPORTS \
        -d $IPADDR 25 -j ACCEPT
```

```
ipchains -A output -i $EXTERNAL_INTERFACE -p tcp ! -y \
        -s $IPADDR 25 \
        -d $ANYWHERE $UNPRIVPORTS -j ACCEPT

# -------------------------------------------------------------------

# POP (110) - Retrieving Mail as a POP Client
# ------------------------------------------

ipchains -A output -i $EXTERNAL_INTERFACE -p tcp \
        -s $IPADDR $UNPRIVPORTS \
        -d $POP_SERVER 110 -j ACCEPT

ipchains -A input -i $EXTERNAL_INTERFACE -p tcp ! -y \
        -s $POP_SERVER 110 \
        -d $IPADDR $UNPRIVPORTS -j ACCEPT

# POP (110) - Hosting a POP Server for Remote Clients
# --------------------------------------------------

ipchains -A input  -i $EXTERNAL_INTERFACE -p tcp \
        -s <my.pop.clients> $UNPRIVPORTS \
        -d $IPADDR 110 -j ACCEPT

ipchains -A output -i $EXTERNAL_INTERFACE -p tcp ! -y \
        -s $IPADDR 110 \
        -d <my.pop.clients> $UNPRIVPORTS -j ACCEPT

# -------------------------------------------------------------------

# IMAP (143) - Retrieving Mail as an IMAP Client
# ---------------------------------------------

ipchains -A output -i $EXTERNAL_INTERFACE -p tcp \
        -s $IPADDR $UNPRIVPORTS \
        -d <my.imap.server> 143 -j ACCEPT

ipchains -A input -i $EXTERNAL_INTERFACE -p tcp ! -y \
        -s <my.imap.server> 143 \
        -d $IPADDR $UNPRIVPORTS -j ACCEPT

# IMAP (143) - Hosting an IMAP Server for Remote Clients
# -----------------------------------------------------

ipchains -A input  -i $EXTERNAL_INTERFACE -p tcp \
        -s <my.imap.clients> $UNPRIVPORTS \
        -d $IPADDR 143 -j ACCEPT
```

```
ipchains -A output -i $EXTERNAL_INTERFACE -p tcp ! -y \
        -s $IPADDR 143 \
        -d <my.imap.clients> $UNPRIVPORTS -j ACCEPT


# ----------------------------------------------------------------------

# NNTP (119) - Reading and Posting News as a Usenet Client
# ---------------------------------------------------------

ipchains -A output -i $EXTERNAL_INTERFACE -p tcp \
        -s $IPADDR $UNPRIVPORTS \
        -d $NEWS_SERVER 119 -j ACCEPT

ipchains -A input -i $EXTERNAL_INTERFACE -p tcp ! -y \
        -s $NEWS_SERVER 119 \
        -d $IPADDR $UNPRIVPORTS -j ACCEPT


# NNTP (119) - Hosting a Usenet News Server for Remote Clients
# ------------------------------------------------------------

ipchains -A input  -i $EXTERNAL_INTERFACE -p tcp \
        -s <my.news.clients> $UNPRIVPORTS \
        -d $IPADDR 119 -j ACCEPT

ipchains -A output -i $EXTERNAL_INTERFACE -p tcp ! -y \
        -s $IPADDR 119 \
        -d <my.news.clients> $UNPRIVPORTS -j ACCEPT

# NNTP (119) - Allowing Peer News Feeds for a Local Usenet Server
# ---------------------------------------------------------------

ipchains -A output -i $EXTERNAL_INTERFACE -p tcp \
        -s $IPADDR $UNPRIVPORTS \
        -d <my.news.feed> 119 -j ACCEPT

ipchains -A input -i $EXTERNAL_INTERFACE -p tcp ! -y \
        -s <my.news.feed> 119 \
        -d $IPADDR $UNPRIVPORTS -j ACCEPT


# ----------------------------------------------------------------------

# TELNET (23) - Allowing Outgoing Client Access to Remote Sites
# -------------------------------------------------------------

ipchains -A output -i $EXTERNAL_INTERFACE -p tcp \
        -s $IPADDR $UNPRIVPORTS \
        -d $ANYWHERE 23 -j ACCEPT
```

```
ipchains -A input -i $EXTERNAL_INTERFACE -p tcp ! -y \
        -s $ANYWHERE 23 \
        -d $IPADDR $UNPRIVPORTS -j ACCEPT

# TELNET (23) - Allowing Incoming Access to Your Local Server
# ----------------------------------------------------------

ipchains -A input  -i $EXTERNAL_INTERFACE -p tcp \
        -s $ANYWHERE $UNPRIVPORTS \
        -d $IPADDR 23 -j ACCEPT

ipchains -A output -i $EXTERNAL_INTERFACE -p tcp ! -y \
        -s $IPADDR 23 \
        -d $ANYWHERE $UNPRIVPORTS -j ACCEPT

# ------------------------------------------------------------------

# SSH client (22) - Allowing Client Access to Remote SSH Servers
# ------------------------------------------------------------

ipchains -A output -i $EXTERNAL_INTERFACE -p tcp \
        -s $IPADDR $UNPRIVPORTS \
        -d $ANYWHERE 22 -j ACCEPT

ipchains -A input  -i $EXTERNAL_INTERFACE -p tcp ! -y \
        -s $ANYWHERE 22 \
        -d $IPADDR $UNPRIVPORTS -j ACCEPT

ipchains -A output -i $EXTERNAL_INTERFACE -p tcp \
        -s $IPADDR $SSH_PORTS \
        -d $ANYWHERE 22 -j ACCEPT

ipchains -A input  -i $EXTERNAL_INTERFACE -p tcp ! -y \
        -s $ANYWHERE 22 \
        -d $IPADDR $SSH_PORTS -j ACCEPT

# SSH (22) - Allowing Remote Client Access to Your Local SSH Server
# -----------------------------------------------------------------

ipchains -A input  -i $EXTERNAL_INTERFACE -p tcp \
        -s $ANYWHERE $UNPRIVPORTS \
        -d $IPADDR 22 -j ACCEPT

ipchains -A output -i $EXTERNAL_INTERFACE -p tcp ! -y \
        -s $IPADDR 22 \
        -d $ANYWHERE $UNPRIVPORTS -j ACCEPT

ipchains -A input  -i $EXTERNAL_INTERFACE -p tcp \
        -s $ANYWHERE $SSH_PORTS \
        -d $IPADDR 22 -j ACCEPT
```

```
ipchains -A output -i $EXTERNAL_INTERFACE -p tcp ! -y \
        -s $IPADDR 22 \
        -d $ANYWHERE $SSH_PORTS -j ACCEPT


# ---------------------------------------------------------------------

# FTP (20, 21) - Allowing Outgoing Client Access to Remote FTP Servers
# ---------------------------------------------------------------------

# Outgoing request

ipchains -A output -i $EXTERNAL_INTERFACE -p tcp \
        -s $IPADDR $UNPRIVPORTS \
        -d $ANYWHERE 21 -j ACCEPT

ipchains -A input -i $EXTERNAL_INTERFACE -p tcp ! -y \
        -s $ANYWHERE 21 \
        -d $IPADDR $UNPRIVPORTS -j ACCEPT

# Normal Port Mode FTP Data Channels

ipchains -A input  -i $EXTERNAL_INTERFACE -p tcp \
        -s $ANYWHERE 20 \
        -d $IPADDR $UNPRIVPORTS -j ACCEPT

ipchains -A output -i $EXTERNAL_INTERFACE -p tcp ! -y \
        -s $IPADDR $UNPRIVPORTS \
        -d $ANYWHERE 20 -j ACCEPT

# Passive Mode FTP Data Channels

ipchains -A output -i $EXTERNAL_INTERFACE -p tcp \
        -s $IPADDR $UNPRIVPORTS \
        -d $ANYWHERE $UNPRIVPORTS -j ACCEPT

ipchains -A input  -i $EXTERNAL_INTERFACE -p tcp ! -y \
        -s $ANYWHERE $UNPRIVPORTS \
        -d $IPADDR $UNPIRVPORTS -j ACCEPT

# FTP (20, 21) - Allowing Incoming Access to Your Local FTP Server
# ---------------------------------------------------------------------

# Incoming request

ipchains -A input  -i $EXTERNAL_INTERFACE -p tcp \
        -s $ANYWHERE $UNPRIVPORTS \
        -d $IPADDR 21 -j ACCEPT

ipchains -A output -i $EXTERNAL_INTERFACE -p tcp ! -y \
        -s $IPADDR 21 \
        -d $ANYWHERE $UNPRIVPORTS -j ACCEPT
```

```
# Normal Port Mode FTP Data Channel Responses

ipchains -A output -i $EXTERNAL_INTERFACE -p tcp \
        -s $IPADDR 20 \
        -d $ANYWHERE $UNPRIVPORTS -j ACCEPT

ipchains -A input  -i $EXTERNAL_INTERFACE -p tcp ! -y \
        -s $ANYWHERE $UNPRIVPORTS \
        -d $IPADDR 20 -j ACCEPT

# Passive Mode FTP Data Channel Responses

ipchains -A input  -i $EXTERNAL_INTERFACE -p tcp \
        -s $ANYWHERE $UNPRIVPORTS \
        -d $IPADDR $UNPRIVPORTS -j ACCEPT

ipchains -A output -i $EXTERNAL_INTERFACE -p tcp ! -y \
        -s $IPADDR $UNPRIVPORTS \
        -d $ANYWHERE $UNPRIVPORTS -j ACCEPT

# --------------------------------------------------------------------

# HTTP (80) - Accessing Remote Web Sites as a Client
# ------------------------------------------------

ipchains -A output -i $EXTERNAL_INTERFACE -p tcp \
        -s $IPADDR $UNPRIVPORTS \
        -d $ANYWHERE 80 -j ACCEPT

ipchains -A input -i $EXTERNAL_INTERFACE -p tcp ! -y \
        -s $ANYWHERE 80 \
        -d $IPADDR $UNPRIVPORTS -j ACCEPT

# HTTP (80) - Allowing Remote Access to a Local Web Server
# --------------------------------------------------------

ipchains -A input  -i $EXTERNAL_INTERFACE -p tcp \
        -s $ANYWHERE $UNPRIVPORTS \
        -d $IPADDR 80 -j ACCEPT

ipchains -A output -i $EXTERNAL_INTERFACE -p tcp ! -y \
        -s $IPADDR 80 \
        -d $ANYWHERE $UNPRIVPORTS -j ACCEPT


# HTTPS (443) - Accessing Remote Web Sites Over SSL as a Client
# -------------------------------------------------------------

ipchains -A output -i $EXTERNAL_INTERFACE -p tcp \
        -s $IPADDR $UNPRIVPORTS \
        -d $ANYWHERE 443 -j ACCEPT
```

```
ipchains -A input -i $EXTERNAL_INTERFACE -p tcp ! -y \
        -s $ANYWHERE 443 \
        -d $IPADDR $UNPRIVPORTS -j ACCEPT

# HTTPS (443) - Allowing Remote Access to a Local SSL Web Server
# ---------------------------------------------------------------

ipchains -A input  -i $EXTERNAL_INTERFACE -p tcp \
        -s $ANYWHERE $UNPRIVPORTS \
        -d $IPADDR 443 -j ACCEPT

ipchains -A output -i $EXTERNAL_INTERFACE -p tcp ! -y \
        -s $IPADDR 443 \
        -d $ANYWHERE $UNPRIVPORTS -j ACCEPT


# -----------------------------------------------------------------

# HTTP Proxy client (8008/8080)
# -----------------------------

ipchains -A output -i $EXTERNAL_INTERFACE -p tcp \
        -s $IPADDR $UNPRIVPORTS \
        -d $WEB_PROXY_SERVER $WEB_PROXY_PORT -j ACCEPT

ipchains -A input -i $EXTERNAL_INTERFACE -p tcp ! -y \
        -s $WEB_PROXY_SERVER $WEB_PROXY_PORT \
        -d $IPADDR $UNPRIVPORTS -j ACCEPT


# -----------------------------------------------------------------

# FINGER (79) - Accessing Remote finger Servers as a Client
# ---------------------------------------------------------

ipchains -A output -i $EXTERNAL_INTERFACE -p tcp \
        -s $IPADDR $UNPRIVPORTS \
        -d $ANYWHERE 79 -j ACCEPT

ipchains -A input -i $EXTERNAL_INTERFACE -p tcp ! -y \
        -s $ANYWHERE 79 \
        -d $IPADDR $UNPRIVPORTS -j ACCEPT

# FINGER (79) - Allowing Remote Client Access to a Local finger Server
# -----------------------------------------------------------------

ipchains -A input  -i $EXTERNAL_INTERFACE -p tcp \
        -s <my.finger.clients> $UNPRIVPORTS \
        -d $IPADDR 79 -j ACCEPT

ipchains -A output -i $EXTERNAL_INTERFACE -p tcp ! -y \
        -s $IPADDR 79 \
        -d <my.finger.clients> $UNPRIVPORTS -j ACCEPT
```

```
# -----------------------------------------------------------------------

# WHOIS client (43)
# -----------------
ipchains -A output -i $EXTERNAL_INTERFACE -p tcp \
         -s $IPADDR $UNPRIVPORTS \
         -d $ANYWHERE 43 -j ACCEPT

ipchains -A input -i $EXTERNAL_INTERFACE -p tcp ! -y \
         -s $ANYWHERE 43 \
         -d $IPADDR $UNPRIVPORTS -j ACCEPT

# -----------------------------------------------------------------------

# Gopher client (70)
# ------------------

ipchains -A output -i $EXTERNAL_INTERFACE -p tcp \
         -s $IPADDR $UNPRIVPORTS \
         -d $ANYWHERE 70 -j ACCEPT

ipchains -A input -i $EXTERNAL_INTERFACE -p tcp ! -y \
         -s $ANYWHERE 70 \
         -d $IPADDR $UNPRIVPORTS -j ACCEPT

# -----------------------------------------------------------------------

# WAIS client (210)
# -----------------

ipchains -A output -i $EXTERNAL_INTERFACE -p tcp \
         -s $IPADDR $UNPRIVPORTS \
         -d $ANYWHERE 210 -j ACCEPT

ipchains -A input -i $EXTERNAL_INTERFACE -p tcp ! -y \
         -s $ANYWHERE 210 \
         -d $IPADDR $UNPRIVPORTS -j ACCEPT

# -----------------------------------------------------------------------
# UDP accept only on selected ports

# TRACEROUTE
# traceroute usually uses -S 32769:65535 -D 33434:33523
# --------------------------------------------------------

# Enabling Outgoing traceroute Requests
# -------------------------------------

ipchains -A output -i $EXTERNAL_INTERFACE -p udp \
         -s $IPADDR $TRACEROUTE_SRC_PORTS \
         -d $ANYWHERE $TRACEROUTE_DEST_PORTS -j ACCEPT
```

```
# Incoming query from the ISP.
# All others are denied by default.
# -------------------------------

ipchains -A input -i $EXTERNAL_INTERFACE -p udp \
        -s $MY_ISP 32769:65535 \
        -d $IPADDR 33434:33523 -j ACCEPT


# ----------------------------------------------------------------------

# DHCP client (67, 68)
# --------------------

# INIT or REBINDING: No lease or Lease time expired.

ipchains -A output -i $EXTERNAL_INTERFACE -p udp \
        -s $BROADCAST_0 68 \
        -d $BROADCAST_1 67 -j ACCEPT

# Getting renumbered

ipchains -A input  -i $EXTERNAL_INTERFACE -p udp \
        -s $BROADCAST_0 67 \
        -d $BROADCAST_1 68 -j ACCEPT

ipchains -A input  -i $EXTERNAL_INTERFACE -p udp \
        -s $DHCP_SERVER 67 \
        -d $BROADCAST_1 68 -j ACCEPT

ipchains -A output -i $EXTERNAL_INTERFACE -p udp \
        -s $BROADCAST_0 68 \
        -d $DHCP_SERVER 67 -j ACCEPT

# As a result of the above, we're supposed to change our IP
# address with this message, which is addressed to our new
# address before the dhcp client has received the update.

ipchains -A input  -i $EXTERNAL_INTERFACE -p udp \
        -s $DHCP_SERVER 67 \
        -d $MY_ISP 68 -j ACCEPT

ipchains -A input  -i $EXTERNAL_INTERFACE -p udp \
        -s $DHCP_SERVER 67 \
        -d $IPADDR 68 -j ACCEPT

ipchains -A output -i $EXTERNAL_INTERFACE -p udp \
        -s $IPADDR 68 \
        -d $DHCP_SERVER 67 -j ACCEPT

# ----------------------------------------------------------------------
```

```
# NTP (123) - Accessing Remote Network Time Servers
# -------------------------------------------------

ipchains -A output -i $EXTERNAL_INTERFACE -p udp \
        -s $IPADDR $UNPRIVPORTS \
        -d <my.time.provider> 123 -j ACCEPT

ipchains -A input  -i $EXTERNAL_INTERFACE -p udp \
        -s <my.time.provider> 123 \
        -d $IPADDR $UNPRIVPORTS -j ACCEPT


# -------------------------------------------------------------------
# Unlimited traffic within the local network.

# All internal machines have access to the firewall machine.

ipchains -A input  -i $LAN_INTERFACE_1 \
        -s $LAN_1 -j ACCEPT

ipchains -A output -i $LAN_INTERFACE_1 \
        -d $LAN_1 -j ACCEPT


# -------------------------------------------------------------------
# Masquerade internal traffic.

# All internal traffic is masqueraded externally.

ipchains -A forward -i $EXTERNAL_INTERFACE -s $LAN_1 -j MASQ


# -------------------------------------------------------------------

echo "done"

exit 0
```

ipfwadm rc.firewall for an Individual System or Home LAN from Chapter 3

All firewall rule examples in this book are based on Red Hat Linux 6.0 using
`ipchains`. However, many systems are running previous Linux releases that built firewalls based on `ipfwadm`. This section lists the same complete firewall script, as it would
appear in `/etc/rc.d/rc.firewall`, built upon `ipfwadm`:

```
#!/bin/sh

echo "Starting firewalling... "

# Some definitions for easy maintenance.
```

```
ANYWHERE="any/0"


# --------------------------------------------------------------------
#  EDIT THESE TO SUIT YOUR SYSTEM AND ISP.

EXTERNAL_INTERFACE="eth0"              # Internet-connected interface
LOOPBACK_INTERFACE="lo"               # or your local naming convention
LAN_INTERFACE_1="eth1"                # internal LAN interface

IPADDR="my.ip.address"                # your IP address
LAN_1="192.168.1.0/24"                # whatever (private) range you use
LAN_IPADDR_1="192.168.1.1"            # your internal interface address

ANYWHERE="any/0"                      # match any IP address
DHCP_SERVER="my.dhcp.server"          # if you use one
MY_ISP="my.isp.address.range"         # ISP & NOC address range
NAMESERVER_1="my.name.server.1"

SMTP_SERVER="any/0"                   # external mail server
SMTP_GATEWAY="my.isp.server"          # external mail relay
POP_SERVER="my.pop.server"            # external pop server, if any
IMAP_SERVER="my.isp.imap.server"      # external imap server, if any
NEWS_SERVER="my.news.server"          # external news server, if any
WEB_PROXY_SERVER="my.www.proxy"       # ISP Web proxy server, if any
WEB_PROXY_PORT="www.proxy.port"       # ISP Web proxy port, if any
                                      # typically 8008 or 8080


LOOPBACK="127.0.0.0/8"                # reserved loopback address range
CLASS_A="10.0.0.0/8"                  # class A private networks
CLASS_B="172.16.0.0/12"              # class B private networks
CLASS_C="192.168.0.0/16"             # class C private networks
CLASS_D_MULTICAST="224.0.0.0/4"      # class D multicast addresses
CLASS_E_RESERVED_NET="240.0.0.0/5"   # class E reserved addresses
BROADCAST_SRC="0.0.0.0"              # broadcast source address
BROADCAST_DEST="255.255.255.255"     # broadcast destination address
PRIVPORTS="0:1023"                    # well-known, privileged port range
UNPRIVPORTS="1024:65535"              # unprivileged port range

TRACEROUTE_SRC_PORTS="32769:65535"
TRACEROUTE_DEST_PORTS="33434:33523"


# ....................................................................
# If your IP address is dynamically assigned by a DHCP server,
# name servers are found in /etc/dhcpc/resolv.conf.  If used, the
# sample ifdhcpc-done script updates these automatically and
# appends them to /etc/dhcpc/hostinfo-$EXTERNAL_INTERFACE or
# /etc/dhcpc/dhcpcd-$EXTERNAL_INTERFACE.info.
```

```
# If using the sample ifdhcpc-done script, the following NAMESERVER
# definitions (one per server, up to 3) will be overridden correctly
# here.

# Otherwise, if you have a static IP address, define both
# your static IP address and the IP address of your external name
# server(s).

if [ -f /etc/dhcpc/hostinfo-$EXTERNAL_INTERFACE ]; then
    . /etc/dhcpc/hostinfo-$EXTERNAL_INTERFACE
elif [ -f /etc/dhcpc/dhcpcd-$EXTERNAL_INTERFACE.info ]; then
    . /etc/dhcpc/dhcpcd-$EXTERNAL_INTERFACE.info
else
    NAMESERVER_1="my.name.server.1"
    IPADDR="my.ip.address"
fi


# ----------------------------------------------------------------------
# EDIT THESE TO MATCH THE NUMBER OF SERVERS OR CONNECTIONS
# YOU SUPPORT.

# X Window port allocation begins at 6000 and increments
# for each additional server running from 6000 to 6063.

XWINDOW_PORTS="6000"                 # (TCP) X Window

# SSH starts at 1023 and works down to 513 for
# each additional simultaneous incoming connection.

SSH_PORTS="1020:1023"                # simultaneous connections


# ----------------------------------------------------------------------

SOCKS_PORT="1080"                    # (TCP) socks
OPENWINDOWS_PORT="2000"              # (TCP) openwindows
NFS_PORT="2049"                      # (TCP/UDP) NFS


# ----------------------------------------------------------------------

# Enable TCP SYN Cookie Protection
echo 1 >/proc/sys/net/ipv4/tcp_syncookies

# Enable IP spoofing protection
# turn on Source Address Verification
for f in /proc/sys/net/ipv4/conf/*/rp_filter; do
    echo 1 > $f
done
```

```
# Disable ICMP Redirect Acceptance
for f in /proc/sys/net/ipv4/conf/*/accept_redirects; do
    echo 0 > $f
done

# Disable Source Routed Packets
for f in /proc/sys/net/ipv4/conf/*/accept_source_route; do
    echo 0 > $f
done

# These are now necessary for masquerading the services
#/sbin/modprobe ip_masq_ftp.o
#/sbin/modprobe ip_masq_raudio.o
#/sbin/modprobe ip_masq_irc.o
#/sbin/modprobe/ip_masq_vdolive.o
#/sbin/modprobe/ip_masq_cuseeme.o
#/sbin/modprobe/ip_masq_quake.o

# -----------------------------------------------------------------

# Flush any existing rules from all chains

ipfwadm -I -f
ipfwadm -O -f
ipfwadm -F -f

# Set the default policy to deny.
ipfwadm -I -p deny
ipfwadm -O -p reject
ipfwadm -F -p deny

# -----------------------------------------------------------------
# LOOPBACK

# Unlimited traffic on the loopback interface.
ipfwadm -I -a accept -W $LOOPBACK_INTERFACE
ipfwadm -O -a accept -W $LOOPBACK_INTERFACE

# -----------------------------------------------------------------
# Refuse any connection from problem sites.

# /etc/rc.d/rc.firewall.blocked contains a list of
# ipfwadm -I -a deny -W $EXTERNAL_INTERFACE -S <address/mask>
# rules to block from any access.

# Refuse packets claiming to be from the banned list
if [ -f /etc/rc.d/rc.firewall.blocked ]; then
    . /etc/rc.d/rc.firewall.blocked
fi
```

```
# -------------------------------------------------------------------
# SPOOFING & BAD ADDRESSES
# Refuse spoofed packets.
# Ignore blatantly illegal source addresses.
# Protect yourself from sending to bad addresses.

# Refuse spoofed packets pretending to be from you or
# from illegal addresses.
ipfwadm -I -a deny   -W $EXTERNAL_INTERFACE -S $IPADDR -o

# Refuse packets claiming to be to or from a Class A private network.
ipfwadm -I -a deny   -W $EXTERNAL_INTERFACE -S $CLASS_A -o
ipfwadm -I -a deny   -W $EXTERNAL_INTERFACE -D $CLASS_A -o
ipfwadm -O -a reject -W $EXTERNAL_INTERFACE -S $CLASS_A -o
ipfwadm -O -a reject -W $EXTERNAL_INTERFACE -D $CLASS_A -o

# Refuse packets claiming to be to or from a Class B private network.
ipfwadm -I -a deny   -W $EXTERNAL_INTERFACE -S $CLASS_B -o
ipfwadm -I -a deny   -W $EXTERNAL_INTERFACE -D $CLASS_B -o
ipfwadm -O -a reject -W $EXTERNAL_INTERFACE -S $CLASS_B -o
ipfwadm -O -a reject -W $EXTERNAL_INTERFACE -D $CLASS_B -o

# Refuse packets claiming to be to or from a Class C private network.
ipfwadm -I -a deny   -W $EXTERNAL_INTERFACE -S $CLASS_C -o
ipfwadm -I -a deny   -W $EXTERNAL_INTERFACE -D $CLASS_C -o
ipfwadm -O -a reject -W $EXTERNAL_INTERFACE -S $CLASS_C -o
ipfwadm -O -a reject -W $EXTERNAL_INTERFACE -D $CLASS_C -o

# Refuse packets claiming to be from the loopback interface.
ipfwadm -I -a deny   -W $EXTERNAL_INTERFACE -S $LOOPBACK -o

# Refuse malformed broadcast packets
ipfwadm -I -a deny   -W $EXTERNAL_INTERFACE -S $BROADCAST_DEST -o
ipfwadm -I -a deny   -W $EXTERNAL_INTERFACE -D $BROADCAST_SRC -o
ipfwadm -O -a reject -W $EXTERNAL_INTERFACE -S $BROADCAST_DEST -o
ipfwadm -O -a reject -W $EXTERNAL_INTERFACE -D $BROADCAST_SRC -o

# Refuse Class D multicast addresses.
ipfwadm -I -a deny   -W $EXTERNAL_INTERFACE -S $MULTICAST -o
ipfwadm -O -a reject -W $EXTERNAL_INTERFACE -S $MULTICAST -o

# Refuse Class E reserved IP addresses.
ipfwadm -I -a deny   -W $EXTERNAL_INTERFACE -S $RESERVED_NET -o
ipfwadm -O -a reject -W $EXTERNAL_INTERFACE -D $RESERVED_NET -o


# addresses defined as reserved by the IANA.
# 0.*.*.*, 1.*.*.*, 2.*.*.*, 5.*.*.*, 7.*.*.*, 23.*.*.*, 27.*.*.*
# 31.*.*.*, 37.*.*.*, 39.*.*.*, 41.*.*.*, 42.*.*.*, 58-60.*.*.*
```

```
ipfwadm -I -a deny    -W $EXTERNAL_INTERFACE -S 1.0.0.0/8 -o
ipfwadm -I -a deny    -W $EXTERNAL_INTERFACE -S 2.0.0.0/8 -o
ipfwadm -I -a deny    -W $EXTERNAL_INTERFACE -S 5.0.0.0/8 -o
ipfwadm -I -a deny    -W $EXTERNAL_INTERFACE -S 7.0.0.0/8 -o
ipfwadm -I -a deny    -W $EXTERNAL_INTERFACE -S 23.0.0.0/8 -o
ipfwadm -I -a deny    -W $EXTERNAL_INTERFACE -S 27.0.0.0/8 -o
ipfwadm -I -a deny    -W $EXTERNAL_INTERFACE -S 31.0.0.0/8 -o
ipfwadm -I -a deny    -W $EXTERNAL_INTERFACE -S 37.0.0.0/8 -o
ipfwadm -I -a deny    -W $EXTERNAL_INTERFACE -S 39.0.0.0/8 -o
ipfwadm -I -a deny    -W $EXTERNAL_INTERFACE -S 41.0.0.0/8 -o
ipfwadm -I -a deny    -W $EXTERNAL_INTERFACE -S 42.0.0.0/8 -o
ipfwadm -I -a deny    -W $EXTERNAL_INTERFACE -S 58.0.0.0/7 -o
ipfwadm -I -a deny    -W $EXTERNAL_INTERFACE -S 60.0.0.0/8 -o

# 65: 01000001   - /3 includes 64 - need 65-79 spelled out
ipfwadm -I -a deny    -W $EXTERNAL_INTERFACE -S 65.0.0.0/8 -o
ipfwadm -I -a deny    -W $EXTERNAL_INTERFACE -S 66.0.0.0/8 -o
ipfwadm -I -a deny    -W $EXTERNAL_INTERFACE -S 67.0.0.0/8 -o
ipfwadm -I -a deny    -W $EXTERNAL_INTERFACE -S 68.0.0.0/8 -o
ipfwadm -I -a deny    -W $EXTERNAL_INTERFACE -S 69.0.0.0/8 -o
ipfwadm -I -a deny    -W $EXTERNAL_INTERFACE -S 70.0.0.0/8 -o
ipfwadm -I -a deny    -W $EXTERNAL_INTERFACE -S 71.0.0.0/8 -o
ipfwadm -I -a deny    -W $EXTERNAL_INTERFACE -S 72.0.0.0/8 -o
ipfwadm -I -a deny    -W $EXTERNAL_INTERFACE -S 73.0.0.0/8 -o
ipfwadm -I -a deny    -W $EXTERNAL_INTERFACE -S 74.0.0.0/8 -o
ipfwadm -I -a deny    -W $EXTERNAL_INTERFACE -S 75.0.0.0/8 -o
ipfwadm -I -a deny    -W $EXTERNAL_INTERFACE -S 76.0.0.0/8 -o
ipfwadm -I -a deny    -W $EXTERNAL_INTERFACE -S 77.0.0.0/8 -o
ipfwadm -I -a deny    -W $EXTERNAL_INTERFACE -S 78.0.0.0/8 -o
ipfwadm -I -a deny    -W $EXTERNAL_INTERFACE -S 79.0.0.0/8 -o

# 80: 01010000   - /4 masks 80-95
ipfwadm -I -a deny    -W $EXTERNAL_INTERFACE -S 80.0.0.0/4 -o

# 96: 01100000   - /4 masks 96-111
ipfwadm -I -a deny    -W $EXTERNAL_INTERFACE -S 96.0.0.0/4 -o

# 126: 01111110   - /3 includes 127 - need 112-126 spelled out
ipfwadm -I -a deny    -W $EXTERNAL_INTERFACE -S 112.0.0.0/8 -o
ipfwadm -I -a deny    -W $EXTERNAL_INTERFACE -S 113.0.0.0/8 -o
ipfwadm -I -a deny    -W $EXTERNAL_INTERFACE -S 114.0.0.0/8 -o
ipfwadm -I -a deny    -W $EXTERNAL_INTERFACE -S 115.0.0.0/8 -o
ipfwadm -I -a deny    -W $EXTERNAL_INTERFACE -S 116.0.0.0/8 -o
ipfwadm -I -a deny    -W $EXTERNAL_INTERFACE -S 117.0.0.0/8 -o
ipfwadm -I -a deny    -W $EXTERNAL_INTERFACE -S 118.0.0.0/8 -o
ipfwadm -I -a deny    -W $EXTERNAL_INTERFACE -S 119.0.0.0/8 -o
ipfwadm -I -a deny    -W $EXTERNAL_INTERFACE -S 120.0.0.0/8 -o
ipfwadm -I -a deny    -W $EXTERNAL_INTERFACE -S 121.0.0.0/8 -o
ipfwadm -I -a deny    -W $EXTERNAL_INTERFACE -S 122.0.0.0/8 -o
ipfwadm -I -a deny    -W $EXTERNAL_INTERFACE -S 123.0.0.0/8 -o
```

```
ipfwadm -I -a deny    -W $EXTERNAL_INTERFACE -S 124.0.0.0/8 -o
ipfwadm -I -a deny    -W $EXTERNAL_INTERFACE -S 125.0.0.0/8 -o
ipfwadm -I -a deny    -W $EXTERNAL_INTERFACE -S 126.0.0.0/8 -o

# 217: 11011001  - /5 includes 216 - need 217-219 spelled out
ipfwadm -I -a deny    -W $EXTERNAL_INTERFACE -S 217.0.0.0/8 -o
ipfwadm -I -a deny    -W $EXTERNAL_INTERFACE -S 218.0.0.0/8 -o
ipfwadm -I -a deny    -W $EXTERNAL_INTERFACE -S 219.0.0.0/8 -o

# 223: 11011111  - /6 masks 220-223
ipfwadm -I -a deny    -W $EXTERNAL_INTERFACE -S 220.0.0.0/6 -o

# -------------------------------------------------------------------
# ICMP


# (4)  Source_Quench
#      Incoming & outgoing requests to slow down (flow control)
ipfwadm -I -a accept -P icmp -W $EXTERNAL_INTERFACE \
        -S $ANYWHERE 4 -D $IPADDR

ipfwadm -O -a accept -P icmp -W $EXTERNAL_INTERFACE \
        -S $IPADDR 4 -D $ANYWHERE

# (12) Parameter_Problem
#      Incoming & outgoing error messages
ipfwadm -I -a accept -P icmp -W $EXTERNAL_INTERFACE \
        -S $ANYWHERE 12 -D $IPADDR

ipfwadm -O -a accept -P icmp -W $EXTERNAL_INTERFACE \
        -S $IPADDR 12 -D $ANYWHERE

# (3)  Dest_Unreachable, Service_Unavailable
#      Incoming & outgoing size negotiation, service or
#      destination unavailability, final traceroute response
ipfwadm -I -a accept -P icmp -W $EXTERNAL_INTERFACE \
        -S $ANYWHERE 3 -D $IPADDR

ipfwadm -O -a accept -P icmp -W $EXTERNAL_INTERFACE \
        -S $IPADDR 3 -D $ANYWHERE

# (11) Time_Exceeded
#      Incoming & outgoing timeout conditions,
#      also intermediate TTL response to traceroutes
ipfwadm -I -a accept -P icmp -W $EXTERNAL_INTERFACE \
        -S $ANYWHERE 11 -D $IPADDR

ipfwadm -O -a accept -P icmp -W $EXTERNAL_INTERFACE \
        -S $IPADDR 11 -D $MY_ISP
```

```
# Allow outgoing pings to anywhere
ipfwadm -O -a accept -P icmp -W $EXTERNAL_INTERFACE \
        -S $IPADDR 8 -D $ANYWHERE

ipfwadm -I -a accept -P icmp -W $EXTERNAL_INTERFACE \
        -S $ANYWHERE 0 -D $IPADDR

# Allow incoming pings from trusted hosts
ipfwadm -I -a accept -P icmp -W $EXTERNAL_INTERFACE \
        -S $MY_ISP 8 -D $IPADDR

ipfwadm -O -a accept -P icmp -W $EXTERNAL_INTERFACE \
        -S $IPADDR 0 -D $MY_ISP


# --------------------------------------------------------------------
# Disallow certain outgoing traffic to protect yourself from mistakes.

# OpenWindows: establishing a connection
ipfwadm -O -a reject -P tcp -y -W $EXTERNAL_INTERFACE \
        -S $IPADDR \
        -D $ANYWHERE $OPENWINDOWS_PORT

# X Window: establishing a connection
ipfwadm -O -a reject -P tcp -y -W $EXTERNAL_INTERFACE \
        -S $IPADDR \
        -D $ANYWHERE $XWINDOW_PORTS

# SOCKS: establishing a connection
ipfwadm -O -a reject -P tcp -y -W $EXTERNAL_INTERFACE \
        -S $IPADDR \
        -D $ANYWHERE $SOCKS_PORT


# --------------------------------------------------------------------
# TCP UNPRIVILEGED PORTS
# Avoid ports subject to protocol & system administration problems.

# NFS incoming connection  (atypical TCP mode)
ipfwadm -I -a deny -P tcp -y -W $EXTERNAL_INTERFACE \
        -D $IPADDR $NFS_PORT

# OpenWindows incoming connection
ipfwadm -I -a deny -P tcp -y -W $EXTERNAL_INTERFACE \
        -D $IPADDR $OPENWINDOWS_PORT

# X Window incoming connection
ipfwadm -I -a deny -P tcp -y -W $EXTERNAL_INTERFACE \
        -D $IPADDR $XWINDOW_PORTS

# SOCKS incoming connection
ipfwadm -I -a deny -P tcp -y -W $EXTERNAL_INTERFACE \
        -D $IPADDR $SOCKS_PORT
```

```
# ----------------------------------------------------------------------
# UDP UNPRIVILEGED PORTS
# Avoid ports subject to protocol & system administration problems.

# NFS incoming request  (normal UDP mode)
ipfwadm -I -a deny -P udp -W $EXTERNAL_INTERFACE \
        -D $IPADDR $NFS_PORT


# ----------------------------------------------------------------------
# NOTE:
#     The symbolic names used in /etc/services for the port numbers
#     vary by supplier.  Using them is less error-prone and more
#     meaningful.


# ----------------------------------------------------------------------
# Required Services

# DNS client modes (53)
# --------------------

ipfwadm -O -a accept -P udp -W $EXTERNAL_INTERFACE \
        -S $IPADDR $UNPRIVPORTS \
        -D $NAMESERVER_1 53

ipfwadm -I -a accept -P udp -W $EXTERNAL_INTERFACE \
        -S $NAMESERVER_1 53 \
        -D $IPADDR $UNPRIVPORTS

# TCP client-to-server requests are allowed by the protocol
# if UDP requests fail. This is rarely seen. Usually, clients
# use TCP as a secondary name server for zone transfers from
# their primary name servers, and as hackers.

ipfwadm -O -a accept -P tcp    -W $EXTERNAL_INTERFACE \
        -S $IPADDR $UNPRIVPORTS \
        -D $NAMESERVER_1 53

ipfwadm -I -a accept -P tcp -k -W $EXTERNAL_INTERFACE \
        -S $NAMESERVER_1 53 \
        -D $IPADDR $UNPRIVPORTS

# DNS server modes (53)
# --------------------

# DNS caching & forwarding name server
# ----------------------------------

# Server-to-server query or response
# Caching only name server uses UDP, not TCP
```

```
ipfwadm -O -a accept -P udp -W $EXTERNAL_INTERFACE \
        -S $IPADDR 53 \
        -D $NAMESERVER_1 53

ipfwadm -I -a accept -P udp -W $EXTERNAL_INTERFACE \
        -S $NAMESERVER_1 53 \
        -D $IPADDR 53

# DNS full name server
# --------------------

ipfwadm -I -a accept -P udp -W $EXTERNAL_INTERFACE \
        -S <my.dns.clients> 53 $UNPRIVPORTS \
        -D $IPADDR 53

ipfwadm -O -a accept -P udp -W $EXTERNAL_INTERFACE \
        -S $IPADDR 53 \
        -D <my.dns.clients> 53 $UNPRIVPORTS

# Zone Transfers
# Due to the potential danger of zone transfers,
# allow TCP traffic to only specific secondaries.

ipfwadm -I -a accept -P tcp    -W $EXTERNAL_INTERFACE \
        -S <my.dns.secondaries> $UNPRIVPORTS \
        -D $IPADDR 53

ipfwadm -O -a accept -P tcp -k -W $EXTERNAL_INTERFACE \
        -S $IPADDR 53 \
        -D <my.dns.secondaries> $UNPRIVPORTS

# ----------------------------------------------------------------------

# AUTH client (113)
# -----------------

ipfwadm -O -a accept -P tcp    -W $EXTERNAL_INTERFACE \
        -S $IPADDR $UNPRIVPORTS \
        -D $ANYWHERE 113

ipfwadm -I -a accept -P tcp -k -W $EXTERNAL_INTERFACE \
        -S $ANYWHERE 113 \
        -D $IPADDR $UNPRIVPORTS

# AUTH server (113)
# -----------------

# Reject incoming queries
```

```
ipfwadm -I -a reject -P tcp -W $EXTERNAL_INTERFACE \
        -D $IPADDR 113

# OR
# Accept incoming queries

ipfwadm -I -a accept -P tcp    -W $EXTERNAL_INTERFACE \
        -S $ANYWHERE $UNPRIVPORTS \
        -D $IPADDR 113

ipfwadm -O -a accept -P tcp -k -W $EXTERNAL_INTERFACE \
        -S $IPADDR 113 \
        -D $ANYWHERE $UNPRIVPORTS

# ---------------------------------------------------------------------
# TCP services on selected ports

# SMTP client (25)
# ---------------

ipfwadm -O -a accept -P tcp    -W $EXTERNAL_INTERFACE \
        -S $IPADDR $UNPRIVPORTS \
        -D $ANYWHERE 25

ipfwadm -I -a accept -P tcp -k -W $EXTERNAL_INTERFACE \
        -S $ANYWHERE 25 \
        -D $IPADDR $UNPRIVPORTS

# ---------------------------------------------------------------------
# OR SMTP client to an ISP account without a local server

ipfwadm -O -a accept -P tcp    -W $EXTERNAL_INTERFACE \
        -S $IPADDR $UNPRIVPORTS \
        -D $SMTP_SERVER 25

ipfwadm -I -a accept -P tcp -k -W $EXTERNAL_INTERFACE \
        -S $SMTP_SERVER 25 \
        -D $IPADDR $UNPRIVPORTS

# SMTP server (25)
# ---------------

ipfwadm -I -a accept -P tcp    -W $EXTERNAL_INTERFACE \
        -S $ANYWHERE $UNPRIVPORTS \
        -D $IPADDR 25

ipfwadm -O -a accept -P tcp -k -W $EXTERNAL_INTERFACE \
        -S $IPADDR 25 \
        -D $ANYWHERE $UNPRIVPORTS
```

```
# -----------------------------------------------------------------------

# POP client (110)
# ---------------

ipfwadm -O -a accept -P tcp    -W $EXTERNAL_INTERFACE \
        -S $IPADDR $UNPRIVPORTS \
        -D $POP_SERVER 110

ipfwadm -I -a accept -P tcp -k -W $EXTERNAL_INTERFACE \
        -S $POP_SERVER 110 \
        -D $IPADDR $UNPRIVPORTS

# POP server (110)
# ---------------

ipfwadm -I -a accept -P tcp    -W $EXTERNAL_INTERFACE \
        -S <my.pop.clients> $UNPRIVPORTS \
        -D $IPADDR 110

ipfwadm -O -a accept -P tcp -k -W $EXTERNAL_INTERFACE \
        -S $IPADDR 110 \
        -D <my.pop.clients> $UNPRIVPORTS

# -----------------------------------------------------------------------

# IMAP client (143)
# ----------------

ipfwadm -O -a accept -P tcp    -W $EXTERNAL_INTERFACE \
        -S $IPADDR $UNPRIVPORTS \
        -D <my.imap.server> 143

ipfwadm -I -a accept -P tcp -k -W $EXTERNAL_INTERFACE \
        -S <my.imap.server> 143 \
        -D $IPADDR $UNPRIVPORTS

# IMAP server (143)
# ----------------

ipfwadm -I -a accept -P tcp    -W $EXTERNAL_INTERFACE \
        -S <my.imap.clients> $UNPRIVPORTS \
        -D $IPADDR 143

ipfwadm -O -a accept -P tcp -k -W $EXTERNAL_INTERFACE \
        -S $IPADDR 143 \
        -D <my.imap.clients> $UNPRIVPORTS

# -----------------------------------------------------------------------
```

```
# NNTP NEWS client (119)
# ---------------------

ipfwadm -O -a accept -P tcp    -W $EXTERNAL_INTERFACE \
        -S $IPADDR $UNPRIVPORTS \
        -D $NEWS_SERVER 119

ipfwadm -I -a accept -P tcp -k -W $EXTERNAL_INTERFACE \
        -S $NEWS_SERVER 119 \
        -D $IPADDR $UNPRIVPORTS


# ------------------------------------------------------------------------

# TELNET client (23)
# ------------------

ipfwadm -O -a accept -P tcp    -W $EXTERNAL_INTERFACE \
        -S $IPADDR $UNPRIVPORTS \
        -D $ANYWHERE 23

ipfwadm -I -a accept -P tcp -k -W $EXTERNAL_INTERFACE \
        -S $ANYWHERE 23 \
        -D $IPADDR $UNPRIVPORTS

# TELNET server (23)
# ------------------

ipfwadm -I -a accept -P tcp    -W $EXTERNAL_INTERFACE \
        -S $ANYWHERE $UNPRIVPORTS \
        -D $IPADDR 23

ipfwadm -O -a accept -P tcp -k -W $EXTERNAL_INTERFACE \
        -S $IPADDR 23 \
        -D $ANYWHERE $UNPRIVPORTS


# ------------------------------------------------------------------------

# SSH client (22)
# ---------------

ipfwadm -O -a accept -P tcp    -W $EXTERNAL_INTERFACE \
        -S $IPADDR $UNPRIVPORTS \
        -D $ANYWHERE 22

ipfwadm -I -a accept -P tcp -k -W $EXTERNAL_INTERFACE \
        -S $ANYWHERE 22 \
        -D $IPADDR $UNPRIVPORTS

ipfwadm -O -a accept -P tcp    -W $EXTERNAL_INTERFACE \
        -S $IPADDR $SSH_PORTS \
        -D $ANYWHERE 22
```

```
ipfwadm -I -a accept -P tcp -k -W $EXTERNAL_INTERFACE \
        -S $ANYWHERE 22 \
        -D $IPADDR $SSH_PORTS

# SSH server (22)
# --------------

ipfwadm -I -a accept -P tcp    -W $EXTERNAL_INTERFACE \
        -S $ANYWHERE $UNPRIVPORTS \
        -D $IPADDR 22

ipfwadm -O -a accept -P tcp -k -W $EXTERNAL_INTERFACE \
        -S $IPADDR 22 \
        -D $ANYWHERE $UNPRIVPORTS

ipfwadm -I -a accept -P tcp    -W $EXTERNAL_INTERFACE \
        -S $ANYWHERE $SSH_PORTS \
        -D $IPADDR 22

ipfwadm -O -a accept -P tcp -k -W $EXTERNAL_INTERFACE \
        -S $IPADDR 22 \
        -D $ANYWHERE $SSH_PORTS


# ----------------------------------------------------------------------


# FTP client (20, 21)
# ------------------

# Outgoing request

ipfwadm -O -a accept -P tcp    -W $EXTERNAL_INTERFACE \
        -S $IPADDR $UNPRIVPORTS \
        -D $ANYWHERE 21

ipfwadm -I -a accept -P tcp -k -W $EXTERNAL_INTERFACE \
        -S $ANYWHERE 21 \
        -D $IPADDR $UNPRIVPORTS

# NORMAL mode data channel

ipfwadm -I -a accept -P tcp    -W $EXTERNAL_INTERFACE \
        -S $ANYWHERE 20 \
        -D $IPADDR $UNPRIVPORTS

ipfwadm -O -a accept -P tcp -k -W $EXTERNAL_INTERFACE \
        -S $IPADDR $UNPRIVPORTS \
        -D $ANYWHERE 20

# PASSIVE mode data channel creation
```

```
ipfwadm -O -a accept -P tcp    -W $EXTERNAL_INTERFACE \
        -S $IPADDR $UNPRIVPORTS \
        -D $ANYWHERE $UNPRIVPORTS

ipfwadm -I -a accept -P tcp -k -W $EXTERNAL_INTERFACE \
        -S $ANYWHERE $UNPRIVPORTS \
        -D $IPADDR $UNPRIVPORTS

# FTP server (20, 21)
# ------------------

# Incoming request

ipfwadm -I -a accept -P tcp    -W $EXTERNAL_INTERFACE \
        -S $ANYWHERE $UNPRIVPORTS \
        -D $IPADDR 21

ipfwadm -O -a accept -P tcp -k -W $EXTERNAL_INTERFACE \
        -S $IPADDR 21 \
        -D $ANYWHERE $UNPRIVPORTS

# PORT MODE data channel responses

ipfwadm -O -a accept -P tcp    -W $EXTERNAL_INTERFACE \
        -S $IPADDR 20 \
        -D $ANYWHERE $UNPRIVPORTS

ipfwadm -I -a accept -P tcp -k -W $EXTERNAL_INTERFACE \
        -S $ANYWHERE $UNPRIVPORTS \
        -D $IPADDR 20

# PASSIVE MODE data channel responses

ipfwadm -I -a accept -P tcp    -W $EXTERNAL_INTERFACE \
        -S $ANYWHERE $UNPRIVPORTS \
        -D $IPADDR $UNPRIVPORTS

ipfwadm -O -a accept -P tcp -k -W $EXTERNAL_INTERFACE \
        -S $IPADDR $UNPRIVPORTS \
        -D $ANYWHERE $UNPRIVPORTS

# -------------------------------------------------------------------

# HTTP client (80)
# ---------------

ipfwadm -O -a accept -P tcp    -W $EXTERNAL_INTERFACE \
        -S $IPADDR $UNPRIVPORTS \
        -D $ANYWHERE 80
```

```
ipfwadm -I -a accept -P tcp -k -W $EXTERNAL_INTERFACE \
        -S $ANYWHERE 80 \
        -D $IPADDR $UNPRIVPORTS

# HTTP server (80)
# ----------------

ipfwadm -I -a accept -P tcp    -W $EXTERNAL_INTERFACE \
        -S $ANYWHERE $UNPRIVPORTS \
        -D $IPADDR 80

ipfwadm -O -a accept -P tcp -k -W $EXTERNAL_INTERFACE \
        -S $IPADDR 80 \
        -D $ANYWHERE $UNPRIVPORTS

# ----------------------------------------------------------------------


# HTTPS client (443)
# ------------------

ipfwadm -O -a accept -P tcp    -W $EXTERNAL_INTERFACE \
        -S $IPADDR $UNPRIVPORTS \
        -D $ANYWHERE 443

ipfwadm -I -a accept -P tcp -k -W $EXTERNAL_INTERFACE \
        -S $ANYWHERE 443 \
        -D $IPADDR $UNPRIVPORTS

# HTTPS server (443)
# ------------------

ipfwadm -I -a accept -P tcp    -W $EXTERNAL_INTERFACE \
        -S $ANYWHERE $UNPRIVPORTS \
        -D $IPADDR 443

ipfwadm -O -a accept -P tcp -k -W $EXTERNAL_INTERFACE \
        -S $IPADDR 443 \
        -D $ANYWHERE $UNPRIVPORTS

# ----------------------------------------------------------------------

# HTTP Proxy client (8008/8080)
# -----------------------------

ipfwadm -O -a accept -P tcp    -W $EXTERNAL_INTERFACE \
        -S $IPADDR $UNPRIVPORTS \
        -D $WEB_PROXY_SERVER $WEB_PROXY_PORT
```

```
ipfwadm -I -a accept -P tcp -k -W $EXTERNAL_INTERFACE \
        -S $WEB_PROXY_SERVER $WEB_PROXY_PORT \
        -D $IPADDR $UNPRIVPORTS

# ------------------------------------------------------------------------

# FINGER client (79)
# -----------------

ipfwadm -O -a accept -P tcp  -W $EXTERNAL_INTERFACE \
        -S $IPADDR $UNPRIVPORTS \
        -D $ANYWHERE 79

ipfwadm -I -a accept -P tcp -k  -W $EXTERNAL_INTERFACE \
        -S $ANYWHERE 79 \
        -D $IPADDR $UNPRIVPORTS

# FINGER server (79)
# -----------------

ipfwadm -I -a accept -P tcp     -W $EXTERNAL_INTERFACE \
        -S <my.finger.clients> $UNPRIVPORTS \
        -D $IPADDR 79

ipfwadm -O -a accept -P tcp -k -W $EXTERNAL_INTERFACE \
        -S $IPADDR 79 \
        -D <my.finger.clients> $UNPRIVPORTS

# ------------------------------------------------------------------------

# WHOIS client (43)
# ----------------

ipfwadm -O -a accept -P tcp     -W $EXTERNAL_INTERFACE \
        -S $IPADDR $UNPRIVPORTS \
        -D $ANYWHERE 43

ipfwadm -I -a accept -P tcp -k -W $EXTERNAL_INTERFACE \
        -S $ANYWHERE 43 \
        -D $IPADDR $UNPRIVPORTS

# ------------------------------------------------------------------------

# Gopher client (70)
# -----------------

ipfwadm -O -a accept -P tcp     -W $EXTERNAL_INTERFACE \
        -S $IPADDR $UNPRIVPORTS \
        -D $ANYWHERE 70
```

```
ipfwadm -I -a accept -P tcp -k -W $EXTERNAL_INTERFACE \
        -S $ANYWHERE 70 \
        -D $IPADDR $UNPRIVPORTS

# -----------------------------------------------------------------------

# WAIS client (210)
# -----------------

ipfwadm -O -a accept -P tcp    -W $EXTERNAL_INTERFACE \
        -S $IPADDR $UNPRIVPORTS \
        -D $ANYWHERE 210

ipfwadm -I -a accept -P tcp -k -W $EXTERNAL_INTERFACE \
        -S $ANYWHERE 210 \
        -D $IPADDR $UNPRIVPORTS

# -----------------------------------------------------------------------

# TRACEROUTE
# traceroute usually uses -S 32769:65535 -D 33434:33523
# -----------------------------------------------------

# Enabling Outgoing traceroute Requests
# -------------------------------------

ipfwadm -O -a accept -P udp -W $EXTERNAL_INTERFACE \
        -S $IPADDR 32769:65535 \
        -D $ANYWHERE 33434:33523

# incoming query from the ISP.
# All others are denied by default.
# ---------------------------------

ipfwadm -I -a accept -P udp -W $EXTERNAL_INTERFACE \
        -S $MY_ISP 32769:65535 \
        -D $IPADDR 33434:33523

# -----------------------------------------------------------------------
# UDP accept only on selected ports


# DHCP client (67, 68)
# --------------------

# INIT or REBINDING: No lease or Lease time expired.

ipfwadm -O -a accept -P udp -W $EXTERNAL_INTERFACE \
        -S $BROADCAST_SRC 68 \
        -D $BROADCAST_DEST 67
```

```
# Getting renumbered

ipfwadm -I -a accept -P udp -W $EXTERNAL_INTERFACE \
        -S $BROADCAST_SRC 67 \
        -D $BROADCAST_DEST 68

ipfwadm -I -a accept -P udp -W $EXTERNAL_INTERFACE \
        -S $DHCP_SERVER 67 \
        -D $BROADCAST_DEST 68

ipfwadm -O -a accept -P udp -W $EXTERNAL_INTERFACE \
        -S $BROADCAST_SRC 68 \
        -D $DHCP_SERVER 67

# As a result of the above, we're supposed to change our IP
# address with this message, which is addressed to our new
# address before the dhcp client has received the update.

ipfwadm -I -a accept -P udp -W $EXTERNAL_INTERFACE \
        -S $DHCP_SERVER 67 \
        -D $MY_ISP 68

ipfwadm -I -a accept -P udp -W $EXTERNAL_INTERFACE \
        -S $DHCP_SERVER 67 \
        -D $IPADDR 68

ipfwadm -O -a accept -P udp -W $EXTERNAL_INTERFACE \
        -S $IPADDR 68 \
        -D $DHCP_SERVER 67

# ----------------------------------------------------------------------

# NTP   (123) - Accessing Remote Network Time Servers
# ----------------------------------------------

ipfwadm -O -a accept -P udp -W $EXTERNAL_INTERFACE \
        -S $IPADDR $UNPRIVPORTS \
        -D <my.time.provider> 123

ipfwadm -I -a accept -P udp -W $EXTERNAL_INTERFACE \
        -S <my.time.provider> 123 \
        -D $IPADDR $UNPRIVPORTS

# ----------------------------------------------------------------------
# Unlimited traffic within the local network.

# All internal machines have access to the firewall machine.

ipfwadm -I -a accept -W $LAN_INTERFACE_1 \
            -S $LAN_1
```

```
ipfwadm -O -a accept -W $LAN_INTERFACE_1 \
            -D $LAN_1

# ------------------------------------------------------------------
# Masquerade internal traffic.

# All internal traffic is masqueraded externally.

ipfwadm -F -a masquerade -W $EXTERNAL_INTERFACE -S $LAN_1

# ------------------------------------------------------------------

echo "done"

exit 0
```

Optimizing the Firewall Rules

Firewall optimization is not a crucial topic for a home system. Chances are good that the Linux network code can handle packets faster than the network connection. Particularly because firewall rules are order-dependent and difficult to construct, optimizing for readability is probably a bigger win than optimizing for speed.

Firewall rules must be ordered from most specific to most general. Within the confines of the order dependencies created by the particular rules you use, rule ordering can be optimized by placing rules for more frequently occurring packets earlier in the firewall rule lists. For example, if you rarely use ftp, chances are good that Web-related traffic will be seen far more often than ftp-related traffic. List traversal ends as soon as the packet matches a rule, so placing the http rules before the ftp rules reduces extra overhead when matching the more common http packets.

Firewall rules can also be optimized in terms of placing input and output rules relative to other rules in their respective chains, rather than grouping the I/O rule pair together. For example, traffic from a Web browser client to a Web server is small relative to the amount of traffic returned from the server in response to the client's URL query. The same is true for ftp. The amount of control traffic passing through port 21 is miniscule relative to the amount of data traffic passing through port 20.

Assume a Linux home computer connected to the Internet. The machine uses the firewall presented in Chapter 3. A static IP address is permanently assigned to the computer's network interface by the ISP. The firewall masquerades Internet connections for a small, private LAN.

The machine runs a local DNS server that first forwards queries to the ISP name server, followed by client-to-server queries to any remote name server in the event the ISP name server does not respond. Full SMTP mail services run locally, but the firewall supports an outgoing POP client connection to retrieve mail from the mail account at the ISP, as well. The site hosts its own Web server. There is no local public FTP server.

As presented in this book, such a firewall script would look like this:

```
#!/bin/sh

echo "Starting firewalling... "

# Some definitions for easy maintenance.

# ------------------------------------------------------------------
# EDIT THESE TO SUIT YOUR SYSTEM AND ISP.

EXTERNAL_INTERFACE="eth0"              # Internet-connected interface
INTERNAL_INTERFACE="eth1"             # LAN-connected interface
LOOPBACK_INTERFACE="lo"               # or your local naming convention

IPADDR="my.ip.address"                # your public IP address
LAN_IPADDR="192.168.1.1"             # internal interface address
LAN_ADDRRESSES="192.168.1.0/24"      # LAN network address

ANYWHERE="any/0"                      # match any IP address

MY_ISP="my.isp.address.range"         # ISP & NOC address range
NAMESERVER_1="my.name.server.1"       # everyone must have at least one

SMTP_SERVER="any/0"                   # external mail server
SMTP_GATEWAY="my.isp.server"          # external mail relay
POP_SERVER="my.pop.server"            # external pop server, if any
NEWS_SERVER="my.news.server"          # external news server, if any
WEB_PROXY_SERVER="my.www.proxy"       # ISP Web proxy server, if any
WEB_PROXY_PORT="www.proxy.port"       # ISP Web proxy port, if any
                                      # typically 8008 or 8080


LOOPBACK="127.0.0.0/8"                # reserved loopback address range
CLASS_A="10.0.0.0/8"                  # class A private networks
CLASS_B="172.16.0.0/12"              # class B private networks
CLASS_C="192.168.0.0/16"             # class C private networks
CLASS_D_MULTICAST="224.0.0.0/4"      # class D multicast addresses
BROADCAST_SRC="0.0.0.0"              # broadcast source address
BROADCAST_DEST="255.255.255.255"     # broadcast destination address
PRIVPORTS="0:1023"                    # well-known, privileged port range
UNPRIVPORTS="1024:65535"             # unprivileged port range
TRACEROUTE_SRC_PORTS="32769:65535"
TRACEROUTE_DEST_PORTS="33434:33523"
SOCKS_PORT="1080"                     # (TCP) socks
OPENWINDOWS_PORT="2000"               # (TCP) openwindows
NFS_PORT="2049"                       # (TCP/UDP) NFS


# ...............................................................
# EDIT THESE TO MATCH THE NUMBER OF SERVERS OR CONNECTIONS
# YOU SUPPORT.
```

```
XWINDOW_PORTS="6000"                    # (TCP) X Window

SSH_PORTS="1020:1023"                   # simultaneous connections

# ------------------------------------------------------------------------

# Enable TCP SYN Cookie Protection
echo 1 >/proc/sys/net/ipv4/tcp_syncookies

# Enable IP spoofing protection
# turn on Source Address Verification
for f in /proc/sys/net/ipv4/conf/*/rp_filter; do
    echo 1 > $f
done

# Disable ICMP Redirect Acceptance
for f in /proc/sys/net/ipv4/conf/*/accept_redirects; do
    echo 0 > $f
done

# Disable Source Routed Packets
for f in /proc/sys/net/ipv4/conf/*/accept_source_route; do
    echo 0 > $f
done

# ------------------------------------------------------------------------

# Flush any existing rules from all chains.
ipchains -F

# Set the default policy to deny
ipchains -P input   DENY
ipchains -P output  REJECT
ipchains -P forward REJECT

# ------------------------------------------------------------------------
# LOOPBACK

# Unlimited traffic on the loopback interface
ipchains -A input  -i $LOOPBACK_INTERFACE -j ACCEPT
ipchains -A output -i $LOOPBACK_INTERFACE -j ACCEPT

# ------------------------------------------------------------------------
# Refuse any connections from problem sites.

# /etc/rc.d/rc.firewall.blocked contains a list of
# ipchains -A input -i $EXTERNAL_INTERFACE -s <address/mask> -j DENY
# rules to block all access.
```

```
# Refuse packets claiming to be from the banned list.
if [ -f /etc/rc.d/rc.firewall.blocked ]; then
    . /etc/rc.d/rc.firewall.blocked
fi


# -------------------------------------------------------------------
# SPOOFING & BAD ADDRESSES
# Refuse spoofed packets.
# Ignore blatantly illegal source addresses.
# Protect yourself from sending to bad addresses.

# Refuse spoofed packets pretending to be from
# the external interface's IP address.
ipchains -A input   -i $EXTERNAL_INTERFACE -s $IPADDR -j DENY -l

# Refuse packets claiming to be to or from a Class A private network.
ipchains -A input   -i $EXTERNAL_INTERFACE -s $CLASS_A -j DENY

# Refuse packets claiming to be to or from a Class B private network.
ipchains -A input   -i $EXTERNAL_INTERFACE -s $CLASS_B -j DENY

# Refuse packets claiming to be to or from a Class C private network.
ipchains -A input   -i $EXTERNAL_INTERFACE -s $CLASS_C -j DENY

# Refuse packets claiming to be from the loopback interface.
ipchains -A input   -i $EXTERNAL_INTERFACE -s $LOOPBACK -j DENY

# Refuse malformed broadcast packets.
ipchains -A input   -i $EXTERNAL_INTERFACE -s $BROADCAST_DEST -j DENY -l
ipchains -A input   -i $EXTERNAL_INTERFACE -d $BROADCAST_SRC  -j DENY -l

# Refuse packets claiming to be from Class D multicast addresses.
# Multicast uses UDP.
ipchains -A input   -i $EXTERNAL_INTERFACE -s $CLASS_D_MULTICAST \
        -j DENY -l

# -------------------------------------------------------------------
# ICMP

# (4)  Source_Quench
#      Incoming & outgoing requests to slow down (flow control)
ipchains -A input   -i $EXTERNAL_INTERFACE -p icmp \
        -s $ANYWHERE 4 -d $IPADDR -j ACCEPT

ipchains -A output -i $EXTERNAL_INTERFACE -p icmp \
        -s $IPADDR 4 -d $ANYWHERE -j ACCEPT

# (12) Parameter_Problem
#      Incoming & outgoing error messages
ipchains -A input   -i $EXTERNAL_INTERFACE -p icmp \
        -s $ANYWHERE 12 -d $IPADDR -j ACCEPT
```

```
ipchains -A output -i $EXTERNAL_INTERFACE -p icmp \
        -s $IPADDR 12 -d $ANYWHERE -j ACCEPT

# (3)  Dest_Unreachable, Service_Unavailable
#      Incoming & outgoing size negotiation, service or
#      destination unavailability, final traceroute response
ipchains -A input  -i $EXTERNAL_INTERFACE -p icmp \
        -s $ANYWHERE 3 -d $IPADDR -j ACCEPT

ipchains -A output -i $EXTERNAL_INTERFACE -p icmp \
        -s $IPADDR 3 -d $MY_ISP -j ACCEPT

ipchains -A output -i $EXTERNAL_INTERFACE -p icmp \
        -s $IPADDR fragmentation-needed -d $ANYWHERE -j ACCEPT

# (11) Time_Exceeded
#      Incoming & outgoing timeout conditions,
#      also intermediate TTL response to traceroutes
ipchains -A input  -i $EXTERNAL_INTERFACE -p icmp \
        -s $ANYWHERE 11 -d $IPADDR -j ACCEPT

ipchains -A output -i $EXTERNAL_INTERFACE -p icmp \
        -s $IPADDR 11 -d $MY_ISP -j ACCEPT

# Allow outgoing pings to anywhere
ipchains -A output -i $EXTERNAL_INTERFACE -p icmp \
        -s $IPADDR 8 -d $ANYWHERE -j ACCEPT

ipchains -A input  -i $EXTERNAL_INTERFACE -p icmp \
        -s $ANYWHERE 0 -d $IPADDR -j ACCEPT

# Allow incoming pings from trusted hosts
ipchains -A input  -i $EXTERNAL_INTERFACE -p icmp \
        -s $MY_ISP 8 -d $IPADDR -j ACCEPT

ipchains -A output -i $EXTERNAL_INTERFACE -p icmp \
        -s $IPADDR 0 -d $MY_ISP -j ACCEPT


# -------------------------------------------------------------------


# UNPRIVILEGED PORTS
# Avoid ports subject to protocol & system administration problems.

# OpenWindows incoming connection
ipchains -A input -i $EXTERNAL_INTERFACE -p tcp -y \
        -d $IPADDR $OPENWINDOWS_PORT -j DENY

# X Window: incoming connection attempt
ipchains -A input -i $EXTERNAL_INTERFACE -p tcp -y \
        -d $IPADDR $XWINDOW_PORTS -j DENY -l
```

```
# SOCKS incoming connection
ipchains -A input -i $EXTERNAL_INTERFACE -p tcp -y \
        -d $IPADDR $SOCKS_PORT -j DENY

# NFS: TCP connections
ipchains -A input -i $EXTERNAL_INTERFACE -p tcp -y \
        -d $IPADDR $NFS_PORT -j DENY -l

# NFS: UDP connections
ipchains -A input -i $EXTERNAL_INTERFACE -p udp \
        -d $IPADDR $NFS_PORT -j DENY -l

# ---------------------------------------------------------------------

# DNS client modes (53)
# --------------------

ipchains -A output -i $EXTERNAL_INTERFACE -p udp \
        -s $IPADDR 53 \
        -d $NAMESERVER_1 53 -j ACCEPT

ipchains -A input  -i $EXTERNAL_INTERFACE -p udp \
        -s $NAMESERVER_1 53 \
        -d $IPADDR 53 -j ACCEPT

ipchains -A output -i $EXTERNAL_INTERFACE -p udp \
        -s $IPADDR $UNPRIVPORTS \
        -d $NAMESERVER_1 53 -j ACCEPT

ipchains -A input  -i $EXTERNAL_INTERFACE -p udp \
        -s $NAMESERVER_1 53 \
        -d $IPADDR $UNPRIVPORTS -j ACCEPT

# TCP client-to-server requests are allowed by the protocol
# if UDP requests fail. This is rarely seen.

ipchains -A output -i $EXTERNAL_INTERFACE -p tcp \
        -s $IPADDR $UNPRIVPORTS \
        -d <my.dns.primary> 53 -j ACCEPT

ipchains -A input -i $EXTERNAL_INTERFACE -p tcp ! -y \
        -s <my.dns.primary> 53 \
        -d $IPADDR $UNPRIVPORTS -j ACCEPT

# ---------------------------------------------------------------------

# AUTH (113)
# ----------
```

```
# Accept Incoming AUTH Requests

ipchains -A input  -i $EXTERNAL_INTERFACE -p tcp \
        -s $ANYWHERE $UNPRIVPORTS \
        -d $IPADDR 113 -j ACCEPT

ipchains -A output -i $EXTERNAL_INTERFACE -p tcp ! -y \
        -s $IPADDR 113 \
        -d $ANYWHERE $UNPRIVPORTS -j ACCEPT

# Accept Outgoing AUTH Requests

ipchains -A output -i $EXTERNAL_INTERFACE -p tcp \
        -s $IPADDR $UNPRIVPORTS \
        -d $ANYWHERE 113 -j ACCEPT

ipchains -A input  -i $EXTERNAL_INTERFACE -p tcp ! -y  \
        -s $ANYWHERE 113 \
        -d $IPADDR $UNPRIVPORTS -j ACCEPT


# -----------------------------------------------------------------------

# HTTP client (80)
# ----------------------------

ipchains -A output -i $EXTERNAL_INTERFACE -p tcp \
        -s $IPADDR $UNPRIVPORTS \
        -d $ANYWHERE 80 -j ACCEPT

ipchains -A input -i $EXTERNAL_INTERFACE -p tcp ! -y \
        -s $ANYWHERE 80 \
        -d $IPADDR $UNPRIVPORTS -j ACCEPT

# HTTP server (80)
# ----------------------------

ipchains -A input  -i $EXTERNAL_INTERFACE -p tcp \
        -s $ANYWHERE $UNPRIVPORTS \
        -d $IPADDR 80 -j ACCEPT

ipchains -A output -i $EXTERNAL_INTERFACE -p tcp ! -y \
        -s $IPADDR 80 \
        -d $ANYWHERE $UNPRIVPORTS -j ACCEPT

# -----------------------------------------------------------------------

# SSL client (443)
# ----------------------------
```

```
ipchains -A output -i $EXTERNAL_INTERFACE -p tcp \
        -s $IPADDR $UNPRIVPORTS \
        -d $ANYWHERE 443 -j ACCEPT

ipchains -A input -i $EXTERNAL_INTERFACE -p tcp ! -y \
        -s $ANYWHERE 443 \
        -d $IPADDR $UNPRIVPORTS -j ACCEPT

# --------------------------------------------------------------------

# NNTP (119) - Reading and Posting News as a Usenet Client
# ---------------------------------------------------------

ipchains -A output -i $EXTERNAL_INTERFACE -p tcp \
        -s $IPADDR $UNPRIVPORTS \
        -d $NEWS_SERVER 119 -j ACCEPT

ipchains -A input -i $EXTERNAL_INTERFACE -p tcp ! -y \
        -s $NEWS_SERVER 119 \
        -d $IPADDR $UNPRIVPORTS -j ACCEPT

# --------------------------------------------------------------------

# POP (110) - Retrieving Mail as a POP Client
# --------------------------------------------

ipchains -A output -i $EXTERNAL_INTERFACE -p tcp \
        -s $IPADDR $UNPRIVPORTS \
        -d $POP_SERVER 110 -j ACCEPT

ipchains -A input -i $EXTERNAL_INTERFACE -p tcp ! -y \
        -s $POP_SERVER 110 \
        -d $IPADDR $UNPRIVPORTS -j ACCEPT

# --------------------------------------------------------------------

# SMTP client (25)
# ---------------------------------------

ipchains -A output -i $EXTERNAL_INTERFACE -p tcp \
        -s $IPADDR $UNPRIVPORTS \
        -d $ANYWHERE 25 -j ACCEPT

ipchains -A input  -i $EXTERNAL_INTERFACE -p tcp ! -y \
        -s $ANYWHERE 25 \
        -d $IPADDR $UNPRIVPORTS -j ACCEPT

# SMTP server (25)
# ---------------------------------------
```

```
ipchains -A input  -i $EXTERNAL_INTERFACE -p tcp \
        -s $ANYWHERE $UNPRIVPORTS \
        -d $IPADDR 25 -j ACCEPT

ipchains -A output -i $EXTERNAL_INTERFACE -p tcp ! -y \
        -s $IPADDR 25 \
        -d $ANYWHERE $UNPRIVPORTS -j ACCEPT


# ------------------------------------------------------------------------

# TELNET (23) - Allowing Client Access to Remote Sites
# --------------------------------------------------------

ipchains -A output -i $EXTERNAL_INTERFACE -p tcp \
        -s $IPADDR $UNPRIVPORTS \
        -d $ANYWHERE 23 -j ACCEPT

ipchains -A input -i $EXTERNAL_INTERFACE -p tcp ! -y \
        -s $ANYWHERE 23 \
        -d $IPADDR $UNPRIVPORTS -j ACCEPT


# ------------------------------------------------------------------------

# SSH client (22) - Allowing Client Access to Remote SSH Servers
# ----------------------------------------------------------------

ipchains -A output -i $EXTERNAL_INTERFACE -p tcp \
        -s $IPADDR $UNPRIVPORTS \
        -d $ANYWHERE 22 -j ACCEPT

ipchains -A input  -i $EXTERNAL_INTERFACE -p tcp ! -y \
        -s $ANYWHERE 22 \
        -d $IPADDR $UNPRIVPORTS -j ACCEPT

ipchains -A output -i $EXTERNAL_INTERFACE -p tcp \
        -s $IPADDR $SSH_PORTS \
        -d $ANYWHERE 22 -j ACCEPT

ipchains -A input  -i $EXTERNAL_INTERFACE -p tcp ! -y \
        -s $ANYWHERE 22 \
        -d $IPADDR $SSH_PORTS -j ACCEPT


# ------------------------------------------------------------------------

# FTP (20, 21) - Allowing Outgoing Client Access to Remote FTP Servers
# ------------------------------------------------------------------------
```

```
# Outgoing request

ipchains -A output -i $EXTERNAL_INTERFACE -p tcp \
        -s $IPADDR $UNPRIVPORTS \
        -d $ANYWHERE 21 -j ACCEPT

ipchains -A input -i $EXTERNAL_INTERFACE -p tcp ! -y \
        -s $ANYWHERE 21 \
        -d $IPADDR $UNPRIVPORTS -j ACCEPT

# Normal Port Mode FTP Data Channels

ipchains -A input  -i $EXTERNAL_INTERFACE -p tcp \
        -s $ANYWHERE 20 \
        -d $IPADDR $UNPRIVPORTS -j ACCEPT

ipchains -A output -i $EXTERNAL_INTERFACE -p tcp ! -y \
        -s $IPADDR $UNPRIVPORTS \
        -d $ANYWHERE 20 -j ACCEPT

# Passive Mode FTP Data Channels

ipchains -A output -i $EXTERNAL_INTERFACE -p tcp \
        -s $IPADDR $UNPRIVPORTS \
        -d $ANYWHERE $UNPRIVPORTS -j ACCEPT

ipchains -A input  -i $EXTERNAL_INTERFACE -p tcp ! -y \
        -s $ANYWHERE $UNPRIVPORTS \
        -d $IPADDR $UNPIRVPORTS -j ACCEPT

# ----------------------------------------------------------------------

# WHOIS client (43)
# ----------------

ipchains -A output -i $EXTERNAL_INTERFACE -p tcp \
        -s $IPADDR $UNPRIVPORTS \
        -d $ANYWHERE 43 -j ACCEPT

ipchains -A input -i $EXTERNAL_INTERFACE -p tcp ! -y \
        -s $ANYWHERE 43 \
        -d $IPADDR $UNPRIVPORTS -j ACCEPT

# ----------------------------------------------------------------------

# TRACEROUTE
# ----------

# Enabling Outgoing traceroute Requests
```

```
# ------------------------------------

ipchains -A output -i $EXTERNAL_INTERFACE -p udp \
        -s $IPADDR $TRACEROUTE_SRC_PORTS \
        -d $ANYWHERE $TRACEROUTE_DEST_PORTS -j ACCEPT

# Enabling Incoming traceroute Requests from the ISP
# --------------------------------------------------

ipchains -A input  -i $EXTERNAL_INTERFACE -p udp \
        -s $MY_ISP $TRACEROUTE_SRC_PORTS \
        -d $IPADDR $TRACEROUTE_DEST_PORTS -j ACCEPT


# ----------------------------------------------------------------

# NTP (123) - Accessing Remote Network Time Servers
# --------------------------------------------------

ipchains -A output -i $EXTERNAL_INTERFACE -p udp \
        -s $IPADDR $UNPRIVPORTS \
        -d <my.time.provider> 123 -j ACCEPT

ipchains -A input  -i $EXTERNAL_INTERFACE -p udp \
        -s <my.time.provider> 123 \
        -d $IPADDR $UNPRIVPORTS -j ACCEPT


# ----------------------------------------------------------------

echo "done"

exit 0
```

Optimizing *ipfwadm* Rule Ordering

In addition to general rule ordering, `ipfwadm` supports one mechanism you can use to optimize your firewall rules. Ports and ICMP message types can be expressed as a list of up to 10 values. A range of values is treated as two values. One range can be defined within any given source or destination port list. Multiple rules can be collapsed into a single rule by grouping the ports or ICMP message types into a single list. A packet will be tested against the single rule, rather than against individual rules for each value in the list.

The following is the previous firewall script, optimized under `ipfwadm`:

```
#!/bin/sh

echo "Starting firewalling... "

# Some definitions for easy maintenance.
```

```
# ------------------------------------------------------------------
# EDIT THESE TO SUIT YOUR SYSTEM AND ISP.

EXTERNAL_INTERFACE="eth0"              # Internet-connected interface
INTERNAL_INTERFACE="eth1"             # LAN-connected interface
LOOPBACK_INTERFACE="lo"               # or your local naming convention

IPADDR="my.ip.address"                # your public IP address
LAN_IPADDR="192.168.1.1"              # internal interface address
LAN_ADDRRESSES="192.168.1.0/24"       # LAN network address

ANYWHERE="any/0"                      # match any IP address

MY_ISP="my.isp.address.range"         # ISP & NOC address range
NAMESERVER_1="my.name.server.1"       # everyone must have at least one

SMTP_SERVER="any/0"                   # external mail server
SMTP_GATEWAY="my.isp.server"          # external mail relay
POP_SERVER="my.pop.server"            # external pop server, if any
NEWS_SERVER="my.news.server"          # external news server, if any
WEB_PROXY_SERVER="my.www.proxy"       # ISP Web proxy server, if any
WEB_PROXY_PORT="www.proxy.port"       # ISP Web proxy port, if any
                                      # typically 8008 or 8080


LOOPBACK="127.0.0.0/8"                # reserved loopback address range
CLASS_A="10.0.0.0/8"                  # class A private networks
CLASS_B="172.16.0.0/12"              # class B private networks
CLASS_C="192.168.0.0/16"            # class C private networks
CLASS_D_MULTICAST="224.0.0.0/4"       # class D multicast addresses
BROADCAST_SRC="0.0.0.0"               # broadcast source address
BROADCAST_DEST="255.255.255.255"      # broadcast destination address
PRIVPORTS="0:1023"                    # well-known, privileged port range
UNPRIVPORTS="1024:65535"              # unprivileged port range
TRACEROUTE_SRC_PORTS="32769:65535"
TRACEROUTE_DEST_PORTS="33434:33523"
SOCKS_PORT="1080"                     # (TCP) SOCKS
OPENWINDOWS_PORT="2000"               # (TCP) OpenWindows
NFS_PORT="2049"                       # (TCP/UDP) NFS


# ..................................................................
# EDIT THESE TO MATCH THE NUMBER OF SERVERS OR CONNECTIONS
# YOU SUPPORT.

XWINDOW_PORTS="6000"                   # (TCP) X Window

SSH_PORTS="1020:1023"                  # simultaneous connections
```

```
# --------------------------------------------------------------------

# Enable TCP SYN Cookie Protection
echo 1 >/proc/sys/net/ipv4/tcp_syncookies

# Enable IP spoofing protection
# turn on Source Address Verification
for f in /proc/sys/net/ipv4/conf/*/rp_filter; do
    echo 1 > $f
done

# Disable ICMP Redirect Acceptance
for f in /proc/sys/net/ipv4/conf/*/accept_redirects; do
    echo 0 > $f
done

# Disable Source-Routed Packets
for f in /proc/sys/net/ipv4/conf/*/accept_source_route; do
    echo 0 > $f
done

# --------------------------------------------------------------------

# Flush any existing rules from all chains.
ipfwadm -I -f
ipfwadm -O -f
ipfwadm -F -f

# Set the default policy to deny
ipfwadm -I -p deny
ipfwadm -O -p reject
ipfwadm -F -p reject

# --------------------------------------------------------------------
# LOOPBACK

# Unlimited traffic on the loopback interface
ipfwadm -I -a accept -W $LOOPBACK_INTERFACE
ipfwadm -O -a accept -W $LOOPBACK_INTERFACE

# --------------------------------------------------------------------
# Refuse any connections from problem sites.

# /etc/rc.d/rc.firewall.blocked contains a list of
# ipfwadm -I -a deny -W $EXTERNAL_INTERFACE -S <address/mask>
# rules to block all access.

# Refuse packets claiming to be from the banned list.
if [ -f /etc/rc.d/rc.firewall.blocked ]; then
    . /etc/rc.d/rc.firewall.blocked
fi
```

```
# ---------------------------------------------------------------------
# SPOOFING & BAD ADDRESSES
# Refuse spoofed packets.
# Ignore blatantly illegal source addresses.

# Refuse spoofed packets pretending to be from
# the external interface's IP address.
ipfwadm -I -a deny    -W $EXTERNAL_INTERFACE -S $IPADDR -o

# Refuse packets claiming to be to or from a Class A private network.
ipfwadm -I -a deny    -W $EXTERNAL_INTERFACE -S $CLASS_A -o

# Refuse packets claiming to be to or from a Class B private network.
ipfwadm -I -a deny    -W $EXTERNAL_INTERFACE -S $CLASS_B -o

# Refuse packets claiming to be to or from a Class C private network.
ipfwadm -I -a deny    -W $EXTERNAL_INTERFACE -S $CLASS_C -o

# Refuse packets claiming to be from the loopback interface.
ipfwadm -I -a deny    -W $EXTERNAL_INTERFACE -S $LOOPBACK -o

# Refuse malformed broadcast packets.
ipfwadm -I -a deny    -W $EXTERNAL_INTERFACE -S $BROADCAST_DEST -o
ipfwadm -I -a deny    -W $EXTERNAL_INTERFACE -D $BROADCAST_SRC -o

# Refuse packets claiming to be from Class D multicast addresses.
# Multicast uses UDP.
ipfwadm -I -a deny    -W $EXTERNAL_INTERFACE -S $MULTICAST -o

# ----------------------------------------------------------------------
# ICMP

# (0)  Echo Reply (pong)
# (3)  Dest_Unreachable, Service_Unavailable
#      incoming & outgoing size negotiation, service or
#      destination unavailability, final traceroute response
# (4)  Source_Quench
#      incoming & outgoing requests to slow down (flow control)
# (8)  Echo Request (ping)
# (12) Parameter_Problem

ipfwadm -I -a accept -P icmp -W $EXTERNAL_INTERFACE \
        -S $ANYWHERE 0 3 4 11 12 -D $IPADDR

ipfwadm -O -a accept -P icmp -W $EXTERNAL_INTERFACE \
        -S $IPADDR 3 4 8 12 -D $ANYWHERE

ipfwadm -I -a accept -P icmp -W $EXTERNAL_INTERFACE \
        -S $MY_ISP 8 -D $IPADDR
```

```
ipfwadm -O -a accept -P icmp -W $EXTERNAL_INTERFACE \
        -S $IPADDR 0 11 -D $MY_ISP


# -----------------------------------------------------------------------

# DNS UDP forwarder mode (53)
# ---------------------------

ipfwadm -O -a accept -P udp -W $EXTERNAL_INTERFACE \
        -S $IPADDR 53 \
        -D $NAMESERVER_1 53

ipfwadm -I -a accept -P udp -W $EXTERNAL_INTERFACE \
        -S $NAMESERVER_1 53 \
        -D $IPADDR 53

# DNS UDP client mode (53)
# ------------------------

ipfwadm -O -a accept -P udp -W $EXTERNAL_INTERFACE \
        -S $IPADDR $UNPRIVPORTS \
        -D $ANYWHERE 53

ipfwadm -I -a accept -P udp -W $EXTERNAL_INTERFACE \
        -S $ANYWHERE 53 \
        -D $IPADDR $UNPRIVPORTS


# -----------------------------------------------------------------------

# HTTP client (80)
# SSL client (443)
# SMTP - sending mail (25)
# AUTH client (113)
# WHOIS client(43)
# Incoming server responses
# ---------------------------

ipfwadm -I -a accept -P tcp -k -W $EXTERNAL_INTERFACE \
        -S $ANYWHERE 80 443 25 113 43 \
        -D $IPADDR $UNPRIVPORTS


# -----------------------------------------------------------------------

# NNTP (119) - Reading and Posting News as a Usenet Client
# --------------------------------------------------------

ipfwadm -I -a accept -P tcp -k -W $EXTERNAL_INTERFACE \
        -S $NEWS_SERVER 119 \
        -D $IPADDR $UNPRIVPORTS
```

```
# --------------------------------------------------------------------

# POP (110) - Retrieving Mail as a POP Client
# ----------------------------------------

ipfwadm -I -a accept -P tcp -k -W $EXTERNAL_INTERFACE \
        -S $POP_SERVER 110 \
        -D $IPADDR $UNPRIVPORTS


# --------------------------------------------------------------------

# HTTP client (80)
# SSL client (443)
# SMTP - sending mail (25)
# AUTH client (113)
# WHOIS client(43)
# Outgoing client requests
# ---------------------------

ipfwadm -O -a accept -P tcp   -W $EXTERNAL_INTERFACE \
        -S $IPADDR $UNPRIVPORTS \
        -D $ANYWHERE 80 443 25 113 43


# --------------------------------------------------------------------

# NNTP (119) - Reading and Posting News as a Usenet Client
# -------------------------------------------------------

ipfwadm -O -a accept -P tcp   -W $EXTERNAL_INTERFACE \
        -S $IPADDR $UNPRIVPORTS \
        -D $NEWS_SERVER 119


# --------------------------------------------------------------------

# POP (110) - Retrieving Mail as a POP Client
# ----------------------------------------

ipfwadm -O -a accept -P tcp   -W $EXTERNAL_INTERFACE \
        -S $IPADDR $UNPRIVPORTS \
        -D $POP_SERVER 110


# --------------------------------------------------------------------

# Web server (80)
# AUTH server (113)
# SMTP - receiving mail (25)
# Handle Incoming Client Requests

ipfwadm -O -a accept -P tcp -k -W $EXTERNAL_INTERFACE \
        -S $IPADDR 80 113 25 \
        -D $ANYWHERE $UNPRIVPORTS
```

```
ipfwadm -I -a accept -P tcp    -W $EXTERNAL_INTERFACE \
        -S $ANYWHERE $UNPRIVPORTS \
        -D $IPADDR 80 113 25


# -------------------------------------------------------------------

# TELNET (23) - Allowing Client Access to Remote Sites
# SSH client (22) - Allowing Initial Client Access to Remote SSH Servers
# FTP client (21) - Allowing Client Command channel Access to Remote FTP Servers
# --------------------------------------------------------------------------

ipfwadm -O -a accept -P tcp    -W $EXTERNAL_INTERFACE \
        -S $IPADDR $UNPRIVPORTS \
        -D $ANYWHERE 23 22 21

ipfwadm -I -a accept -P tcp -k -W $EXTERNAL_INTERFACE \
        -S $ANYWHERE 23 22 21 \
        -D $IPADDR $UNPRIVPORTS


# -------------------------------------------------------------------

# SSH client (22) - Allowing Client Access to Remote SSH Servers
# -------------------------------------------------------------

ipfwadm -O -a accept -P tcp    -W $EXTERNAL_INTERFACE \
        -S $IPADDR $SSH_PORTS \
        -D $ANYWHERE 22

ipfwadm -I -a accept -P tcp -k -W $EXTERNAL_INTERFACE \
        -S $ANYWHERE 22 \
        -D $IPADDR $SSH_PORTS


# -------------------------------------------------------------------

# UNPRIVILEGED PORTS
# Avoid ports subject to protocol & system administration problems.

# X Window incoming connection
# SOCKS incoming connection
# NFS incoming connection  (atypical TCP mode)

ipfwadm -I -a deny -P tcp -y -W $EXTERNAL_INTERFACE \
        -D $IPADDR $XWINDOW_PORTS $SOCKS_PORT $NFS_PORT

# NFS incoming request  (normal UDP mode)
ipfwadm -I -a deny -P udp -W $EXTERNAL_INTERFACE \
        -D $IPADDR $NFS_PORT


# -------------------------------------------------------------------

# FTP (20, 21) - Allowing Outgoing Client Access to Remote FTP Servers
```

```
# ----------------------------------------------------------------------

# Passive Mode FTP Data Channels

ipfwadm -I -a accept -P tcp -k -W $EXTERNAL_INTERFACE \
        -S $ANYWHERE $UNPRIVPORTS \
        -D $IPADDR $UNPRIVPORTS

# Normal Port Mode FTP Data Channels

ipfwadm -I -a accept -P tcp    -W $EXTERNAL_INTERFACE \
        -S $ANYWHERE 20 \
        -D $IPADDR $UNPRIVPORTS

# ----------------------------------------------------------------------

# FTP (20, 21) - Allowing Outgoing Client Access to Remote FTP Servers
# ----------------------------------------------------------------------

# Passive Mode FTP Data Channels

ipfwadm -O -a accept -P tcp    -W $EXTERNAL_INTERFACE \
        -S $IPADDR $UNPRIVPORTS \
        -D $ANYWHERE $UNPRIVPORTS

# Normal Port Mode FTP Data Channels

ipfwadm -O -a accept -P tcp -k -W $EXTERNAL_INTERFACE \
        -S $IPADDR $UNPRIVPORTS \
        -D $ANYWHERE 20

# ----------------------------------------------------------------------

# NTP (123) - Accessing Remote Network Time Servers
# ------------------------------------------------

ipfwadm -O -a accept -P udp -W $EXTERNAL_INTERFACE \
        -S $IPADDR $UNPRIVPORTS \
        -D <my.time.provider> 123

ipfwadm -I -a accept -P udp -W $EXTERNAL_INTERFACE \
        -S <my.time.provider> 123 \
        -D $IPADDR $UNPRIVPORTS

# ----------------------------------------------------------------------

# TRACEROUTE
# ----------

# Enabling Outgoing traceroute Requests
# -------------------------------------
```

```
        ipfwadm -O -a accept -P udp -W $EXTERNAL_INTERFACE \
               -S $IPADDR $TRACEROUTE_SRC_PORTS \
               -D $ANYWHERE $TRACEROUTE_DEST_PORTS

        # Enabling Incoming traceroute Requests from the ISP
        # ---------------------------------------------------

        ipfwadm -I -a accept -P udp -W $EXTERNAL_INTERFACE \
               -S $MY_ISP $TRACEROUTE_SRC_PORTS \
               -D $IPADDR $TRACEROUTE_DEST_PORTS

        # (11) Time_Exceeded
        #      Outgoing timeout conditions,

        ipfwadm -O -a accept -P icmp -W $EXTERNAL_INTERFACE \
               -S $IPADDR 11 -D $MY_ISP


        # ----------------------------------------------------------------------

        # PING
        # ----

        # allow incoming pings from trusted hosts
        ipfwadm -I -a accept -P icmp -W $EXTERNAL_INTERFACE \
               -S $MY_ISP 8 -D $IPADDR

        ipfwadm -O -a accept -P icmp -W $EXTERNAL_INTERFACE \
               -S $IPADDR 0 -D $MY_ISP


        # ----------------------------------------------------------------------

        # DNS TCP client mode (53)
        # ------------------------

        # TCP client-to-server requests are allowed by the protocol
        # if UDP requests fail. This is rarely seen.

        ipfwadm -I -a accept -P tcp -k -W $EXTERNAL_INTERFACE \
               -S $ANYWHERE 53 \
               -D $IPADDR $UNPRIVPORTS

        ipfwadm -O -a accept -P tcp    -W $EXTERNAL_INTERFACE \
               -S $IPADDR $UNPRIVPORTS \
               -D $ANYWHERE 53


        # ----------------------------------------------------------------------

        echo "done"

        exit 0
```

Optimizing *ipchains* Rules with User-Defined Chains

In addition to general rule ordering, ipchains supports user-defined rule lists, or chains, you can use to optimize your firewall rules. Passing a packet from one chain to another based on values in the packet header provides a means to selectively test the packet against a subset of the input, output, or forward rules, rather than testing the packet against every rule in the list until a match is found.

For example, using the nonoptimized firewall script, an input packet from an NTP time server must be tested against approximately 40 input rules before the packet matches its ACCEPT rule. Using user-defined chains to optimize the firewall, the same input packet is tested against approximately 15 rules before matching its ACCEPT rule.

In ipchains, rules are used to pass packets between chains, as well as to define under what conditions the packet is accepted or denied. If a packet doesn't match any rule in the user-defined chain, control returns to the calling chain. If the packet doesn't match a chain selection rule, the packet isn't passed to that chain for testing against the chain's rules. The packet is simply tested against the next chain selection rule.

The following is the previous firewall script, optimized under ipchains:

```sh
#!/bin/sh

echo "Starting firewalling... "

# Some definitions for easy maintenance.


# ------------------------------------------------------------------
# EDIT THESE TO SUIT YOUR SYSTEM AND ISP.

EXTERNAL_INTERFACE="eth0"              # Internet-connected interface
LAN_INTERFACE="eth1"                   # LAN-connected interface
LOOPBACK_INTERFACE="lo"                # or your local naming convention

IPADDR="my.ip.address"                 # your public IP address
LAN_IPADDR="192.168.1.1"               # internal interface address
LAN_ADDRESSES="192.168.1.0/24"         # LAN network address

ANYWHERE="any/0"                       # match any IP address

MY_ISP="my.isp.address.range"          # ISP & NOC address range
NAMESERVER_1="my.name.server.1"        # everyone must have at least one

SMTP_SERVER="any/0"                    # external mail server
SMTP_GATEWAY="my.isp.server"           # external mail relay
POP_SERVER="my.pop.server"             # external pop server, if any
NEWS_SERVER="my.news.server"           # external news server, if any
WEB_PROXY_SERVER="my.www.proxy"        # ISP Web proxy server, if any
WEB_PROXY_PORT="www.proxy.port"        # ISP Web proxy port, if any
                                       # typically 8008 or 8080
```

```
LOOPBACK="127.0.0.0/8"              # reserved loopback address range
CLASS_A="10.0.0.0/8"                # class A private networks
CLASS_B="172.16.0.0/12"             # class B private networks
CLASS_C="192.168.0.0/16"            # class C private networks
CLASS_D_MULTICAST="224.0.0.0/4"     # class D multicast addresses
BROADCAST_SRC="0.0.0.0"             # broadcast source address
BROADCAST_DEST="255.255.255.255"    # broadcast destination address
PRIVPORTS="0:1023"                  # well-known, privileged port range
UNPRIVPORTS="1024:65535"            # unprivileged port range
TRACEROUTE_SRC_PORTS="32769:65535"
TRACEROUTE_DEST_PORTS="33434:33523"
SOCKS_PORT="1080"                   # (TCP) socks
OPENWINDOWS_PORT="2000"             # (TCP) openwindows
NFS_PORT="2049"                     # (TCP/UDP) NFS


# ----------------------------------------------------------------------
# EDIT THESE TO MATCH THE NUMBER OF SERVERS OR CONNECTIONS
# YOU SUPPORT.

XWINDOW_PORTS="6000"                # (TCP) X Window

SSH_PORTS="1020:1023"               # simultaneous connections

# ----------------------------------------------------------------------

# Enable TCP SYN Cookie Protection
echo 1 >/proc/sys/net/ipv4/tcp_syncookies

# Enable IP spoofing protection
# turn on Source Address Verification
for f in /proc/sys/net/ipv4/conf/*/rp_filter; do
    echo 1 > $f
done

# Disable ICMP Redirect Acceptance
for f in /proc/sys/net/ipv4/conf/*/accept_redirects; do
    echo 0 > $f
done

# Disable Source-Routed Packets
for f in /proc/sys/net/ipv4/conf/*/accept_source_route; do
    echo 0 > $f
done

# ----------------------------------------------------------------------

# Flush any existing rules from all chains
ipchains -F
ipchains -F spoofed
ipchains -F tcp-c-o
```

```
ipchains -F tcp-s-i
ipchains -F udp-c-o
ipchains -F udp-s-i
ipchains -F tcp-c-i
ipchains -F tcp-s-o
ipchains -F misc-out
ipchains -F misc-in
ipchains -F icmp-in
ipchains -F icmp-out
ipchains -F log-in
ipchains -F log-out

ipchains -X spoofed
ipchains -X tcp-c-o
ipchains -X tcp-s-i
ipchains -X udp-c-o
ipchains -X udp-s-i
ipchains -X tcp-c-i
ipchains -X tcp-s-o
ipchains -X misc-out
ipchains -X misc-in
ipchains -X icmp-in
ipchains -X icmp-out
ipchains -X log-in
ipchains -X log-out

# Set the default policy to deny
ipchains -P input   DENY
ipchains -P output  REJECT
ipchains -P forward REJECT

# ---------------------------------------------------------------------
# LOOPBACK INTERFACE

# Unlimited traffic on the loopback interface
ipchains -A input  -i $LOOPBACK_INTERFACE -j ACCEPT
ipchains -A output -i $LOOPBACK_INTERFACE -j ACCEPT

# ---------------------------------------------------------------------
# LAN INTERFACE

ipchains -A input  -i $LAN_INTERFACE -j ACCEPT
ipchains -A output -i $LAN_INTERFACE -j ACCEPT

# ---------------------------------------------------------------------
# User-Defined Chains

ipchains -N spoofed
ipchains -N tcp-c-o
ipchains -N tcp-s-i
ipchains -N udp-c-o
```

```
ipchains -N udp-s-i
ipchains -N tcp-c-i
ipchains -N tcp-s-o
ipchains -N misc-out
ipchains -N misc-in
ipchains -N icmp-in
ipchains -N icmp-out
ipchains -N log-in
ipchains -N log-out


# --------------------------------------------------------------------
# EXTERNAL INTERFACE Spoofed Source Address CHAIN  (spoofed)

# Refuse any connections from problem sites.

# /etc/rc.d/rc.firewall.blocked contains a list of
# ipchains -A spoofed -s <address/mask> -j DENY
# rules to block all access.

# Refuse packets claiming to be from the banned list.
if [ -f /etc/rc.d/rc.firewall.blocked ]; then
    . /etc/rc.d/rc.firewall.blocked
fi


# --------------------------------------------------------------------
# SPOOFING & BAD ADDRESSES
# Refuse spoofed packets.
# Ignore blatantly illegal source addresses.
# Protect yourself from sending to bad addresses.

# Refuse spoofed packets pretending to be from
# the external interface's IP address.
ipchains -A spoofed -s $IPADDR -j DENY -l

# Refuse packets claiming to be to or from a Class A private network.
ipchains -A spoofed -s $CLASS_A -j DENY

# Refuse packets claiming to be to or from a Class B private network.
ipchains -A spoofed -s $CLASS_B -j DENY

# Refuse packets claiming to be to or from a Class C private network.
ipchains -A spoofed -s $CLASS_C -j DENY

# Refuse packets claiming to be from the loopback interface.
ipchains -A spoofed -s $LOOPBACK -j DENY

# Refuse packets claiming to be from Class D multicast addresses.
# Multicast uses UDP.
ipchains -A spoofed -s $CLASS_D_MULTICAST -j DENY -l
```

```
# Refuse malformed broadcast packets.
ipchains -A spoofed -s $BROADCAST_DEST -j DENY -l

# ----------------------------------------------------------------
# EXTERNAL INTERFACE - TCP Client Output CHAIN (tcp-c-o -p tcp)


# HTTP client (80)

ipchains -A tcp-c-o -p tcp \
        -d $ANYWHERE http -j ACCEPT

# ----------------------------------------------------------------

# NNTP (119) - Reading and Posting News as a Usenet Client

ipchains -A tcp-c-o -p tcp \
        -d $NEWS_SERVER nntp -j ACCEPT

# ----------------------------------------------------------------

# POP (110) - Retrieving Mail as a POP Client

ipchains -A tcp-c-o -p tcp \
        -d $POP_SERVER pop-3 -j ACCEPT

# ----------------------------------------------------------------

# SMTP client sending mail (25)

ipchains -A tcp-c-o -p tcp \
        -d $ANYWHERE smtp -j ACCEPT

# ----------------------------------------------------------------

# AUTH client (113)

ipchains -A tcp-c-o -p tcp \
        -d $ANYWHERE auth -j ACCEPT

# ----------------------------------------------------------------

# TELNET (23) - Allowing Client Access to Remote Sites

ipchains -A tcp-c-o -p tcp \
        --destination-port telnet -j ACCEPT

# ----------------------------------------------------------------
```

```
# SSH client (22) - Allowing Client Access to Remote SSH Servers

ipchains -A tcp-c-o -p tcp \
        --destination-port ssh -j ACCEPT

# --------------------------------------------------------------------

# FTP (20, 21) - Allowing Outgoing Client Access to Remote FTP Servers

# Passive Mode FTP Data Channels

ipchains -A tcp-c-o -p tcp \
        --destination-port $UNPRIVPORTS -j ACCEPT

# Normal Port Mode FTP Data Channels

ipchains -A tcp-c-o -p tcp ! -y \
        --destination-port ftp-data -j ACCEPT

# outgoing request

ipchains -A tcp-c-o -p tcp \
        --destination-port ftp -j ACCEPT

# --------------------------------------------------------------------

# SSL client (443)

ipchains -A tcp-c-o -p tcp \
        -d $ANYWHERE https -j ACCEPT

# --------------------------------------------------------------------

# WHOIS client (43)

ipchains -A tcp-c-o -p tcp \
        --destination-port whois -j ACCEPT

# --------------------------------------------------------------------

# DNS TCP client mode (53)

# TCP client-to-server requests are allowed by the protocol
# if UDP requests fail. This is rarely seen.

ipchains -A tcp-c-o -p tcp \
        -d $ANYWHERE domain -j ACCEPT
```

```
# --------------------------------------------------------------------
# EXTERNAL INTERFACE - TCP Server Input CHAIN (tcp-s-i -p tcp)

# HTTP client (80)

ipchains -A tcp-s-i -p tcp \
        -s $ANYWHERE http -j ACCEPT

# --------------------------------------------------------------------

# NNTP (119) - Reading and Posting News as a Usenet Client

ipchains -A tcp-s-i -p tcp \
        -s $NEWS_SERVER nntp -j ACCEPT

# --------------------------------------------------------------------

# POP (110) - Retrieving Mail as a POP Client

ipchains -A tcp-s-i -p tcp \
        -s $POP_SERVER pop-3 -j ACCEPT

# --------------------------------------------------------------------

# SMTP client sending mail (25)

ipchains -A tcp-s-i -p tcp \
        -s $SMTP_GATEWAY smtp -j ACCEPT

# --------------------------------------------------------------------

# AUTH client (113)

ipchains -A tcp-s-i -p tcp \
        -s $ANYWHERE auth -j ACCEPT

# --------------------------------------------------------------------

# TELNET (23) - Allowing Client Access to Remote Sites

ipchains -A tcp-s-i -p tcp \
        --source-port telnet -j ACCEPT

# --------------------------------------------------------------------

# SSH client (22) - Allowing Client Access to Remote SSH Servers

ipchains -A tcp-s-i -p tcp \
        --source-port ssh -j ACCEPT
```

```
# -------------------------------------------------------------------

# FTP (20, 21) - Allowing Outgoing Client Access to Remote FTP Servers

# Passive Mode FTP Data Channels

ipchains -A tcp-s-i -p tcp \
        --source-port $UNPRIVPORTS -j ACCEPT

# Outgoing request

ipchains -A tcp-s-i -p tcp \
        --source-port ftp -j ACCEPT

# -------------------------------------------------------------------

# SSL client (443)

ipchains -A tcp-s-i -p tcp \
        -s $ANYWHERE https -j ACCEPT

# -------------------------------------------------------------------

# WHOIS client (43)

ipchains -A tcp-s-i -p tcp \
        --source-port whois -j ACCEPT

# -------------------------------------------------------------------

# DNS TCP client mode (53)

# TCP client-to-server requests are allowed by the protocol
# if UDP requests fail. This is rarely seen.

ipchains -A tcp-s-i -p tcp \
        -s $ANYWHERE domain -j ACCEPT


# -------------------------------------------------------------------
# EXTERNAL INTERFACE - UDP Client Output CHAIN (udp-c-o)

# UDP peer forwarder mode (53)
# --------------------------

ipchains -A udp-c-o -p udp \
        --source-port domain \
        -d $NAMESERVER_1 domain -j ACCEPT
```

```
# UDP client mode (53)
# ------------------

ipchains -A udp-c-o -p udp \
        --source-port $UNPRIVPORTS \
        -d $ANYWHERE domain -j ACCEPT


# ----------------------------------------------------------------------

# NTP (123) - Accessing Remote Network Time Servers

ipchains -A udp-c-o -p udp \
        --source-port $UNPRIVPORTS \
        -d <my.time.provider> ntp -j ACCEPT

# ----------------------------------------------------------------------
# EXTERNAL INTERFACE - UDP Server Input CHAIN (udp-s-i)

# UDP peer forwarder mode (53)
# --------------------------

ipchains -A udp-c-o -p udp \
        -s $NAMESERVER_1 domain \
        --destination-port domain -j ACCEPT

# UDP client mode (53)

ipchains -A udp-s-i -p udp \
        -s $ANYWHERE domain \
        --destination-port $UNPRIVPORTS -j ACCEPT


# ----------------------------------------------------------------------

# NTP (123) - Accessing Remote Network Time Servers

ipchains -A udp-s-i -p udp \
        -s <my.time.provider> ntp \
        --destination-port $UNPRIVPORTS -j ACCEPT

# ----------------------------------------------------------------------
# EXTERNAL INTERFACE - Client Input CHAIN (tcp-c-i -p tcp)

# HTTP server (80)

# Accept Incoming HTTP Requests

ipchains -A tcp-c-i -p tcp \
        --destination-port http -j ACCEPT
```

```
# ----------------------------------------------------------------------

# AUTH server (113)

# Accept Incoming AUTH Requests

ipchains -A tcp-c-i -p tcp \
        --destination-port auth -j ACCEPT

# ----------------------------------------------------------------------

# UNPRIVILEGED PORTS
# Avoid ports subject to protocol & system administration problems.

# OpenWindows incoming connection
ipchains -A tcp-c-i -p tcp -y \
        --destination-port $OPENWINDOWS_PORT -j DENY

# X Window: incoming connection attempt
ipchains -A tcp-c-i -p tcp -y \
        --destination-port $XWINDOW_PORTS -j DENY -l

# SOCKS incoming connection
ipchains -A tcp-c-i -p tcp -y \
        --destination-port $SOCKS_PORT -j DENY

# NFS: TCP connections
ipchains -A tcp-c-i -p tcp -y \
        --destination-port $NFS_PORT -j DENY -l


# ----------------------------------------------------------------------
# EXTERNAL INTERFACE - Server Output CHAIN (tcp-s-o -p tcp)

# HTTP (80)

# Accept Incoming AUTH Requests

ipchains -A tcp-s-o -p tcp \
        --source-port http -j ACCEPT

# ----------------------------------------------------------------------

# AUTH (113)

# Accept Incoming AUTH Requests

ipchains -A tcp-s-o -p tcp \
        --source-port auth -j ACCEPT
```

```
# --------------------------------------------------------------------
# EXTERNAL INTERFACE - Misc Output CHAIN (misc-out)


# SSH client (22) - Allowing Client Access to Remote SSH Servers

ipchains -A misc-out -p tcp \
        --source-port $SSH_PORTS \
        --destination-port ssh -j ACCEPT


# --------------------------------------------------------------------

# TRACEROUTE

# Enabling Outgoing traceroute Requests to anywhere

ipchains -A misc-out -p udp \
        --source-port $TRACEROUTE_SRC_PORTS \
        --destination-port $TRACEROUTE_DEST_PORTS -j ACCEPT

# Enabling Incoming traceroute Requests from the ISP

# (3)  Dest_Unreachable, final traceroute response
# (11) Time_Exceeded - intermediate traceroute response

ipchains -A misc-out -p icmp \
        --icmp-type port-unreachable -d $MY_ISP -j ACCEPT

ipchains -A misc-out -p icmp \
        --icmp-type time-exceeded -d $MY_ISP -j ACCEPT


# --------------------------------------------------------------------

# PING

# Allow outgoing pongs to trusted hosts
ipchains -A misc-out -p icmp \
        --icmp-type echo-reply -d $MY_ISP -j ACCEPT

# --------------------------------------------------------------------
# EXTERNAL INTERFACE - Misc Input CHAIN (misc-in)


# SSH client (22) - Allowing Client Access to Remote SSH Servers

ipchains -A misc-in -p tcp ! -y \
        --source-port ssh \
        --destination-port $SSH_PORTS -j ACCEPT
```

```
# -------------------------------------------------------------------

# FTP (20, 21) - Allowing Outgoing Client Access to Remote FTP Servers

# Normal Port Mode FTP Data Channels

ipchains -A misc-in -p tcp \
        --source-port ftp-data \
        --destination-port $UNPRIVPORTS -j ACCEPT


# -------------------------------------------------------------------

# NFS: UDP connections
ipchains -A misc-in -p udp \
        --destination-port $NFS_PORT -j DENY -l


# -------------------------------------------------------------------

# TRACEROUTE

# Enable Incoming traceroute Requests from the ISP

ipchains -A misc-in -p udp \
        -s $MY_ISP $TRACEROUTE_SRC_PORTS \
        --destination-port $TRACEROUTE_DEST_PORTS -j ACCEPT


# -------------------------------------------------------------------

# PING

# Allow incoming pings from trusted hosts
ipchains -A misc-in -p icmp \
        -s $MY_ISP echo-request -j ACCEPT


# -------------------------------------------------------------------
# INCOMING ICMP CHAIN

ipchains -A icmp-in -p icmp --icmp-type echo-reply -j ACCEPT
ipchains -A icmp-in -p icmp --icmp-type destination-unreachable -j ACCEPT
ipchains -A icmp-in -p icmp --icmp-type source-quench -j ACCEPT
ipchains -A icmp-in -p icmp --icmp-type time-exceeded -j ACCEPT
ipchains -A icmp-in -p icmp --icmp-type parameter-problem -j ACCEPT


# -------------------------------------------------------------------
# OUTGOING ICMP CHAIN

ipchains -A icmp-out -p icmp --icmp-type fragmentation-needed -j ACCEPT
ipchains -A icmp-out -p icmp --icmp-type source-quench -j ACCEPT
ipchains -A icmp-out -p icmp --icmp-type echo-request -j ACCEPT
```

```
ipchains -A icmp-out -p icmp --icmp-type parameter-problem -j ACCEPT


# ------------------------------------------------------------------------
# Filter Packets

ipchains -A input  -i $EXTERNAL_INTERFACE -j spoofed
ipchains -A input  -i $EXTERNAL_INTERFACE -p tcp  ! -y \
         -d $IPADDR $UNPRIVPORTS -j tcp-s-i
ipchains -A input  -i $EXTERNAL_INTERFACE -p udp \
         -d $IPADDR -j udp-s-i
ipchains -A input  -i $EXTERNAL_INTERFACE -p icmp \
         -d $IPADDR -j icmp-in
ipchains -A input  -i $EXTERNAL_INTERFACE -p tcp \
         -s $ANYWHERE $UNPRIVPORTS \
         -d $IPADDR -j tcp-c-i
ipchains -A input  -i $EXTERNAL_INTERFACE \
         -d $IPADDR -j misc-in
ipchains -A output -i $EXTERNAL_INTERFACE -p tcp ! -y \
         -s $IPADDR \
         -d $ANYWHERE $UNPRIVPORTS -j tcp-s-o
ipchains -A output -i $EXTERNAL_INTERFACE -p tcp \
         -s $IPADDR $UNPRIVPORTS -j tcp-c-o
ipchains -A output -i $EXTERNAL_INTERFACE -p udp \
         -s $IPADDR -j udp-c-o
ipchains -A output -i $EXTERNAL_INTERFACE -p icmp \
         -s $IPADDR -j icmp-out
ipchains -A output -i $EXTERNAL_INTERFACE \
         -s $IPADDR -j misc-out


# ------------------------------------------------------------------------
# FORWARDING & MASQUERADING CHAIN

ipchains -A forward -i $EXTERNAL_INTERFACE -s $LAN_ADDRESSES -j MASQ

# ------------------------------------------------------------------------
# Log Denied Packets

ipchains -A input  -i $EXTERNAL_INTERFACE -j log-in

ipchains -A output -i $EXTERNAL_INTERFACE -j log-out

# ------------------------------------------------------------------------

echo "done"

exit 0
```

Special-Purpose Support Scripts

Periodically, someone will write and ask whether I have a script to perform some special function, such as allow everything or deny (almost) everything. The four most frequently requested scripts are presented here.

Allow Everything

The `accept-all` script is a debugging tool. Every once in a while, you might need to check whether a particular service is unavailable due to something the firewall rules are doing.

A description of `accept-all`, formatted as a `man` page is:

NAME:

`accept-all`   Allow all network traffic.

SYNOPSIS:

`accept-all`

DESCRIPTION:

Flush any current firewall rules and set the default to accept.

Must be executed as root.

The `accept-all` shell script contains:

```
#!/bin/sh

# Remove all existing rules belonging to this chain
ipchains -F input
ipchains -F output
ipchains -F forward

# Set the default policy of the chain to accept.
ipchains -P input    ACCEPT
ipchains -P output   ACCEPT
ipchains -P forward ACCEPT
```

Deny Everything

The `deny-all` script is partially a debugging tool, partially a stop-gap when a new firewall script contains syntax errors and isn't completing, and partially a panic measure. Every once in a while, you might need to block access from the Internet and start over.

A description of deny-all, formatted as a man page is:

NAME:

deny-all   Block Internet network traffic.

SYNOPSIS:

deny-all

DESCRIPTION:

Flush any current firewall rules and set the default policies for the external network interface to deny.

Must be executed as root.

The deny-all shell script contains:

```
#!/bin/sh

LOOPBACK_INTERFACE="lo"
LAN_INTERFACE="eth1"

# Remove all existing rules belonging to this chain
ipchains -F input
ipchains -F output
ipchains -F forward

# Set the default policy of the chain to deny
ipchains -P input   DENY
ipchains -P output  REJECT
ipchains -P forward REJECT

ipchains -A input  -i $LOOPBACK_INTERFACE  -j ACCEPT
ipchains -A output -i $LOOPBACK_INTERFACE  -j ACCEPT

# Enable access to the firewall machine from the LAN
ipchains -A input  -i $LAN_INTERFACE  -j ACCEPT
ipchains -A output -i $LAN_INTERFACE  -j ACCEPT
```

Blocking an IP Address

block-ip is useful if a remote site is misbehaving and you want to block incoming packets from it immediately, without taking the time to edit the firewall script and reinitialize the firewall. block-ip both inserts a firewall rule in the input chain and adds the rule to the file containing any other sites you are blocking.

A description of `block-ip`, formatted as a `man` page is:

NAME:

`block-ip`   Deny incoming packets from an address.

SYNOPSIS:

`block-ip <address>[/mask]`

DESCRIPTION:

Insert a firewall deny rule at the head of the `input` chain. *address* may be a fully qualified hostname, an IP address, or an IP address range specified as an address and mask.

If `/etc/rc.d/rc.firewall.blocked` does not exist, it is created. The firewall rule is also appended to the end of `/etc/rc.d/rc.firewall.blocked` so the rule remains permanently included in the blocked list.

Must be executed as root.

The `block-ip` shell script contains:

```
#!/bin/sh

EXTERNAL_INTERFACE="eth0"

# If the blocked file doesn't exist, create it.
if [ ! -f /etc/rc.d/rc.firewall.blocked ]; then
    touch /etc/rc.d/rc.firewall.blocked
fi

# insert the rule at the head of the existing input chain
ipchains -i input -i $EXTERNAL_INTERFACE -s $1 -j DENY

# append the new rule to the end of the blocked file
echo ipchains -i input -i $EXTERNAL_INTERFACE -s $1 -j DENY \
    >> /etc/rc.d/rc.firewall.blocked
```

Unblocking an IP Address

If you want to remove a deny rule from the list of globally denied remote sites immediately, without taking the time to edit the firewall script and reinitialize the firewall, unblock-ip is useful to remove an existing firewall rule from the input chain. You must manually remove the rule from /etc/rc.d/rc.firewall.blocked.

A description of unblock-ip, formatted as a man page is:

NAME:

unblock-ip   Remove a firewall DENY rule.

SYNOPSIS:

unblock-ip <*address*>[/mask]

DESCRIPTION:

Delete an existing firewall deny rule from the input chain. *address* may be a fully qualified hostname, an IP address, or an IP address range specified as an address and mask. *address* must exactly match the argument used to create the deny rule.

Must be executed as root.

The unblock-ip shell script contains:

```
#!/bin/sh

EXTERNAL_INTERFACE="eth0"

ipchains -D input -i $EXTERNAL_INTERFACE -s $1 -j DENY
```

DHCP: Firewall Support with a Dynamic IP Address and Name Servers

The Linux DHCP client program has been dhcpcd historically. As of Red Hat Release 6.0, dhcpcd is replaced with a new client program, pump. dhcpcd is still included in the Linux distribution, however. Although the newer pump works fine for a ppp dial-up connection, pump does not adequately support a permanent network connection. Sites with a cable modem or DSL connection, for example, need to continue using dhcpcd.

DHCP provides your public IP address, name server addresses, network mask, broadcast address, and possibly the DHCP server address. This information can change at each bootup, as well as at the end of each DHCP lease period. When the firewall is initialized, the script needs to include IPADDR and the NAMESERVER addresses. The information provided by DHCP is stored in different places, depending on the Linux release you're running. The following shell commands can be inserted in the firewall script at some point after any hard-coded definitions of IPADDR, NAMESERVER, and DHCP_SERVER:

```
# The IP address, $IPADDR, is defined by dhcp

if [ -f /etc/dhcpc/hostinfo-$EXTERNAL_INTERFACE ]; then
    # Red Hat Release < 6.0 - dhcpcd
    . /etc/dhcpc/hostinfo-$EXTERNAL_INTERFACE
elif [ -f /etc/dhcpc/dhcpcd-$EXTERNAL_INTERFACE.info ]; then
```

```
        # Red Hat Release 6.0 - dhcpcd
        . /etc/dhcpc/dhcpcd-$EXTERNAL_INTERFACE.info
        DHCP_SERVER=$DHCPSIADDR
    else
        echo "rc.firewall:  dhcp is not configured."
        ipchains -F
        ipchains -P input  DENY
        ipchains -P output DENY
        ipchains -A input  -i $LOOPBACK_INTERFACE -j ACCEPT
        ipchains -A output -i $LOOPBACK_INTERFACE -j ACCEPT
        ipchains -A input  -i $LAN_INTERFACE -j ACCEPT
        ipchains -A output -i $LAN_INTERFACE -j ACCEPT
        exit 1
fi

# If using the sample ifdhcpc-done script, any previous definitions of
# IPADDR, NAMESERVER, and DHCP_SERVER will be overridden correctly here.
```

dhcpcd-${DEVICE}.exe (post–Red Hat 6.0 Release)

As of Red Hat Release 6.0, the /sbin/dhcpcd client program has been refurbished. There are a number of subtle differences between the current dhcpcd and previous versions.

The mechanism for specifying a program to execute after dhcpcd gets a new IP address is to create an executable file called /etc/dhcpc/dhcpcd-${DEVICE}.exe, where ${DEVICE} is the name of your Internet-connected network interface—for example, eth0 or eth1. Support for dhcpcd's -c option is deprecated.

Unlike prior versions, the current dhcpcd does not execute dhcpcd-eth0.exe at start up if the new IP address assignment is the same address as the last time dhcpcd ran. dhcpcd-eth0.exe is executed only when the IP address changes. This is an important, but subtle, difference from prior versions of dhcpcd.

The /etc/dhcpc directory is not created by the Linux installation scripts. You must create the directory yourself:

```
mkdir /etc/dhcpc
```

/etc/resolv.conf is modified directly. dhcpcd creates a backup copy of the file, /etc/resolv.conf.sv, before writing to /etc/resolv.conf. dhcpcd restores resolv.conf from the backup copy when the program exits. How the file was treated in previous releases varied by release. Some wrote directly to resolv.conf. Some wrote to a file, /etc/dhcpc/resolv.conf, and expected /etc/resolv.conf to be a symbolic link to /etc/dhcpc/resolv.conf.

The information dhcpcd receives from the DHCP server is stored in /etc/dhcpc/dhcpcd-${DEVICE}.info, where ${DEVICE} is the name of the network interface, such as eth0 or eth1. The information is stored as shell variable assigments, so the file can be included in other scripts. For example, the file contains definitions for IPADDR, NETMASK, NETWORK, BROADCAST, GATEWAY, DOMAIN, and the DHCP server address, DHCPSIADDR.

Updating Dynamic Addresses and Installing the Firewall from /etc/dhcpc/dhcpcd-${DEVICE}.exe

Because dhcpcd-eth0.exe is executed each time the IP address changes, the script file is a handy place from which to reexecute the firewall script. If the firewall rules aren't reinitialized with the new IP address, your own firewall will suddenly block you from sending network traffic to the Internet.

The script is also a handy place to update any dynamic data used in other configuration files. The following sample script updates your IP address in /etc/hosts. It copies the name server addresses from /etc/resolv.conf into /etc/dhcpc/dhcpcd-eth0.info as shell variable assignments usable by the firewall script. If you run a forwarding name server, the script updates /etc/named.conf with the name server addresses and updates /etc/resolv.conf to point to your local name server:

```
#!/bin/bash


# Get the hostinfo
. /etc/dhcpc/dhcpcd-eth0.info

# Update domainname
domainname $DOMAIN

# Update /etc/hosts
# Replace <you> with your hostname.
sed -e "s/^.*<you>/$IPADDR        <you>.$DOMAIN      <you>/" /etc/hosts \
        > /var/tmp/hosts
cp /var/tmp/hosts /etc/hosts
rm /var/tmp/hosts


# -----------------------------------------------------------------
# Update /etc/rc.d/rc.firewall with the current name servers
# from /etc/resolv.conf.

# The following 2 sections support a caching-only name server.
# /etc/named.conf, /etc/dhcpc/resolv.conf and /etc/resolv.conf are modified.

# Update /etc/named.conf forwarders to be the original
# name servers from /etc/resolv.conf.

let cnt=1
fgrep nameserver /etc/resolv.conf | sed -e "s/nameserver //" |
    while read naddr
    do
        echo "NAMESERVER_$cnt=\"$naddr\"" >> /etc/dhcpc/dhcpcd-eth0.info
        let cnt=$cnt+1
    done
```

```
. /etc/dhcpc/dhcpcd-eth0.info

awk '/forwarders {/ { active = 1; print }             \
                /};/ {                                \
                    if ( active == 1 ) {              \
                        active = 0;                   \
                        print "\t\t" f1 ";";          \
                        print "\t\t" f2 ";";          \
                        print "\t\t" f3 ";";          \
                    }                                 \
                }                                     \
                                                      \
                {                                     \
                    if ( active == 0 )                \
                        print;                        \
                } '                                   \
    f1="$NAMESERVER_1" f2="$NAMESERVER_2" f3="$NAMESERVER_3" /etc/named.conf \
        > /var/tmp/named.conf

cp /var/tmp/named.conf /etc/named.conf
rm /var/tmp/named.conf


# ----------------------------------------------------------------

# Update /etc/resolv.conf for local caching name server.
# Replace the name servers with an entry for the local server.

# Save the original
cp /etc/resolv.conf /etc/dhcpc/resolv.conf.bak

echo "domain $DOMAIN" > /var/tmp/resolv.conf
echo "nameserver 127.0.0.1" >> /var/tmp/resolv.conf

cp /var/tmp/resolv.conf /etc/dhcpc/resolv.conf
rm /var/tmp/resolv.conf


# ----------------------------------------------------------------

sh /etc/rc.d/rc.firewall
echo "Firewalling enabled." > /dev/console

cp /etc/dhcpc/resolv.conf /etc

exit 0
```

DHCP support in */sbin/ifup*

In Red Hat Release 6.0, pump is the default DHCP client, not dhcpcd. To use dhcpcd, the network interface initialization script, /sbin/ifup, must be modified. Replace the lines in the if $PUMP block with the following lines:

```
if [ -n "$PUMP" ]; then
```

```
        echo -n "Determining IP information for $DEVICE..."
        if /sbin/dhcpcd; then
            /etc/rc.d/rc.firewall
        else
            echo "failed."
            exit 1
        fi
    else
```

If dhcpcd detects a new IP address at startup, it will execute /etc/dhcpc/ dhcpcd-eth0.exe. If dhcpcd succeeds at startup, the firewall is initialized from /sbin/ifup. In the case where dhcpcd succeeds but the IP address has not changed, the firewall is installed from /sbin/ifup, but /etc/dhcpc/dhcpcd-eth0.exe is not executed. In the case where dhcpcd succeeds and the IP address has changed, the firewall script is executed twice, first from /etc/dhcpc/dhcpcd-eth0.exe and then from /sbin/ifup.

ifdhcpc-done (pre–Red Hat 6.0 Release)

Prior to Red Hat Release 6.0, the DHCP client mechanism was somewhat different from what it is now. At startup from /sbin/ifup, dhcpcd is executed with the option, -c /etc/sysconfig/network-scripts/ifdhcpc-done. dhcpcd executes ifdhcpc-done at each startup and each time the IP address changes dynamically.

The /etc/dhcpc directory may or may not be created by the Linux installation scripts. If the directory doesn't exist, you must create the directory yourself:

```
mkdir /etc/dhcpc
```

/etc/resolv.conf is not modified directly. Name server information is written to a file, /etc/dhcpc/resolv.conf. Either /etc/resolv.conf is expected to be a symbolic link to /etc/dhcpc/resolv.conf, or the ifdhcpc-done script copies /etc/dhcpc/resolv.conf to /etc/resolv.conf.

The information dhcpcd receives from the DHCP server is stored in /etc/dhcpc/hostinfo-${DEVICE}, where ${DEVICE} is the name of the network interface, such as eth0 or eth1. The information is stored as shell variable assignments, so the file can be included in other scripts. For example, the file contains definitions for IPADDR, NETMASK, BROADCAST, and GATEWAY.

Updating Dynamic Addresses and Installing the Firewall from
/etc/sysconfig/network-scripts/ifdhcpc-done

The purpose of the ifdhcpc-done script is to execute at initialization and each time the IP address changes. It waits until dhcpcd has completed its initialization and then copies the name server information to /etc/resolv.conf.

The script is a handy place to update any dynamic data used in other configuration files. The following sample script updates your IP address in /etc/hosts. It copies the name server addresses from /etc/dhcpc/resolv.conf into /etc/dhcpc/hostinfo-eth0 as shell variable assigments usable by the firewall script. If you run a forwarding name server, the script updates /etc/named.conf or /etc/named.boot with the name server addresses and updates /etc/dhcpc/resolv.conf to point to your local name server. /etc/dhcpc/resolv.conf is copied to /etc/resolv.conf. Finally, the firewall script, /etc/rc.d/rc.firewall, is executed:

```
#!/bin/sh

SLEEPPIDFILE=/var/run/dhcp-wait-${IFNAME}.pid

# If the wait file doesn't exist, either the parent timed out or
# the dhcp server is issuing a new IP address.

if [ -f $SLEEPPIDFILE ]; then
    SLEEPPID=`cat $SLEEPPIDFILE`
    rm -f $SLEEPPIDFILE
    kill $SLEEPPID
fi

# Get the pid of the process, which is waiting for this to complete.


# ----------------------------------------------------------------
# Get the hostinfo
. /etc/dhcpc/hostinfo-eth0

# Update domainname
domain=`fgrep domain /etc/dhcpc/resolv.conf | sed -e "s/domain //"`
domainname $domain

# Update /etc/hosts
# Some services will break without this, unless you use localhost

# Replace <you> with your hostname.
sed -e "s/^.*<you>/$IPADDR          <you>.$domain       <you>/" /etc/hosts \
        > /var/tmp/hosts
cp /var/tmp/hosts /etc/hosts
rm /var/tmp/hosts


# ----------------------------------------------------------------
# Update $hostinfo with the current name servers from /etc/resolv.conf.
# Thanks to Roger Goun for the idea of appending these to $hostinfo and
# getting rid of the temporary file.
```

```
let cnt=1
fgrep nameserver /etc/dhcpc/resolv.conf ¦ sed -e "s/nameserver //" ¦
    while read naddr
    do
        echo "NAMESERVER_$cnt=\"$naddr\"" >> /etc/dhcpc/hostinfo-eth0
        let cnt=$cnt+1
    done


# ----------------------------------------------------------------
# The following 2 sections support a caching-only name server.
# The first section supports the BIND included in Red Hat 5.1 and earlier.
# The second section supports the BIND included in Red Hat 5.2 and newer.

# Update /etc/named.boot or /etc/named.conf forwarders to be the original
# name servers from /etc/resolv.conf.

# ----------------------------------------------------------------

# NOTE: This is for Red Hat versions 5.1 and OLDER.

#forwarders=""
fgrep nameserver /etc/dhcpc/resolv.conf ¦ sed -e "s/nameserver //" ¦
    while read naddr
    do
        forwarders=$forwarders" "$naddr
    done

sed -e "s/^forwarders.*$/forwarders    $forwarders/" /etc/named.boot \
    > /var/tmp/named.boot
#p /var/tmp/named.boot /etc/named.boot
rm /var/tmp/named.boot

# ----------------------------------------------------------------

# Note : This is for Red Hat versions 5.2 and NEWER.

let cnt=1
fgrep nameserver /etc/dhcpc/resolv.conf ¦ sed -e "s/nameserver //" ¦
    while read naddr
    do
        case $cnt in
            1 ) forwarder1=$naddr ;;
            2 ) forwarder2=$naddr ;;
            3 ) forwarder3=$naddr ;;
        esac
        let cnt=$cnt+1
    done
```

```
awk '/forwarders {/ { active = 1; print }        \
              /}/;/ {                             \
                  if ( active == 1 ) {            \
                      active = 0;                 \
                      print "          " f1 ";";  \
                      print "          " f2 ";";  \
                      print "          " f3 ";";  \
                  }                               \
              }                                   \
                                                  \
              {                                   \
                  if ( active == 0 )              \
                      print;                      \
              } '                                 \
    f1=$forwarder1 f2=$forwarder2 f3=$forwarder3 \
    /etc/named.conf > /tmp/named.conf

cp /var/tmp/named.conf /etc/named.conf
rm /var/tmp/named.conf


# ----------------------------------------------------------------------
# Update /etc/resolv.conf for local caching name server.
# Replace the name servers with an entry for localhost.

# Save the original
cp /etc/dhcpc/resolv.conf /etc/dhcpc/resolv.conf.bak

echo "domain $domain" > /var/tmp/resolv.conf
echo "search $domain firewall.lan" > /var/tmp/resolv.conf
echo "nameserver 127.0.0.1" >> /var/tmp/resolv.conf

cp /var/tmp/resolv.conf /etc/dhcpc/resolv.conf
rm /var/tmp/resolv.conf

# ----------------------------------------------------------------------

cp /etc/dhcpc/resolv.conf /etc

sh /etc/rc.d/rc.firewall
echo "Firewalling enabled." > /dev/console
```

C

Glossary

THIS GLOSSARY DEFINES TERMS AND ACRONYMS used in the book. Multiword terms are alphabetized on the major noun in the term, followed by a comma and the rest of the term.

ACCEPT   A firewall-filtering rule decision to pass a packet through to its next destination.

accept-everything-by-default policy   A policy that accepts all packets that don't match a firewall rule in the chain. Therefore, most firewall rules are DENY rules defining the exceptions to the default accept policy.

ACK   The TCP flag that acknowledges receipt of a previously received TCP segment.

application gateway   *See* proxy, application gateway.

AUTH   TCP service port 113, associated with the identd user authentication server.

authentication   The process of determining that an entity is who or what it claims to be.

authorization   The process of determining what services and resources an entity can use.

bastion   *See* firewall, bastion.

BIND   Berkeley Internet Name Domain, the Berkeley UNIX implementation of the DNS protocol.

BOOTP   Bootstrap Protocol, which is used by diskless workstations to discover their IP address and the location of the boot server, and to initiate the system download over tftp prior to booting. BOOTP was developed to replace RARP.

BOOTPC   UDP service port 68, associated with the BOOTP and DHCP clients.

bootpd   The BOOTP server program.

BOOTPS   UDP service port 67, associated with the BOOTP and DHCP servers.

broadcast   An IP packet that is addressed and sent to all interfaces connected to the same network.

CERT   Computer Emergency Response Team, an information coordination center and Internet security emergency prevention center formed at the Software Engineering Institute of Carnegie Mellon University after the Internet Worm incident in 1988.

CGI   Common gateway interface. CGI programs are local programs executed by the Web server on behalf of the remote client. CGI programs are often Perl scripts, so these programs are often called CGI scripts.

chain   The list of rules defining what packets can come in and what can go out through a network interface.

checksum   A number produced by performing some arithmetic computation on the numeric value of each byte in a file or packet. If the file is changed, or the packet corrupted, a second checksum produced for the same object will not match the original checksum.

choke   *See* firewall, choke.

chroot   Both a program and a system call that defines a directory to be the root of the file system, and then executes a program to run confined to that virtual file system.

circuit gateway   *See* proxy, circuit gateway.

class, network address   One of five classes of network addresses. An IPv4 address is a 32-bit value. The address space is divided into class A through E addresses, depending on the value of the first 4 most significant bits in the 32-bit value. The class A network address space maps 126 separate networks, each addressing over 16 million hosts. The class B network address space maps 16K networks, each addressing up to 64K hosts. The class C network address space maps 2 million networks, each addressing up to 254 hosts. Class D is used for multicast addresses. Class E is reserved for unspecified or experimental purposes.

client/server model   The model for distributed network services, in which a centralized program, a server, provides a service to remote client programs requesting that service, whether the service is receiving a copy of a Web page, downloading a file from a central repository, performing a database lookup, sending or receiving electronic mail, performing some kind of computation on client-supplied data, or establishing human communication connections between two or more people.

control-panel   A set of basic system administration tools wrapped in a GUI interface. A newer, fuller-featured program is linuxconf.

COPS   The Computer Oracle and Password System, a suite of programs that together check for a large set of potential security vulnerability areas on a UNIX system.

`Crack`   A password-guessing program.

`cron`   A system daemon, called `crond`, and configuration files and scripts that run system tasks at scheduled times.

daemon   A basic system services server running in the background.

DARPA   Defense Advanced Research Projects Agency.

data link layer   In the OSI reference model, the second layer, which represents point-to-point data signal delivery between two adjacent network devices, such as the delivery of an Ethernet frame from your computer to your external router. (In the TCP/IP reference model, this functionality is included as part of the first layer, the subnet layer.)

default policy   A policy for a firewall ruleset—whether for an `input` chain, an `output` chain, or a `forward` chain—that defines a packet's disposition when the packet doesn't match any rule in the set. *See also* accept-everything-by-default policy and deny-everything-by-default policy.

denial-of-service attack   An attack based on the idea of sending unexpected data or flooding your system with packets in such a way as to disrupt or seriously degrade your Internet connection, tying up local servers to the extent that legitimate requests can't be honored, or in the worst case, crashing your system altogether.

`DENY`   A firewall filtering rule decision to silently drop a packet without returning any notification to the sender.

deny-everything-by-default policy   A policy that drops all packets that don't match a firewall rule in the chain. Therefore, most firewall rules are `ACCEPT` rules defining the exceptions to the default deny policy.

DHCP   Dynamic Host Configuration Protocol, which is used to dynamically assign IP addresses and provide server and router information to clients without registered IP addresses. DHCP was developed to replace BOOTP.

`dhcpcd`   One of the DHCP client programs that locates a DHCP server, requests an IP address, and renews its lease on the address it is assigned.

`dhcpd`   The DHCP server program, which listens for client requests for an available server and requests for an IP address assignment, and periodically renews the clients' leases on the addresses.

DMZ   The demilitarized zone, a perimeter network containing machines hosting public services, separated from a local, private network. The less secure public servers are isolated from the private LAN.

DNS   Domain Name Service, a global Internet database service primarily allowing clients to look up host IP addresses, given their fully qualified host and domain name, and to look up fully qualified hostnames, given their IP address.

dual-homed   A computer that has two or more network interfaces. *See also* multihomed.

dynamically assigned address   IP addresses temporarily assigned to a client network interface by a central server, such as a DHCP server. Dynamically assigned addresses are normally assigned to customer or employee machines from a pool of registered IP addresses owned by an ISP or business.

Ethernet frame   Over an Ethernet network, IP datagrams are encapsulated in Ethernet frames.

filter, firewall   A firewall packet-filtering rule, or packet screen, defining the characteristics of the packet, which, if matched, determines whether the packet is to be allowed through the network interface or is to be dropped. Filters are defined in terms of a packet's source and destination addresses, source and destination ports, protocol type, TCP connection state, and ICMP message type.

finger   A user information lookup program.

firewall   A computer, router, or application program that enforces a set of security policies by tightly controlling access to system and network resources.

firewall, bastion   A firewall that has two or more network interfaces and is the gateway or connection point between those networks, most typically between a LAN and the Internet. Because a bastion firewall is the single point of connection between networks, the bastion is secured to the greatest extent possible.

firewall, choke   A LAN firewall that has two or more network interfaces and is the gateway or connection point between those networks. One side connects to a DMZ, perimeter network between the choke firewall and a bastion firewall. The other network interfaces connect to internal, private LANs.

firewall, packet-filtering   A firewall implemented at the network and transport layers that filters network traffic on a packet-by-packet basis, making routing decisions based on information in the IP packet header.

firewall, screened-host   A single-host firewall that requires local users to specifically connect to the firewall machine in order to access the Internet from the firewall machine. A screened-host firewall does not route traffic between networks. In addition to packet filtering, screening is performed either via NAT or application proxies. As shown in Figure C.1, in a single-host firewall system, the packet-filtering functionality of a bastion firewall is combined with the public server functions associated with public server machines in a DMZ network.

firewall, screened-subnet   A firewall system incorporating a bastion firewall and DMZ network to screen a LAN from direct Internet access. The DMZ network, housing public servers, is a separate network or separate subnet from any private LAN. Figure C.2 shows the two basic screened-subnet firewall configurations.

flooding, packet   A denial-of-service attack where the victim host or network is sent more packets of a given type than the victim can accommodate.

forward   To route packets from one network to another in the process of delivering a packet from one computer to another.

fragment   An IP packet containing a piece of a TCP segment.

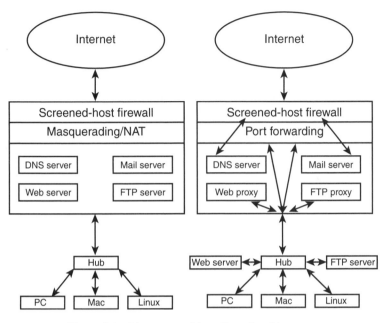

Figure C.1 Two screened–host firewall architectures.

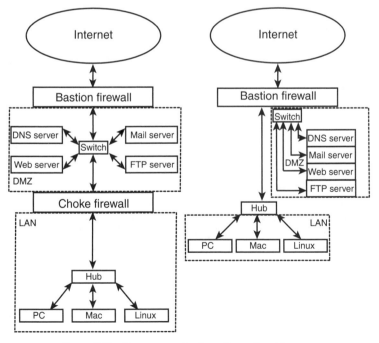

Figure C.2 Two screened–subnet firewall architectures.

FTP File Transfer Protocol. The protocol and programs used to copy files between networked computers.

FTP, anonymous FTP service accessible to any client that requests the service.

FTP, authenticated FTP service accessible to predefined accounts, which must be authenticated prior to using the service.

gateway A computer or program serving as the conduit, or relay, between two networks.

hosts.allow, hosts.deny TCP wrappers's configuration files are /etc/hosts.allow and /etc/hosts.deny.

HOWTO In addition to the standard man pages, Linux includes user-supplied online documentation on numerous topics, in many languages, and in multiple formats. The HOWTO documents are coordinated and maintained by the Linux Documentation Project.

HTTP Hypertext Transfer Protocol, used by Web servers and browsers.

hub A hardware signal repeater used to physically connect multiple network segments, extend the distance of a physical network, or connect network segments of different physical types.

IANA Internet Assigned Numbers Authority.

ICMP Internet Control Message Protocol. A network-layer IP status and control message.

identd The user authentication (AUTH) server.

ifstatus A system program that checks the system's network interface configurations and reports any interfaces in debug or promiscuous mode.

IMAP Internet Message Access Protocol, used to retrieve mail from mail hosts running an IMAP server.

inetd A network superserver that listens for incoming connections to service ports used by servers that it manages. When a connection request arrives, inetd starts a copy of the requested server to handle the connection.

inetd.conf inetd's configuration file.

innd The UNIX Usenet network news server.

IP Internet Protocol.

IP address A unique numeric identifier assigned to a specific network or a specific device's network interface on a network. This is a software address, directly translatable to a human-readable host or network name. Host network interface IP addresses are also associated with one or more hardware network interface addresses.

IP datagram An IP network layer packet.

ipchains With the introduction of the new implementation of the IPFW firewall mechanism in Linux, the new firewall administration program.

IPFW IP firewall mechanism.

ipfwadm Prior to the introduction of ipchains, the Linux IPFW firewall administration program.

IRC Internet Relay Chat, used for written electronic communication between networked individuals and groups.

ISP   Internet service provider.

`klogd`   The kernel logging daemon that collects operating system error and status messages from the kernel message buffers, and in conjunction with `syslogd`, writes the messages to a system log file.

LAN   Local area network.

`localhost`   The symbolic name often given to a machine's loopback interface in `/etc/hosts`.

loopback interface   A special software network interface used by the system to deliver local network messages destined to the local machine, bypassing the hardware network interface and associated network driver.

`man page`   The standard UNIX online documentation format. Manual pages are written for almost all user and system administration programs, as well as system calls, library calls, device types, and system file formats.

masquerading   The process of replacing an outgoing packet's local source address with that of the firewall or gateway machine so that the LAN's IP addresses remain hidden. The packet appears to come from the gateway machine rather than from an internal machine on the LAN. The process is reversed for incoming response packets from remote servers. The packet's destination address, the firewall machine's IP address, is replaced with the address of the client machine in the internal LAN. IP masquerading is more generally called network address translation, or NAT.

MD5   A cryptographic checksum algorithm used to ensure data integrity by creating digital signatures, called message digests, of objects.

MTU   Maximum transmission unit, the maximum packet size based on the underlying network.

multicast   An IP packet specially addressed to a class D, multicast IP address. Multicast clients are registered with the intermediate routers to receive packets addressed to a particular multicast address.

multihomed   A computer that has two or more network interfaces. *See also* dual-homed.

name server, primary   An authoritative server for a domain or a zone of the domain space. The server maintains a complete database of hostnames and IP addresses for this zone.

name server, secondary   A backup or peer to a primary name server.

`named`   The DNS name server.

NAT   Network address translation, or IP masquerading, the process of replacing a packet's local source address with that of the firewall or gateway machine, so that the LAN's IP addresses remain hidden. The packet appears to come from the gateway machine rather than from an internal machine on the LAN. The process is reversed for incoming response packets from remote servers. The packet's destination address, the firewall machine's IP address, is replaced with the address of the client machine in the internal LAN.

netstat   A program that reports various kinds of network status based on the various network-related kernel tables.

network layer   In the OSI reference model, the third layer, which represents end-to-end communication between two computers, such as the routing and delivery of an IP datagram from your source computer to some external destination computer. In the TCP/IP Reference Model, this is referred to as the second layer, the Internet layer.

NFS   Network File System, used to share file systems between networked computers.

NIS   Network Information Service, used to centrally manage and provide user account and host information.

nmap   A fairly new network security auditing (i.e., port scanning) tool that includes many of the newer scanning techniques in use today.

NNTP   Network News Transfer Protocol, used by Usenet.

NTP   Network Time Protocol, used by xntpd and ntpdate.

ntpdate   A client program that contacts one or more NTP time servers to request the current time.

OSI (Open Systems Interconnection) reference model   A seven-layer model developed by the International Organization for Standardization (ISO) to provide a framework or guide for network interconnection standards.

OSPF   The Open Shortest Path First routing protocol for TCP/IP, which is the most commonly used routing protocol today. The gated routing daemon uses OSPF.

packet   An IP network datagram.

packet filtering   *See* firewall, packet-filtering.

PATH   The shell environmental variable defining which directories the shell should search for unqualified executable commands, and the order in which the shell should search those directories.

peer-to-peer   A communication mode used for communication between two server programs. A peer-to-peer communication protocol is often, but not always, different from the protocol used to communicate between the server and a client.

physical layer   In the OSI reference model, the first layer, which represents the physical medium used to carry the electrical signals between two adjacent network devices, such as copper wire, optical fiber, packet radio, or infrared. In the TCP/IP reference model, this is included as part of the first layer, the subnet layer.

PID   Process ID, which is a process's unique numeric identifier on the system, usually associated with the process's slot in the system process table.

ping   A simple network analysis tool used to determine whether a remote host is reachable and responding. ping sends an ICMP Echo Request message. The recipient host returns an ICMP Echo Reply message in response.

POP   Post Office Protocol, used to retrieve mail from mail hosts running a POP server.

port   In TCP or UDP, the numeric designator of a particular network communication channel. Port assignments are managed by the IANA. Some ports are assigned to particular application communication protocols as part of the protocol standard. Some ports are registered as being associated with a particular service by convention. Some ports are unassigned and free to be dynamically assigned for use by clients and user programs:

- **privileged**   A port in the range from 0 to 1023. Many of these ports are assigned to application protocols by international standard. Access to the privileged ports requires system-level privilege.

- **unprivileged**   A port in the range from 1024 to 65535. Some of these ports are registered as used by convention by certain programs. Any port in this range can be used by a client program to establish a connection with a networked server.

port scan   A probe of all or a set of a host computer's service ports, typically service ports that are often associated with security vulnerabilities.

`portmap`   An RPC manager daemon, used to map between a particular RPC service number a client is requesting to access, and the service port the associated server is bound to.

probe   To send some kind of packet to some one service port on a host computer. The purpose of a probe is to determine whether a response is generated from the target host.

proxy   A program that creates and maintains a network connection on behalf of another program, providing an application level conduit between a client and a server. The actual client and server have no direct communication. The proxy appears to be the server to the client program, and appears to be the client to the server program. As shown in Figure C.3, application proxies are generally categorized into application gateways and circuit gateways.

proxy, application gateway   Similar to a screened-host firewall that is implemented at the system configuration and application levels. Only the computer running the application gateway has direct access to the Internet. Network traffic is never automatically forwarded through the application gateway machine. All Internet access is done through the gateway program. External access is allowed only to the gateway machine. Internal access is allowed only to the gateway machine. Local users must either log into the gateway machine and access the Internet from there, or else connect to the application gateway and authenticate themselves there first. A proxy server is usually implemented as a separate application for each proxied service. The application-level proxy server understands the application's specific communication protocol. Each proxy application appears to be the server to the client program, and appears to be the client to the real server. Special client programs, or specially configured client programs, connect to the proxy server instead of to a remote server. The proxy establishes the connection to the remote server on the client application's behalf, after substituting the client's source address with its own. Examples of application-level gateways are the Apache Web server proxy and the application-specific proxies included in the TIS Firewall Toolkit.

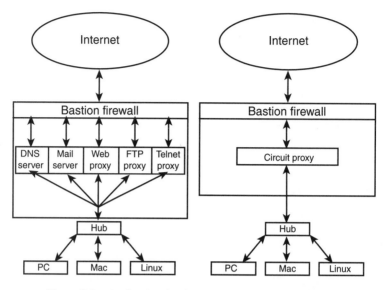

Figure C.3 Application-level and circuit-level proxy gateways.

proxy, circuit gateway   A proxy server, which can be implemented as either separate applications for each service being proxied, or as a generalized connection relay that doesn't have any specific knowledge about the application protocols. The circuit-level relay creates a virtual, software-managed connection circuit between a client and server program. Unlike appplication-level proxies, the intermediate connection steps are performed transparently to the user. SOCKS is a circuit-level proxy system.

QoS   Quality of service.

RARP   Reverse Address Resolution Protocol, which was developed to enable diskless machines to ask servers for their IP address based on their MAC hardware address.
REJECT rule   A firewall-filtering rule decision to drop a packet and return an ICMP error message to the sender.
resolver   The client side of DNS. The resolver is implemented as library code that is linked to programs requiring network access. The DNS client configuration file is `/etc/resolv.conf`.
RFC   Request for Comment, a note or memo published through the Internet Society or the Internet Engineering Task Force. Some RFCs become standards. RFCs typically concern a topic related to the Internet or the TCP/IP protocol suite.
RIP   Routing Information Protocol, an older routing protocol still in use today, especially within a large LAN. The `routed` daemon uses RIP.
RPC   Remote-procedure call.
rule   *See* firewall and filter.

runlevel   A booting and system state concept taken from System V UNIX. A system normally operates at one of runlevels 2, 3, or 5. Runlevel 3 is the default, normal, multiuser system state. Runlevel 2 is the same as 3, without NFS services running. Runlevel 5 is the same as 3, with the addition of the X Window Display Manager, which presents an X-based login and host-selection screen.

SATAN   Security Administrator Tool for Analyzing Networks, a tool to help identify security vulnerabilities in network service configurations.

screened host   *See* firewall, screened-host.

screened subnet   *See* firewall, screened-subnet.

script   An executable ASCII shell script, such as a file containing `sh`, `csh`, `bash`, `ksh`, or `perl` commands.

segment, **TCP**   A TCP message.

setgid   A program that, when executed, assumes the group ID of the program's owner, rather than the group ID of the process running the program.

setuid   A program that, when executed, assumes the user ID of the program's owner, rather than the user ID of the process running the program.

shell   A UNIX command interpreter, such as `sh`, `ksh`, `bash`, and `csh`.

smrsh   Sendmail Restricted Shell.

SMTP   Simple Mail Transport Protocol, used to exchange mail between mail servers, and between mail programs and mail servers.

SNMP   Simple Network Management Protocol, used to manage network device configuration from a remote workstation.

socket   The unique network connection point defined by the pairing of an IP address with a particular TCP or UDP service port.

SOCKS   A popular circuit gateway proxy package available from NEC.

spoofing, **source address**   Forging the source address in an IP packet header to be that of some other address.

SSH   Secure shell protocol, used for more strongly authenticated, encrypted network connections.

SSL   Secure Socket Layer protocol, used for encrypted communication. SSL is most commonly used by Web servers and browsers for exchanging personal information for e-commerce.

statically assigned address   Permanently assigned, hard-coded IP addresses, whether publicly registered addresses or private class addresses.

strobe   A basic TCP port scanner.

subnet   A subnetwork addressing scheme, which is a means of using IP address masks to internally divide a single Internet network address space into multiple internal network address spaces. The address space appears as a single network to the Internet, but appears as multiple networks, or LANs, internally. This is done by using some of the host ID bits in the IP address as if they were an extension to the network ID section of the IP address. For example, the `192.168.30.0` network address space, masked as `255.255.255.0/24`, could be subnetted into two internal networks by using the high bit from the fourth quad, masked as `255.255.255.128/25`. The result is two internal network address spaces, each with 126 usable addresses.

subnet layer In the TCP/IP reference model, the first layer, which represents both the physical medium used to carry the electrical signals between two adjacent network devices, such as copper wire, optical fiber, packet radio, or infrared. It also includes point-to-point data signal delivery between two adjacent network devices, such as the delivery of an Ethernet frame from your computer to your external router.

SUNRPC Service port 111, which is used by the `portmap` daemon to map incoming requests to RPC services to the service port the associated server is bound to.

SYN The TCP connection synchronization request flag. A `SYN` message is the first message sent from a program seeking to open a connection with another networked program.

`syslog.conf` The system logging daemon's configuration file.

`syslogd` The system logging daemon, which collects error and status messages generated by system programs that post messages using the `syslog()` system call.

TCP Transmission Control Protocol, used for reliable, ongoing network connections between two programs.

`tcp_wrapper` An authorization scheme used to control which local services are available to which remote hosts on the network.

`tcpd` TCP wrapper service, which is provided for `inetd`-managed services by the `tcpd` program.

TCP/IP reference model An informal network communication model developed when TCP/IP became the de facto standard for Internet communication among UNIX machines during the late 1970s and early 1980s. Rather than being a formal, academic ideal, the TCP/IP reference model is based on what manufacturers and developers finally came to agree upon for communication across the Internet.

TFTP Trivial File Transfer Protocol, the protocol used to download a boot image to a diskless workstation or router. The protocol is a UDP-based, simplified version of FTP.

three-way handshake The TCP connection establishment protocol. When a client program sends its first message to a server, the connection request message, the `SYN` flag is set and accompanied by a synchronization sequence number the client will use as the starting point to number all the rest of the messages the client will send. The server responds with an acknowledgment (`ACK`) to the `SYN` message, along with its own synchronization request (`SYN`). The server includes the client's sequence number incremented by one. The purpose of the acknowledgment is to acknowledge the message the client referred to by its sequence number. As with the client's first message, the `SYN` flag is accompanied by a synchronization sequence number. The server is passing along its own starting sequence number for its half of the connection. The client responds with an `ACK` of the server's `SYN-ACK`, incrementing the server's sequence number by one to indicate receipt of the message. The connection is established.

`tiger` A collection of scripts and C programs designed to check for security vulnerabilities that could allow someone to gain unauthorized `root` access.

TOS   Type of Service, the field in the IP packet header that was intended to provide a hint as to the preferred routing policy or packet-routing preference.

traceroute   A network analysis tool used to determine the path from one computer to another across the network.

transport layer   In the OSI reference model, the fourth layer, which represents end-to-end communication between two programs, such as the delivery of a packet from a client program to a server program. In the TCP/IP reference model, this is referred to as the third layer, also the transport layer. However, the TCP/IP Layer 3 transport level abstraction includes the concept of the OSI layer five session layer, which includes the concepts of an orderly and synchronized exchange of messages.

tripwire   A program that builds and maintains a database of MD5 digital signatures for all or a set of files and directories on the system. Its purpose is to detect unauthorized additions, deletions, or changes to files.

TTL   Time-to-live, an IP packet header field that is a maximum count of the number of routers the packet can pass through before reaching its destination.

UDP   User Datagram Protocol, used to send individual network messages between programs, without any guarantee of delivery or delivery order.

unicast   An IP packet sent point-to-point, from one computer's network interface to another's.

UUCP   UNIX-to-UNIX Copy Protocol.

WAIS   Wide Area Information Service, now known as an Internet search engine.

WAREZ   A repository of pirated software.

world-readable   File system objects—files, directories, entire file systems—that are readable by any account or program on the system.

world-writable   File system objects—files, directories, entire file systems—that are writable by any account or program on the system.

WWW   World Wide Web.

X Window   The UNIX graphical user interface window display system.

xntpd   The NTP network time server, which can both provide the current time to networked clients and exchange time information with other servers.

zone transfer   The process of copying an authoritative DNS name server's database of hostnames and IP addresses belonging to a contiguous section of a domain to a secondary name server.

Index

I-J

P

New Riders Books for Professionals

UNIX/Linux Titles

Solaris Essential Reference

By John P. Mulligan

1st Edition

350 pages, $24.95

ISBN: 0-7357-0023-0

Looking for the fastest, easiest way to find the Solaris command you need? Need a few pointers on shell scripting? How about advanced administration tips and sound, practical expertise on security issues? Are you looking for trustworthy information about available third-party software packages that will enhance your operating system? Author John Mulligan—creator of the popular Unofficial Guide to Solaris Web site (sun.icsnet.com)—delivers all that and more in one attractive, easy-to-use reference book. With clear and concise instructions on how to perform important administration and management tasks and key information on powerful commands and advanced topics, *Solaris Essential Reference* is the reference you need when you know what you want to do and you just need to know how.

Linux System Administration

By M Carling and James T. Dennis

1st Edition

450 pages, $29.99

ISBN: 1-56205-934-3

As an administrator, you probably feel that most of your time and energy is spent in endless firefighting. If your network has become a fragile quilt of temporary patches and workarounds, then this book

is for you. For example, have you had trouble sending or receiving your email lately? Are you looking for a way to keep your network running smoothly with enhanced performance? Are your users always hankering for more storage, more services, and more speed? *Linux System Administration* advises you on the many intricacies of maintaining a secure, stable system. In this definitive work, the author addresses all the issues related to system administration, from adding users and managing files permission to Internet services and Web hosting to recovery planning and security. This book fulfills the need for expert advice that will ensure a trouble-free Linux environment.

Developing Linux Applications

By Eric Harlow

1st Edition

400 pages, $34.99

ISBN: 0-7357-0021-4

We all know that Linux is one of the most powerful and solid operating systems in existence. And as the success of Linux grows, there is an increasing interest in developing applications with graphical user interfaces that really take advantage of the power of Linux. In this book, software developer Eric Harlow gives you an indispensable development handbook focusing on the GTK+ toolkit. More than an overview on the elements of application or GUI design, this is a hands-on book that delves deeply into the technology. With in-depth material on the various GUI programming tools and loads of examples, this book's unique focus will give you the information you need to design and launch professional-quality applications.

Linux Firewalls

By Robert Ziegler

Fall 1999

400 pages, $35.00

ISBN: 0-7357-0900-9

New Riders is proud to offer the first book aimed specifically at Linux security issues. While there are a host of general UNIX security books, we think it is time to address the practical needs of the Linux network. Author Robert Ziegler takes a balanced approach to system security, discussing topics like planning a secure environment, firewalls, and utilizing security scripts. With comprehensive information on specific system compromises, and advice on how to prevent and repair them, this is one book that every Linux administrator should have on their shelf.

GIMP Essential Reference

by Alex Harford

1st Edition, Fall 1999

350 pages, $24.95

ISBN: 0-7357-0911-4

GIMP Essential Reference is designed to fulfill a need for the computer expert. It is made to bring someone experienced in computers up to speed with the GNU Image Manipulation Program. It provides essential information on using this program effectively. This book is targeted at you if you want to efficiently use the GIMP. *GIMP Essential Reference* will show you how to quickly become familiar with the advanced user interface using a table-heavy format that will allow users to find what they're looking for quickly.

GIMP Essential Reference is for users working with GIMP who know what they want to accomplish, but don't know exactly how to do it.

KDE Application Development

by Uwe Thiem

1st Edition, Fall 1999

450 pages, 39.99

ISBN: 1-57870-201-1

KDE Application Development offers a head start into KDE and Qt. The book will cover the essential widgets available in KDE and Qt, and it offers a strong start without the "first try" annoyances which sometimes make strong developers and programmers give up. This book explains KDE and Qt by writing a real application from the very beginning stages, where it can't do anything but display itself and offer a button to quit. Then it will finally bring the user to a full-featured application. The process of developing such an application takes the potential KDE developer through all stages of excitement.

GIMP

by Carey Bunks

1st Edition, Winter 2000

350 pages, $39.99

ISBN: 0-7357-0924-6

This title is a technical and inspirational reference covering the intricacies of the GIMP's feature set. Even if you have little background in image manipulation, you can succeed at using the GIMP to achieve your goals, using this book as a guide. Keeping in mind that all tools are not created equal, author Carey Bunks provides an in-depth look at the GIMP's most useful tools. The content focuses on the intermediate to advanced topics of interest to most users, like photo touchup and enhancement, compositing, and animations. Invaluable is the conceptual approach of the author, in which he avoids the cookbook approach to learning image manipulation and helps you become self-sufficient.

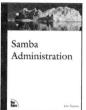

Samba Administration

by John Terpstra

1st Edition, Winter 2000

400 pages, $35.00

ISBN: 0-7357-0903-3

The world of today's system administrators is filled with many different types of network operating systems, protocols, and hardware configurations all under the requirements of demanding and sometimes less than savvy users. Many administrators turn to the Samba product to help them share services between systems.

Samba Administration provides the sysadmin with the necessary technical background on the SMB architecture, compiling the source and installation, managing clients and servers, and dealing with the inexplicable.

Inside Linux

by Michael Tobler

1st Edition, Winter 2000

650 pages, $49.99

ISBN: 0-7357-0940-8

With in-depth complete coverage on the installation process, editing and typesetting, graphical user interfaces, programming, system administration, and managing Internet sites, *Inside Linux* is the only book "smart" users new to Linux will need if you have an understanding of computer technology and are looking for just the right reference to fit your sophisticated needs. This book guides you to a high level of proficiency with all the flavors of Linux, and helps you with crucial system administration chores. *Inside Linux* is different than other books available because it's a unique blend of a how-to and a reference guide.

Development Titles

GTK+/Gnome Development

By Havoc Pennington

400 pages, $29.99

ISBN: 0-7357-0078-8

GTK+ /Gnome Develpment provides the experienced programmer the knowledge to develop X Window applications with the powerful GTK+ toolkit. The author provides the reader with a checklist of features every application should have, advanced GUI techniques, and the ability to create custom widgets. The title also contains reference information for more experienced users already familiar with usage, but require knowledge of function prototypes and detailed descriptions. These tools let the reader write powerful applications in record time.

Python Essential Reference

By David Beazley

300 pages, $34.95

ISBN: 0-7357-0901-7

This book describes the Python programming language and its library of standard modules. Python is an informal language that has become a highly valuable software development tool for many computing professionals. This language reference covers Python's lexical conventions, built-in datatypes, control flow, functions, statements, classes, and execution model. This book also covers the contents of the Python library as bundled in the standard Python distribution.

MySQL

by Paul DuBois

1st Edition, Fall 1999

450 pages, $39.99

ISBN: 0-7357-0921-1

MySQL will teach you how to use the tools provided by the MySQL distribution itself, covering installation, setup, daily use, security, optimization, maintenance, and troubleshooting. It also discusses important third-party tools, such as the Perl DBI and Apache/ PHP interfaces that provide access to MySQL. These tools are used by a significant number of people who employ MySQL particularly for tying MySQL to Web sites.

GLibC: A Comprehensive Reference to GNU/Linux LibC

by Jeff Garzik

1st Edition, Winter 2000

400 pages, $40.00

ISBN: 1-57870-202-X

GLibC comprises over 1,800 functions. This title is a complete reference work encompassing a single-volume version that gives quick coverage to each function. It includes a searchable index to provide added value, and it is slated to become an Open Source titles available for free download online. The book content consists of an index of functions by category (networking, threading, string, etc), and then an alphabetical function listing.

Lotus Notes and Domino Titles

Domino System Administration

By Rob Kirkland

1st Edition Fall 1999

500 pages, $29.99

ISBN: 1-56205-948-3

Your boss has just announced that you will be upgrading to the newest version of Notes and Domino when it ships. As a Premium Lotus Business Partner, Lotus has offered a substantial price break to keep your company away from Microsoft's Exchange Server. How are you supposed to get this new system installed, configured, and rolled out to all of your end users? You understand how Lotus Notes works—you've been administering it for years. What you need is a concise, practical explanation about the new features, and how to make some of the advanced stuff really work. You need answers and solutions from someone like you, who has worked with the product for years, and understands what it is you need to know. *Domino System Administration* is the answer—the first book on Domino that attacks the technology at the professional level, with practical, hands-on assistance to get Domino running in your organization.

Lotus Notes and Domino Essential Reference

By Dave Hatter &
Tim Bankes
1st Edition
700 pages, $45.00
ISBN: 0-7357-0007-9

You're in a bind because you've been asked to design and program a new database in Notes that will keep track of and itemize a myriad of inventory and shipping data for an important client. The client wants a user-friendly interface, without sacrificing speed or functionality. You are experienced (and could develop this app in your sleep), but feel that you need to take your talents to the next level. You need something to facilitate your creative and technical abilities, something to perfect your programming skills. Your answer is waiting for you: *Lotus Notes and Domino Essential Reference.* It's compact and simply designed. It's loaded with information. All of the objects, classes, functions, and methods are listed. It shows you the object hierarchy and the overlaying relationship between each one. It's perfect for you. Problem solved.

Networking Titles

Cisco Router Configuration and Troubleshooting

By Mark Tripod
1st Edition
300 pages, $34.99
ISBN: 0-7357-0024-9

Want the real story on making your Cisco routers run like a dream? Why not pick up a copy of *Cisco Router Configuration and Troubleshooting* and see what Mark Tripod has to say? His company is the one responsible for making some of the largest sites on the Net scream, like Amazon.com, Hotmail, USAToday, Geocities, and Sony. In this book, he provides advanced configuration issues, sprinkled with advice and preferred practices. You won't see a general overview on TCP/IP—he talks about more meaty issues like security, monitoring, traffic management, and more. In the troubleshooting section, Mark provides a unique methodology and lots of sample problems to illustrate. By providing real-world insight and examples instead of rehashing Cisco's documentation, Mark gives network administrators information they can start using today.

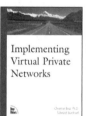

Implementing Virtual Private Networks

By Tina Bird and Ted
Stockwell
1st Edition Fall 1999
300 pages, $32.99
ISBN: 0-7357-0047-8

Tired of looking for decent, practical, up-to-date information on virtual private networks? *Implementing Virtual Private Networks,* by noted authorities Dr. Tina Bird and Ted Stockwell, finally gives you what you need—an authoritative guide on the design, implementation, and maintenance of Internet-based access to private networks. This book focuses on real-world solutions, demonstrating how the choice of VPN architecture should align with an organization's business and technological requirements. Tina and Ted give you the information you need to determine whether a VPN is right for your organization, select the VPN that suits your needs, and design and implement the VPN you have chosen.

Understanding Data Communications, Sixth Edition

By Gilbert Held
6th Edition Summer 1999
550 pages, $34.99
ISBN: 0-7357-0036-2

Updated from the highly successful fifth edition, this book explains how data communications systems and their various hardware and software components work. Not an entry-level book, it approaches the material in a textbook format, addressing the complex issues involved in internetworking today. A great reference book for the experienced networking professional, written by noted networking authority, Gilbert Held.

DCE/RPC over SMB

by Luke Leighton
1st Edition, Fall 1999
400 pages, $39.99
ISBN: 1-57870-150-3

When Microsoft's systems were locked into offices and chained to small LANs, they were relatively safe. Now as they've been unleashed onto the Internet, they are more and more vulnerable to attack. Security people, system and network administrators, and the folks writing tools for them all need to be familiar with the packets flowing across their networks. It's the only way to really know how much trouble a system is in. This book describes how Microsoft has taken DCE/RPC (Distributed Computing Environment/ Remote Procedure Calls) and implemented it over SMB (Server Message Block) and TCP/IP. SMB itself runs over three transports: TCP/IP, IPX/SPX, and NETBEUI.

Luke Leighton presents Microsoft Developer NT system calls (including what some such calls would be, if they were documented) and shows what they look like over-the-wire by providing example C code to compile and use. This gives administrators and developers insights into how information flows through their network, so that they can improve efficiency, security, and heterogeneous transfers.

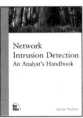

Intrusion Detection: An Analyst's Handbook

by Stephen Northcutt
1st Edition
350 pages, $34.99
ISBN: 0-7357-0868-1

Get answers and solutions from someone who has been in the trenches with *Network Intrusion Detection: An Analyst's Handbook* Author Stephen Northcutt, original developer of the Shadow intrusion detection system and former Director of the United States Navy's Information System Security Office at the Naval Security Warfare Center, lends his expertise to intrusion detection specialists, security analysts, and consultants responsible for setting up and maintaining an effective defense against network security.

New Riders

We Want to Know What You Think

To better serve you, we would like your opinion on the content and quality of this book. Please complete this card and mail it to us or fax it to 317-581-4663.

Name_____

Address _____

City _____ State _____ Zip _____

Phone _____

Email Address _____

Occupation _____

Operating System(s) that you use _____

What influenced your purchase of this book?

❑ Recommendation ❑ Cover Design
❑ Table of Contents ❑ Index
❑ Magazine Review ❑ Advertisement
❑ New Riders' Reputation ❑ Author Name

How would you rate the contents of this book?

❑ Excellent ❑ Very Good
❑ Good ❑ Fair
❑ Below Average ❑ Poor

How do you plan to use this book?

❑ Quick reference ❑ Self-training
❑ Classroom ❑ Other

What do you like most about this book?
Check all that apply.

❑ Content ❑ Writing Style
❑ Accuracy ❑ Examples
❑ Listings ❑ Design
❑ Index ❑ Page Count
❑ Price ❑ Illustrations

What do you like least about this book?
Check all that apply.

❑ Content ❑ Writing Style
❑ Accuracy ❑ Examples
❑ Listings ❑ Design
❑ Index ❑ Page Count
❑ Price ❑ Illustrations

What would be a useful follow-up book to this one for you? _____

Where did you purchase this book? _____

Can you name a similar book that you like better than this one, or one that is as good? Why?

_____

_____

How many New Riders books do you own? _____

What are your favorite computer books? _____

_____

What other titles would you like to see us develop? _____

_____

Any comments for us? _____

_____

_____

_____

Linux Firewalls, 0-7357-0900-9

Fold here and tape to mail

Place
Stamp
Here

New Riders Publishing
201 W. 103rd St.
Indianapolis, IN 46290

New Riders | How to Contact Us

Visit Our Web Site

www.newriders.com

On our Web site, you'll find information about our other books, authors, tables of contents, indexes, and book errata. You can also place orders for books through our Web site.

Email Us

Contact us at this address:
newriders@mcp.com

- If you have comments or questions about this book
- To report errors that you have found in this book
- If you have a book proposal to submit or are interested in writing for New Riders
- If you would like to have an author kit sent to you
- If you are an expert in a computer topic or technology and are interested in being a technical editor who reviews manuscripts for technical accuracy

newriders-sales@mcp.com

- To find a distributor in your area, please contact our international department at the address above.

newriders-pr@mcp.com

- For instructors from educational institutions who wish to preview New Riders books for classroom use. Email should include your name, title, school, department, address, phone number, office days/hours, text in use, and enrollment in the body of your text along with your request for desk/examination copies and/or additional information.

Write to Us

New Riders Publishing
201 W. 103rd St.
Indianapolis, IN 46290-1097

Call Us

Toll-free (800) 571-5840 + 9 + 7494
If outside U.S. (317) 581-3500. Ask for New Riders.

Fax Us

(317) 581-4663